Educating Psyche

IMAGINATION, EMOTION AND THE UNCONSCIOUS IN LEARNING

BERNIE NEVILLE

THIRD EDITION

David Lovell Publishing
Melbourne Australia

Published in 2014 by

David Lovell Publishing
PO Box 44, Kew East
Victoria 3102 Australia
tel/fax +61 3 9859 0000
publisher@davidlovellpublishing.com

© Copyright 1989, 2014 Bernie Neville

This work is copyright. Apart from any fair dealing for the purposes of private study, research, criticism or review, as permitted under the Copyright Act, no part may be reproduced by any process without written permission. Inquiries should be addressed to the publisher.

Front cover photo: Lee Pettet
Typeset in 11.75/15 Perpetua
This edition printed through Amazon CreateSpace

National Library of Australia Cataloguing-in-Publication data

Neville, Bernard, 1938–
Educating psyche : imagination, emotion and the
unconscious in learning / Bernie Neville.
3rd ed.

  ISBN 9781863551434 (pbk)

  Includes bibliographical references and index.
  Learning, Psychology of. Education – Philosophy.
  Education – Psychological aspects.Educational psychology.
370.15

This book brings together multiple perspectives in understanding the importance of authentic holistic practices in the teaching and learning of children. Neville provides the spaces to challenge and redefine current educational paradigms and rediscover the essentialities of process, the imagination and creative thought. In these times of standardization and neo-liberalism, Neville deepens our awareness of the significance of the soul in education, the natural rhythms of growth, and spirituality in our interconnectedness with children.

Dr Marni Binder, Associate Professor, School of Early Childhood Studies, Ryerson University, Toronto, Canada

This third edition of *Educating Psyche* is timely. Principals, teachers and teacher educators are facing a tumultuous time in education with both Hermes' market place and Apollo's reductionist presences dominating. Neville makes this visible in the early chapters. The present reality manifesting is not created by educators, but rather economists and administrators. Neville's work allows those in the field to be more articulate about what is occurring. The other significant aspect of this book is that Neville provokes educators to consider themselves as creators of reality, rather than being passively positioned by Hermes and Apollo. A very welcome book for anyone who cares about education for and of future generations.

Dr Andrea Gallant, Deakin University

Energized by the instant mobility of their digital worlds, young people can escape boredom with ease. Guiding their decision-making takes courage to recognize, value and celebrate their inner worlds. For this to happen, *Educating Psyche* provides an inspirational catalyst for reflection on what really matters in schooling.

Professor Margaret Robertson, La Trobe University

This is one of my favourite books on education, now revised and updated – what a delight! Woven through the text are ideas on teaching, learning, philosophy, consciousness and what it is to be human. Bernie Neville has the rare gift of being able to combine ideas from many perspectives and relate them to our everyday lives. While teachers and would-be teachers love this book, it is about far more than education.

Dr Peta Heywood, La Trobe University

Over the past twenty years I've seen *Educating Psyche* open minds and hearts of practitioners in education and social change. It inspires new ways of thinking, feeling and acting, providing clear guidelines in putting its wealth of ideas into practice. I'm excited to use this new edition with trainee teachers and social ecologists.

Dr Catherine E. Camden Pratt, University of Western Sydney

Contents

Introduction to the Third Edition	vii
Introduction to the First Edition	ix
1. Psyche in the Classroom	1
2. The Power of Suggestion	31
3. Magic and Manipulation	65
4. Use Your Imagination	97
5. The High, the Deep and the Ordinary	137
6. Catching the Light	175
7. The Search for Spontaneity	211
8. Sitting Quietly	249
9. Eros and Associates	283
10. Being Alive	325
11. Being in Five Minds	345
12. The Gods in the Classroom	381
Bibliography and Further Reading	433
Index of Names	442

For Helen

Introduction to the Third Edition

by Jack Miller

Educating Psyche has for two decades been a seminal text in holistic education. In 1999 the Foundation for Educational Renewal identified it as one of the most important books on education in its ten year review of the field.

The original text focused primarily on educating the soul through a variety of means including imagery, psychodrama and contemplative practices. Bernie Neville explored the work of Jung, Coué, Assagioli, Lozanov, Moreno, Erikson and Wallas and showed how their ideas could be employed by teachers in classrooms. As I mentioned in the introduction to the second edition, 'the best books on education are a blend of theory and practice, and *Educating Psyche* continually connects the two.' This original core of *Educating Psyche* remains but it is a tribute to Bernie Neville that he continues to explore new ideas.

In the second edition, Dr Neville explored how the Greek gods can be used a metaphors for understanding teaching and learning. In an imaginative exploration of archetypes he describes how gods such as Hestia, Hades and Aphrodite can appear in the classroom. For example, 'Hestia represents the place of stillness from which we come and to which we go' and can thus provide a basis for pursuing contemplative practices in the classroom.

In this latest edition, Neville has used the work of Whitehead, Egan and Gebser to broaden the conceptual frame for his earlier writing. These thinkers describe broad developmental patterns that can provide a frame for understanding student growth. The work of Gebser has long been of interest to Bernie Neville and in this edition of *Educating Psyche* he is able to integrate Gebserian thinking with the notion of educating the soul. Gebser's theory provides a five stage model of human development with five types of mind: archaic, magic, mythic, mental and integral. This last stage, which can also called spiritual, includes the previous stages and allows the individual to move beyond dualistic thinking and adopt multiple perspectives to see holistically. He argues that it is important that teachers do not rush children through the stages but honour each one. So much of education today is about thrusting an academic curriculum on young children and denying who they are as children.

The entire body of Neville's work provides a powerful counter to present-day factory-like models of schooling that are promoted by departments of education and the media. Politicians and administrators who take on the task of formulating education policy could benefit greatly from reading this text and reflecting on how the ideas here could be brought into practice. Exploration and application of the ideas in *Educating Psyche* could lead to the life-affirming education which is so desperately needed.

Professor John (Jack) P. Miller
Ontario Institute for Studies in Education at the
University of Toronto

Introduction to the First Edition (1989)

by Colin Wilson

On a shelf above my bed I have a dozen or so books to which I return again and again. They include Robert L. Heilbroner's *The Worldly Philosophers*, Stuart Chase's *Proper Study of Mankind*, E. T. Bell's *Men of Mathematics*, Horace Freeland Judson's *The Eighth Day* and Douglas Hotstadter's *Gödel, Escher, Bach*. When I receive a bound copy of Bernie Neville's *Educating Psyche*, it will immediately be assigned a place of honour on this shelf.

The point about the shelf is that the books are not about subjects that I would normally regard as my special field (philosophy, criminology, the paranormal); but each book is such an enthralling introduction to its particular topic – economics, social science, mathematics, molecular biology, symbolic logic – that I can acquire a vast amount of specialist knowledge in the most painless manner imaginable. And as soon as I began to read the typescript of *Educating Psyche*, I realized that I had stumbled upon another one of those convenient and fascinating books that offer an introduction to a whole new field of twentieth century knowledge.

Education is not, I must admit, a subject to which I give a great deal of thought. One of the first great modem educationalists, Rudolf Steiner, recognized that its central aim is to arouse in pupils a passionate desire to educate themselves, and this insight has always struck me as the foundation of any sensible educational theory. But how is it to be done? It might be compared to a mother attempting to train her baby to feed itself. But, then, the baby already possesses the most important motivation: hunger. How many children have a 'hunger' for the nine-times tables or the rules of grammar? Education consists of not only leading the horse to water but trying to persuade it that it is thirsty. And that – to be honest – is a task that demands more patience than I possess.

Educating Psyche

But as I read *Educating Psyche*, it soon became clear that Bernie Neville has a more interesting and constructive approach to the problem. And as soon as I began reading the section on Freud and Coué, I realized that he is dealing with the problem that interests me above all others: the remarkable undiscovered powers of the human mind. I had always been fascinated by the mystery of hypnosis. And when I came upon the new science of split-brain physiology, I realized that this had provided the basic solution. It reveals that we have two people living inside our skulls, in the left and right cerebral hemispheres. The person you call 'you' lives in the left; the person who lives a few millimetres away is a total stranger. Moreover, you are unaware of his existence for most of the time. Under hypnosis, the 'you' is put to sleep, but the stranger remains awake. And his powers are far greater than 'yours'. So the hypnotist tells you that you will lie across two chairs, with your head on one and your feet on the other, and that, although several people will stand on your stomach you will not bend in the middle, the 'stranger' does it with no difficulty at all.

Neville quotes the following extremely important passage of Coué:

> You must know that we have in ourselves two beings. The first one is the conscious, voluntary being we know, and the second one, behind the first being, is the subconscious or imaginative being ... We don't pay attention to this being, and we are perfectly wrong, because it is this second being which runs us entirely ... If it is this second being which runs us, and we learn how to run it, through it we learn to run ourselves [see p. 34 below].

The moment I read this, I realized that Neville is on to something of tremendous importance. I must admit that I have never read Coué. All I knew about him was that he had discovered auto-suggestion, and that he was the author of the much derided phrase: 'Every day and in every way I am getting better and better.' And, as I went on reading, I continued to learn things I knew nothing about: Professor Dahl's treatment of Rachmaninov, about Vogt and Schultz and Romen and Lozanov and Silva. I had heard something about 'Silva mind control', for my wife bought a book about it, and she swears that, when she gets into the right state of mind, she can invariably find a parking space. I do not doubt her, for I have often

Introduction to the First Edition

noticed that I can get parking spaces when I am in a relaxed and confident frame of mind, and that if I am tense and irritable, they always seem to be full. (Most of us are usually in a kind of 'in between' state in which we may or may not be lucky.) And this in turn made me see that it has something to do with Jung's synchronicity, which seems (at its simplest level) to be some strange power of the subconscious mind to cause coincidences.

This is why I went on reading Neville's book in an increasing state of excitement, and why I wrote to his publishers saying that I would regard it as a privilege to introduce it. It is not simply because he seems to me to be propounding an immensely important theory of 'creative' education, but because everything he says has implications that go beyond education – unless we define education in its very broadest sense as the evolution of the soul. (Keats, we may recall, once defined life as 'a vale of soul-making'.) It is one of those books that fills the reader with a curious sense of optimism, a feeling that important discoveries lie just around the corner, and that you or I might be the ones who stumble upon them.

Another important insight came when I was reading his fascinating chapter on Milton Erickson. Talking about the differences between trance and hypnosis, Neville writes: 'A group of children listening open-mouthed as their teacher reads a story is in trance. So is the child who sits gazing out of a window instead of doing his sums. So is the friend whose eyes glaze over as soon as you start talking about your fascinatingly clever two-year-old.' And he goes on to point out that people in trance are unusually receptive to suggestion. For the hundredth time, I put down the typescript to think about it. (I always find this to be a sure sign of an important book.) It would be ideal if you had a kind of second self who could sit next to you, begin talking about his clever two-year-old, and then implant all kinds of useful suggestions. Then I saw that, in fact, something of the sort can be done, not only in 'trance' but in sleep. If, before I fall asleep, I deliberately induce in myself a feeling of marvellous optimism and hopefulness (it helps if I have received an unexpected royalty cheque that day), I can then relax into sleep carrying the optimism with me. If I wake up an hour or so later, the optimism is still there, and I can strengthen it by simply reminding myself how pleasant it is to be lying in a warm bed. Once the process is begun, it is easy to maintain, and 1 find that I wake up the next morning feeling thoroughly refreshed and prepared to take on the most 'boring' problems. (In fact, no problem is boring; it is we who are bores.) I offer this as an extremely useful way of maintaining yourself in a state of purposeful vitality.

The basic method, of course, was discovered by the Austrian psychiatrist Viktor Frankl, who called it 'the law of reverse effort'. He came across the case of a boy who stuttered badly, and who was chosen to play the part of a stutterer in the school play. On stage, he found he couldn't stutter for the life of him, and that he stopped stuttering thereafter. Frankl, like Erickson, used this technique on his patients. One patient, for example, was a clerk in the days when ledgers had to be filled in by hand. In a a state of anxiety about his personal life, his handwriting was getting worse and worse, and the more anxious he became about it, the worse it got. Frankl told him: 'Go home and tell yourself that you are going to develop the worst handwriting in the whole world. Write as badly as you possibly can.' After an hour of trying to write badly, the clerk found that he couldn't write badly any more.

A similar discovery was made by a remarkable friend of mine called Alfred Reynolds in the last months of the Second World War. He was in British intelligence, and was given the task of 'de-nazifying' young Nazis. Alfred is half-Jewish, and these blond-haired Junkers eyed him with distaste and mistrust. But, instead of lecturing them on the virtues of democracy, Alfred simply asked them to tell him about their beliefs — why they were Nazis, why they admired Hitler. And as they talked, he just sat and listened, making no attempt to interrupt, but merely interjecting questions when the discussion seemed to be running out of steam. Within two or three days, they had de-converted themselves, merely by engaging in heated discussions about the fundamental principles of politics and social organization. They had come to recognize that this kind of free, intelligent discussion would have had no place in Hitler's Germany. And they simply ceased to be Nazis. (Amusingly enough, they all transferred their allegiance to Alfred, who became head of a flourishing European movement called 'Die Brücke' (the bridge) immediately after the war.)

Introduction to the First Edition

Alfred's method was 'socratic', and we may recollect that Socrates described himself as a 'midwife' of truth, one who merely helped it to be born – you may recall the passage in the *Meno* in which he gets an ignorant slave to solve a geometrical problem simply by asking him the right questions. Quite clearly, the whole thing depends upon the peculiar genius of the teacher (using genius in its precise sense of some natural aptitude or talent). The trouble is – as Neville points out in his chapter on Coué – that, although the method may be worked out to the last detail, it can seldom be passed on to the teacher's successors, for it seems to depend upon that indefinable genius of its creator. This seems to be the fundamental paradox of education, the paradox that has continued to defy all the theorists.

Yet I would suggest that, in this book, Neville has come close to solving it. Although his conclusions, as set out in the last chapter, seem to me to be logical and satisfying, I feel that the most exciting thing about the book is not its conclusions, but the sparks his mind throws off in such abundance in reaching them. Neville himself obviously possesses the peculiar genius of the educator to a very high degree. I do not know what he is like in the classroom, but on paper he is an inspiration. He shows us that the essence of education is becoming excited about ideas. And the moment we become excited about ideas, we begin to grasp the answer to the question that Neville poses on the first page – 'whether we are manifestations of reality or the creators of it'. When the mind recognizes its power to grasp the nature of reality, it also recognizes its power to order and create reality. (One of the peculiar paradoxes of this state may even be the power to induce 'synchronicities'.) In short, the ultimate definition of education is the power to uncover humanity's hidden evolutionary potential.

PSYCHE IN THE CLASSROOM

*O*nce, in a certain land, there dwelt a King and Queen who had three daughters — the eldest charming for her bodily grace, the second equally charming for her wit and intelligence. Even when they were children, everyone admired these two. But as time went on it began to be noised abroad that the third and youngest was after all the fairest of the three. The name of this one was Psyche. She was retiring, shy perhaps, nor had she all the gifts of her sisters; but it was seen that there was something unearthly in her beauty, some strange light in her countenance which entranced those who gazed upon it. Indeed it was whispered here and there that she was fairer than Aphrodite herself, whom all Nature adores. And some, actually deserting the temples and the service of the foam-born goddess, came and paid their worship to the lovely maiden.

Lucius Apuleius, *The Golden Ass*

Educating Psyche

WHEN I WAS IN THE EARLY STAGES of writing this book I had a dream.

I was at a faculty meeting at the university where I was working. My colleagues and I were discussing, as we often did, ways in which we might change our programs in order better to cope with changing needs and changing resources. There was not much energy in the discussion. I had a feeling that there was something very significant at issue, but that we were all playing safe by avoiding it. Eventually I got impatient and, feeling somewhat self-conscious, began to speak my mind. Somehow the staff room was transformed into a vast auditorium and I was on stage addressing an audience of thousands. It was a very long speech. I don't know what I said, but at one point I recall saying something about Wilhelm Reich. At this point I seem to have lost my audience. Some went to sleep. Others were chatting to each other or shuffling their feet. A couple of my colleagues were standing in one of the side aisles; I suspected that they were sniggering at my predicament. I wanted to stop talking but I was trapped on stage, becoming more and more self-conscious, less and less coherent, and not knowing how to stop. At length I paused, got everyone's attention and delivered my final sentence, which was still ringing in my ears when I awoke: 'The question with which I must ultimately wrestle is whether we are manifestations of reality or creators of it.'

It sounded sort of significant. It also sounded a bit pretentious.

The script of this dream will be recognized by many teachers who have dreamed their own versions of it. At least in my dream I had all my clothes on. I also had a sense of having the last word, and managed to escape back into waking.

Of course, the last word was not much of a statement. My dream ego was only saying that a particular metaphysical question was one that affected me personally, one that I had to ultimately wrestle with. It didn't suggest an answer to the question which has been thoroughly argued by materialists and idealists, positivists and phenomenologists, physicalists and vitalists, Darwinists and Lamarckians, determinists and voluntarists. Neither did it suggest that if I wrestled hard enough I would come up with an answer. After all, Shakespeare and Tolstoy, for all their wrestling, were also only able to express the complexity of the question.

The mythologies of our culture dealt with such questions long before philosophers gave us the words that now enable us to argue about them. Our monotheistic myth sees God as both creator and manifestor of reality: 'In the beginning God created heaven and earth ... and God said, "Let there be light".'[1] Our polytheistic myths present us with a division of labour. In the Greek version, manifestation is attributed to Apollo, imaged in the clear light of the sun, who makes everything obvious, who shows things as they are. Creativity, the life-impulse, belongs to another god, Eros, a much more complex and paradoxical figure.

When Freud was looking for a god-image to personify the sexual energy that he was convinced was at the root of all human action, he thought of Eros. But Freud did Eros an injustice in defining him so narrowly. Eros is indeed the son of Aphrodite, goddess of sexual love, but he does not really grow up until he manages to leave his mother. For gods, as for humans, growing up comes through relationship, through finding a lover. Eros finds Psyche.

PSYCHE'S STORY

Psyche's myth tell us that when Eros, to the dismay of his mother, falls in love with the mortal Psyche and marries her, he insists on coming to her only in darkness so that she will not recognize him. Her sisters tell her that her husband must be a monster and she is at last persuaded to shine a light on his face as he sleeps. Of course she loses him. She wanders the world seeking him, becomes the slave of Aphrodite, is given impossible tasks to perform including going to hell and bringing back the beauty of Death in a casket, and is at last reunited with Eros.

The myth of Psyche, whom the ancient Greeks recognized in the butterfly and whom medieval writers saw as an image of the soul in search of God, is a myth of transformation. It is the story of how the soul is drawn by love through a slow, painful, shadowy initiation into a new way of being. T. S. Eliot describes the experience as arriving back where we started and knowing the place for the first time.[2] Gilbert Durand calls Psyche's story a myth of the metamorphosis of perception.[3] It is a story of finding Eros through encounters with animals, insects, plants and the Queen of Death. It is a story of blunders and ambivalence, of self-abasement, of stumbling over shadows towards reunion with the divine.

The Psyche story as we know it best is a literary re-working of the Greek myth by the Roman writer Apuleius.[4] Apuleius was a devotee of the Egyptian goddess Isis and had been initiated into her mysteries. His story of Psyche carries echoes of the myth of Isis, of the Greek Persephone, the Sumerian Inana, the Japanese Izanami and the Indian Urvasi. These myths are not identical by any means, but they seem to derive from a common basic metaphor of the human condition.

Against the myth of Psyche and Eros stands the myth of Apollo, the myth that celebrates the clear light of the sun. It is the myth of logic, rationality, detached observation, scientific enquiry, spiritual enlightenment, obviousness, understanding exactly what is what. Durand suggests that this myth took hold of European culture in the seventeenth century and has maintained a grip ever since. In the nineteenth century the myth of Dionysos (impulse, ecstasy and the irresistible irrational) took hold of the romantic imagination and the myth of Prometheus (the technocrat, the engineer, the instrumentalist) inspired the industrial age. More recently, Hermes, god of merchants and thieves, has taken a high profile, claiming that the world is nothing but a marketplace where anything and everything can be bought, sold or bartered. But in universities and schools Apollo has so far held his ground. Dionysos has never had much influence in the classroom, except in marginalized subjects like drama. Prometheus has always been careless of the future and his present attempts to take control of schooling may in the long run turn out to mark the end of an era rather than the beginning of one. While politicians of all parties are enthusiastic worshippers of Hermes, and many school administrators fall in behind them, teachers on the whole prefer not to imagine themselves to be in the retail business. For the moment, at any rate, Apollo dominates the philosophy and psychology of teaching and learning.

The glories of Apollo are many and great, but one-sided. We can indeed be grateful that we have inherited from the Enlightenment a simple faith in the immediate light of sense-evidence. It has served us well and will, presumably, continue to do so. But we need to be aware at the same time of the perspective of Psyche, who tells us that understanding is not so simple, that reality is not manifested so clearly and directly but through shadows, images, and subtle intuitions.

In those fields of study that interest me most deeply, the worship of Apollo maintains its place as the establishment religion. Those basic human issues of survival and growth which were once worked out through the joy and pain of enduring relationships, through the nourishment of poetry, through the excitement of comic and tragic drama, through the splendour of ceremony and the spell of religious initiation, are now presented in a language which turns metaphors into abstractions. It is a language that belittles the soul and sneers at its mysteries, which classifies, categorizes, sterilizes and often bores the listener.

The language of conventional academic psychology is a language without soul. Too great a faith in Apollo's promise to uncover the essence of things leads psychologists to pin the struggling soul-psyche-butterfly in their specimen cabinet and attempt to comprehend it through meticulous measurement.

Like the Greeks, who knew better than to confine their worship to one god, if we want to worship Apollo wholeheartedly we must acknowledge Eros as well. Apollo can give us only manifested reality. It is Eros who introduces us to process, experience, relationship, the creative moment. Like Apollo, Eros is a powerful god who shows himself in whole cultures and cultural movements as well as in individual behaviour. Those who give him due worship may be blessed in the warmth of their relationships, in the richness of their experience, in the joy of their becoming. Yet, unfortunately, some fall so completely under his spell that they forget how to think at all. They have no taste for contaminating their romantic visions with theory or research or 'negative' notions of reality. They have no patience with organization or structure. Some of them label themselves 'humanistic' or 'transpersonal' psychologists or devote themselves to 'alternative' schools or ways of teaching. They are inclined to confuse chaos with creativity and impulsiveness with spontaneity. Under Eros' spell, even some holistic educators forget that the exercise of a keen, critical mind is as just as much a part of being 'whole' as the experience of unity consciousness.

Educating Psyche

Psyche, of course, is not a god, at least not when her story begins. She is a human who has all the problems humans are accustomed to have in dealing with these unpredictable beings.

Psyche does not seek out Eros. On Apollo's instruction, her parents have abandoned her on a mountain top, and she is standing there clad in her funeral-gown when Eros arrives. Aphrodite, envious of Psyche's beauty, has sent her son to fire his love-darts at her so that she will fall in love with a monster. Instead, Eros himself is smitten and carries her off to a beautiful palace in the valley where her days are peaceful and boring and the nights are spent in the arms of her unknown lover. Apollo, who is responsible for Psyche's presence on the mountain top, does not enter the narrative again, but the Apollo-image of light is powerfully present.

Psyche's days are full of light and spent in a beautiful environment, yet she is bored. The daylight only shows her the 'things' of which her world consists. It is only at night, when she can no longer see, that she knows the god who comes to her. This knowledge, shadowy, incomplete, and unreflective though it is, satisfies her. It is only after the visit of her sisters, who come to relieve her day-time boredom, that she seeks to know her divine lover in a different way. The jealous sisters, who have never experienced the god in darkness, persuade her that true knowledge comes through light: she must shine a lamp on her lover's face. Psyche takes the light and sees Eros' face for a moment. A drop of hot oil wakes him and he vanishes, leaving Psyche in the dark with her lamp and no god to shine it on. Whereas previously she had experience of the god without knowledge, now she has knowledge without experience. In her grief, Psyche passes through the valley of the shadow of death before she can be reunited with Eros, in the fullness of light and the fullness of experience, in happily-ever-after-land.

When the Greeks took Psyche as a metaphor of the human mind-soul they envisaged a much larger entity than what we are accustomed to call 'mind'. We are inclined to think that consciousness is the mind, and it is a long time since it has been very fashionable to speak of soul at all. Our prejudice extends to assuming that the abstract, rational processes that consciousness is so fond of are the standard human mode of operating. Actually, abstract conceptualization was a fairly late achievement in the mind's (or brain's) development, and it still occupies the mind for only a fraction of the time. The original and basic unit of mental activity, which remains the total psyche's preferred way of operating, is the image. The Greeks had great respect for abstract intellect and its achievements, but they knew it was a tiny lamp in the surrounding darkness, which drives away reality in the moment of observing it: Psyche encompasses the shadows as well as the light, and other senses besides sight.

When mind, however, sets out to examine itself scientifically it adopts the perspective of Apollo and the methods of rational, logical thinking. It hopes to set itself out in the clear light of day and examine all its component parts and the ways they fit together.

UNDERSTANDING PSYCHE

Freud, who initiated the systematic study of the psyche at the end of the nineteenth century, did so in homage to Apollo. He was intent on writing science according to the positivistic, reductionist model he admired. Freud's original enthusiasm was for neurophysiology. He was attracted by the project of uncovering the relationship between mental processes and the physiology of the brain. When he realized that he did not have the patience to commit himself to this task with little hope of swift success, he switched his commitment to the project of uncovering the facts about mind as mind, and left the science of brain-mind relations to others.

A hundred years later the science is still in its infancy. Brain physiologists are not in agreement as to whether the mind is reducible to biological processes, as Freud assumed, or is an independent non-material entity. Neither do they have consensus when they attempt to map the brain and locate the different functions of the mind in it or when they try to reduce its processes to electricity and chemistry. However, though there are vast areas of the brain of which they know very little they can now tell us a lot about mind-brain. We are assured that there is much more information yet to come about left-brain right-brain differentiation, about imaging and perception, about short-term and long-term memory, about 'on-line' and 'off-line' processing, about brain plasticity, about the living presence within us of not only a human brain but of a mammalian and a reptilian brain as well. The work of physiologists brings teachers up against the evidence that the brain has greatly under-used capacities.

Freud's language was very different from that of the physiologists, but his sense of what he was doing was the same – uncovering the 'facts' about the mind. Both Freud and Jung were committed to the Apollonic ideal of empirical science but they could not find an adequate scientific language to pin down and label exactly what the mind is. They had to fall back on myth, metaphor and poetry, Psyche's own language. All the same, Freud stuck determinedly to the Apollonic fantasy that he could discover exactly what mind is and lay it before the world clearly, systematically and without ambiguity. While he did not succeed and his science now appears to us inadequate in many ways, his images are still powerful and contribute greatly to our understanding of the mind.

It was Jung who stood as the leading apologist for Psyche in the twentieth century. In some ways Jung was a more modest scholar than Freud. He did not share Freud's drive to produce a single, coherent, systematic, Apollonic theory to explain all human behaviour. Like Freud, he had a lot of faith in the clear light of the intellect but, unlike Freud, he did not need to defend his thinking against the paradoxes and contradictions that sabotaged every attempt to be consistent; indeed, he seems rather to have enjoyed them. Jung explored Psyche by the accumulation of images; he did not attempt to explain Psyche by reducing her to a 'nothing but'.

Jung wrote little about education, but the re-evaluation of Psyche which he and other depth psychologists have undertaken offers a great deal to teachers in the attempt to understand what education might involve and to find the best ways of going about it.

Freud struggled to persuade the world that mind is larger than consciousness, but he found the conscious and unconscious minds to be at war. For Jung, on the other hand, the evidence declared that conscious and unconscious were essentially in harmony as parts of a greater whole. This greater whole, the composite of all human mental activities, he called the psyche.

In his early writings Jung made the distinction between the personal and collective unconscious. He had first of all to show that his idea of the personal unconscious was less narrow than Freud's. Then he had to account for the evidence that some of the contents of the unconscious were universal rather than individual. Later he decided that these terms were not very useful, preferring to write about the personal psyche to emphasize the whole mind, rather than to set ego and unconscious against each other as Freud did. When he found that the expression 'collective unconscious' was misinterpreted he chose to substitute the term 'objective psyche' in his later writing.

For Jung, the personal psyche is the total personality. In its thing-aspect it is made up of several components (ego, persona, shadow, anima/animus) and an organising centre that Jung called the self. The psyche is also distinguished by attitudes (introversion and extraversion) and functions (sensing, intuition, thinking and feeling). The psyche is inhabited by clusters of ideas and feelings which Jung called complexes. The ego is one of these, but there are others that are unconscious.

For Jung, the personal psyche was not the central psychological reality; it was only a part of the whole that he called the objective psyche. He concluded from his study of dreams that there is a dimension that operates prior to and independently of our individual conscious functioning. We find it difficult to grasp the idea that our experience of an individual 'I' is somehow a secondary phenomenon, that the universe does not revolve around the ego, that our personal consciousness is just the momentary expression, at a point in space and time, of the cosmos. Yet that is what Jung implies. Galileo and Copernicus had it easy in comparison.

One way of imaging the objective psyche is as an energy field. It is not perceivable in itself, but through the patterns formed by observable events that come under its influence, just as we cannot see a magnetic field but can see the patterns that iron filings form within it. Jung called the patterns of image, emotion and drive that shape themselves in the fundamental psychic energy field the archetypes. They have often been called gods.

CREATING REALITY

In Greek thinking the gods were personifications of primal energy as it manifested itself to and in humanity. For contemporary Jungian thinkers like James Hillman, these personifications are ways of understanding the world of nature and human consciousness. 'They are formulated ambiguously, as metaphors for modes of experience and as numinous borderline persons. They are cosmic perspectives in which the soul participates.'[5] We do not have to believe literally in Apollo and Eros (or Jesus and Satan) to take them seriously. They are culturally confirmed images that represent psychological truth.

Jung found it easy enough to write about the psyche as a thing, an empirically established fact, but he was conscious of the limitations of so doing. He was more comfortable writing from a perspective in which 'hard, concrete reality' is perceived as a world of meaningfully structured images. He pointed out that 'everything of which we are conscious is an image'[6] and that 'every psychic process is an image and an imagining'.[7] Not only is the psyche's whole activity that of imagining but the psyche actually 'creates reality every day'.[8] This is a perspective that, in Western thinking, goes back to Pythagoras and beyond. It maintains that we can approach reality (what Kant called the forever unknowable 'thing in itself') only through constructing a pattern of symbols. Everything we can say about life, truth or consciousness is an 'as if'. Reality is something we constantly create.[9]

Jung found that one way to avoid reducing the psyche to a thing was to take his cue from mythology and write of Psyche as a person. He found that through this image he could come closer to conveying the idea of psyche as a process or as a perspective. Hillman follows this lead. For him, psyche or soul is 'that unknown human factor which makes meaning possible, which turns events into experiences, and which is communicated in love'.[10] It is a perspective that sees all realities as essentially symbolic and metaphorical. Psyche permeates everything, even the fictions, fantasies and facts of objective science. Whatever Apollo displays as physically and literally real is always also a metaphor. Where intellect seeks reality, soul finds poetry.

It is a perspective that must be adopted also when looking at the psyche itself, or Psyche herself. The myth tells us that truth is very elusive, that while the clear light of intellectual abstraction can give us a moment of brilliant insight, this is only one element in the process. The rest of the process is presented in images of love-making in the darkness, of going down again into the shadows, of confronting all the elements (earth, air, fire, water), of negotiations with the gods, of love, hate and death, of finding community in other living creatures.

We can learn a great deal about the mind from those who are interested essentially in establishing 'the facts' (whether the facts of neuroscience or the facts of phenomenology) and building elegant theories upon them. However, Psyche is not content with Apollo's point of view. Valuable as it is, it is only one point of view. Psyche has her own point of view, in which left-brain, right-brain, old-brain, new-brain and the rest are images which join the images of Vergil, Goethe, Blake and Shakespeare in pointing to a reality greater than themselves. When it comes to examining these images, Apollo can provide a number of fashionable lamps to use (Darwinist, structuralist, critical theorist, constructivist, antideconstructionist, polymetatransintercreationist) that, as often as not, will declare they are manifesting reality even as they are creating a new set of images. But there is much more to understanding than this. Where Apollo wants to analyse these images, Psyche must go down into them and experience them.

THE SOUL PERSPECTIVE

Whether we think of the psyche in thing-terms as the whole of the mind, or think of Psyche in process-terms as the soul-perspective, it is apparent that it, or she, gets little acknowledgement in the schooling system. Classical and medieval writers distinguished the soul from both spirit and body. For them, soul was a sort of link between spirit (intellect) and body; soul was the aspect of us which feels, loves, images, prays, responds to beauty. In the seventeenth century the idea of soul was discarded as unnecessary and unscientific, suitable only for religious language. It is only very recently that soul has begun to find its way back into the language of psychology.

It is intellect that dominates conventional schooling. Even body gets a recognition not allowed to soul. The specifically soul-making subjects – literature, drama, music, the visual and tactile arts – are progressively 'de-souled' as the child proceeds through the school. The infant or primary teacher may read a poem or story or show a picture because it may nurture or enrich the children or 'stimulate their imagination'. Moving up through secondary school, there is less and less time for such luxuries. When it comes to the public examinations which dominate secondary schooling, there can be no marks for being grabbed by a poem or painting or sonata, unless this translates into a motivation to analyse the artifact thoroughly and competently. The arts are often seen as not much more than a recreational diversion from the real studies.

The 'real' subjects are taught without soul. There is rarely a sense that we are dealing with metaphor. Mathematics in secondary school becomes a set of algorithms rather than the quest for a language to contain the uncontainable. The excitement of this quest seems to be confined to the first years of primary schooling and the last years of tertiary. The sciences talk only the language of facts. In the technology-based subjects, the possibilities for soul-making are neglected in an obsession with utility.

This one-sidedness in conventional teaching makes it not only narrow but ineffective, a concern which has been dealt with through many overlapping metaphors. Some writers use the image of the brain and decry the tendency in schooling to access only one part of it and ignore the rest. Others locate their metaphor in the computer and find teachers wanting in their assumption that all processing is 'on-line' while the evidence points to our enormous capacity for 'off-line' processing. Whatever the mind is, consciousness is not to be identified with it. Mind seems to be a tiny part of the whole. Pavlov saw it as a tiny, moving speck of light surrounded by shadow. He could have been thinking of Psyche's lamp.

It is my purpose in this book to explore this shadowy area and to see whether our understanding of it can help our teaching. This is not to diminish intellect, which is largely the instrument of our exploration. Apollo does not need an apologist yet, though he is clearly under challenge from Prometheus the technologist and Hermes the merchant, even in schools. This book will be somewhat one-sided, taking the perspective of Psyche, whose love is not Apollo but Eros. However, we must realize that Psyche's one-sidedness is one that reflects on itself reflecting, which embraces complexity rather than singleness and irony rather than belief. Psyche prefers *both-and* to *either-or*. One element in the perspective of soul is the acknowledgement that it is only a perspective, one image among many.

THE POLYTHEISTIC CLASSROOM

Psyche seeks her daemon lover largely in darkness, but from time to time there is a flicker of light, as when I dream and recall my dream. My dream-ego was not reflecting on uncertainty, incompleteness or insubstantiality. It was up on stage being very earnest about something. What it was saying was very important and needed very much to be said. My Apollonic consciousness was making clear what was what. It had something to do with teaching, it had something to do with depth psychology and it involved ideas that sensible academics do not take very seriously. But the message obviously wasn't getting across. As far as the audience was concerned all this earnestness was counter-productive. They didn't learn anything by being told, certainly not by being preached at. The only thing that caught their attention eventually, if only for a moment, was the statement of a personal dilemma and the formulation of an ultimate question that concerned themselves.

I can recognize in the interaction between dream-ego and audience something of my ambivalence as a teacher. On the one hand I believe that there are things that children have to know, if they are to have any power over their lives or find any pleasure in them. Some of these things are derived from our guesses about what sort of future these children are growing into. Some of them come from our experience of the past. Likewise in training and educating teachers I believe that there are things that student teachers have to know if they are to cope in any sense in the classroom. I cannot depend on them staying in the profession long enough to learn by experience if they do not take suitable skills and attitudes into it in the first place. And I do not want them to be a burden to their pupils. There are also certain ideas about teaching which have had great influence on me and which I would like my students to confront and understand. As a teacher I give in to the urge to label things, to make them clear, to make the occasional categorical statement that 'This is the way things are!' I become a devotee of Apollo, finding and proclaiming the truth about things.

Educating Psyche

Archetypal psychologists suggest that all behaviour is archetypally constellated. All our thinking and behaving is done within one archetypal fantasy or another.[11] When Jung referred to archetypes as 'modes of apprehension', he was suggesting that not only the ways we perceive the world, but the ways we think about it, feel it and make judgments about it are shaped by particular patterns which people once called gods and represented in the stories about them. We may no longer be accustomed to talk about Apollo and the rest, but our behaviour is still largely framed by the same patterns and energies that earlier peoples acknowledged as gods. So, when I think about education in this essentialist way, my thinking is shaped not only by the Apollo image. It is also shaped by the image of Zeus, patriarch of the gods, who insists that everything worth knowing is already known and needs only to be passed on the next generation of students.

But, clearly, this is not the only way of imagining education. I have come to believe that we learn very little by being told the answers to questions we have not asked. It seems to me that learning originates in the experiences of the learner, not those of the teacher. A great deal of what we learn, we learn by a sort of absorption, or we just 'pick it up' through experience, as we go along, without the need for teaching. It is only in schools that we abandon this natural way of learning. In schools, we tell children (or adults) things we consider important and then we expect them to remember what we tell them. I believe we tell them largely in vain. The learning they do has little to do with our telling.

Through one eye I can see education to be concerned with a body of knowledge that the adult-generation is engaged in transmitting to the child-generation. This essential curriculum is dictated by the wisdom of the past and the needs of the future. There may be strong conflict as to exactly what it is that should be taught to all children. Some may even see the content itself as relatively inconsequential and stress that it is the skills gained in learning the content that constitute the essential core of the curriculum. Whatever we disagree about (sex education, peace education or grammar, for instance) we may still agree that something, whatever it is, is essential. Essentialist education by its nature tends to make everyone the same: the child as the inheritor of society's wisdom and the manifestation of society's values. Obviously Apollo and Zeus have a hand in it.

Through my other eye I see that the content of education is not particularly important. What matters is that children have the experience of thinking, not that they learn to think particular thoughts. From this perspective, what matters is that children experience the process of learning, not that they store pieces of information in their brains. Teaching is not about imparting knowledge but about facilitating learning. Schooling should be concerned with the growth of the individual child, which will occur if the child is fortunate enough to be placed in a supportive, nourishing, stimulating, resource-rich environment. What is fully human in society's value system will be learned as it needs to be learned. The teacher has only to be there, to respond authentically to the child's needs and questionings as they arise from moment to moment. The child will gain the knowledge and skills needed to live each moment. The teacher has no need to impose. As for coping with the 'real world' after schooling, the child will learn to do this as naturally as he or she has learned to do everything else. Education understood in this way enables every child to be different: the child as creator of its own life and, perhaps even, of a new society. It is the work of Eros and of other 'young' gods, such as Dionysos, Hermes, Artemis and Persephone, who each have their own slant on it.[12]

If it is not possible in this case to keep both eyes wide open, at least we can keep blinking very quickly. Many teachers manage to juggle the two perspectives without doing themselves damage. They value the tribal culture and use it as a vehicle for helping their students to grow, to create, to become individuals. They ensure that in their spontaneous exploration of the world the children have the opportunity to pick up the knowledge and skills that will enable them to appreciate and contribute to that culture. However, the schooling system as a whole comes down firmly for one value or the other. At the present time the essentialist approach is dominant. It is not particularly rational, as most of the essentialist curriculum is only essential because it has been there for years. The rigidity of this irrational essentialism is perhaps a defence against the chaos that would doubtless overwhelm us were we to relax our grip for a moment. The free schools and open classrooms that were ready to sweep the world in the 1970s may have retreated to the fringes of the schooling system but, it seems, they and their subversive values will swoop on us again if we are not ceaselessly vigilant!

In this contemporary essentialism we can see Apollo's power being challenged by Prometheus. The Apollonian pursuit of knowledge for its own sake is now apparently a luxury that even the richest societies cannot afford. The pursuit of knowledge for the understanding it may give us of society is not cost-efficient and is likely to be subversive. It is the needs of industry and economic development which provide the justification for re-sourcing education. Prometheus rules – at least for the moment.

Prometheus, the futurist and technologist, crafted man in the first place, and gave him fire (stolen from the gods) and the other gifts of industry. But in giving men these gifts in defiance of the gods, Prometheus cruelly took from them the foresight that might help keep them from catastrophe. Prometheus came to a sticky end.[13] The myth suggests that man's one-sided obsession with technology will lead him in the same direction, for Promethean arrogance ignores both the gods from whom technology comes and the hell to which such dangerous gifts might consign us. (Lest the reader assume that the use of the masculine form in this paragraph is a sexist slip, I must point out that in Greek mythology this scenario involves men only. Women arrive later, to Prometheus' great dismay.)

If we look at the root meaning of 'manifestation' (*manus*, hand; *festus*, struck) we find that it originally applied to crafting. Manifestation was first of all the work of Prometheus. Apollo's work of manifesting reality by throwing light upon it came later. It is no accident that the Promethean view not only sees production as the end of our endeavour, but sees the child itself as a product.

Apollo and Prometheus are great gods, but they have their faults. The gods (or archetypes) have negative as well as positive qualities. The Apollo-perspective may have inspired the greatest philosophical and scientific achievements, but the same Apollo is also to be found behind all kinds of rigid and dogmatic fundamentalism – religious, political and scientific – that insist on taking metaphors literally. Prometheus is heroic in his mission of making man master of his fate, and is dazzling in his inventiveness.

Psyche in the Classroom

Yet he is often mean-minded, amoral, obsessive in his materialism and careless of the future. When Apollo or Prometheus control the classroom, the teaching may be either good or bad within its own terms. From the Psyche perspective it is incomplete, however competent it is.

Yet we don't find completeness by banishing Apollo, Prometheus or Zeus from the classroom and substituting another god. Classrooms dominated by any single god tend to be toxic places. Without the critical consciousness of Apollo to provide some balance, Eros will be bitchy and vengeful, Dionysos will be self-indulgent and destructive, Artemis will be paranoid and defensive. We especially need to keep a careful eye on Hermes. The god of transformation is also the god of thieves and liars. For some years, Hermes has been negotiating a takeover of education, making it simply another commodity with no value other than its exchange value. He seems to be currently negotiating a deal with Prometheus, so that skills and technologies cease to be of value in themselves, or of value in improving human lives, and become instead commodities to be traded, with no value other than their market value. Homer portrayed the gods squabbling in their palace on Mount Olympus. We can still hear them squabbling within ourselves and within our classrooms.

In my dream, the dream-ego started off by seeing things simply and trying to state them clearly and forcefully. If the experience which followed is a caricature of teaching, it is one that is frequently approached by reality, a caricature of a particular style of teaching which we might call 'direct'. We are all familiar with such teaching and in some places it is the standard. Good direct teaching successfully transfers information from teacher to student, generally thought to be a rational, intellectual operation. I suggest, however, that where direct teaching or lecturing is engaging, stimulating, entertaining and successful, it gets much of its success from operations which are not at all intellectual in the usual sense of the word: through modelling, through image and metaphor, through suggestion, through emotional contagion, through projection, through transference, through the unconscious mental sets of the listeners, through non-verbal and subliminal communication. Psyche is not to be confused with her lamp.

Direct teaching is tied to an Apollonic or Promethean view of the curriculum, to a model of teaching in which the teacher has the information and the student awaits it. Ideally the student asks questions, at least internally, and the teacher answers: the teacher demonstrates and the student copies. The student becomes more knowledgeable and skilful. However, Apollo and Prometheus are too proud: even in those areas of education that are concerned solely with the manifestation and reproduction of knowledge and skills, direct teaching has limited effectiveness.

Indirect teaching methods are more powerful than direct methods even in teaching an essentialist curriculum. In a non-essentialist approach they are the basic means by which a teacher works. They can call on capacities of the brain only marginally available to direct teaching. They emulate the way in which children and adults 'pick up' information, skills and values more or less unconsciously as they go about the business of living. In addition, the skilful teacher integrates conscious and unconscious processes in a way that not only creates a new understanding of the content but works towards the development of the child as a balanced and integrated individual. All of this indirectness and peripheral vision and movement towards wholeness is Psyche-stuff, shaped by the life force of Eros and Dionysos, by Artemis' engagement in the rhythms of the natural world, and by Hermes' assurance that the journey is more important than the destination.

Indirect and experiential methods are often criticized as being wasteful of time. Why spend a lot of time on an elaborate game on the environment or the French Revolution when you could just tell them what you want to tell them and be done with it? Why spend valuable class time having the chemistry class work out a formula from their own observations and calculations when you can just tell them plainly and get them to write it down and memorize it? Why send them off to the library researching a topic for hours when you could give them a one page summary that contains all the essential information and the correct opinions as well? Wouldn't it be quicker to tell the French class the vocabulary they need instead of having them waste time puzzling over the strange words in a text. We have little enough time to 'get through' *Macbeth* without putting hours into thoroughly workshopping and producing a scene. Why engage in a long discussion when all they need to know is the five main points that you are going to write on the board at the end of it?

Now for the five main points!

- The mechanisms of the brain are such that indirect 'unconscious' learning is more permanent than learning through direct verbal instruction.
- Indirect teaching methods involve emotion, intentionality and the handling of concrete objects, all of which reinforce learning.
- Learning through indirect methods often involves conscious or unconscious processes that lead to insight. Insights immediately become part of one's knowing rather than something to be remembered.
- Indirect methods, including genuine dialogue, are open-ended as far as content is concerned. If they are not closed down at the limits of the teacher's present knowledge they can generate entirely new understandings. Even the teacher can learn something.
- Verbal instruction is productive if it comes after indirect learning: to clarify, to answer questions, to provide labels for the ideas that have arisen. In other words, it is effective in teaching what is already known but not adequately verbalized. Instruction directed at complete ignorance and disinterest raises no ripples at all. It is certainly not time-effective.

Arguments like these can be set out in ways that are sufficiently logical, rational and systematic to be persuasive. The Apollonic implications will perhaps be sufficient to teach the reader what I want to teach. However, Psyche's myth sees it differently.

DOWNWARDS AND INWARDS

In Psyche's story there are three steps which precede the fullness of knowledge. First, the vague, inchoate, inarticulate knowledge that comes in the dark. Then the shining of the light and the recognition of what we knew all along. Third, the grounding and testing in concrete experience, while that illumination remains only a memory. Only after all this do the knower and the known truly meet.

Educating Psyche

I cannot teach the importance of the soul perspective, the benefits of indirect teaching methods or even facts about the brain to someone who does not in a sense 'know' it already. Socrates said as much 2500 years ago, and developed a teaching method based on this understanding. Yet when Socrates or any other teacher shines the lamp in the right direction so that someone finds words to express what before was vaguely felt, the experience may be exhilarating but the learning is only half-way there. With or without the teacher's help the learner must go on a journey, sometimes painful, sometimes tedious, to ground that knowledge in experience in the 'real world'. Otherwise Eros flees and is gone forever.

The movement downwards and inwards is a central image in the Psyche story. Psyche has to leave the bright world of exterior things and go down into the darkness of the underworld in order to find the beauty of Persephone, Queen of Life and Death. The myth reminds us that the Apollonic sunlight of what Jung calls the 'extroverted attitude' – reaching out to the external, day-to-day, obvious world – shows us only one face of reality. The other is to be found in the introverted attitude, going downwards and inwards to the depths of ourselves and learning there the depths of things.

The observant and sensitive teacher sees and responds to this inward movement in her pupils. As she presents and explains a concept that is new to her class, she notices the engagement and puzzlement of those pupils in whom her words find some resonance as they search within their subjective inchoate knowledge, for the point at which they already know what the teacher is talking about. She knows the delight of seeing the light come into her students' eyes as her concept begins to make sense. She notices also the blankness in the faces of those for whom her words are only words, who, if they carry her words downwards and inwards, find they have nowhere to place them. So the teacher searches for new words and new images and tries again to connect with what the children already know darkly. When she succeeds she is immediately rewarded.

As she drives home from school she may herself follow Psyche's path downwards and inwards as she reflects on the day's activity. She may not be aware she is reflecting on it. She is not thinking thoughts about it at all. Yet from time to time she is aware of an idea emerging, an understanding, fully or partly formed, of something which happened during the day. She has not thought things through to a sensible conclusion. Rather, she has gone down with Psyche to the underworld, the realm of invisibility, and brought back a fragment of the beauty of Persephone, the Queen of Death, that is, of finality, of purpose, of ultimate meaning.

This movement from the outer to the inner and back again is a basic human rhythm. In an extroverted society like ours there is some danger that we will override this rhythm and neglect these necessary moments of inwardness. Our organism protects us from this to some extent by periodically falling asleep. Many adults formalize the inward movement by setting time aside for meditation, jogging, quiet. What many teachers overlook is that children also need the opportunity to turn inward, not only to grow as balanced, healthy individuals but also to learn effectively what they are being taught.

As long as there has been a notion of soul it has been associated with depth. The early Greek philosopher Heraclitus said: 'You could not find the ends of the psyche though you travelled every way, so deep is its logos'.[14] The soul is not to be found in the near and far of things but in the depth of things. As James Hillman says: 'to study soul we must go deep, and when we go deep, soul is involved'.[15] The soul perspective looks for the non-obvious, the invisible, the poem hidden in the 'hard reality'.

Yet my attempts to explain the Psyche-myth and my dream show my faith in Apollo as much as my faith in Psyche. If I was more single-mindedly devoted to Psyche I might let the images speak for themselves or expand them through poetry or narrative. Some devotees of Psyche argue that she can only be grasped through vague, sentimental ideas, that the vaguer our ideas are the better they reflect her. I cannot agree. Precision is difficult to achieve but the attempt does her honour. However, in attempting to translate Psyche from a goddess to a psychological concept, we have to remember that abstract, conceptual Apollonic language can only go part of the way. The natural language of Psyche is metaphor, and we may get our best understanding of Psyche by layering metaphor upon metaphor. This is not vagueness. It is, at best, a peculiarly subtle form of precision.

Educating Psyche

PSYCHE'S WORK

Obviously, for all my intentions, I cannot escape the dilemma of my dream-ego. I stand on the stage and harangue my audience about the futility of standing on a stage haranguing one's audience. If I have any audience still with me, I need to make certain undertakings to increase the chances that writing and reading this book will be some sort of educational experience. I must undertake to do some thinking as I write, to wrestle with a question or two rather than simply pass on ready-made ideas – not an easy task in the age of the web browser when plagiarism is so easy and so rewarding. And I must remember that the myth of Psyche is a myth of relationship, that it shows the mind's encounter with the world to be inextricably linked with the encounter with another person. I must undertake to engage in dialogue with the reader, to ask questions and to listen for answers. And I must try not to cheat by avoiding questions that seem too hard.

One of the questions I find too hard is how the process of teaching and learning is related to questions of ultimate meaning, yet my dream shows me asking myself this question. My question is not about the treatment of ultimate meaning in the curriculum, which can be answered readily enough, theoretically at least. In schools grounded in a religious ideology, questions of ultimate meaning are dealt with explicitly. At the fundamentalist end of the spectrum they are dealt with directly and dogmatically. At the liberal end they may be taught in an exploratory and open-ended way, but the questions and answers are formed by the template of orthodoxy. In a secular school all such questions are dealt with indirectly. The children pick up their notions of meaning while studying literature, science, art, technology, history, politics, music, mathematics. They are lucky if they have a teacher who is sensitive to such questions. They are even luckier if their teacher has the skills to help them articulate and explore the vague notions that emerge.

Meaning is Psyche's work. It is the depth in things that Psyche must search out. It is a fragment of the beauty of Persephone, Queen of Life and Death. Psyche's confrontation with Persephone is not to be read any more literally than the rest of the myth. There is no one-to-one correspondence between the image and some concrete reality. For sure, Psyche must confront the reality of physical death, but Death is a more complex image than that. This confrontation is an image of transformation, of letting go what we are in order to become what we may be. It is also an image of ultimate meaning, of the end-point towards which our existence is facing. Psyche is permitted to bring back from the underworld only a fragment of this beauty, and this beauty must be kept locked in a casket, possessed but not seen.

EDUCATION AS EVOLVING PROCESS

For hundreds of years the ancient Greek philosophers grappled with the meaning of the universe.

The Greeks greatly admired the attempts of their philosophers to grapple with the meaning of the universe through the power of reason, but they had no expectation that mere rationality would ever be equal to this task. Their most intense exploration of the ultimate questions was through mythology, ritual, poetry and drama, all integrated in the celebration of the god Dionysos.

Dionysos is the brother of Apollo, and in most respects his opposite or shadow. His myths are full of images of darkness, of impulse, of vitality, of intoxication, of ecstasy. He has characteristics of both Eros and Psyche, but the gift of Dionysos is not insight or love. It is the spontaneous flow in which the ultimate question of what we are doing here is answered not in words but in action.

The ultimate question is not my concern here, but I do have a modest question about the function of teaching and learning in the universe. Is learning a manifestation only of what is there already, or can it be truly creative? Does it make a transformative contribution to the process of evolution? And what is the function of knowing in the evolution of the individual person? What am I to make of the physicist Wolfgang Pauli's statement that 'the process of knowing is connected with the religious experience of transmutation undergone by him who acquires knowledge?'[16]

Merely asking these questions implies that we are seeing the world from Eros' point of view. The Eros-perspective cares nothing for a static universe of things-in-themselves. It sees the life-impulse always moving towards its own continuation. It sees life expressed not in things but in the relationships between things. When it looks towards learning it sees the creative evolution of the individual, transformation, the emergence of hidden potentials. Eros is the youngest of the gods, unpredictable and occasionally malicious, but always insufferably romantic.

When Pauli writes of discovery in science as a transforming experience, he echoes the images of the Psyche myth. Knowing is somehow like religion, it binds us to the god. Psyche is set on the lonely mountain top, threatened by dreadful monsters. What she yearns for is love. What she gets is Love itself. Her curiosity and yearning brings her to union with the god and the transforming gift of immortality. What she comes to comprehend is her own and the universe's becoming.

The image of evolving or becoming is central to depth psychologies, as well as to the humanistic and existential psychologies that focus on the conscious aspects of this process. Roberto Assagioli's system of psychosynthesis is built on the premise that the human person grows naturally from unconscious to personal to transpersonal living and that this process can be facilitated by bringing consciousness to bear on it in specific ways.[17] Abraham Maslow saw human beings as moving instinctually towards self-actualization and beyond it to the transpersonal.[18] Carl Rogers was convinced that an 'actualising tendency' was the crucial dynamic in human development.[19] Jung's writing on individuation and the emergence of the self places humanity on the growing edge of a new evolutionary phase.

Alfred Adler and Otto Rank who, like Jung, were originally close associates of Freud, both developed a conception of the person as an organism drawn towards a meaning that is inherent in his or her individual life by dynamic forces neither wholly conscious nor wholly unconscious. Ira Progoff tried to avoid the conscious-unconscious dichotomy by talking about the 'organic psyche'. For him, the evolution of the 'integral personality' comes about through the action of archetypal images.

> In the human species the guiding images that are active in the seed of protoplasm have advanced to the point where they are able to communicate themselves. They become perceivable by the organism itself, and they are expressed with varying degrees of clarity and

emotion ... But whatever their aspect and quality, they represent what the psyche is as it manifests itself. They are the specific forms in which the psyche comes forth in human development and takes its place in the forefront of evolution.[20]

Such a concept of evolution owes more to Plato than it does to Darwin. Freud may have been impressed by the reductionist materialism of Darwin, but his legacy has fallen into the hands of those who would give more attention to Teilhard, Bergson, Lamarck, Goethe and Wordsworth.

Alfred North Whitehead argued that what we think of as our personal growth in understanding is our participation in the becoming of the cosmos. We are drawn, with the whole universe, towards the realization of beauty, harmony, intensity, complexity, enjoyment and peace. Each moment is a moment of creation in which we either contribute to this becoming or submit to the drag of the past and go on repeating ourselves.[21] Yet, even if we feel inclined to grasp this as the truth about our place in the universe, we should be restrained by Whitehead's own statement that this is a half-truth at best.[22]

The Psyche-perspective does not try to pin down truth in one form or the other, but accepts each of them as an 'as if'. Psyche is, after all, a butterfly. When put the question, 'Are we manifestations of reality or creators of it?' Psyche happily answers, 'Yes.' A little disappointing for those who came to watch her wrestle. Actually Psyche does not wrestle at all. She is courageous, committed, enduring, but wrestling is not her style. Wrestling is for Ares or Herakles, and a masculine consciousness. Psyche's consciousness is feminine.[23]

The soul has always been spoken of as feminine. In the classical languages soul was feminine and spirit masculine and many modern languages still carry this differentiation. Jung often uses the word anima synonymously for psyche and implies by it a feminine consciousness. For Jung, all human beings are psychologically androgynous. Immature people will identify fully with either their feminine self or their masculine self. If their identification is feminine (anima) they will have a repressed masculine consciousness (animus) and vice versa. As they mature or 'individuate' they will learn to own all their possibilities and cease to limit their identification to one self or the other.

Educating Psyche

In the meantime, most girls in our culture (through a combination of hormonal balance and early conditioning) will have a feminine consciousness and most boys a masculine. The masculine consciousness needs no exposition here. It dominates most classrooms, even many taught by women. The feminine consciousness is the consciousness of Psyche, characterized by receptivity, intuition, inwardness, a centrality of relationship, a sensitivity to beauty, a grounding in and comfort with what Carl Rogers calls 'organismic experiencing'.

To put it in this way is not to sentimentalize the feminine. All of these characteristics have negative as well as positive aspects and implications. It is not even women that we are talking about. It is a kind of consciousness that our culture manages to devalue and suppress not only in most men but in many women as well. It is perhaps unfortunate that the notions of feminine and masculine, anima and animus, have a gender-connotation, but in the absence of neutral words we have to make do with them. The Greeks themselves did not unambiguously give the goddesses 'feminine' attributes and the gods 'masculine' ones. The 'masculine' consciousness is represented in many of the myths of Athena and Artemis, not to mention the Amazons. And Dionysos, Eros and Hephaistos are almost as much figures of 'feminine' consciousness as Psyche herself.

When we look at conventional teaching we see it working hard at producing incomplete people. Traditional teaching methods come out of a masculine consciousness, whether Apollonine or Promethean, and assume a masculine consciousness in students. Boys are given little opportunity or reward to handle knowledge through their feminine consciousness. Girls, whose preferred or 'natural' way of learning is through a feminine consciousness, may have difficulty with the masculine mode of teaching. If girls are allowed to be intuitive and receptive and relationship-centred in class, it is often only because in the schooling system girls are devalued along with these Psyche-skills. Yet there are ways of teaching which emerge from the understanding of the human personality represented in the Psyche myth. To teach in these ways is to do something to redress an imbalance that we have long mistaken for the god-given and unshakeable order of things. We can start by abandoning the fantasy that the intellect with which our ego identifies so readily is our whole mind, our psyche.

The person on stage in my dream, all revved up to wrestle with ultimate questions, is certainly not my psyche. It is my dream-ego, the actor in the dream to whom my waking identity and consciousness seems to be attached. The fact that he makes his proclamations from the stage suggests that he represents my persona, my public self. The rest of me, my psyche, my total personality, is out in the dimly lit theatre. I would do well to receive the dream as a statement from all my selves, not just with the performing, self-conscious, thinking, wrestling self who gets all the good lines to say.

When my dream-ego got to the point of saying something earnest and significant, it said, 'The question with which I must ultimately wrestle is whether we are manifestations of reality or creators of it.' I awoke with a sense that this shift between 'I' and 'we' was somehow important.

The dream-ego with which my waking 'I' so readily identifies includes the audience in the dilemma. The 'I' which gets its kicks out of wrestling with ultimate questions has to do so on behalf of and in interaction with all my other selves: the bored, the busy, the cynical, the ironic, the apathetic, the impatient. The earnest pomposity with which I harangue my many selves has to be deflated by my whispers and sniggers. When I proclaim the significance of Wilhelm Reich and his ideas (homage to Aphrodite and Eros!) I have to listen to myself yawning. Reality is plural. So is personality.

The acceptance of this multiplicity of selves and the multiplicity of realities is one of the characteristics of the soul perspective. Soul cannot flourish in a classroom where everyone is expected to learn the same things and be pointed towards the same image of excellence, where there is only one way of being a teacher and one way of being a student. It flourishes where diversity is both a means and an end, where Saturn, Aphrodite, Dionysos, Persephone, Apollo, Eros, Hera, Hades, Jesus and Godzilla all get to express themselves.

Soul flourishes where images are honoured, where literature, art, drama and history are presented as a means of nourishment and not merely as intellectual pursuits, where enlivening images are sought in the sciences so that they too will enrich the imagination, feelings and relationships. In technology-based subjects, soul will flourish where the experience of crafting is taken seriously.

Fortunately schools contain many teachers who have learned to design and use curriculum to expand their own and their students' imagination, and many who provide for their students the experience of a healthy personality, characterized by humour, compassion, imagination, irony and a relish for ambiguity and complexity. And if Psyche's sacred marriage to Eros has been consummated, they will be able to announce the birth of Psyche's daughter Voluptas (pleasure) and display in their own lives (occasionally at least) what Hillman calls an 'animal flow of life' from which morality and choice issue spontaneously and naturally.

NOTES Chapter 1. Psyche in the Classroom

[1] Genesis 1:1-3.
[2] T. S. Eliot, 'Little Gidding' in *Complete Poems and Plays*.
[3] G. Durand, 'Psyche's View, *Spring*, 1981, p. 13.
[4] Apuleius, *Metamorphoses*.
[5] J. Hillman, *Archetypal Psychology*, p. 35.
[6] C. G. Jung, *Collected Works* 13:75.
[7] ibid., 11:889.
[8] ibid., 6:78.
[9] Alfred North Whitehead's process philosophy likewise asserts that the universe is not composed of 'things' at all, but of moments of experience. Every so-called 'thing' (including ourselves) is an accumulation of such moments – the current moment that we subjectively experience and all past moments that we now 'prehend'. The universe is not composed of 'its' at all, and subjectivity is not confined to humans.
[10] Hillman, op. cit., p. 16.
[11] The main contemporary voice in archetypal psychology is James Hillman. Hillman argues that the proper work of psychology is seeing through our personal and collective experience to the archetypal image behind it. He argues that we always see the world metaphorically. In fact, according to Hillman, we have no other way of seeing it.

> All consciousness depends on fantasy images. All we know about the world, about the mind, the body, about anything whatsoever, including the spirit and the nature of the divine, comes through images and is organized by fantasies into one pattern or another ... Because these patterns are archetypal, we are always in one or another archetypal configuration, one or another fantasy, including the fantasy of soul and the fantasy of spirit

(James Hillman, 'Peaks and Vales: The Soul/Spirit Distinction as Basis for the Differences between Psychotherapy and Spiritual Discipline', in J. Needleman and D. Lewis, *On the Way to Self-Knowledge*).

[12] Dionysos is the god of new life, impulse and creative energy. Artemis is the god of female initiation, feminine intuition and harmony with nature. Hermes is the god of travellers, of exchange and of transformation. He is constantly on the move, with no particular commitment. Persephone, like Dionysos, is simultaneously a god of death and of new life, which are not construed as opposites but as different aspects of transformation.

[13] Prometheus defended and supported human beings in defiance of Zeus. Consequently he was punished by being nailed to a rock at the boundary of the universe, while an eagle daily devoured his liver.

[14] Heracleitus, *Cosmic Fragments*, p. 45.

[15] Hillman, op. cit., p. 29.

[16] W. Pauli, *The Interpretation of Nature and Psyche*, p. 208.

[17] See R. Assagioli, *Psychosynthesis*.

[18] See A. Maslow, *The Further Reaches of Human Nature*.

[19] See C. Rogers, *On Becoming a Person*.

[20] I. Progoff, *Depth Psychology and Modern Man*, p. 13.

[21] See A. N. Whitehead, *Process and Reality*.

[22] 'There are no whole truths; all truths are half-truths. It is trying to treat them as whole truths that plays the devil.' Whitehead in L. Price, *Dialogues of Alfred North Whitehead*.

[23] For a discussion of Psyche as a myth of feminine consciousness, see E. Neumann, *Amor and Psyche*, and R. Johnson, *She*.

Note that in using the expressions 'feminine consciousness' and 'masculine consciousness' we are using a metaphor based ultimately on biology. The same polarization is often represented by the symbolism of Yin and Yan. It is often also portrayed under the metaphor of 'Eastern' versus 'Western' consciousness. Suzuki develops this image at length:

> The Western mind is:
>
> analytical, discriminative, differential, inductive, individualistic, intellectual, objective, scientific, generalising, conceptual, schematic, impersonal, legalistic, organising, power-wielding, self-assertive, disposed to impose its free-will on others, alienated from nature (it exists to be utilized) and eloquent.
>
> The Eastern mind can be characterized:
>
> synthetic, totalizing, integrative, indiscriminative, deductive, non-systematic, intuitive, non-discursive, subjective, spiritually individualistic and socially group-minded, in harmony with nature. (D Suzuki, 'Lectures on Zen Buddhism' in *Zen Buddhism and Psychoanalysis*, p. 5).

All the significant researchers in the past hundred years have come to the conclusion that the human mind is bifocal, from Freud who wrote about primary and secondary process, through Pavlov who referred to first and second signal systems, to Bateson who distinguished between analog and digital mental processes. A physiological basis for such distinctions is alleged to exist in the difference between the left and right hemispheres of the brain: verbal and logical thinking appear to be operations of the left hemisphere; pictorial and synthetic thinking appear to be functions of the right, as does the awareness and expression of emotional states. Attention to detail appears to be a left brain function while awareness of wholes resides in right brain; the left brain works in active mode whereas the right brain works in receptive mode. All of this is, of course, an oversimplification, as most mental activities engage both hemispheres.

For a useful introductions to research and thinking on hemispheric lateralization see R. Ornstein, *The Psychology of Consciousness* and W. Dell, *Notes for a New Mind*.

THE POWER OF SUGGESTION

One day the disciples came to the Buddha and said,
'Tell us, master. Are you a god?'
'No', said the Buddha, 'I am not a god.'
'Are you a demon, then?' said the disciples.
'No', said the Buddha. 'I am not a demon.'
'Are you a prophet?' said the disciples.
'No', said the Buddha.
'Then tell us, master. What are you?' said the disciples.
'I am awake', said the Buddha.

Zen story

FREUD DID NOT DISCOVER THE UNCONSCIOUS or invent it. When he began to work as a mind-doctor he did so within a well-established tradition, and paid due reverence to it. The controversy his ideas aroused only echoed the arguments that had been going on for a century (in France particularly) concerning the nature of the unconscious and its role in psychiatric treatment.

In the later years of the nineteenth century the argument had been centred on hypnosis, though it was only at the end of the century that the phenomenon got this name. Before it got a name and a physiological (but incorrect) explanation, it simply did not exist as far as the scientific establishment was concerned. Though people with remarkable powers had been finding careers in entertainment, religion or healing for thousands of years, and though there had been notorious and influential healers like Mesmer demonstrating their skills in Europe for a hundred years or more, the guardians of scientific medicine regarded them as charlatans.

It was a demonstration of hypnosis that set Freud thinking in the direction which led to psychoanalysis. He was fascinated by the effect of posthypnotic suggestions, where a fully awake subject would open a door or take off his coat in response to a cue that had previously been given him in trance. If asked why he was opening the door he would give a perfectly reasonable reply. Yet it was obvious that the real reason for opening the door had nothing to do with his rational mind. He must have another, unconscious mind which was directing his actions. And if this was true of this action, why might it not be true of all his behaviour? Freud used hypnosis for some time in his practice, but eventually decided that psychoanalysis could do without it.

While Freud was forming his school and developing his theoretical system in Vienna, a group of medical hypnotists was making hypnosis scientifically respectable at Nancy in France. Like Freud, they theorized about the nature of the unconscious, but came to a very different conclusion. Freud emphasized that the unconscious represented something essentially nasty, with unsavoury forces trying to push their way through into consciousness. The hypnotists at Nancy saw the unconscious as a positive force. The unconscious tended to move the person towards doing what was best for him or herself. While psychoanalysis was directed to enabling the person to control the unconscious forces, the hypnotists were inclined to invite the unconscious to express itself in behaviour. While Freud perceived the unconscious as dominating the personality, they were more impressed by its opposite aspect – its receptivity. They found the unconscious only too ready to receive and respond to suggestions made to it.

There was a great deal in common between the Vienna school and the Nancy school. Both were intent on making their art respectable through a passionately scientific approach, both were centred around a strong and attractive personality, surrounded by enthusiastic disciples, both suffered the antipathy of the scientific medical establishment, and both had visions of conquering the world.

EVERY DAY IN EVERY WAY

The strong and attractive personality at Nancy was Emile Coué. Unlike his colleagues he was not a doctor, but a pharmacist with a scientific bent and a gift for healing. Like Freud he was originally impressed by the power of hypnosis, but as his skills and reputation increased he found that he could cure people by making suggestions to them in their normal waking state. He found that he could heal people by merely giving them the expectation that they would be healed and then the suggestion that they were healing. He reached the conviction that the healer was not much involved in the process at all. His patients had only to suggest to themselves that their ailments were being cured and the healing would take place.

The craft of the faith-healer is an ancient one, but in our culture not a very respected one. Coué was adulated as a miracle worker, but what sets him aside from the religious and occult traditions of faith-healing is the serious attempt which he and his associates made to work within the framework of science. However, those who looked to Coué for elaborate scientific explanations of his miracles were disappointed. The method he developed through experimentation rested on two simple ideas which he was reluctant to elaborate in a detailed, systematic manner: all successful suggestion is auto-suggestion, and auto-suggestion is nothing but the action of the imagination.

Coué made much of the conflict between will and imagination, though his use of these words sounds a little vague to us. By will, he generally seems to mean the conscious mind. By imagination he sometimes means our ability to visualize possibilities. More often he simply means the unconscious.

> It is imagination that is the most important quality of man. You must know that we have in ourselves two beings. The first one is the conscious, voluntary being we know, and the second one, behind the first being, is the subconscious or imaginative being, or imagination as you call it.
>
> We don't pay attention to this being, and we are perfectly wrong, because it is this second being which runs us entirely ...
>
> If it is the second being which runs us, and we learn how to run it, through it we learn to run ourselves. Do you understand? I repeat, because it is most important. It is our unconscious being which runs us. We learn how to run it. Through it we learn to run ourselves.[24]

Coué's method of taking charge of the imagination or unconscious is through verbal self-suggestion.

> As long as you live, every morning, before getting up, and every night, as soon as you are lying in bed, shut your eyes, and repeat twenty times, with your lips, loud enough to hear your own words, without trying to think of what you are saying – if you think of it, it is well; if you don't think of it, it is well – counting on a little string, providing yourself with a little string of knots, 'Day by day, in every way, I am getting better and better.'
>
> In this little phrase there are three important words, 'In every way', which includes all the suggestions. Thus it is quite useless to make particular suggestions, as they are all included in three words 'in every way', but you must pay attention to make the suggestion, the auto-suggestion, very simply. Try it like this, in a monotonous manner, without any effort, as they recite the litanies in church.[25]

Coué was fond of demonstrating that if you clench your fist and keep repeating the words 'I cannot open my hand', it is impossible to open it. The only way your hand will open is if you allow, even for an instant, the thought (that is, the words) 'I can'. Then your hand opens without effort.

The Power of Suggestion

For him this is an analogy of our self-imposed illnesses and our self-imposed physical and mental limitations.

Interest in self-suggestion was not confined to France. Coué had disciples and imitators in England, North America and Australia, and the same methods had been independently developed by others. One of the most celebrated illustrations of the power of self-suggestion was the story of the loss and return of Rachmaninoff's creative abilities. After the poor reception given to his First Symphony, Rachmaninoff had withdrawn from his friends and become deeply depressed. He found it impossible to write music for two years, and became convinced that he would not compose again. He was close to suicide when his friends persuaded him to visit the Moscow physician and hypnotist, Nicolai Dahl. Dahl treated him for three months, constantly repeating to him in trance: 'You will begin to write again. You will write easily. Inspiration flows freely in you.' He taught Rachmaninoff self-hypnosis so that he could practise on his own.

Under Dahl's treatment, Rachmaninoff found that inspiration began to come to him. As he continued the practice he found music coming from within him and demanding to be written down. In this way he composed his Second Piano Concerto in C Minor, which was first performed in Moscow in 1901 and dedicated to Dahl.

Such a recipe for health is rather too simple and cheap to remain popular for long, unless it can be associated with a charismatic figure to whom one can make a pilgrimage. Auto-suggestion in the Nancy model did not sweep the world. It showed some promise of doing so in the 1920s, but had trouble coping with the Great Depression. It occasionally re-emerges as a phenomenon such as that expounded in *The Power of Positive Thinking*,[26] *The Silva Mind Control Method*[27] or *Psychocybernetics*.[28]

An important factor in this is the evidence that while people like Coué can work seeming miracles, their imitators cannot. Even after disciples and commentators have examined the methods of the master in detail and turned them into a set of techniques, there is still something essential missing. Coué, being an admirably modest person, denied that he had any specific powers, and was uncomfortable with adulation. Nevertheless he was very conscious of the part that his own status had in giving people an expectation that their ills would be cured. He paradoxically used this faith in him to give force to his suggestion to his patients that they could take control of their own healing. Specific suggestions relating to their ailments did not come until they had been prepared for healing by his obvious assurance, by the impact of meeting people who had already been cured, and by a relaxed and joyous environment. He maintained that no sort of technique could be effective without such preparation, but after such preparation cures could be sometimes effected by a word. The precise nature of this preparation was not important. What mattered was that it generated an expectation of assistance, or what in religious contexts is called 'faith'. Coué tried very hard to turn his over-dependent patients' faith in him into faith in their own power to heal themselves.[29]

The so-called 'placebo effect' has been well documented in medicine. Most of us have been cured by a placebo at some time or other. It worked particularly well when we were children. Mother could take away the pain of a bruise by 'kissing it better' or by putting iodine on it. It continues to be effective with us as adults, as every doctor is aware. The placebo effect is sometimes represented as evidence of the stupidity of human beings. It should be seen, rather, as evidence of the human organism's ability to heal itself, and of the role of suggestion in allowing it to do so.

AUTOGENIC TRAINING

While the doctors at Nancy were moving from hypnosis to self-suggestion as a cure for the world's ills, a group of doctors in Germany were making a similar journey, over a somewhat different route. For instance, Vogt started with conventional medical hypnosis, but found he could train people to induce in themselves autohypnotic states by a sequence of suggestions similar to those used in hypnosis. Vogt's first interest was in the use of such a technique in psychoanalysis but he soon came to see these self-induced states to be of interest in themselves. This interest was taken up in the 1920s by Schultz, who was impressed by the clinical possibilities of hypnosis but disliked the passivity and dependence associated with it. He noticed that people in this quasi-hypnotic state experienced heaviness and warmth in their limbs, and set out to discover if they could reverse the experience or induce a hypnotic trance by self-suggesting heaviness and warmth. Out of these experiments, influenced also by a study of yoga, he developed a system called autogenic training (AT).[30]

Autogenic training is done in two stages. In the basic stage the trainee repeats standard formulas to affect physical functions: to induce sensations of heaviness and warmth in the arms, legs and solar plexus, to induce coolness in the forehead, to regulate heartbeat and breathing rhythm.[31] The trainee who has gained control over these functions (usually after training for a few minutes a day for several weeks) can then use specific formulas to eliminate sickness and pain, to take voluntary control over body mechanisms (e.g., blood pressure, blood sugar) or improve memory and powers of concentration. With the basic training the trainee can go at will into a state of deep relaxation. In the advanced stage the trainee learns to create mental images, to meditate on these images and to receive answers from the unconscious speaking through them.

Schultz discovered that training was most effective when the trainee recited the formulas casually, without effort, with what he called 'passive concentration'. He also discovered that stage one was a healing process in itself. Trainees reported that physical disorders and personality problems seemed to disappear when they learned to spend time in the state of self-suggested relaxation. This echoes the discovery by hypnotists of the Nancy school of the 'healing trance'. They found that patients who were left in a trance for some time without specific suggestions were sometimes freed from their symptoms. The contemporary American hypnotist Milton Erickson sometimes induced a trance in a patient and left him or her for some time with the vague suggestion that their unconscious would work something out. The same phenomenon is observed in Ainslie Meares' use of 'mental ataraxis', a deeply relaxed meditative state, in the treatment of mental and physical disorders, including cancer.[32]

There has been a great deal more interest in autogenic training in the former Soviet Union and Eastern Europe than elsewhere. This is due, no doubt, in part to the fact that the study of suggestion and self-suggestion was legitimized by its compatibility with a materialist philosophy and by the interest and contribution of two prestigious figures, Pavlov and Stanislavsky. At any rate, the outcomes of autogenic training have been well documented, both within the laboratory and outside it. The continued support for research in autogenic training in Eastern Europe can be attributed in part to its demonstrated effectiveness in the training of athletes. The technique has gone through a number of modifications, most recently through the research of Romen in the USSR.

Romen has simplified the autogenic training procedure, and claims to have considerably shortened the time required to become proficient. The trainees are taught to actively submerge themselves in a special state of calm and muscular relaxation, by alternatively tensing and relaxing their muscles.. Then they switch to self-suggestions of calm and relaxation. When they have mastered the ability to submerge themselves in a pronounced state of calm and relaxation, they progress to self-suggestion, visualizing the effects they want to achieve. Romen asserts that 'through active self-suggestion, one can within three weeks learn to exert a considerable degree of direct, voluntary influence on the flow of psychophysiological processes of the organism.'[33]

Schultz' interests were medical. By contrast, Romen's research work has been devoted to discovering how healthy people can learn to control bodily and mental functions that are conventionally thought to be involuntary. He provides laboratory evidence that ordinary people, without experience of yoga or hypnosis can, by self-suggestion:

— raise or lower their skin temperature through several degrees;
— speed up or slow down their heart-beat;
— raise or lower their blood pressure;
— raise or lower their blood-sugar;
— engage in 'automatic writing';
— contract isolated muscles (e.g., breathe with one lung);
— eliminate sensitivity to pain (local or general anaesthesia);
— increase their skin sensitivity;
— shorten reaction time;
— increase the speed, accuracy and selectivity of perception;
— increase the ability to memorize and recall information;

— increase the ability to recover from fatigue;
— induce catalepsy (including the 'catalyptic bridge' where the body can rigidly support its own weight when suspended between two chairs, with the head on one and the feet on the other).

There is significance in Romen's discovery that, after the trainee has learned to achieve the state of 'self-submergence', and has learned to make suggestions while in that state, it becomes no longer necessary to enter that state in order to make suggestions successfully. He or she can control breathing or blushing, sharpen perception, eliminate pain or fatigue or generate perfect recall by a self-suggestion made in the midst of normal occupations.

For Romen, working within the Pavlovian tradition, the concept of 'the unconscious' is unnecessary. His interest is in psychophysiology and his discoveries and explanations are made within this model and use its language. Nevertheless, his findings confirm those of an uncritical pychodynamicist like Coué. And they reflect the same aspect of mind as is pictured in the myth of Psyche – its extraordinary receptivity when it stops trying to master experience and is content simply to receive it.

One phenomenon which has clearly emerged in Romen's research is the way successful suggestion is dependent on 'set'. We are all familiar with the experience of perceiving what we expect to perceive, or failing to perceive something because we are not mentally prepared for it at the moment, or because we do not believe that it exists. Once the organism has perceived something the first time it will readily perceive the same or similar events again.

The theory of mental sets was largely developed by the Soviet psychologist Uznadze. His basic idea was that the relationship between a stimulus affecting a human being and the behavioural response is never direct. It is always mediated by the person's psychological set. The person's interaction with the environment is constantly organising and reorganising such sets. Sometimes the process is conscious. More often it is entirely unconscious. We may even have a conscious set which is in conflict with an unconscious set, as when we believe we are highly motivated to do something yet never get around to doing it.

Uznadze's theory is essentially physiological. He was interested in the way experience sets up patterns of response in the brain, which then mediate between further stimulus and response. Even the stimulus which we receive subliminally and which elicits no apparent response works to form a new set or to change an existing set and thus to shape a future response. Some sets are unstable, that is, they only last for a particular situation. Others are fixed and firmly established. They may have been established by social rituals and expectations, by traditions, or by traumatic events. At any rate, experiences which tend to destabilize such sets generally generate resistance and anxiety, though the source of this anxiety may not be recognized.

What Romen discovered was that in a state of muscular relaxation, and more particularly in the specific state of self-suggested 'self-submergence', a set is more easily established or changed than in the normal waking state. An appropriate set can be established not only for a new perception, but also for a new action or reaction. Where past experience has already created a set it can be successfully changed or displaced by either verbal self-suggestion or by imagining the intended action. Once the new set is established it can be activated by a simple suggestion without the preliminary relaxation.

For the past fifty years biofeedback has been used with success for the same purposes as AT to achieve relaxation and meditative states and gain control of 'involuntary' physical functions-blood pressure, emotional states, headaches. As with 'self-submergence', once the subject discovers that he or she is in control, the technology can be thrown away. The new set has been established. For many people the Promethean fantasy of hi-tech gives biofeedback a credibility not possessed by soft approaches like relaxation methods, so that for them it is a much more effective placebo.[34]

The educational possibilities of AT and its various derivations are considerable. Any rational society would be interested in teaching its children a simple and tried method of controlling physical and emotional tension, controlling pain, bleeding, fatigue and boredom, improving memory, improving physical and intellectual performance. Since the technique has been successfully used with children for medical purposes, the development of educational uses should offer no great challenge or risk. However, schooling systems everywhere are inclined to develop their own unshakeable sets. We may have to wait till micro-technology makes biofeedback available on a mass scale. If this more credible placebo does become widely available, events which are now impossible may, perhaps, become boringly commonplace.

SUGGESTOPEDIA

One person who did not wait for the sunrise is Georgi Lozanov.[35] Like Schultz and Romen, his initial interest in suggestion was medical. He was impressed by the curative effects of hypnotic and non-hypnotic suggestion in ailments that did not seem to have a psychological origin. Like Schultz and Romen he examined yoga and was fascinated by the yogis' extraordinary feats of memory, and by the similar feats of memory specialists in non-literate cultures. He was puzzled also by the unusual ability possessed by isolated individuals in his own country (Bulgaria) to do complicated mathematical operations almost instantaneously and without effort.

William James takes the blame or the credit for first saying that we use only ten per cent of our mental potential. The statement has been repeated so often that it has gained for some the status of unassailable truth. However James reached his conclusion about the mind, there does appear to be evidence now that, as far as the brain is concerned, a large part simply doesn't appear to do much. It is this 'reserve capacity' which challenged Lozanov.

Like Coué he initially used hypnosis in psychotherapy. Like Coué he found that successful suggestion could be made without hypnosis. As his interest shifted to the phenomenon of hypermnesia – the ability of some people under hypnosis to recall past events in great detail – he discovered that with receptive subjects he could get the same result through suggestion without hypnosis. Moreover he found that through suggestion alone he could empower people to learn and recall vast amounts of new material, far more than conventionally thought possible.

Lozanov does not have much use for the term 'the unconscious', though he speaks a great deal about 'unconscious mental activity'. He prefers to use the word 'paraconscious' (more or less unconscious) because he is not interested so much in the instinctive-atavistic layers of the unconscious as in the constant flowing and merging between conscious and unconscious mental activity.

For Lozanov, like Romen, the 'set' is a central postulate in his theory of how suggestion works. He believes that the brain has an apparatus for foreseeing the results of actions that have not yet been carried out. This apparatus is influenced mainly, but not entirely, by past experience. According to past experience and incoming information, the brain selects the most probable event and prepares for it. The information the brain uses in constructing the set is largely unconscious, as is the set itself. Such unconsciously transmitted and recorded information is the basis of our more or less stable relationship to our social environment. Information transmitted and recorded consciously will not usually be assimilated into the complex of mental sets unless it is confirmed by information received unconsciously. In other words, when the teacher makes a statement to the class, and the teacher's subliminal non-verbal messages contradict the spoken word, it is these non-verbal messages of which neither teacher nor child is aware which influence the future behaviour of the children.

Suggestion operates through this sort of paraconscious activity. For Lozanov it is a simple stimulus-response, direct, automatic, precise, fast, economical in its use of energy. In suggestion, the flow of information goes straight into the areas of unconscious mental activity. Persuasion, on the other hand, takes a side-track via critical-logical reflection and decoding, and often runs into obstacles.

Lozanov's theory comes in direct line from Pavlov. For an understanding of paraconscious remembering, he turns to Pavlov's image of consciousness as a mobile light spot on the cortex, surrounded by a shadow, an area which is not fully excited but not fully inhibited either. The activity in that shadow is not experienced as consciousness but it takes place nevertheless. When someone speaks to us, for example, we deal consciously with a very limited range of the information. Usually we hear the basic idea, analyse it and form an answer. But this is not all we perceive or react to.[36] The speaker's choice of words, interaction, sentence structure, posture, facial expression, odour, age, dress, movements, are all received, as is contextual

The Power of Suggestion

information like background noise. Indeed, we can easily switch our attention to any of these. In addition, there is accompanying information that we cannot receive without special training or the assistance of technology: for example, imperceptible changes in facial expression, skin colour, odour, or the speaker's bioelectrical field. The whole pattern is recorded and shapes our intuitive reaction to the speaker. Children form their impressions of the world through this sort of paraconscious mental reactivity long before their logical-critical abilities are developed, and it remains the mechanism through which their basic assumptions are established.

Lozanov's instructional technique is based on the evidence that the connections made in the brain through this mechanism (which he calls non-specific mental reactivity) are more durable than those made through conscious processing. Besides the laboratory evidence for this, we know from our experience that we often remember what we have perceived peripherally, long after we have forgotten what we set out to learn. If we think of a book we studied months or years ago, we will find it easier to recall peripheral details – the colour, the binding, the typeface, the table at the library where we sat while studying it – than the content on which we were concentrating. If we think of a lecture we listened to with great concentration, we may recall the lecturer's appearance and mannerisms, our place in the auditorium, the person sitting next to us, the failure of the air-conditioning, much more easily than the ideas we went to learn. Even if these peripheral details are a bit elusive, they come back readily in hypnosis or when we relive the event imaginatively, as in psychodrama. The details of the content of the lecture, on the other hand, may have gone forever.

This phenomenon can be partly attributed to the common counterproductive approach to study (making extreme efforts to memorize, tensing muscles, inducing fatigue), but it also simply reflects the way the brain functions. Lozanov therefore made indirect instruction (suggestion) central to his teaching system. In suggestopedia, as he called his method, consciousness is shifted away from the curriculum to focus on something peripheral. The curriculum then becomes peripheral and is dealt with by the reserve capacity of the brain.

The suggestopedic foreign language session provides a good illustration. It consists in the reading of vocabulary and text while the class is listening to a concert of classical music. The session is in two parts. In the first part the music is classical (Mozart, Beethoven, Brahms) and the teacher reads the text slowly and solemnly, with attention to the dynamics of the music. The students follow the text in their books. This is followed by several minutes of silence. In the second part they listen to baroque music (Bach, Corelli, Handel) while the teacher reads the text in a normal speaking voice. During this time they have their books closed. During the whole session their attention is passive; they listen to the music but make no attempt to learn the material.

Before they attend the language session the students have been carefully prepared. Through meeting with the staff and satisfied students they develop the expectation that learning will be easy and pleasant and that they will successfully learn several hundred words of the foreign language during the class. In a preliminary session the teacher introduces them to the material to be covered, but does not 'teach' it. Likewise the students are instructed not to try to learn it during this introduction.

Some hours after the session proper there is a follow-up class at which the students are stimulated to recall the material presented. Once again the approach is indirect. The students do not focus their attention on trying to remember the vocabulary, but focus on using the language to communicate (e.g., through games or improvised dramatizations). Such methods are not unusual in language teaching. What is distinctive in the suggestopedic method is that they are devoted entirely to assisting recall. The 'learning' of the material is assumed to be automatic and effortless, accomplished while listening to music. The teacher's task is to assist the students to apply what they have learned paraconsciously, and in doing so to make it easily accessible to consciousness. Another difference from conventional teaching is the evidence that students can regularly learn 1000 new words of a foreign language during a suggestopedic session, as well as grammar and idiom.

Lozanov experimented with teaching by direct suggestion during sleep, hypnosis and trance-states, but found such procedures unnecessary. Hypnosis, yoga, autogenic training, Silva mind-control, religious ceremonies, EST, bio-feedback, faith healing are all associated with successful suggestion, but none of their techniques seem to be essential to it. Such rituals may be seen as placebos. Lozanov acknowledges that the ritual surrounding suggestion in his own system is also a placebo, but maintains that without such a placebo people are unable or afraid to tap the reserve capacity of their brains. Like any placebo it must be dispensed with authority to be effective. Just as a doctor calls on the full power of autocratic suggestion by insisting that the patient take precisely this white capsule precisely three times a day before meals, Lozanov is categoric in insisting that the suggestopedic session be conducted exactly in the manner designated, by trained and accredited suggestopedic teachers.

While suggestopedia has gained some notoriety through success in the teaching of modem languages, few teachers are able to emulate the spectacular results of Lozanov and his associates. We can, perhaps, attribute mediocre results to an inadequate 'placebo effect'. The students have not developed the appropriate set. They are often not motivated to learn through this method. They do not have enough 'faith'. They do not see it as 'real teaching', especially as it does not seem to involve the 'work' they have learned to believe is essential in learning. Lozanov could deal with such doubt through the authority of his personality and could impart this authority to other teachers in his institute. The ritual placebo system he elaborated may not be effective for particular students in particular places but if this is so teachers must develop an alternative ritual. And when they set out this ritual and proclaim its efficacy, their words must be supported by their paraconscious communication. If they want the system to be magic they must act as though it is. Once the magic has unlocked their students' capacities, freed them from their learned limitations, the magic can be debunked and abandoned. Meanwhile, since we appear to be unwilling to acknowledge our true capacity to learn but are willing to accept the suggestion that we will learn spectacularly through a particular technique, the placebo must continue to be used.

A teacher working according to Lozanov's principles will set out to gear instruction to the reserve capacity of the brain. While making full use of the students' mental processes, the teacher will also find ways to ensure that the students receive, retain, process and creatively utilize information below the level of awareness. He or she will not accept conventional estimates of the brain's capacities.

In teaching practice this involves the creation of a climate of trust and confidence, in which learning is a relaxed, pleasant experience. The teacher establishes personal and professional credibility (Lozanov prefers the word 'authority') so that students are prepared to give their attention and energy to activities that don't make immediate sense to them. Their assumptions about themselves and about learning are unfrozen, generating a readiness for new experience.

The method favours aesthetically satisfying presentation of information (through drama, art, dance, etc.) and indirect approaches to teaching, (games, simulations, dramatic enactments, project work, films, newspaper production), where the stuff of the curriculum is picked up incidentally while the students have their attention on something else. There is a concentration on wholes before parts, structures before detailed information, and a readiness to withhold one's energy and skills from 'teaching' the content. Children are allowed to learn through peripheral attention and are enabled to use the information they did not know they were learning. Sharpness of observation and a sensitive control over one's non-verbal communication are promoted, and acknowledgement made that the brain can assimilate a great deal of complex information – much more than it has the chance to process in the typical classroom.

Many teachers arrive at a similar perception of 'good teaching' via a variety of other routes. In fact, the consideration of the Psyche myth in the previous chapter leads to just this preference for the indirect, the subliminal, the intuitive, the dramatic, the aesthetic and the receptive. What distinguishes the Lozanov approach from other teaching methods, both behaviouristic and humanistic, is its perspective on the critical impact of direct suggestion – verbal and non-verbal – on the unconscious mind. To those who accuse him of 'brainwashing', Lozanov replies, 'If we don't know the real effect of suggestive influences that are all around us – from television, cinema, music and the environment – then we are being brainwashed. By becoming aware of suggestion, for the first time we are no longer victims of our culture.'[37] Rather than conditioning individuals, suggestopedic techniques make them aware of their potentials, and give them more choices.

MIND CONTROL

Another innovator who has undertaken the paradoxical task of using suggestion to increase people's freedom is the Mexican-American Jose Silva. His approach is of particular relevance here because his starting point was his own children's failure at school and his desire to discover a technique that would increase their ability to handle schoolwork. Like Coué, Schultz and Lozanov, he was initially impressed by the possibilities of hypnosis, but he soon found that a self-suggested state of deep relaxation had all the advantages of hypnosis without its limitations. He revived Coué's general affirmation, 'Every day, in every way, I get better and better'. He devised an extremely simple method by which anyone, even young children, could enter a state of consciousness in which they could receive, process and recall information more efficiently.

Here is all you have to do, according to Silva, to reach the Alpha, or meditative, state of mind.

> When you awaken in the morning, go to the bathroom, if necessary, then return to bed. Set your alarm for fifteen minutes later in case you drift off to sleep during the exercise. Close your eyes and look upward, behind your eyelids, at a 20 degree angle. For reasons not fully understood, this position of the eyes alone will trigger the brain to produce Alpha.
>
> Now, slowly, at about two-second intervals, count backward from one hundred to one. As you do this, keep your mind on it, and you will be in Alpha the very first time.[38]

In continuing practice over several weeks, the count-down is reduced from one hundred to five. Then the Alpha-state can be 'anchored' by joining the thumb and two first fingers of either hand and self-suggesting (while in this state): 'Whenever I join my fingers like this for a serious purpose I will instantly reach this level of mind to accomplish what I desire.' Those who have gained this proficiency can alter their mode of consciousness instantaneously and at will, and can keep the brain alert at frequencies (Alpha and Theta) that are usually associated with daydream and sleep.

The brain at slower frequencies is both more receptive and more accessible.[39] In the Silva method one goes 'into Alpha' or to one's 'level' in order to receive both information and suggestions. Children are taught to use the three-finger trick while listening to new and important information. If they have to learn a text they read it on to tape in their Beta state, then go into Alpha and play it back. Holding their three fingers together assists their recall.

In the early development of suggestopedia Lozanov believed that slowing down the students' brainwaves (e.g., by reading the material slowly, in rhythm with the slow movement of a baroque concerto) was an essential element of his technique. Later he decided that this, like hypnotic trance, was unnecessary and was merely a useful placebo. Students could engage in accelerated learning as long as they truly believed they could, just as Romen's trainees no longer needed their self-submergent state once they had discovered what they were capable of. It is likely that the Silva method and other methods like it will prove themselves to be merely placebos which seduce people into accessing the unused capacity of their brain.

While Coué's every-day-every-way-better-and-better slogan can sound like a bit of a joke when detached from the turn of the century optimism from which it emerged, the technique of self-suggestion itself has gained a good deal of legitimacy in recent years. Lozanov and Silva are only two among many who have turned from hypnosis to self-suggestion after experiencing the limitations of the former: its efficacy with only a small proportion of the population, its tendency to generate dependency between hypnotist and subject, and the likelihood that what is learned under hypnosis will only be recalled under hypnosis.

AUTOHYPNOSIS

While the state of consciousness in autohypnosis (self-suggestion) has some similarities to the hypnotic state, there is an essential difference in that it remains under the control of consciousness.

There is certainly a narrowing of awareness, but awareness is never lost completely, unless, of course, you fall asleep. Autogenic training and the trance of Silva Mind Control are forms of autohypnosis, but these are merely ritualizations of a very ordinary process.[40] A sudden shock, long-distance driving or running, watching television, can all put us into a hypnotic trance. In autohypnosis we can take control of the process. We can easily and quickly put ourselves into a state of consciousness in which relaxation can exist side by side with mental clarity and mental activity. All the effects researched by Romen in his study of autogenic training become possible with a little practice. Above all, self-hypnosis is safe. There is no way a person can be 'stuck' in such an altered state of consciousness. There is no evidence that anyone ever came to any harm through practising the technique.

Unfortunately, there is a good deal of superstition attached to hypnosis of any kind, and the use of the word in any description of what a teacher is doing is likely to arouse antagonism. Nevertheless, teaching children techniques of relaxation and stress management that use self-suggestion is an eminently useful thing to do. When they have gained some proficiency in this area they can be shown how to use the same skills to improve their concentration and ability to learn, as in the Silva method. Plenty of excellent material is available on self-hypnosis, to enable the teacher to take the essential step of learning the technique before attempting to teach it to someone else. Nevertheless, while waiting to obtain the literature from the library or elsewhere, he or she can experiment with a self-induction and a few suggestions.[41]

The Silva method of counting down slowly from ten (or a hundred) to one is a common form of induction. It is often accompanied by a visualization which involves images of descent, for example, riding down on an escalator, or in a lift.

Other common inductions include:

— gazing at an object (e.g. a lighted candle) while suggesting to yourself that your eyelids are getting heavier and heavier ... are closing;
— thinking the thought 'Yes' over and over, as you gaze at the candle flame;
— placing a coin in your hand and suggesting that your hand will

slowly turn over. Let your hand turn over so that the coin drops and you go into trance.

You may need to use a fairly lengthy induction on the first few occasions, but thereafter you will be able to do it very quickly. Have a standard formula for bringing yourself out of trance, for example, counting to five or saying, 'Now I will awake refreshed and alert.'

Glove anaesthesia is a useful technique for controlling pain. While in trance suggest that your hand is beginning to tingle, is becoming numb, that the skin is thick and insensitive. The suggestion can be made that when this hand touches a painful part of the body the pain will cease.

The five finger exercise has proved very effective in dealing with tension or depression. While in a trance go through the following steps.

- Touch your thumb to your index finger. As you do so, go back to a moment in your life when you felt tired and relaxed.
- Touch your thumb to your middle finger. As you do so, go back to a moment in your life when you felt really loved and loving.
- Touch your thumb to your ring finger. As you do so go back to a moment in your life when you really felt good about yourself, e.g., after receiving a well-deserved compliment.
- Touch your thumb to your little finger. As you do so, go back to the most beautiful place you have ever been.[42]

By 'anchoring' these experiences and the associated feelings in the finger touch it is possible to elicit the feelings in future simply by going through the four movements in turn without being in trance.

Stress management does not figure in the curriculum of conventional schools. Nevertheless, many children are under stress, and where schooling revolves around success in competitive examinations, stress is endemic. The reduction of stress is a byproduct of all the methods discussed in this chapter, and on this basis alone they deserve to be adapted to the ordinary classroom. The power of suggestion to increase the children's ability to handle the curriculum and to perform under pressure is a bonus.

Hypnosis, auto-suggestion and the specific techniques of Romen, Lozanov and Silva are based in the first place on our peculiar readiness to

The Power of Suggestion

accept suggestions from ourselves and others while in an 'altered state of consciousness'. We know we can induce such a state through mental exercises, meditation, exhaustion, self-suggestion, biofeedback or simply listening to a story. We know, besides, that we spontaneously go into a state of ordinary trance many times a day.

There are some fairly obvious indications when someone is going into this trance state. Eyes stare off into the distance, breathing slows down, and the person sighs or yawns or does not notice when they are spoken to. There are also other more subtle indications: skin becomes shiny, pupils dilate, eyelids droop, limbs become immobile. The hypnotist Milton Erickson trained himself from boyhood to recognize such signs that a person was becoming suggestible, and the list has been expanded and systematized by those who have studied his techniques.[43]

Sometimes our trance is deep enough for us to 'lose' half an hour through amnesia (a frequent occurrence in long-distance driving). Sometimes we just find ourselves humming or whistling or daydreaming. Sometimes we become pleasantly social. Sometimes we become unable to concentrate and our work is seriously disrupted.

Recent research seems to indicate that the shifts between our alert state and this light trance state are not haphazard, but follow a regular and consistent pattern according to our biological rhythms. In any case teachers can train themselves to recognize the state in their students and, instead of being irritated and frustrated by their drowsiness and inattention, can learn to take advantage of it. Students in this state may be less able to concentrate on 'intellectual' work, but they are more relaxed, more open to suggestions, more imaginative. Instead of blaming the children and grinding on, the flexible teacher will change his or her method of teaching. What we experience as apathy and mental exhaustion is often only the organism's resistance to a kind of activity that is out of phase with this physiological cycle.

The early afternoon is one period when most students' (and teachers') biological clocks are set for some kind of introverted, receptive activity (or for fantasy, story-telling, conversation or acting out). Primary teachers seem to understand this better than secondary teachers, and to use more flexibility and imagination in dealing with it. The teacher who is locked into seeing teaching only in terms of rational, linear processes will ensure that much of his or her effort goes for nothing. The teacher whose repertoire includes the use of suggestion and other non-rational techniques ought to be more effective. The natural flow of the organism can be utilized rather than resisted.

Coué's experience led him to the conviction we can take control of our organism through suggestion. He found a simple and effective way of running the unconscious, by giving it repeated verbal suggestions while in a relaxed, passive, attentive state. His idea has not been discredited since then. It has been confirmed both by 'hard' research and by the 'soft' research of shared human experience. The technique of 'positive affirmation' has proved so powerful and successful that cults have been built around it. The hype of such cults makes many teachers suspicious of the practice itself, associating it with manipulation and brain-washing. This is understandable but unreasonable. Taking control of one's life as Coué and Lozanov envisage is to allow the conscious mind (the will, in Coué's language) to form and instruct the unconscious, instead of being controlled by it. The unpersuaded teacher might try Coué's formula for physical, psychological and moral health: 'Every day, in every way, I get better and better'. Or Willis Harman's formula for changing not only oneself but the world.

> The exercise is this. Simply affirm, a number of times a day, day after day, for six months, the following statements, imagining the full meaning of each statement to the fullest extent possible:
> > I am not separate.
> > I can trust.
> > I can know.
> > I am responsible.
> > I am single-minded.[44]

Choosing to recite such phrases as if you fully believe them may change some of your unconsciously held beliefs about yourself.

The sports coach who psyches up athletes by getting them to repeat formulas to convince them of their strength, skill and determination to succeed knows that the repetition of verbal formulas can change attitudes and behaviour. Perhaps if teachers in other fields had the same experience we would hear the occasional chant of 'Maths is fun', or 'I am typing faster and more accurately every day.' Consciously held beliefs can be changed through persuasion. Unconsciously held beliefs demand another approach. Where conscious and unconscious beliefs are in conflict, the conscious mind can deliberately influence the mental set through affirmation and imagination. To reprogram old unconscious beliefs about limitations, or to program in new ones such as 'I can do it', 'I can know the solution to this problem', 'I really believe in myself', is essentially a matter of visualising and verbalising the new belief. When this is done persistently it displaces the old belief and takes over its power to form our behaviour.

When it comes to teaching a skill like this, business organizations can set up a seminar in psychocybernetics[45] or something with an equally technical-sounding name, then show their sales representatives how to reach their sales goals by visualising and affirming success. Teachers as a rule do not have, or do not give themselves, the same freedom. The conventions of most classrooms are not devised to allow such interruptions to the real-work. Nevertheless the techniques are available, appropriate and adaptable, even if only to teach students to make rhythmic self-suggestion or self-affirmations while jogging, cycling or doing aerobics.

BYPASSING CONSCIOUSNESS

One technique which has hardly been used in the classroom but has proved effective in other contexts is the deliberate use of subliminal suggestion.[46] There are plenty of CDs now available which, according to their promoters, will relax you, improve your memory, tennis or sex life, make you feel good, or increase your marketing skills. Usually recordings have an audible track of music or natural sound, and one or more below-threshold tracks containing suggestions to the listener on how to feel and behave.

The technology is now readily available for multi-track recording, and it is not particularly difficult or expensive for teachers to make their own recordings for particular purposes. Subliminal suggestions can be directed to getting the students to relax, to improve their sense of competence in a particular subject, to persuade them that they will understand and remember what is being taught. A subliminal track may simply repeat information to be remembered. If several tracks are running simultaneously they should be distinguished by some means such as using different voices. Negative statements (e.g., 'I am not anxious') should be avoided. The tape of relaxing music can be played during a rest period or as a background when the teacher is giving a lesson.

Ethical questions about using such a technique are resolved by explaining to the class beforehand what messages they will be hearing subliminally. This may also increase the effectiveness of the technique by generating an appropriate mental set and an expectancy of learning.

The ethical questions around hypnosis and suggestion have been debated often enough. While hypnosis remains in popular mythology the ultimate manipulation, experience seems to bear out Adler's assertion that even in trance we only respond to suggestions to do what (at some level) we want to do anyway.[47] This was put another way by Coué when he maintained that all successful suggestion is auto-suggestion. According to Coué and his friends, and contemporary hypnotists such as Milton Erickson, our unconscious minds know what is good for us. It is consciousness and all its acquired assumptions that inhibits us from living at our full potential. Suggestion bypasses the inhibitions of consciousness and lets the organism move towards self-realization. Adler tells us that it is only those suggestions, direct and indirect, which are compatible with this movement that have lasting influence.

> It is impossible to have a lasting influence upon an individual whom one is harming. One can influence another individual best when he is in the mood in which he feels his own rights are guaranteed. This is a very important point in pedagogy. Perhaps it is possible to conceive or even carry out some other form of education, but a system of education which takes this point into consideration will be adequate for the reason that it is connected with the most primitive instinct in man, the feeling of his relatedness to man and the cosmos.[48]

Not everyone will take as optimistic a view as Adler. We have seen enough of the influence of Hitler, the Rev. Jim Jones and various opportunistic or malevolent gurus to wonder how skilful the human organism is at

The Power of Suggestion

sorting out good suggestions from bad. It is reasonable enough to argue, as humanistic psychologists do, that the individual will persistently seek what is for his or her greater self-realization (love, personal power, self-esteem, transcendence) and that it is merely the means to these ends (violence, racism, conspicuous consumption) that are sometimes poorly chosen. Reasonable as it is, it is only one way of looking at the evidence. We need to acknowledge that this romantic vision is only a partial one; it needs to be balanced by the tragic vision and comic vision. Too enthusiastic a worship of Eros is inclined to lead to the neglect of Senex and Hera, the deeply conservative gods of absolute values and social obligations. Resisting Freud's pessimistic view of the human organism as trapped in the relentless pursuit of self-gratification can lead us to a view as one-dimensional as his.

Hitler and Jones certainly knew how to use the techniques of suggestion to manipulate others to their own ends. It is not necessarily much help to us to be told that the Nazis' sadism and infantile dependence on their superman were but distorted expressions of each man's own basic human needs to be loved and acknowledged. And when we see the power of the cinema to make pathological violence acceptable and the ability of the print and electronic media to shift public opinion according to the interests of their masters, it is not very comforting to be told that 'it is impossible to have a lasting influence upon an individual whom one is harming'. A temporary influence can be nasty enough.

Yet Adler's argument, one-sided as it is, is worth attending to, as it has practical implications for teaching. Teachers often wish that their students were more receptive. Unfortunately, the things that they want them to receive are often seen by the children as irrelevant, or incompatible with what they want. When students and teachers want the same things, problems of management and problems of learning seem to disappear together. Coué, Adler and many before and after them have deeply believed that human beings essentially want what is truly good for them. Perhaps the best starting point for capitalising on the extraordinary receptivity of the human mind is just this one: to want what is truly good for one's pupils, to listen seriously to their statements of what they want, and to accept these stated wants as the point from which teacher and pupil can begin to work together. Teachers do not have to make assumptions about what the child 'really' wants, though there are plenty of theorists willing to say what basic human needs these wants express or disguise. However, they do have to genuinely desire the good of their pupils. And they have to be sensitive to their tendency to use their pupils in their own pursuit of power, acknowledgement and a regular pay-packet.

Suggestion is one of the many ways available for manipulating and harming children. The more powerful a technique is for good the more capacity it seems to have for doing harm. But, on the whole, more damage seems to be done by ignorance, incompetence and malice than by knowledge, skill and concern.

SELF-REMEMBERING

We can turn our usual understanding of hypnotic suggestion on its head by viewing our normal state as hypnotic trance and looking for ways of waking out of it. If a medical hypnotist successfully suggests to a patient that bleeding will stop or that an operation will be painless, we see it as a demonstration of the power of suggestion. Why not rather say that we all have the ability to control our pain and bleeding yet have somehow accepted the suggestion that we cannot? From this perspective we are all in what Charles Tart calls 'consensus trance'.[49]

Freud's speculations on the unconscious were stimulated by his experience with hypnosis. His contemporary, Gurdjieff, was also an accomplished hypnotist whose observations convinced him that hypnosis is a major and ordinary part of everyday life. He saw that people constantly move in and out of trance states and that their habitual behaviour has the characteristics we associate with formal hypnosis: automatized body movements, narrow focus of attention, distorted perception. He was persuaded that our whole lives are lived in a trance induced by our culture; all the beliefs, reactions and behaviours that we see as normal are the product of cultural suggestion. In his travels researching exotic religious traditions, he was looking for techniques that might enable us to wake out of our trance and discover who and what we really are.[50]

The Power of Suggestion

While many of Gurdjieff's ideas are on the fringes of credibility (this statement demonstrates how deeply I am stuck in 'consensus trance'), the techniques that he developed in his attempted Westernization of the wisdom of the Orient have a great deal to commend them. They are aimed at de-automatizing our perception, feelings and behaviour. Exercises such as systematic self-observation and self-remembering certainly give us a sense of being alive. They are also appropriate classroom exercises.

Self-observation is simply 'paying more attention to everything in your world and everything in yourself'.[51] For example, a teacher might focus on the class's attention on how they are sitting at their desks.

> How are you sitting? Is your weight more on one buttock than on the other? Is your weight forward or back? Is your position balanced? Is your back-bone straight, or curved, or leaning to one side? Where are your arms? Are they supporting you? Are their positions symmetrical? Is your head tilted to one side? Which side? Is your neck twisted? What contact do your feet have with the floor? Are you comfortable in this position? Are there strains? Is there pressure on your chest? Your belly? Are there any 'shoulds' associated with the way you sit? Is your breathing free and unrestricted? Is there any feeling associated with this posture? What happens when you change it? And so on.

Self-remembering involves a deliberate expansion of consciousness with the aim of being able to keep the whole of your being in awareness. It involves including your body, instincts and feelings in consciousness as well as your thoughts. It establishes a centre of consciousness which is outside the usual automated pattern of identification and behaviour. You might try the following exercise.

> Sit upright in a comfortable chair. Close your eyes. For the first half minute or so just relax and pay attention to the fact that you are there.
>
> Now focus your attention on your right foot. Just pay attention to whatever sensations there are, at this moment, in your right foot. Don't reject any sensation or try to hold on to any sensation. When you are in touch with your right foot, just keep paying attention to it for half a minute. If you drift away, come gently back to it. Shift

your attention focus to the lower part of your right leg. Sense it for half a minute.

And so on. Don't go to a new part of the body until you have made contact with the preceding part.

When the parts of the body have been sensed individually, broaden your focus. Sense both feet simultaneously, then both feet and legs, then feet legs and arms, then the whole body.

Broaden your focus further. While attending to the sensations in your whole body, listen to whatever sounds there are around you. Then open your eyes and simultaneously sense, listen and look.

This is not as easy as it sounds. Attention tires easily but certainly improves with practice. For Gurdjieff, waking out of our trance involves not only a keener awareness of our inner and outer worlds but, more particularly, greater flexibility and control in our behaviour.

Gurdjieff's exercises seem to contrast strongly with Schultz and Romen's autogenic training or Coué and Silva's affirmations, but they work to the same ends. Autogenic training starts in trance induction but only as a step to giving us conscious control of our organism so that the trance induction can be abandoned. Coué's technique was also designed to give us conscious control of our 'robot'. Biofeedback does the same. Gurdjieff would hardly have argued with Coué's statement that, 'It's our unconscious being which runs us. We learn to run it. Through it we learn to run ourselves.'[52]

THE FIVE-MINDED ANIMAL

Freud, Coué and their associates developed the notion that we have two minds: a conscious, reflecting mind and another mind which can control our behaviour for better or worse without any awareness or reflection at all.

Since they developed their original insights and techniques, this notion has been addressed in numerous ways. We have evidence now from quite diverse sources that it makes sense to think of our minds as not just double, but multiple.

Kieran Egan writes of us as 'five-minded animals', proposing that:

The Power of Suggestion

> We have, you might say, a fivefold mind, or, more dramatically, we are a five-minded animal, in whom different kinds of understanding jostle together and fold on one another, to some degree remaining 'somewhat distinct'.[53]

Egan is a developmental psychologist, whose starting point is Piaget's observation that as children grow to adolescence and maturity they pass through a series of defined stages in which they become capable of thinking in quite new and different ways. Egan labels our five minds somatic, magic, romantic, philosophic and ironic, making it clear that we do not leave one way of thinking behind when another becomes dominant. We still think somatically after we have grown to be adults capable of philosophic and ironic thinking. This bodily, unreflective mode of awareness remains the ground of our more complex ways of dealing with our experience.

Egan was not the first to develop such an idea. In the 1940s, the cultural philosopher Jean Gebser collected evidence from many sources to sustain the argument there are five distinct 'structures of consciousness' which may be dominant in a particular culture. He called these structures archaic, magic, mythical, mental and integral.[54] In the 1960s, biologist Paul Maclean developed his theory of the 'triune brain', arguing that the human brain comprizes an ancient 'reptilian' brain (the seat of instincts in the brain-stem), a 'mammalian' brain (the seat of emotions in the limbic system) as well as a 'neo-mammalian' brain (the seat of thinking in the cerebral cortex). He compared the human brain to a car driven simultaneously by three people with different ideas of where they are going.[55] Since MacLean developed his theory we find research on brain lateralization suggesting that even the two hemispheres of the neo-mammalian brain may not be always driving in the same direction.

The thrust of these theories is that, while we may be inclined to identify with our ability to think rationally and logically, there are other minds or 'structures of consciousness' alive in us of which our rational minds may be scarcely aware, in spite of the fact that they may dominate a great deal of our behaviour. Some of these minds are older and simpler, in an evolutionary sense, than our 'rational' minds, and operate on very different rules from the rules of rational decision-making. We note the dimness of consciousness of our archaic mind when we have a trance or meditation experience, immersed in our environment with little sense of ourselves as individuals. We connect with the world through our magic mind when we let ourselves be healed by placebos or engage in the rituals by which we keep our world a safe place. We are in our mythic consciousness when we accept without question our tribal stories, including the story about who we are and what we are doing here. Our mental mind looks at evidence, thinks logically and seeks the truth about things. Most of the time, all our minds are at work. While we busy ourselves thinking rationally, our 'archaic' or 'somatic' mind maintains its trance and keeps our 'robot' working, our 'magic' mind connects the concrete objects of our experience through the rituals, obsessions and superstitions by which we try to control our world and manage our fear, and our 'mythic' mind remains embedded in the cultural narratives in which we find the meaning of our lives. But that is not all. According to Gebser we also have an emerging spiritual or 'integral' mind, which transcends the limitations of time, space, culture and logic to keep us in touch with reality. We can experience the world through a multi-perspectival kind of consciousness which acknowledges that magical and mythical ways of thinking have the same legitimacy as rational thinking.

Modern science has typically seen magic and myth as very inadequate ways of understanding the world, overlooking the evidence that the rational thinking on which science depends is itself a very inadequate way of understanding and dealing with the world, even in science. Gebser proposed that the twentieth century was witnessing the emergence of a way of thinking which re-owns and re-values these older, simpler 'structures of consciousness' and, more significantly, integrates them in an entirely new way of understanding and dealing with the world.

Egan is saying something very similar when he calls the fifth and most complex of our five minds 'ironic' and suggests that the irony resides in our ability to process our experience simultaneously though our philosophic or rational mind on the one hand and our somatic, magic and romantic minds on the other. If we can do this (for him a sign of mature psychological development) truth becomes complex and ambiguous. Our different minds form different conclusions and express them in different ways. The message my

The Power of Suggestion

body (somatic) gives me that you are afraid of me conflicts with my intellect's (philosophic) assessment that you admire me. My ironic comments on the situation will be both true and untrue. If my listeners have only their philosophic minds 'turned on', they will miss my meaning entirely.

Gebser and Egan do not need a theory of the unconscious. They simply recognize that much of our knowing does not occur in our mental-rational-philosophic awareness. Much of it occurs in our body, and we may be hardly aware of it at all. Much of it is embedded in group rituals and stories and we may rarely reflect on it. Much of it is beyond the reach of the teacher's conventional show-and-tell approach to imparting knowledge. Fortunately, there are other ways of teaching.

NOTES Chapter 2. The Power of Suggestion

[24] E. Coué, *How to Practice Suggestion and Auto-suggestion*, p.125.
[25] ibid.
[26] See N. V. Peale, *The Power of Positive Thinking*.
[27] See J. Silva, *The Silva Mind Control Method*.
[28] See A. Maltz, *Psychocybernetics: A New Way to Get More Living Out of Life*.
[29] Herbert Benson, in *Beyond the Relaxation Response*, discusses what he calls 'the faith factor'. It appears not to matter greatly what the patient has faith in (a favourite doctor, a new drug, a particular form of prayer); the faith in itself has a significant impact on the process of healing. Studies of healing centres such as Lourdes suggest that healing is only available to the faithful; cynics and sceptics fail to reap the benefits.
[30] See J. H. Schultz and W. Luthe, *Autogenic Training*.
[31] The trainee repeats the verbal formulas for a few minutes only, without trying to achieve anything. According to Schultz, repeating the formulas for a longer period gives the unconscious mind the suggestion that the effect does not take place immediately. Standard formulas are:

> My right hand is heavy and warm (left hand, right foot, left foot).
> My belly is warm.
> My forehead is cool.
> My heartbeat is slow and regular.
> It breathes me; it breathes me.

[31] See A. Meares, *Relief Without Drugs*.
[32] A. S. Romen, *Self-suggestion and Its Influence on the Human Organism*, p. 118.
[33] Alyce and Elmer Green, who must be credited with the major contribution to the development of biofeedback techniques, began their work in a

medical context (the Menninger Foundation) in 1964. One of their first studies was in the use of electronic feedback to accelerate autogenic training. It is not suggested that biofeedback technology produces its clinical results only through the placebo effect; it is essentially an educational tool. The electronic devices enable subtle, normally unconscious physiological changes (skin temperature, electrical activity in the brain, muscle tension, electrical resistance of the skin) to be picked up. We can learn to connect changes in meter reading with changes in our mental state, or with particular mental activities such as suggestion or visualization. As we learn to manipulate an external object, the meter, in so doing we learn to regulate our nervous system through subtle changes in our state of consciousness. The machines then become unnecessary as the brain is now able to control physiological changes that previously remained under the control of the limbic system without coming into awareness. See E. E. Green and A. M. Green, *Beyond Biofeedback*.

[35] See G. Lozanov, *Suggestology and Outlines of Suggestopedy*.

[36] Whitehead points out that consciousness is just the tip of our experience:

> Consciousness flickers; and even at its brightest, there is a small focal field of clear illumination, and a large penumbral region of experience which tells of intense experience in dim apprehension. The simplicity of clear consciousness is no measure of the complexity of complete experience. Also, this character of our experience suggests that consciousness is the crown of experience, only occasionally attained, not its necessary base (*Process and Reality*, p. 267).

[37] Cited in S. Krippner, *Human Possibilities*, p. 133.

[38] Silva, *Mind Control*, p. 28. There are four major brain rhythms. Beta (13 to 26 cycles per second) is associated with active thinking. Alpha (8 to 13 cps) is associated with a more relaxed state (daydreaming, watching television commercials) without organized thought. Theta (4 to 8 cps) is associated with deep reverie; it appears as consciousness slips towards unawareness. Delta (0 to 4 cps) is primarily associated with deep sleep.

[39] There is plenty of evidence that we are peculiarly receptive to suggestions while our brains are producing Theta-waves. However, while most people can produce Alpha simply by closing their eyes and relaxing, it is difficult to produce Theta waves without going to sleep. Having learned to do this through some technique such as autogenic training, meditation or biofeedback, we still have to learn to maintain the Theta state while making suggestions to ourselves. Conventional hypnosis produces the Theta state and then makes suggestions without disturbing the subject's passivity. Self-suggestion is a little more complex, since any intentional activity destroys the passive, receptive state that is essential to the production of Theta waves. Coué, Schultz and Silva insist that suggestions should be made

casually, passively, without effort. The biofeedback researchers, Alyce and Elmer Green, found that the production of Theta waves is least inhibited if a suggestion of visualization is constructed beforehand so that it can be inserted into the 'field of mind' with as little 'thinking' as possible (see Green & Green, op. cit., p. 575).

For a review of evidence of our ability to access and program the unconscious in the Alpha-Theta state, see E. E. Green and A. M. Green, 'Biofeedback and States of Consciousness' and T. Budzinski, 'Clinical applications of non-drug-induced State', both in B. Wolman and M. Ullman, *Handbook of States of Consciousness*.

[40] There is some evidence that our left (rational) cerebral hemisphere has a limited range of operation. When it is either over-stimulated or deprived of stimulation it breaks down and the right hemisphere takes over. Without a fully functioning left hemisphere we are unable to screen sensory input critically and hence become less resistant to suggestion and less able to inhibit the feelings and fantasies that may emerge from our unconsciousness. We find over-stimulation as a prelude to a faith-healing trance in many religious cults. The same phenomenon is utilized in the techniques of 'brain-washing' and interrogation. On the other hand, minimising the stimulation the brain receives has the same effect, as is demonstrated in various hypnotic inductions and meditative techniques as well as in religious chanting or drumming and in experiences of sensory deprivation. It also appears that the left hemisphere is more sensitive to fatigue than the right, which acts as a 'back-up computer' while the left hemisphere is resting. See Budzinski, op. cit., p. 448f.

[41] A simple approach to auto-hypnosis will be found in M. Davies, M. McKay and E. Robbins Eshelman, *The Relaxation and Stress Reduction Workbook*. Other useful books are R. Stone, *Autohypnosis*; A. Burke, *Self-Hypnosis: New Tools for Deep and Lasting Transformation* and A. Eason, *The Secrets of Self-Hypnosis*.

[42] From Davies et al, op. cit., pp. 67f.

[43] E. Rossi, 'Altered states of consciousness in everyday life', in Wolman and Ullman, op. cit., p. 100.

[44] W. Harman and H. Reingold, *Higher Creativity*, p. 226.

[45] See A. Maltz, *Psychocybernetic Principles for Creative Living*.

[46] On subliminal perception and suggestion, see N. F. Dixon, *Subliminal Perception: The Nature of a Controversy* and *Preconscious Processing* There has been a recent revival of scientific interest in subliminal perception, though the existence of the phenomenon is still disputed. Dixon concludes from the research evidence that the brain may respond to external stimuli which, for one reason or another, are not consciously perceived. 'The effects of such a stimulus may be almost as varied as those of sensory inflow which does reach consciousness. They include the evoking or determination of

cortical potentials, changes in the EEG, the production of electrodermal responses, and changes in sensory threshold. They also include effects on memory, the influencing of lexical decisions, and such subjective manifestations as changes in conscious perceptual experience, dreams and the evoking of appropriate effects' (*Preconscious Processing*, p. 262).

[47] A. Adler, *Understanding Human Nature*, p. 63.
[48] ibid., p. 161.
[49] See C. Tart, *Waking Up: Overcoming the Obstacles to Human Potential*. Gurdjieff's ideas will be found in *Beelzebub's Tales to his Grandson*, *Meetings with Remarkable Men* and *Views From the Real World* and in P. D. Ouspensky's *In Search of the Miraculous*. A good introduction is Tart's *Waking Up*.
[51] Tart, op. cit., p. 193. Similar exercises influenced by the work of Alexander and Feldenkrais will be found in R. Masters and J. Houston, *Listening to the Body*.
[52] Coué, op. cit., p. 118.
[53] K. Egan, *The Educated Mind*, p. 80.
[54] See J. Gebser, *The Ever-Present Origin*.
[55] See P. MacLean, 'The paranoid streak in man', in A. Koestler and J. Smythies, *Beyond Reductionism* and *The Triune Brain in Evolution*.

Others who have contributed in different ways to this image of 'multiple minds' are developmental psychologist Robert Kegan and neuroscientist Merlin Donald. See Kegan, R., *In Over Our Heads: The Mental Demands of Modern Life* and Donald, M. D., *Origins of the Modern Mind*. See also Chapter 12, below.

MAGIC AND MANIPULATION

*I*t is our less conscious thoughts and our less conscious actions which mainly mould our lives and the lives of those who spring from us.
Samuel Butler, *The Way of All Flesh*

AS AN EXPERIMENTAL AND CLINICAL HYPNOTIST, Milton Erickson was much admired and much discussed. Extraordinarily curious and constantly experimenting, he had a quite uncanny ability to put people in a trance by a word or a gesture, even by shaking hands with them, and could do this while his subject was declaring a refusal to be hypnotized. Had Erickson lived a few centuries earlier he would no doubt have been tried for witchcraft for his magic power to take people into trance and the magic healing he wrought on them while they were in that state.

Erickson was reluctant to pin down the exact elements in his technique which were so powerful and equally reluctant to develop a systematic theory to explain them. Fortunately for us, his success in dealing with difficult cases through hypnosis led to his methods being examined in detail by a number of observers with a taste for classification and systematic theorising. Through Erickson's own case histories and the commentaries of Haley, Rossi, Grinder, Bandler and others, we have a great deal of information about the communication patterns of someone who was, as communicators go, something of a virtuoso.

In presenting Milton Erickson as a model for teachers wishing to deal productively with 'the unconscious' in their pupils, we need to clarify what Erickson understood by the words 'unconscious', 'trance' and 'hypnosis'.

THE BACK OF YOUR MIND

Erickson often referred to the 'conscious mind' and 'unconscious mind' when talking to his patients. When dealing with people who might have trouble with these terms, he would talk about 'the front of your mind' and 'the back of your mind'. He did not have an elaborate theory of the unconscious but spoke of it as a separate mind which functions outside our awareness, having its own wisdom and stored information. Functioning independently of the conscious mind, the unconscious mind, essentially positive, can learn, make decisions and direct behaviour. If the conscious mind does not intervene the unconscious will see that the person does what is best for him or herself. Erickson's approach as a therapist was to bypass or 'depotentiate' the conscious mind and make suggestions directly to the unconscious, aiming to set the patient's unconscious free from domination by the conscious mind so that it could be directed away from self-destructive behaviour. His patient's unconscious, he believed, contained not hostile forces, but positive ones waiting to be let out.[56]

His understanding of hypnosis and trance was equally simple. For Erickson, the two phenomena are quite independent. Hypnosis is suggestion. Trance is a state of focused attention. Both are very ordinary. A group of children listening open-mouthed as their teacher reads a story are in trance. So is the child who sits gazing out the window instead of doing his sums. So is the friend whose eyes glaze over as soon as you start talking about your fascinatingly clever two-year-old. A common feature of trance is that the person coming out of trance can remember nothing about it. Another is that people in trance are more receptive to suggestion.

Hypnosis (suggestion) does not require trance. Erickson found that he could bypass the conscious mind and make suggestions directly to the unconscious by making the conscious mind bored, confused or distracted. He found that while trance makes people suggestible, they can reject suggestions even in deep trance.

Erickson preferred stories and metaphors to theories. Certainly, stories from his own case histories give the flavour of Ericksonian therapy better than complex explanations. He once described how he dealt with a child who was brought to him with a 'learning difficulty'. This boy could not write or, at least, not in the conventional manner. He was able to write backwards, upside down and from right to left. Parents and teachers had tried the usual strategies of prohibition, punishment and promised rewards without any success. Erickson began by acknowledging the boy's superiority as a writer. He was able to write skilfully in these three different ways while he, the doctor, could only manage one. He immediately set out in all seriousness to learn to write backwards, asking the child to assist him. To maintain his superiority the boy set out to learn to write in yet another way — the conventional way — with the satisfaction that while the doctor was still struggling with his second writing technique, he was on his fourth.

Looking at this as a sample of Erickson's teaching style, certain elements are fairly easily detected. Erickson works with the boy's energy rather than against it, operating on the hunch that the energy is bound up in demonstrating that parents and teachers can't push him around. The hypnotist nowhere gives a directive: he does not even give a direct suggestion to the boy that he should learn to write. Rather, he establishes a situation in which the boy will give this suggestion to himself, a situation where he will gain rather than lose status by learning to write. The issue of learning to write correctly is not even raised. Above all, the practitioner accepts and takes seriously the boy's own frame of reference, and finds a way to label the boy's behaviour as positive.

EVERYDAY HYPNOSIS

Erickson often uses experiences with his own children to illustrate his points. In the following example he shows how he responds to a child on the child's terms. In dealing with his three-year-old son he uses hypnosis, but it is not what people usually call hypnosis.

> Three-year-old Robert fell down the back stairs, split his lip, and knocked an upper tooth back into the maxilla. He was bleeding profusely and screaming loudly with pain and fright. His mother and I went to his aid. A single glance at him lying on the ground screaming, his mouth bleeding profusely and blood spattered on the pavement, revealed that this was an emergency requiring prompt and adequate measures.
>
> No effort was made to pick him up. Instead, as he paused for breath for fresh screaming, I told him quickly, and simply, sympathetically and emphatically, 'That hurts awful, Robert. That hurts terrible.'
>
> Right then, without any doubt, my son knew that I knew what I was talking about. He could agree with me and he knew that I was agreeing completely with him. Therefore he could listen respectfully to me, because I had demonstrated that I understood the situation fully. In paediatric hypnotherapy there is no more important problem than so speaking to the patient that he can agree with you and respect your intelligent grasp of the situation as he judges it in terms of his own understandings.
>
> Then I told Robert, 'And it will keep right on hurting.' In this

simple statement, I named his own fear, confirmed his own judgement of the situation, demonstrated my good intelligent grasp of the entire matter and my entire agreement with him, since right then he could foresee only a lifetime of anguish and pain for himself.

The next step for him and for me was to declare, as he took another breath, 'And you really wish it would stop hurting.' Again, we were in full agreement, and he was ratified and even encouraged in this wish. And it was his wish, deriving entirely from within him and constituting his own urgent need. With the situation so defined, I could then offer a suggestion with some certainty of its acceptance. This suggestion was, 'Maybe it will stop hurting in a little while, in just a minute or two.' This was a suggestion in full accord with his own needs and wishes, and, because it was qualified by a 'maybe it will', it was not in contradiction to his own understandings of the situation. Thus he could accept the idea and initiate his responses to it.[57]

As he did this, a shift was made to another important matter, important to him as a suffering person, and important in the total psychological significance of the entire occurrence – a shift that in itself was a primary measure in changing or altering the situation

Erickson goes on to describe how he ensured that Robert understood that his parents recognized how catastrophic his injury was, so that he could have some narcissistic distinction in his misfortune.

> He needed to know that his misfortune was catastrophic in the eyes of others as well as in his own, and he needed tangible proof that he himself could appreciate. By my declaring it to be 'an awful lot of blood', Robert could again recognize the intelligent and competent appraisal of the situation in accord with his own actually unformulated, but nevertheless real, needs. The question about the goodness, redness, and strongness of the blood came into play psychologically in meeting the personal meaningfulness of the accident to Robert. In a situation where one feels seriously damaged, there is an overwhelming need for a compensatory feeling of satisfying goodness. Accordingly, his mother and I examined the blood upon the pavement, and we both expressed the opinion that it was good, red, strong blood. In this way we reassured him, but not on an emotionally comforting basis only; we did so upon the basis of an instructional, to him, examination of reality.

However, we qualified that favourable opinion by stating that it would be better if we were to examine the blood by looking at it against the white background of the bathroom sink. By this time Robert had ceased crying, and his pain and fright were no longer dominant factors. Instead, he was interested and absorbed in the important problem of the quality of his blood.

His mother picked him up and carried him to the bathroom, where water was poured over his face to see if the blood 'mixed properly with water' and gave it a 'proper pink colour'. Then the redness was carefully checked and reconfirmed, following which the 'pinkness' was reconfirmed by washing him adequately, to Robert's intense satisfaction, since his blood was good, red and strong and made water rightly pink.

Then came the question of whether or not his mouth was 'bleeding right' and 'swelling right'. Close inspection, to Robert's complete satisfaction and relief, again disclosed that all developments were good and right and indicative of his essential and pleasing soundness in every way.

Next came the question of suturing his lip. Since this could easily evoke a negative response, it was broached in a negative fashion to him, thereby precluding an initial negation by him, and at the same raising a new and important issue. This was done by stating regretfully that, while he would have to have stitches taken in his lip, it was most doubtful if he could have as many stitches as he could count. In fact, it looked as if he could not even have ten stitches, and he could count to twenty. Regret was expressed that he could not have seventeen stitches, like his sister, Betty Alice, or twelve, like his brother, Allan; but comfort was offered in the statement that he would have more stitches than his siblings Bert, Lance or Carol. Thus the entire situation became transformed into one in which he could share with other older siblings a common experience with a comforting sense of equality and even superiority. In this way he was enabled to face the question of surgery without fear or anxiety, but with hope of high accomplishment in cooperation with the surgeon and imbued with the desire to do well the task assigned to him, namely, to 'be sure to count the stiches'. In this manner, no reassurances were needed, nor was there any need to offer further suggestions regarding freedom from pain.

Only seven stitches were required, to Robert's disappointment, but the surgeon pointed out that the suture material was of a newer and better kind than any that his siblings had ever had, and that the scar would be an unusual 'W' shape, like the letter of his Daddy's college. Thus the fewness of the stitches was well compensated.[58]

Erickson points out that at no time was Robert given a false statement, nor was he forcibly reassured in a manner contradictory to his understandings. A community of understanding was established and then, one by one, matters of vital interest to him were thoughtfully considered and decided in ways that he was satisfied to agree with. 'Hypnosis', as Erickson uses the term, began with the first statement.

This is what Erickson calls 'everyday hypnosis'. It starts with his acceptance of Robert's experience of the situation: 'It hurts awful, and it's going to keep right on hurting.' This establishes his credibility and disposes Robert to accept the series of suggestions which follow. There is also the element of trance, the 'everyday trance' which consists in fixing Robert's attention on one part of his experience (through curiosity) so that other aspects (e.g., pain) are not in consciousness.

CHANGE WITHOUT INSIGHT

The following case provides another illustration of Erickson's hypnotic technique. This sixteen-year-old girl was a chronic thumbsucker, to the annoyance of her parents and everyone else. Her parents had tried everything even having her prayed for publicly in church and making her wear a sign declaring that she was a thumbsucker. The school psychologist had interpreted the girl's behaviour to her as an aggressive act, and she seemed to go along with this interpretation. When her parents approached Erickson as a last resort, he made them promise that after the girl became his patient, they would absolutely ignore her thumbsucking for a whole month, no matter what happened.

> The girl came unwilling to the office with her parents. She was nursing her thumb noisily. I dismissed her parents and turned to face the girl. She moved her thumb sufficiently to declare she didn't like 'nut doctors'.

I replied, 'And I don't like the way your parents ordered me to cure your thumbsucking. Ordering me, huh! It's your thumb and your mouth, and why in hell can't you suck it if you want to? Ordering me to cure you! The only thing I am interested in is why, when you want to be aggressive about thumbsucking, you don't really get aggressive instead of piddling around like a baby that doesn't know how to suck a thumb aggressively. What I'd like to do is tell you how to suck your thumb aggressively. What I'd like to do is tell you how to suck to irk the hell out of your old man and your old lady. If you're interested, I'll tell you. If you aren't, I'll just laugh at you.'

The use of the word 'hell' arrested her attention completely – she knew that a professional man ought not to use that kind of language to a high school girl who attended church regularly. Challenging the inadequacy of her aggressiveness, a term the school psychologist had taught her, commanded her attention still more.

The offer to teach her how to irk her parents, referred to so disrespectfully, elicited even more complete fixation of her attention, so that to all intents and purposes she was in a hypnotic trance. Then in an intent tone of voice, I said, 'Every night after dinner, just like a clock, your father goes into the living room and reads the newspaper from the front page to the back. Each night when he does that, go in there, sit down beside him, really nurse your thumb good and loud, and irk the hell out of him for the longest twenty minutes he has ever experienced.

'Then go in the sewing room, where your mother sews for one hour every night before she washes dishes. Sit down beside her and nurse your thumb good and loud and irk the hell out of the old lady for the longest twenty minutes she ever knew.

'Do this every night and do it good. And on the way to school, figure out carefully just which crummy jerk you dislike most, and every time you meet him, pop your thumb in your mouth and watch him turn his head away. And be ready to pop your thumb back if he turns to look again.

'And think over all your teachers and pick out the one you really dislike and treat that teacher to a thumb pop every time he or she looks at you. I just hope you can be really aggressive.'

After some desultory irrelevant remarks, the girl was dismissed and her parents were summoned into the office. They were reminded of the absoluteness of their promise. I said that if they kept their promise faithfully, the girl's thumbsucking would cease.

Magic and Manipulation

On the way home the girl did not suck her thumb and she was silent the entire trip. The parents were so pleased that they telephoned to report their gratification. That evening to her parents' horror, the girl obeyed instructions. The parents also obeyed the instructions not to oppose the thumsucking. They reported unhappily by telephone the next day. I reminded them of their promise and of my statement about the girl's prognosis.

Each night for the next few evenings the girl was faithful in her performance. Then it began to pall on her. She began to shorten the time, then she began late and quit early, the finally she skipped, and then she forgot!

In less than four weeks the girl had discontinued her thumbsucking, both at home and elsewhere. She became increasingly interested in much more legitimate teenage activities of her own group. Her adjustments improved in all regards.

The girl was seen again in a social setting about a year later. She recognized me, viewed me thoughtfully for a few minutes, and then remarked, 'I don't know whether I like you or not, but I am grateful to you.'[59]

Erickson refers to the girl's 'hypnotic state' but he clearly has not 'hypnotized' her in the usual sense of the word. He has used no formal trance induction but has simply fixed her attention and by so doing put her in the state of ordinary trance that we all slip in and out of all day. He regularly used formal inductions to lead patients into a state of deep trance, blocking out the influence of the conscious mind so that the unconscious could be addressed simply and directly. He emphasized, however, that trance is not really necessary and that the unconscious can be addressed in our normal waking state. It is the repertoire of techniques he developed to do this which make his work of immediate relevance to teaching.

Erickson was not interested in giving his patients insight into their behaviour. Many of them knew exactly what they wanted to do or stop doing and, in going the rounds of the therapists, had got plenty of insight. His approach was to ignore insight altogether and aim directly at the desired change of behaviour through suggestions made to the unconscious mind. In attempting this he realized that he was in competition with all the other sources of suggestion that were addressing (or assaulting) his patient's unconscious.

Educating Psyche

Our perception of ourselves and our world is largely a product of suggestion. So is our socialization. We are constantly responding automatically to the suggestions which come to us from our environment, and we carry many of those suggestions through into our behaviour without the slightest awareness of what has happened. Fortunately our tendency to respond to suggestion is not indiscriminate: we respond automatically and positively to suggestions from those who have somehow gained the right to make them (either personally or by association), and we are much less receptive to those to whom we are hostile or indifferent.

However, there does seem to be a tendency to go along with suggestions when they get through to our unconscious without being mediated by our conscious minds. When we realize that someone is suggesting something to us we are much more likely to resist. When we hear commands we are even more likely to resist, momentarily and automatically, though we may then decide to do what we are told. Happily, most people in our culture do not carry out commands automatically. Undiscriminating obedience is no longer seen as desirable. The picture of the autocratic mind-controlling hypnotist comes from a time and culture where automatic, unthinking obedience was highly valued, at least in women and children.

The reality of modern hypnosis is very different. Certainly Erickson's technique is far removed from that of the autocratic hypnotist. In dealing with Robert he gave no commands, but he guided Robert's behaviour in the direction he chose by first establishing rapport and then suggesting in conversation that the child would feel satisfaction and self-esteem rather than distress and pain. In treating the teenage thumbsucker he first took her side against her parents. This, and his unexpected language, startled and confused her conscious mind so that he was able to slip in the suggestion that she was entirely in control of her thumb-sucking: 'It's your thumb and your mouth, and why in hell can't you suck it if you want to.' Her conscious mind was so occupied with his outburst that she was not aware of the implicit suggestion that since she could choose to suck her thumb, she could also choose not to. Nevertheless this suggestion registered in her unconscious. In the context of this suggestion, he gave her a directive to increase her thumbsucking, not to give it up. There was here a suggestion implicit that these were the only two choices open to her. This was of course untrue, but that did not matter, because she was too occupied to reflect on it. In the choices she made she was able to discharge her resistance not only to her parents, but also to the 'nut doctor'.

CHOOSING TO CHANGE

Erickson emphasized the futility of trying to change behaviour by telling or advising people how to behave. Instead, his strategy was to influence his patients through indirect suggestion so that they freely chose to change, often without any awareness that they had been influenced.

> A boy was brought to me who was supposed to be in the seventh grade in school, but he couldn't read. His parents insisted that he could read, and he was deprived in every possible way as they tried to force him to read. His summers were always ruined by tutors. He reacted by not reading.
> I started working with the boy by saying, 'I think your parents are rather stubborn. You know that you can't read, I know that you can't read. Your parents have brought you to me and they insist I teach you how to read. Between you and me, let's forget about it. I should do something for you, and I really ought to do something that you like. Now, what do you like most?' He said, 'Every summer I've wanted to go fishing with my father.'
> I asked him where his father fished. He told me that his father, who was a policeman, fished in Colorado, in Washington, in California, and even planned to go to Alaska. He had fished all along the coastline, I started wondering if he knew the names of the towns where those fishing spots were located. He got out a map of the West, and we tried to locate the towns. We weren't reading the map; we were looking for the names of towns. You look at maps, you don't read them.
> I would confuse the location of certain cities, and he would have to correct me. I would try to locate a town named Colorado Springs and be looking for it in California, and he had to correct me. But he was not reading, he was correcting me. He rapidly learned to locate all the towns we were interested in. He didn't know he was reading the

names. We had such a good time looking at the map and finding good fishing spots. He liked to come and discuss fish and the various kinds of flies used in catching fish. We also looked up different kinds of fish in the encyclopedia.

Near the end of August, I said, 'Let's play a joke on your teachers and on your parents. You've been told you'll be given a reading test when school starts. Your parents are going to be anxious about how you'll do, and so will your teacher. So you take the first-grade reader and you carefully stumble through it. Botch it up thoroughly. Do a better job on the second-grade reader, and a somewhat better one on the third-grade reader. Then do a beautiful job on the eight-grade reader.' He thought that was a wonderful joke. He did it just that way. Later he played truant and came over to tell me about the appalled look on his parents' faces and his teacher's face.

If he had read the first-grade reader correctly, it would have been an acknowledgement of failure on his part. But when he misread that and then went beyond the seventh grade to do the eight-grade reading well, that made him the winner. He could confound his teacher, bewilder his parents, and be the acknowledged winner.[60]

Erickson's approach as a teacher in this case came from his conviction that our limitations are learned. The boy is not refusing to read. He really 'knows' that he can't read. He has devoted some years to learning that. Erickson begins by accepting this belief without question. The energy which was going into maintaining this belief and resisting change is easily directed to doing what the boy likes to do. He learns to read while having the satisfaction of resisting learning to read.

UNLEARNING LIMITATIONS

All of Erickson's work as a therapist was directed to freeing individuals from their learned limitations. He followed the same approach when teaching other therapists about hypnosis. He believed that our conscious minds are programmed by our rationalistic, reductionist civilization in a way that severely limits our beliefs and behaviour. Our conscious mind learns a great deal about what we can't do. Our unconscious minds, in Erickson's view, are a lot smarter.

And it is very important for a person to know their unconscious is smarter than they are. There is a great wealth of stored material in the unconscious. We know the unconscious can do things and it's important to assure your patient that it can. They have to be willing to let their unconscious do things and not depend so much on their conscious mind. This is a great aid to their functioning. So you build your technique around instructions that allow their conscious mind to withdraw from the task and leave it all up to the unconscious.[61]

To 'leave it all to the unconscious' may seem too radical a prescription for teachers, charged as they are with passing on the culture's view of what is true, good, beautiful and possible. Erickson was, of course, acting on the assumption that there is a natural desire for growth within the person, an assumption shared by many teachers. Teachers, however, tend to the illusion that their activities are principally involved with the conscious and rational. However, teaching, for better and for worse, deals with 'the back of the mind' as much as 'the front of the mind'. And good teaching involves freeing the child from learned limitations. Erickson's discovery that this is best achieved through indirect suggestion goes contrary to conventional wisdom in pedagogy, just as it did in therapy.

INDIRECT SUGGESTION

Erickson's techniques have been thoroughly analysed in an attempt to work out exactly what he was doing which was so effective. The elements of his communication style have been extracted and discussed by many writers. Grinder, Bandler and Cameron, for example, analyse Erickson's use of language in great detail and use it as the basis for a whole new technology of communication which they call neurolinguistic programming (NLP).[62]

In looking for practical applications of Ericksonian technique outside the field of medical hypnosis, there is a tendency to reduce it to a set of clever formulas. This seems particularly true of those who get enthusiastic about NLP. There is also a tendency to see these techniques as cunning ways of controlling people. This is certainly an aspect of them, but it is a long way from Erickson's perception that the people who came to him as patients were stuck in self-destructive beliefs and behaviour which they could not control and that his techniques were a means of freeing them.

Ericksonian therapy clearly offers a model with application to teachers' problems in classroom management, but this is not all. To be true to Erickson's ideas we need to examine as well the ways that indirect suggestion can be used to give the child access to the information, memories, potentials for action and creativity locked in his or her unconscious.

In using indirect suggestion it is important to understand that the language of the unconscious mind is different from the language of the conscious mind. The unconscious does not deal in ideas; it deals in images. It tends to see the pictures rather than to hear the words; it hears the melody rather than the lyrics. It receives not the communication but the metacommunication (communication about the communication) that comes with the accompanying non-verbal signals. It does not register negatives at all.

When Daddy breaks up a fight between his children by giving Billy a cuff over the ear and shouting, 'How many times have I told you not to hit people?' Billy's conscious mind may hear the verbal message and act on it or he may be aware of two conflicting messages and get confused. His unconscious only registers the non-verbal message. Likewise, while a teacher is keeping the children's conscious minds occupied with language and ideas, their unconscious minds are busy with the hidden curriculum. This comes to them through images. Some of these images come from the system and environment in which their schooling takes place. Some of them come from the actions, emotional tone, intonation and gestures which express the attitudes and unexamined assumptions of the teacher. Below the awareness of both teacher and child are pictures and a melody. For better or worse, these register in the child's unconscious, which receives the message without reflection, processes it, and stores it as a guide for behaviour. When it emerges into consciousness it emerges as an unchallengeable assumption about the nature of things.

The tendency of the unconscious to see the pictures and not hear the ideas may account for some of the difficulty teachers have in influencing their students' attitudes on emotionally charged topics such as racism, sexism and violence. Teachers with an emotional commitment in these areas are sometimes frustrated to find that teaching about racism, for instance, only seems to worsen racist attitudes and behaviour. For one thing, a strong emotional commitment can sometimes mask a basic and unacknowledged ambivalence, and this ambivalence will be expressed in one's metacommunications. For another, the unconscious records the pictures and does not hear the don'ts. Third, what the teacher is saying is competing with direct and indirect suggestions from many other sources.

This is not the whole story, but in so far as it is part of it, there are implications for the way teachers can productively handle such topics. In the first place the teacher should acknowledge the 'everyday neurosis' that generates her own ambivalence, owning that she has a 'shadow', an unacknowledged tendency to racism, sexism and violence. This may give more control over her communication. Second, the lesson might be about peace rather than violence, gender and race equality rather than gender and race discrimination. Last, in order to compete with other influences, the teacher can target the unconscious by teaching other subjects in a non-racist, non-sexist, non-violent way and by consciously and strategically using the techniques of indirect suggestion to reinforce this message.

BEING CREDIBLE

Very often the teacher is not heard by a child or adolescent because the teacher lacks credibility. Credibility for Erickson was an aspect of rapport, and the establishment of rapport was the essential first step in the therapeutic interaction. Establishing rapport with someone attractive, who is willing to like and admire us, is no great problem, at least in the short term. Rapport with someone who is hostile and antagonistic is another matter. For Erickson, rapport did not involve getting his patient to like him; that was of little importance to him. He found that the patient's antipathy could be as useful in manipulating a change in behaviour as affection, and more useful than dependence. The essence of rapport for him was to let the patient know that in some important aspects of reality as it was experienced by the patient at that moment, Erickson and the patient understood each other perfectly.

'It hurts. It hurts awful.'
'I don't like the way your parents ordered me to cure you.'

Carl Rogers was expressing the same priority when he emphasized empathic understanding as the first of the key conditions for a productive helping relationship, including the teacher-pupil relationship. The skill to express accurate empathy is one that can be acquired through practice, and practice is most required to deal with the occasions when the other person is indifferent or antagonistic.[63]

People like Rogers, Erickson, Fritz Perls and Virginia Satir possess a quite extraordinary ability to establish rapport. NLP theorists have analysed their verbal and non-verbal behaviour microscopically, broken it down into discrete techniques and developed an elaborate terminology.

One of the phenomena for which they have a name is *mirroring*. This is the process of offering back to a person part of that person's non-verbal behaviour. It is actually something we do all the time, adjusting our posture, gestures and voice modulation to those of the person we are talking to. It has been demonstrated that when two people are talking in a truly attentive way, there are constant minute changes in both the speaker's and the listener's non-verbal expression which are exactly synchronous with the words. When we feel 'intuitively' hostile to people, it is likely that they are either not mirroring us, or are doing it in too obvious a way.

Erickson's genius was in taking control of natural processes like this. When Erickson was attempting to establish rapport with a patient he would subtly match his posture, his breathing, his gestures, his voice rhythms to those of the patient. Adopting the patient's physical way of being in the world, he really got a sense of what it felt like to be that person. The patient, without knowing why, felt understood.

He would mirror the vocabulary and language patterns of the patient, as we all do when we really want to communicate with someone. He would also mirror the patient's representational system. That is to say, if the patient used largely visual imagery, Erickson would do the same: 'I *see* that life is pretty *gloomy* for you right now. It *looks* as though you don't have a *clear* idea of what you want.' Or kinesthetic: 'I *feel* we'll get *stuck* if we *mess around* with this any longer.' People show distinct and consistent preferences in imagery.

All this becomes very complex and technical when the psycholinguists get hold of it, but verbal and non-verbal mirroring is something we do automatically and unconsciously when we are giving our attention to someone we care about and are genuinely interested in. The trick is in learning to do as much in dealing with someone with whom one is not naturally in sympathy. When we try to make such unconscious behaviour conscious we experience a good deal of awkwardness, but in this instance practice is well rewarded with an ability to tune in at will to others.

While there is some overlap between the concerns and techniques of the therapist and those of the teacher, there are also obvious and significant differences. One characteristic of the teacher's task which limits the applicability of therapeutic techniques is that most of it involves dealing with groups rather than individuals. Where a teacher has to confront an individual student and change his or her behaviour, it must often be done in public and under institutional pressure. It is one thing for Erickson, in the privacy of his consulting room, to take a child's side against his or her parents, as a means of establishing rapport. A teacher attempting to deal with a hostile or angry child within the classroom does not have the same freedom to attack parents or other teachers. Nevertheless, it is in dealing with hostility that Erickson's views and methods are most enlightening.

DISCHARGING RESISTANCE

Erickson's first principle for handling resistance is to go with it and not against it. The second is to try to find something positive in the resistance and accentuate that. The child may be wrong-headed, but his provocative or alienated behaviour is the best way he knows of coping with his world at this moment. It's not only an Ericksonian principle that if you want him to learn anything you must start where he is.

> 'You'd really rather be somewhere else?'
> 'You hate being pushed around, don't you?'
> 'You'd rather talk to your friends than listen to me?'

Educating Psyche

The aim of such reflective statements is to transform a determination to be uncooperative into a feeling of being understood. Erickson developed a number of ways of dealing with the reluctant or resistant learner, his intention being to take the energy of the resistance and turn it in a productive direction. He by no means regarded resistance as a bad thing, but was amused by how easy he found it to manipulate people's choices through their resistance.

As an example, say that you have a bunch of marbles only one of which is a solid colour. You tell a child that you are going to write down on paper which marble he is going to choose. You take the position that you are going to predict and force the child to accept your choice. The child accepts the challenge and maintains that you cannot predict his choice. You then begin describing the various marbles as his possibilities: the blue one with white stripes, the brown and white, and so on. He hears you describing all the marbles in a seemingly random manner. He does not notice that you always pick a colour combination. He can escape by picking a marble with no colour combination – the solid colour marble that you previously wrote down as his eventual choice.

In this case you create the resistance by saying, 'I can predict your choice.' You insisted that he was going to choose one of the colour combinations you mentioned, but he puts an end to your speculations by choosing the solid colour you had previously predicted when you wrote it down. The child does not how you did it, yet there was a genuine rationale for predicting his choice. The child is now intrigued and open to other things you say to him.

The same procedure can work with a resistant adult. You look at the bookcase in your office and say that you can predict which book the patient will choose. You then mention all the various possibilities of choice: the dark books with light printing and those that are the reverse, the multicoloured bindings, the odd-sized books, and others. You carefully avoid mentioning just one book. Patients invariably resist all the possibilities you mention and pick the one you did not. Patients experience a surprise upon finding out that you had written down their choice before the game started. Their resistance tends to remain in the bookcase, and they are now simply open and curious about what you are up to.[64]

Magic and Manipulation

People don't need to be in therapy to fall for this trick. Playing this sort of game with friends or pupils is a good way to polish one's skills in suggestion while gaining a reputation as a mind reader.

When he wanted a patient to do A, Erickson would often argue vehemently for B, an even less attractive alternative. He would eventually let the patient win that battle and the patient having discharged his resistance on B, would go ahead and do A with satisfaction. When dealing with a married couple who were continually fighting he would direct them to have a fight, but specify the time and place. The couple was likely to 'spontaneously' stop fighting.

A teacher may have a daily ritual of reading a story to the children while they sit on a mat at her feet. All except Jason. Jason simply refuses to sit on the mat and listen. He doesn't disrupt the others; he simply goes and does something else when the teacher asks the children to sit and listen. No amount of persuading or cajoling has any effect. Eventually the teacher decides to let Jason express his resistance. She tells the children that it's time for them all to sit on the mat ... *except Jason*. Jason looks confused for a minute and then sits on the mat with the others.

Another Ericksonian approach to discharging resistance and negativity is to get the student's 'no' away from the immediate issue and gradually replace it by 'yes'. For example, the teacher has instructed the class to read quietly at their desks and Alex is clearly refusing to do so. The teacher asks Alex a series of questions which (knowing Alex) are likely to get the answer 'no', all about things far removed from the read-at-your-desk issue. Alternatively, she simply engages Alex in conversation about something he is known to dislike doing:

'I notice that Mr Y had you picking up papers in the yard at lunchtime ...'

Alex gets a chance to be negative about something. The teacher then moves closer to the reading situation with questions which anticipate a 'yes' answer:

'I suppose you'd prefer to be messing around with Sam.'
'Would you rather be sitting closer to the window while you are doing this?'

According to this script, Alex is soon reading happily by the window, having forgotten all about his earlier refusal to do so.

As in so many of Erickson's approaches, questions of manipulation and autonomy can be argued forever without reaching a satisfying conclusion. One view of the situation is that the teacher is allowing Alex to grow, which is what Alex is *really* striving for all the time, in fearful, wrongheaded, limiting ways; that the teacher simply liberates Alex from an inhibiting emotional state so that he can make a free choice to learn; that every time a teacher smiles or says a kind word a child's behaviour is 'manipulated'. We can't remove 'manipulation' without removing people.

A more direct approach to the Alex episode is to move straight into establishing a yes-set so that when a suggestion is made the unconscious will be receptive. Reflective statements are used with this intent. So are truisms and tautologies. Erickson's transcripts are full of unchallengeably fatuous remarks made with the intention of getting his patient nodding internally.

In the classroom:

> 'Sooner or later you'll get tired of looking out the window.'
>
> 'You don't know how long you can keep this up without getting bored.'
>
> 'People sometimes say things they later regret.'

All these statements are unarguably true.

To make the most of a reflective statement, you can tack a suggestion on to it with an 'and'.

> 'You're bored to death AND you're waiting for me to do something really interesting.'
>
> 'Sooner or later you'll get tired of looking out the window AND you'll want to work with the others."
>
> 'You don't know how long you can keep this up AND you're wondering what I'm going to say next.'
>
> 'You've been wasting your time all the term AND you don't have to waste your time any longer.'
>
> 'You have a very good reason for calling me a bitch AND there are probably a few other things you would like to tell me.'

Magic and Manipulation

'It's lovely day outside AND we're ready to work quietly for the next half hour.'

There is a strong tendency for the assent to the first clause to carry over to the second, especially if the teacher keeps talking so that the children cannot pause, reflect and reject the suggestion. It's not necessary for them to agree consciously with what is said. The suggestion acts most effectively if they do not reflect on it at all.

With an actively aggressive child, one safe way of developing a yes-set is to suggest behaviour which is already happening.

'You can sit down now', as the child begins to sit.
'You might like to move around a bit', as the child starts to get up.

Erickson learned to detect minute gestures and changes in posture so that he could actually tell what his patients were about to do before they were properly aware of it themselves. He could time his suggestion to the very beginning of a movement, so that the patient had the sense of following suggestions rather than leading them.[65] This skill was invaluable in trance induction. However, even without this highly developed observational power it is possible to have this sort of effect, as people are generally not very aware of what their bodies are doing. As in the earlier cases you can use this observation to lead into a suggestion.

'You can sit down now, and get on with your work.'
'You might like to move around the room a bit and help the others.'

DIRECTING BY SUGGESTION

Erickson was essentially a directive therapist. He had a clearly defined goal, the removal of the patient's symptoms, and he manipulated the patient in that direction by any means he thought might work. Yet he avoided giving directives, unless manipulating resistance. His patients chose to change behaviour, and chose voluntarily and, as they thought, spontaneously. Likewise, many teachers manage to teach towards specific goals without, it seems, giving directives. In analyses of teacher talk in classrooms, this is one of the dimensions on which it is relatively easy to categorize teachers. The teaching style of some centres around giving instructions. Others rarely give instructions of any kind, yet their classes may function smoothly and learn effectively without management problems. It seems to have nothing to do with being conservative or radical in their attitudes and teaching methods. Among them are benevolent despots, creative anarchists and charismatic narcissists. They simply don't give orders. What they seem to have in common is a rapport with their class and the ability to direct by suggestion. They say:

'You don't need to talk now', instead of, 'Be quiet.'

'You don't have to move', for, 'Be still.'

'You don't need to remain standing', for, 'Sit down.'

'You can get out your books', for, 'Get out your books.'

'You may do the next five problems', for, 'Do the next five problems'.

For Erickson the difference was a critical one. *Permissive suggestions* such as these achieve a subtly different effect from commands. They give the child an opportunity to choose rather than a requirement to submit, and they do not generate resistance as a command does.

Slightly more complex are the *implied suggestions*.

'You may not understand this poem fully on the first reading' (implies that you'll understand it on a subsequent reading).

'You won't want to start writing immediately' (implies you'll want to start writing soon).

'You won't be able to concentrate on these problems till you're seated comfortably' (implies that when you're comfortable you'll be able to concentrate).

'I don't suppose you can work properly while I'm staring at you' (implies that when I look away you will work).

'I don't know when you'll change your behaviour' (implies that you'll change your behaviour).

There is nothing new or startling about it. Our everyday communication is full of implied suggestions. Our perception of ourselves and our abilities has come through a long process of unconsciously hearing such suggestions. If you tell a child: 'You will never be any good at maths because you are a girl' the statement can be reflected on, talked about and rejected as absurd. If the same message is given indirectly, through implications expressed either verbally or through gesture, tone or facial expression, the child receives the suggestion unconsciously and gradually comes to accept it as irrefutable. Fortunately, this is true also of positive suggestion.

Psychological implication is an essential part of our style of communication. Erickson's contribution in this as in other areas lies in his demonstration that one can take some control over this process and use it with intention.

A related way of dealing with resistance is through giving multiple tasks, rather than single tasks. For example:

> 'Robin, when you've put that book away can you come over here and help me organize this?'

This has a quite different effect from the three separate commands: 'Put the book away.' 'Come here.' 'Help me.' It is easy for Robin to refuse separate tasks, but refusal of combined tasks is complicated, especially if one of them is attractive. The effort it takes Robin to decide which of them she is refusing is itself a deterrent to refusal. Robin may perform the tasks unwillingly, but she may prefer to do so rather than go to the effort of analysing the situation.

BINDS AND DOUBLE BINDS

A further and very characteristic technique of Erickson's, especially in dealing with a resistant or antagonistic patient, was the bind. It is best illustrated by an anecdote.

> My first well-remembered intentional use of the double bind occurred in early boyhood. One winter day with the weather below zero, my father led a calf out of the barn to the water trough. After the calf had satisfied his thirst, they turned back to the barn but at the doorway the calf stubbornly braced its feet and, despite my father's desperate

pulling on the halter, he could not budge the animal. I was outside playing in the snow and, observing the impasse, began laughing heartily. My father challenged me to pull the calf into the barn. Recognising the situation as one of unreasoning stubborn resistance on the part of the calf, I decided to let the calf have full opportunity to resist since that was what it apparently wished to do. Accordingly I presented the calf with a double bind by seizing it by the tail and pulling it away from the barn while my father continued to pull inward. The calf promptly chose to resist the weaker of the two forces and dragged me into the barn.[66]

Erickson used the bind and double bind in very subtle ways both to induce trance and to enable his patients to change their behaviour while acting out their resistance to change. He gives an example of a six-year-old nail-biter.

I know your father and mother have been asking you, Jimmy, to quit biting your nails. They don't seem to know that you're just a six-year-old boy. And they don't seem to know that you will naturally quit biting your nails just before you're seven years old. And they really don't know that! So when they tell you to stop biting your nails, just ignore them![67]

This is an example of the therapeutic double bind. The more Jimmy enjoys biting his nails to irritate his parents the more he reinforces the suggestion that he will give up nail-biting. He is not aware that Erickson knows that he is approaching his seventh birthday.

Discussion of binds and double binds is inclined to get technical. In essence, a bind gives someone an illusion of choice between comparable alternatives, as in the parental trick question: 'Do you want to go to bed now or after this program?' Either response gets the parents what they want provided the child is naive enough to fall for it. Likewise the teacher says: 'Do you prefer to do the test tomorrow or on Monday?' The choice is a phony one, but it is likely to leave the students in quite a different frame of mind from the statement, 'You will do the test on Monday.' The unconscious has received the suggestion that it is choosing to do the test and directs energy to the task rather than waste it in resistance.

Magic and Manipulation

Both of these illustrations are examples of time-binds, as is the following: 'Will you be ready to stop distracting the class today or do we have to wait for tomorrow?' If the implicit suggestion in this bind is received unconsciously, it may well be worth waiting till tomorrow for its effect.

Here are other examples, without the time element.

> 'Do you want to do that work on your own or would you like me to come and help you?' (said as an offer, not a threat).
>
> 'Do you want to study this topic the hard way or the easy way?'
>
> 'Which of these experiments do you want to do first?'
>
> 'Would you like to explain your behaviour standing up or sitting down?'

Such binds are common in teacher-talk and parent-talk.

In spite of the faulty logic in binds, the rational mind can deal with them and make a choice. If given time to reflect the child can spot the faulty logic and reject the suggestion. In a *double bind*, on the other hand, the rational mind has no way out. If it tries it only gets confused. For Erickson, a major use of the double bind was in inducing trance in resistant patients.

> 'Will you begin to feel numb in the fingers or the back of the hand first?'
>
> 'Would you like to have your hands on your thighs or on the arms of the chair when you go into trance?'
>
> 'If your unconscious is ready for you to go into trance your left hand will rise. If not, your right hand will rise.'

He found that such a bind was often enough to put the patient into trance.

While many teachers would no doubt appreciate the ability to put an aggressive or hyperactive child into trance occasionally, this can hardly be seen as a legitimate use of the double bind in the classroom. Nevertheless, in dealing with provocative or antagonistic behaviour, Erickson's technique for getting cows into barns may be more effective than persuasion, command or reactive violence.

'I want you to keep banging that desk until I tell you to stop.'

'I'd like you to keep doing that until you start to feel silly.'

As a response to abusive language: 'From now on, I insist that you call me a ... every time you talk to me.'

Some will see such a use of *psychological binds* as nasty and manipulative. It is certainly manipulative. For Erickson, manipulation is a legitimate activity when we are engaged in manipulating someone out of self-defeating behaviour. It may be nasty, too, if it comes out of hostility, or an aggressive or defensive need to win points against the student. If the teacher is acting out of antagonism this will be communicated non-verbally and this episode will mark another round in the battle. The non-verbal communications of the teacher who is genuinely interested in freeing the child from learned destructive attitudes and behaviour patterns will be quite different. It doesn't matter that the child is unaware of them; they will register just the same. While both teachers use the technique skilfully and 'successfully' the criteria for success are quite distinct. One teacher is happy to get an angry submission. The other aims at a genuine, if confused, choice to behave in a socially acceptable fashion.

To take the Ericksonian approach is first of all to accept the student's resistance and hostility as legitimate within the student's frame of reference, to take it seriously from the student's point of view, instead of being enmeshed in one's own reactions to attack. At the same time, one sees this behaviour as an unproductive, uncreative, frustrating pattern that the child is trapped in, and offers a way out of it.

When following a therapeutic model in writing about teaching, there is a tendency to overlook some complexities in the teaching situation that do not exist in individual therapy. The therapist's responsibility is to the client, and this responsibility can be pursued at length. The teacher's responsibility is divided, and he or she is under pressure to find instant solutions to behaviour problems, in order to get on with the real job, which involves the other twenty children in the class. At times the teacher may have to settle for angry submission, if it enables the class to proceed. Major personality change may need to be postponed for a few days. In the school, institutional pressures may make it difficult to follow through when the teacher has mis-

Magic and Manipulation

calculated the nature of the resistance and a pupil responds to an attempted bind by 'calling the teacher's bluff'. When Erickson found a technique did not have the desired result he just went on acknowledging and permitting whatever the patient was doing. This may not be possible in the classroom. The situation in the classroom is also complicated by status issues. If a technique makes a student look ridiculous in front of a peer group, it may lose more than it gains.

In spite of all these limitations there are occasions when the use of a reverse bind is appropriate and effective. Rossi explains the effectiveness of this sort of bind.

> The reverse set double bind permits the subject both to resist and to yield! People with problems are, in fact, usually caught between conflicting impulses. They are caught in ambivalence between resisting and yielding to various impulses and trends within themselves. An effective approach to resolving this dilemma is to allow both the resistance and the yielding to be expressed. It does not make sense from a rational point of view – but it does make sense from an emotional point of view – to free and express all the impulses that were locked up in mutual contradiction.[68]

In another illustration from Erickson, the presenting problem was a fourteen-year-old girl who had developed the idea that her feet were much too large. The mother came alone to Erickson and described the situation. For three months the girl had been becoming more and more withdrawn, and she didn't want to go to school or to church or to be seen on the street. The girl would not allow the subject of her feet to be discussed, and she would not go to a doctor to talk about them. No amount of reassurance by her mother had any influence and the girl was becoming more and more seclusive. Erickson reports:

> I arranged with the mother to visit the home on the following day under false pretences. The girl would be told that I was coming to examine the mother to see if she had the flu. It was a pretence, and yet the mother wasn't feeling well and I suggested that an examination would be appropriate. When I arrived at the home, the mother was in

bed. I did a careful physical examination of her, listening to her chest, examining her throat, and so on. The girl was present. I sent her for a towel, and I asked that she stand beside me in case I needed something. She was very concerned about her mother's health. This gave me an opportunity to look her over. She was rather stoutly built and her feet were not large.

Studying the girl, I wondered what I could do to get her over this problem. Finally I hit upon a plan. As I finished my examination of the mother, I manoeuvred the girl into a position directly behind me. I was sitting on the bed talking to the mother, and I got up slowly and carefully and then stepped back awkwardly. I put my heel down squarely on the girl's toes. The girl, of course, squawked with pain. I turned on her and in a tone of absolute fury and said, 'If you would grow those things large enough for a man to see, I wouldn't be in this sort of situation. The girl looked at me, puzzled, while I wrote out a prescription and called the drugstore. That day the girl asked her mother if she could go out to a show, which she hadn't done in months. She went to school and church, and that was the end of a pattern of three months' seclusiveness. I checked later on how things were going, and the girl was friendly and agreeable. She didn't realize what I had done, nor did her mother. All her mother noticed was that I had been impolite to her daughter when I visited that day. She couldn't connect that with the daughter's return to normal activity.[69]

The double bind is not restricted to use with problems in behaviour. Consider the following examples:

'You will probably learn how to do this in spite of yourself.'

'Try very hard not to remember what I'm about to say to you.'

The word 'try' in itself contains a bind, in that it suggests failure. It is a favourite word of stage hypnotists. 'Try to lift your hand' suggests an inability to raise the hand. 'The harder you try to move it, the more impossible it is to move.' This suggestion is powerful even without an induction. Unfortunately the same powerful suggestion may operate inadvertently when the teacher says: 'Try to read the passage without a single mistake.'

Magic and Manipulation

EMBEDDED COMMANDS

Besides containing a bind, the directive 'Try not to remember what I am about to say to you' contains an *embedded command*. The embedding of commands in conversational statements is one of the more sophisticated Ericksonian techniques, which has been turned into a technology by NLP practitioners. In the case above, while the conscious mind is coping with what it hears as a command to forget what it has not yet heard, the unconscious not only hears the suggestion of failure in the word 'try' but may also hear the command, 'Remember what I am about to say to you.' For this command to register, the speaker must mark this phrase, or at least the words 'remember' ,'I' and 'say', by speaking them with an unexpected inflection, by pausing before them, or by associating them with a gesture.

Embedded commands are a favourite technique for demonstrating 'everyday hypnosis'. The hypnotist may address the audience: 'Think we'd better start from scratch. Nobody really knows how hypnotism works.' Immediately, a number of people begin to scratch their noses. The hypnotist has *marked* 'scratch' and 'knows' in some way. One of Erickson's typical techniques was to talk to a patient in a rambling, anecdotal fashion, interspersing suggestions in the monologue. The patient would come away knowing that something had changed, but not knowing what or how, or what Erickson's rather boring story had to do with it.

To improvise such a monologue as Erickson did may seem a little daunting, but there is nothing to prevent a teacher from dealing with a classroom problem by telling or reading a story into which suggestions have been embedded. For example, a teacher who is concerned about racial tensions or prejudices in his or her classroom might talk about going to a rock concert. Interspersed in the story, with no necessary regard to the grammatical structure or logical form of narrative, are phrases like 'people are different'; 'differences very interesting'; 'enjoy being together'. There might be a remark that when you are having a friendly *race*, it *doesn't matter* who wins. And so on. The advantage of a story is that listening to a story often puts one into a receptive, trance state anyway. Erickson's stories tended to meander without, it seems, ever getting to the point. They were low-key with lots of falling inflections and unexpected pauses which seemed to have no relation to the grammar or the sense (one way of marking key phrases). He claimed that by never quite getting to the point he created a mental set of expectancy, in which the unconscious was particularly receptive to suggestions. Very often his stories were parables. He might deal with a person with sexual problems by telling a story about a friend's attempts to raise some money or his own experience in growing tomatoes. The resolution in Erickson's story, when it eventually came, would be translated unconsciously by the patient as a solution to his or her own problem. Like Jesus, he saw no value in explaining the metaphor, and the patient went off wondering why Erickson had spent the last hour talking about tomatoes or money, and feeling relieved that he'd now thought of a solution to the problem.

The analysis and refinement of Erickson's techniques goes on and on. In the hands of the rare expert they appear magical. For the teacher beginning to experiment, they may seem at first to have no effect at all. It takes a great deal of practice to achieve a fraction of what Erickson seemed to do intuitively and easily. To achieve any sort of skill at all, part of that practice must be spent on acquiring something of Erickson's capacity for detailed observation and his sense of timing. For someone whose genius was in the field of communication, he had some initial disadvantages. He was colour blind, tone deaf, dyslexic, and partially paralysed after two polio attacks. He compensated for his handicaps by developing extraordinary powers of observation. He learned to detect minute gestures, changes of skin colour, eye movements, changes in vocal tone and breathing patterns, and learned to associate them with changes in the internal processes of his patients. He could judge the exact moment when a suggestion would be most effective. Add to this an extraordinarily original mind and a love of the unexpected, and any attempt to emulate him becomes somewhat frustrating. On the other hand, all the skills described here, both the observational skills and the interventionist skills, can be acquired through practice, and practice does not have to be restricted to the classroom.

Erickson's idea of the unconscious is a very simplistic one. He was essentially a practitioner and had little patience for working out a theory that was logically consistent. Had recent research on brain hemisphere specialization been conducted before he developed his ideas, he might have preferred to use left-brain/right-brain as his metaphor, instead of conscious/unconscious. If he had been familiar with recent research on the structure of the brain and its relation to consciousness he might have preferred to speak of somatic or magical knowing rather than of the unconscious. A lot of NLP theorists make use of the left-brain/right-brain model. However, whatever the adequacy of the language he used, he certainly pointed to the limitations of conventional notions of teaching.

Fears about manipulation in the classroom are real and justified. Teachers who are malicious or neurotic as well as skilful can use Ericksonian techniques for their own self-serving ends rather than those of their students. It may even be argued that the manipulatively managed classroom is somehow a worse environment than the violent, oppressive, apathetic or chaotic one. It does seem, however, that both children and adults are better able to cope with suggestions which go contrary to their purposes than they are able to cope with violence, oppression, apathy or chaos without being affected for the worse. When we read Erickson's case histories, indirect suggestion appears as a subtle and powerful tool. If teachers can become aware of how they and their students are swimming in a sea of suggestions to the extent that they are, in Lozanov's words, 'victims of their culture', they will seize all the powerful and subtle tools they can find to alter their victim status.

NOTES Chapter 3. Magic and Manipulation

[56] Erickson's distinction between 'front of your mind' and 'back of your mind' thinking (or conscious and unconscious as Erickson uses the terms) can be readily conceptualized as a distinction between left-brain and right brain processes.
[57] Haley, *Uncommon Therapy*, p. 189.
[58] ibid., p. 190.
[59] ibid., pp. 195f.
[60] ibid., pp. 204f.
[61] M. Erickson, E. Rossi & S. Rossi, *Hypnotic Realities*, p. 7.
[62] The literature on NLP is extensive and some of it examines the teaching-learning process specifically. See J. Grinder and R. Bandler, *The Structure of Magic*; B. F. Cleveland, *Master Teaching Techniques* and L. Harper, *Classroom Magic*.
[63] There is an immense gap in sensibility between the empathic understanding

of a Carl Rogers and the rapport of a neurolinguistic programmer. Rogers saw the person, not the details of the person's behaviour, and was acutely aware of the person's feeling state. The neurolinguistic programmer establishes rapport not by trying to share the client's experience of the world but by reflecting the client's physical behaviour, e.g., by paying close attention to the client's breathing or the rising and falling intonations of the client's voice, and unobtrusively moving a finger to this rhythmic pattern. The client perceives this subliminally and senses that the therapist has tuned in. Where the person-centred therapist respects absolutely the client's capacity to find an adequate way of coping with present problems, NLP aims at making the client's behaviour more functional in a specific way.

In the language of archetypal psychology we can assign NLP to Prometheus the scientist and technician, for whom the highest wisdom is to find out how things work and use this knowledge efficiently. Rogers' work on the other hand is guided by Eros, the god of relatedness. It is worth noting also that the guiding energy for Erickson himself seems to come less from Prometheus than from Hermes, the Trickster.

[64] Erickson, Rossi and Rossi, op. cit., p. 222.
[65] Actually, you may notice the child (or adult) moving before he or she is aware that that it what they are going to do. There is laboratory evidence that our body often starts to move before we are aware of what we are about to do.
[66] Haley, op. cit., p. 72.
[67] ibid., p. 217.
[68] Erickson, Rossi & Rossi, op. cit., p. 72.
69 Haley, op.cit., p. 198.

4

USE YOUR IMAGINATION

The dynamic principle of fantasy is play, which belongs also to the child, and as such it appears to be inconsistent with the principle of serious work. But without this playing with fantasy no creative work has ever come to birth. The debt we owe to the play of imagination is incalculable.

Carl Jung

ONE OF THE CONSEQUENCES OF Jung's break with Freud in 1913 was that Jung was plunged into a state of confusion, disorientation and inner uncertainty that he later described as his 'confrontation with the unconscious'. Not only had he lost his friend and mentor, and with him the friendship of the whole Viennese circle, but he had lost his grip on the whole psychoanalytic framework which he had devoted years of his life to building. He found himself struggling to understand what had happened and his struggle led into depression and frustration. He turned to sculpture, painting, mountain walks, talking to rocks and trees, trying to find a way to deal with the images and feelings that were overwhelming him.

Jung sensed strongly that the only way to deal with this flood was through his imagination. He let his emotions express themselves in images, and found that a number of specific images emerged. These he accepted as 'mediators', communicating meaning from the unconscious. He found that by personifying his feelings in this way he could differentiate himself from them and avoid being swept away by the flood. By this means he could confront them and relate to them, with a sense that he had some control over the process.

Among the person-images that inhabited his imagination at this time was an ageless wise man whom Jung called Philemon, who was sometimes accompanied by a young woman. Jung accepted these figures as real, and learned to converse with them, coming to see that Philemon possessed qualities and wisdom far superior to those possessed by Jung's conscious personality, and realising also the presence within himself of a woman, whom he called Anima.

ACTIVE FANTASY

For some years, this inner exploration was Jung's whole work. He took notes of his conversations with these images, and painted and sculpted a great deal in an attempt to record what he was learning, even though he did not understand what it was. Whether we regard Jung's internal life during this period as a sort of voluntary psychosis or merely as an interesting mental exercise, the fact remains that his immense theoretical works of later years were based on what he learned through this experience.

Jung took his images seriously. His experience of them was of autonomous beings, not manufactured or owned by the conscious self. He discovered from them that the unconscious Jung was very different from the personality with which he identified. Through dialogue with these personifications and through wrestling with the question whether they represented the 'I' or the 'Other', he was forced to abandon his unsuccessful attempt to force his thinking into the framework of psychoanalysis. When he started writing again (1916) he introduced the distinction between the personal and collective unconscious, the concepts of anima, animus and persona, and the principle of individuation. By 1921 he had started his discussion of archetypes and had developed his psychology of types and his notion of the self. All of this speculation, which has been as influential as it was innovative in modern European psychology, he claimed to have initiated in the years of his 'breakdown', when he encountered his soul. He eventually came to believe that this 'purposive introspection' was the basic condition for any creative act.

Jung speculated not only on what he had learned during this period of purposive introspection, but also on how he had learned it. He was not alone in his attempt to understand this process and use it therapeutically. He was familiar with the experience of the ancient world and of some non-European cultures in relating to internal images and also with the Christian spiritual tradition of imaginative meditation and inner dialogue. Besides this, imagination had become an object of scientific investigation in late nineteenth century Europe, involving major figures like Janet and Binet. They encouraged their patients to converse with the figures thrown up by the unconscious in directed visualization, believing that such figures expressed their various unconscious sub-personalities. A great deal of interest centred on the peculiarly vivid images experienced by many people just before going to sleep (hypnogogic imagery). By the time Jung was clear enough about his own technique to give it its final name – active imagination – a number of comparable techniques of therapeutic imagining had been invented.

Educating Psyche

For Jung, the 'active' attitude implied in his technique was all-important. He wished to distinguish it from passive fantasy, where the contents of the unconscious break through into consciousness without any participation by the ego.

> It is probable that passive fantasies always have their origin in an unconscious process that is antithetical to consciousness, but invested with approximately the same amount of energy as the conscious attitude, and therefore capable of breaking through the latter's resistance. Active fantasies, on the other hand, owe their existence not so much to this unconscious process as to a conscious propensity to assimilate hints or fragments of lightly-toned unconscious complexes and, by associating them with parallel elements, to elaborate them in clearly visual form. It is not necessarily a question of a dissociated psychic state, but rather of a positive participation of consciousness ...
>
> Active fantasy is one of the highest forms of psychic activity. For here the conscious and the unconscious personality of the subject flow together into a common product in which both are united.[70]

Jung's technique was not, then, a free association of images — either trivial recollections or affect-laden images from the deeper levels of the conscious. Neither was it a guided fantasy. He saw in it not so much a way of dealing with pathology as a means by which a person could bring conscious and unconscious processes into harmony, without the necessary assistance of a therapist. He looked to images not as hiding reality (as Freud perceived them) but as revealing it. In active imagination it was possible to pursue that revelation through direct participation in processes usually unconscious, something a dream will rarely allow. For Jung the imaginal drama was being played out in the unconscious all the time, only occasionally coming to the attention of the conscious self. Through active imagination the conscious self could enter the drama.

> The point is that you start with any image, for instance, just with that yellow mass in your dream. Contemplate it and carefully observe how the picture begins to unfold or to change. Don't try to make it into something, just do nothing but observe what its spontaneous changes are. Any mental picture you contemplate in this way will sooner or later change through a spontaneous association that causes a slight

alteration of the picture. You must carefully avoid impatient jumping from one subject to another. Hold fast to the one image you have chosen and wait until it changes by itself. Note all these changes and eventually step into the picture yourself, and if it is a speaking figure at all then say what you have to say to that figure and listen to what he or she has to say.

Thus you can analyse your unconscious but also give your unconscious a chance to analyse yourself, and therewith you gradually create the unity of conscious and unconscious without which there is no individuation at all. If you apply this method, then I can come in as an occasional adviser, but if you don't apply it, then my existence is of no use for you.[71]

At the time that Jung was exploring his own unconscious and developing his technique, Johannes Schultz was experimenting with and developing autogenic training. Schultz had a much more mechanistic model of the mind and a much more systematic approach to experience than Jung. In attempting to find a way of using the healing power of hypnosis without the associated dependence, he taught his subjects to achieve a sort of hypnotic state through self-suggested relaxation, and discovered that while in this state of consciousness they had an increased ability to visualize, and sometimes experienced spontaneous and vivid imagery. He found also that through progressive visualization exercises, this ability to imagine could be developed to the point where they could hold conversations with imaginary people. Furthermore, just as they could affect their state of consciousness by achieving a particular physical state, they could also affect their physical functioning by using their imagination. Schultz's understanding of the processes was essentially psychophysiological. He sought and found evidence relating to the psychosomatic aspects of health and sickness, and demonstrated that just as disturbances in the imagination affect the functioning of the body, the reverse is also true. The body can be made to function more harmoniously and healthily through constructive imagining. Schultz's demonstration that the imagination could systematically be trained for this purpose was taken up by Roberto Assagioli and incorporated in his technique of psychosynthesis.

During these same years, Robert Désoillé was developing the use of guided fantasy in psychotherapy.[72] He would have his patients insert themselves in one of his imaginary 'archetypal' situations (e.g., meeting a dragon, going into a cave). He would guide the patient through the fantasy, using the latter's responses to situations as the basis of his diagnosis. In addition he would 'script' the fantasy as it went along, to meet the particular patient's needs. Though his work shows the influence of Jung, he was, like Schultz, more curious about the operations of the brain than about the nature of 'the unconscious'. One of his contributions was to gather evidence that the 'happy ending' to a fantasy actually had a physiological effect. If a conflict could be resolved metaphorically, in guided fantasy, it would tend also to be resolved in the body and the personality.

The guided fantasy or directed day-dream is an easier tool to utilize than Jung's active imagination. Jung's technique is based on the premise that the dreaming which goes on in the unconscious all the time is essentially compensatory to the narrow view of identity and reality held by our conscious selves. The technique involves detecting subtle, subliminal signals, 'hints or fragments of highly toned unconscious complexes', and letting them emerge into consciousness as visual images. To get in tune with the unconscious process without either controlling it or being submerged in it requires delicacy, dedication and practice. Jung assumed that people taking on the exercise would have been prepared for it in analysis.

Guided imagery initiates a different sort of arrangement with the unconscious. In Désoillé's approach the therapist provides a basic script based on the universal images that recur in primitive and modern art forms, in myths, fairytales, dreams and psychotic hallucinations. His understanding is that there is a mechanism in the brain which is somehow represented by such symbols and which operates through them. The particular form the image takes belongs to the individual and it is this aspect that the therapist uses in diagnosis. Désoillé argued that since we know through mythology the critical importance of particular images there is no need to wait for the patient to generate his or her own in the consulting room. The patient can enter immediately into these ancient and fundamental dramas, to act them out, and find catharsis and enlightenment.

If we wish to find in all of this some hint of how application might be made to our thinking about the process of education and the practice of teaching, the source we are likely to find most helpful is the system of psychosynthesis, developed by Roberto Assagioli.[73] Like Jung, Assagioli was an early convert to psychoanalysis and a later refugee from it. His break with the Freudian circle came when he realized that he could not accept Freud's pessimistic view of the unconscious. For Assagioli the unconscious had to contain the best of us as well as the worst of us. Human beings seemed to him to be almost as scared of their creativity, spontaneity, altruism and spirituality as they were of their violence and sadism.

Imagination plays a central part in Assagioli's method. Though his thinking shows plenty of Jungian influence, his approach is much more practical than Jung's, and much more explicit about the 'how' of therapy. He created many techniques, and adapted many that he had borrowed from Schultz, Désoillé and other European therapists, as well as from Eastern and Western meditative traditions. While psychosynthesis can be discussed as an approach to the whole process of education, our interest here is in the techniques he developed to exploit the power of the imagination. Many of these can be readily translated into classroom practice, even to the content-centred practice of the conventional classroom.

Assagioli's psychology is, in part, an old-fashioned 'faculty' psychology. While all the faculties are to be brought into harmonious union, and engaged in the organism's instinctive growth towards completeness, Assagioli showed most interest in two faculties or functions of the self — imagination and will. The development of these functions is a worthwhile end in itself. Attention paid to training the imagination, in particular, is a preparation for effective use of the visualization techniques that are fundamental to psychosynthesis.

THE SKILFUL IMAGINATION

If 'training the imagination' sounds somewhat old-fashioned, it may be preferable to talk of imagining as a skill which, like language, significantly affects the child's ability to learn, to develop peer and adult relationships, to pursue goals and to experience pleasure.

While the capacity to imagine appears to be wired into the human organism in much the same way as the potential for language, it does not emerge and develop independently. The growing child's developing imagination depends not only on the maturation of the brain, but also on a number of interpersonal and environmental conditions. Besides providing these conditions (e.g. security, affection, acknowledgement, time and space for expression) the teacher can enter into the process directly and actively through teaching the skills of imaging and providing practice.

> Close your eyes and imagine the following objects, tastes, smells and sounds. Hold the image in your mind for a couple of minutes. If it disappears, bring your attention back to it without effort.
> — a green triangle, a red rose, a gold star;
> — a hand writing your name on a blackboard;
> — the touch of velvet, of glass, of a cool breeze;
> — the taste of a peach, of a lemon, of an olive;
> — the smell of eucalyptus, of a flower, of cut grass;
> — the sound of bells, of a baby crying, of someone calling your name.

This training can be extended by consciously attending to the many dimensions of the five senses and learning to manipulate them in imagining.

> Visualize a red rose ... make it redder ... change its colour gradually to gold ... make it bigger ... smaller ... make it fold up into a bud ... look at the background ... open the rose again ... shine more light on it ... make it darker ... make it fuzzy ... clear ... faint ...
> Smell it ... touch it with your tongue ... make the fragrance more intense ... fainter ...
> Touch the rose with your hand ... make the petals damp ... dry ... soft ... rough ... crush it against your cheek ...

These are basic drills which work surprisingly well with children and adults and quickly increase powers of concentration and the vividness of imagination. There is no question that, in most people, imagination is poorly developed but improves readily with a little training. Such training in the classroom should require no justification. Simple exercises like those above can easily be fitted into a teaching program. The children's improved concentration and ability to visualize are worthwhile goals in themselves. Besides that, they can be exploited for more effective teaching of the curriculum.

TELLING STORIES

Primary teachers should need no reminder of the value of telling stories. Unfortunately, as children progress through their schooling they encounter teachers who have never learned this value, have forgotten it, or have decided that there are more important things to do in school.

What such teachers forget is that a great deal of what we know we know as story.

Our basic assumptions – the things we take so completely for granted that we never reflect on them – are embedded in the story of who we are and where we come from. We did not make up this story. We inherited it from our parents, our family, our religious tradition and more widely from our culture. This story is not about 'facts', though it may pretend to be. Rather, it is a way of imagining the world and asserting that our lives have meaning. We 'pick up' this story when we are very young without wondering whether it is 'true' or not, and we may carry it into adulthood without bothering whether there is any objective evidence to support it. Our culture reproduces itself through the repetition of its story.

Our cultural narrative is expressed in lots of different ways in the stories we tell our children. For instance, we may tell stories which carry the message that good people get rewarded and bad people get punished, stories that marrying the one you love leads to living happily ever after, stories that boys grow up by going on heroic journeys and girls grow up by waiting quietly at home, stories which imply that everything will turn out all right in the long run. The assumptions and values embedded in these stories are inclined to persist even when the facts of life seem to contradict them.

Some children grow up hearing and observing the story that the best way of dealing with conflict is through violence, the story that men have the right to beat women and children, the story that they belong to a superior race and should treat inferior races with contempt, the story that you can't trust anybody. The values and assumptions in these stories also persist into adulthood.

Teachers know well enough that assumptions like these do not easily collapse under the weight of reasonable argument. 'Objective facts' make little impact on deep assumptions. When teachers are confronted with violent, racist or sexist assumptions in their students they may well attempt to deal with them through instruction, by laying out a set of propositions based on what are to them indisputable principles and evidence. Such an approach will only convince those who don't need convincing.

Propositional knowledge is only one kind of knowledge. Narrative knowledge resides in a different part of the brain and is quite different; it is not easily translated into propositions. Besides this we have experiential knowledge, the knowledge that we carry in our bodies and could not articulate if we tried to. If we want to change our students' self-destructive or anti-social attitudes and assumptions, we need to stop arguing with them or forcing them to comply and instead devote our energies to telling them a different story and providing an experience from which they pick up a different message.

It seems that the 'natural' mode of learning for children is through story, that for them life is story, not a lot of 'facts'. They uncritically accept the picture of the world that they inherit from those who care for them. In adolescence they may gain the capacity to reflect objectively on the evidence and decide what is 'true', but even then it is not guaranteed. And even if teachers are successful in their task of teaching adolescents to observe objectively and think rationally, their students never leave behind their reliance on story to express what is important in their lives. This is obvious enough to their English and History teachers. It is a pity that more of their Science and Mathematics teachers don't acknowledge it. Story is not just a way of entertaining: it is a powerful way of teaching.

GUIDED VISUALIZATION

The two following examples of guided visualization are taken from *What We May Be*, by Piero Ferrucci.

Use Your Imagination

The Sun

Visualize yourself on the beach at dawn. The sea is almost motionless as the last bright stars fade away.

Feel the freshness and the purity of the air. Watch the water, the stars, the dark sky.

Take some time to experience the silence before sunrise, the stillness filled with all possibilities.

Slowly, the darkness melts and colours change. The sky over the horizon becomes red, then golden. Then the sun's first rays reach you, and you watch it slowly emerging from the water.

With half the sun's disc visible and the rest still below the horizon, you see that its reflection in the water is creating a path of golden, shimmering light leading from you all the way to its very heart.

The temperature of the water is pleasant, and you decide to go in. Slowly, start to swim in the golden radiance. You feel the light-filled water touching your body. You experience yourself floating effortlessly and moving pleasurably in the sea.

The more you swim toward the sun, the less aware you are of the water, and the more the light around you increases. You feel enveloped in a beneficent, golden light which permeates you completely.

Your body is bathing now in the vitality of the sun. Your feelings are pervaded by its warmth. Your mind is illuminated by its light.[74]

The Bell

Imagine that you are lying on the grass of a meadow surrounded by hills. Feel the softness of the grass under your body, and smell the fragrance of the flowers around you. Look at the sky above.

Nearby there is a small country church. It has a bell which you can hear pealing. Its sound is both pure and joyful. It travels through the ether and reaches you. It is your sound, a sound capable of evoking and stimulating your unknown, concealed joy.

Now you hear the bell again. This time its peal is louder. Feel its resonance within you. Realize that it is awakening your dormant potentialities. Then listen to this sound as it gradually fades, and be aware of the moment when sound ends and silence begins.

Once more, you hear the bell pealing. The sound is somehow

closer to you, and you can feel it vibrating within you, in each one of your cells, in each one of your nerves. And at some moment, if only for a second, you become that sound, pure, boundless, vibrating.[75]

There is a good deal of evidence that our bodies are unable to distinguish clearly between fantasy and external reality. Even without the evidence from psychophysiological research we know this from our experience of waking up trembling from a nightmare, of salivating when we imagine eating a lemon, of being sexually stimulated by a fantasy, of 'feeling our blood go cold' as we listen to a ghost story. Similar biological mechanisms operate in imagined experiences like the two examples above. The fragmented, dispersed chaotic energies of our organism are aligned, harmonized and made purposive by the imagined experience, just as they would be by a 'real' one. People do feel better, more serene or more energized after such a visualization. If this sort of exercise is repeated regularly, it can markedly change people's self-image, attitudes and behaviour.

The shelves of pop psychology in libraries and bookshops have plenty of titles like *Using Creative Visualization to Get Rich and Improve Your Golf Stroke* and *Taking Control of Your Life through Positive Imagery*, and there are also a number of serious treatments available of the use of imagery in therapy and healing. Many of these books are extremely valuable for their understanding of the nature and use of imagery.[76] However, even books that purport to be specifically concerned with education, such as Diana Whitmore's excellent *Psychosynthesis and Education*, limit their concern to a broad, humanistic view of education, ignoring the trivial matter of the curriculum which largely defines what teachers do in class. Such publications contain visualizations suitable for use in the classroom, which can assist children and adolescents to increase their self-esteem, to deal with their identity struggles and their relationships, to cope with stress, to develop goals. It is more difficult to find models for using visualization to improve their learning of mathematics and history.

Fortunately, it is not particularly difficult to script guided visualizations around curriculum content. Through such a device children can enter and participate in historical events, chemical processes, social conflicts, futurist scenarios. They can have some empathic identification with Einstein or

Use Your Imagination

Mozart or with a molecule or enzyme, to gain some understanding of an event or process 'from the inside'.

Such a technique depends for its effectiveness on the validity of Assagioli's conviction that we know a lot more than we know we know. One of the central exercises of psychosynthesis is a meditation on the words 'I know'.

> Sit quietly ... breathe deeply ... relax.
> Let your attention shift from your head down through your body to a point just below your solar plexus ... to your centre ... let it rest there ...
> Now, from your centre say I KNOW ... just rest on these words ... then repeat it ...
> In spite of my confusion ... in spite of the difficulty I have in understanding things ... I know that deep down inside myself, I KNOW ...
> Just rest quietly in the certainty that you know ... and that when you need to, you can make that knowledge conscious.

In a classroom following the principles of psychosynthesis, such a meditation would be used regularly as an affirmation by the students of their inner knowledge and their ability to find their own direction.

More pragmatically, it can be used as a warm-up to learning or recalling a segment of the curriculum.

A useful visualization exercise to enable students to become aware of what they have already learned either consciously or unconsciously is to have them fantasize going on a short journey which ends at a door of a room. On the door they find the words 'The Room of X' (X being the content to be explored). They enter and find within the room an assortment of objects, pictures, diagrams, etc. from which they can learn all there is to know about X. Alternatively, they may find a large picture book, and examine the pictures as they turn the pages one by one. Or they may meet someone who gives them information or advice. Or they may find themselves standing in a beam of light which infuses them with knowledge and understanding of the subject.

A guided visualization can be presented as a 'set piece' to introduce or enlarge on a topic. In this case it can be conducted with some ritual. Silence, directed relaxation and a gradual setting up of the scene lead to a serious encounter with the idea or event, often through identification with a character. The visualization may be carefully written out beforehand, and read with some solemnity. This can be a useful, and sometimes powerful, experience. Alternatively, it can be done spontaneously and without ceremony, when it suddenly seems an appropriate way of dealing with a question. 'Just imagine that you are ...' The more often the technique is used the more effective it will be. Whether scripted or improvised, for best effect it will be more than 'visualization'. Though the words 'fantasy', 'imagination' and 'visualization' are for convenience used interchangeably, it must not be forgotten that we have more senses than one. The teacher directing a visualization will deliberately introduce hearing, touching, tasting and smelling images to reinforce the visual.

DIALOGUE WITH IMAGINAL FIGURES

In order to get in touch with our 'inner knowing', Assagioli suggests entering into dialogue with symbolic figures such as 'the Wise Old Man', 'the Wise Old Woman' or guru-figures taken from history or mythology. In dialogue with such imagined figures we can seek information or advice and receive it. For Assagioli such personifications are essentially internal projections and such dialogues are a productive way of talking to ourselves. He found many people unable or unwilling to acknowledge their own wisdom, projecting it instead on to teachers, gurus or anyone who claimed authority, only giving credit to their own ideas when they heard them expressed by someone else. Internalising such projections involves owning the ideas and acknowledging one's suppressed wisdom.

In the schooling context, it is not difficult to direct a class through guided visualization to a meeting with a historical figure, the creator of a scientific theory, social movement or work of art. Alternatively, students can be taken through a warm-up visualization to an encounter with a character from a story, novel or play. The teacher can suggest the questions they might ask, and give them time to hear the replies. It is useful, at least sometimes, to have them shift identity between interviewer and interviewee. Speaking out of the persona of, say, Darwin, Demeter, Desdemona or Dostoevsky, adolescents can experience an understanding distinctly different from what has been expressed through their limited, everyday consciousness. They will also have the opportunity in this sort of exercise to own qualities in themselves that they do not claim in their limited, everyday identification. The goal of psychosynthesis is to own all of these fragments of ourself that our consciousness is unaware of. It is not essential that we have a sophisticated psychological understanding of this process. It is sufficient for the process to take place in imagination for it to influence self-image and behaviour in the 'real world'.

FREE DRAWING

It is not unusual for teachers to use some sort of art activity to help children to work through and remember the facts and ideas that have been presented in a lesson. It has been well demonstrated that pictures are more easily remembered than words, and a picture that emerges from a consideration of issues discussed in class is an invaluable reinforcement of the students' memory for these ideas. The conventional way of using art activity in the non-art class assumes that useful drawings are pictorial, naturalistic or at least rationally constructed. Free drawing as a technique in psychosynthesis demands a different approach. The teacher is interested in what is not so easily expressed rationally, in feelings and attitudes that are either not in awareness or not yet readily verbalized. The exercise is as likely to come before the topic is dealt with in class as it is to come after. The suggested title should be one that is not too easily translated photographically.

> Before beginning to draw, take a few deep breaths, relax, and just rest without thinking about anything.
> Now let the title of your drawing float around in your mind a bit.
> Get in touch with how you feel about this topic, in a vague sort of way, without giving that feeling a name.
> Now let your hand draw. Don't try to control it, just let it do the drawing by itself, while your mind repeats the title over and over. Do this in a casual sort of way, without using up your energy by concentrating too hard.

Just watch your hand and see what it does. Allow it to draw any way it likes. Let the image that emerges through your hand be whatever it wants to be.

When you've finished your drawings we can see something of what we know and feel about this topic.

While many primary teachers are used to the idea of free drawing of some kind, and some junior secondary teachers are prepared to see it as useful as well as recreational, the technique virtually disappears in higher secondary and adult classes. Nevertheless, it is just as valuable at these levels. Teachers who are able to overcome their own and their students' conservatism with regard to teaching methods have found that time taken to elicit a personal, non-verbal response to a stimulus-word like 'entropy', 'momentum', 'discrimination', 'tragedy', 'family' or 'revolution' is time found to be productively spent as the class proceeds from personal to shared response to exploratory dialogue to systematic investigation.

MANDALA DRAWING

When Jung was seeking a way out of his own loss of meaning, one of the techniques he found useful was the drawing of mandalas. He drew one balanced circular pattern after another, attempting by this means to construct some order in his chaotic thoughts and feelings.

Utilising mandala drawing as a way of terminating class study of a particular topic in social studies may seem a trivial application of the technique compared to Jung's use of it and its long religious history. Nevertheless, it is effective in this context. The mandala circle is sometimes divided into segments, sometimes patterned in free form. In either case it is a symbol of completeness and the exercise of expressing within it a particular aspect of our experience, is a means of giving coherence to our thoughts and feelings. Both primary and secondary students can get excitement and satisfaction out of using the mandala form to express the essence of something they have experienced or studied. Where appropriate the mandala can be drawn, painted or pasted as a group exercise.

Use Your Imagination

ALMOST AUTOMATIC WRITING

Automatic writing can be produced in a trance state or in deep relaxation. In this phenomenon the unconscious expresses itself directly in writing without any control by the conscious mind. The message appears to come from a particular unconscious sub-personality of the writer, sometimes masquerading as a historical personage or a disembodied spirit. The technique was used commonly by the hypnotherapists of the late nineteenth century in dealing with fragmented personalities.

The techniques of psychosynthesis are most effective with a degree of relaxation, but Assagioli, like Freud and Jung, moved right away from the use of trance in his therapy. Psychosynthesis exercises are performed in a relaxed normal waking state. Automatic writing within this system will not be strictly automatic. Nevertheless, as in many other psychosynthesis techniques, there can be a deliberate lowering of the 'mental threshold' through relaxation, to invite unconscious material to emerge. In the educational context this means inviting unacknowledged understanding and information to come into consciousness.

The effectiveness of any teaching technique depends a good deal on suggestion. This technique in particular is likely to prove useless if undertaken 'cold' by a teacher and class who don't really expect it to work. One way of increasing the likelihood of a satisfactory experience is by embedding the exercise in a ritual.

> You can take your pens and two blank sheets of paper and put them on the table in front of you. Sit quietly and do nothing for a moment. Let your mind stop hanging on to the thoughts that come into it. Just let them float away until your mind is empty. Pause.
>
> During the past few classes we've been talking about X ... Imagine you've got a movie screen in your mind and that when I mention X a lot of different pictures flash on the screen ... or maybe there's only one picture. Just let the pictures come and go ...
>
> Now let the pictures stop. In a moment, when I say NOW, there will be one more picture. This time it will be the picture of a person ... someone who can tell you a lot about this topic ... someone who has a special understanding of it ...

NOW!

Look at this person for a moment ... until he or she fades away ...

Open your eyes ...

Now take your pen and one of those sheets of paper and write a letter to that person asking any questions you like about the topic, and about the person's involvement in it ...

It is now time to finish your letter, fold it, and post it. (There may be an appropriate ritual for posting, and a brief visualization of the letter travelling through space and time to its destination.)

To reply, this person has to use your hand, and pen and paper, but does not need your mind. Place the other sheet of paper in front of you and take the pen in your hand. I'll now play you some music. Let your hand write a reply to your letter while you are listening to the music, and don't worry if it looks like nonsense ...

Now that you've got a reply to your letter, close your eyes and rest a little. Then we can see if we can make sense of it.

Exercises like this don't have to be carried out in high seriousness. A relaxed, casual, light-hearted approach is possibly more productive. A lot of giggling in psychosynthesis exercises is likely to be an indication of resistance, but it is better at first to accept this resistance as legitimate and allow the students to avoid real involvement in the exercise rather than insist on total seriousness, as though the exercise had some deep quasi-religious significance.

Even if the result of this correspondence is not demonstrably knowledgeable or wise, the students have been learning to appreciate and utilize processes other than the rational-logical ones to which they are restricted in much of their education, especially at higher levels. In so doing they are not only becoming more efficient learners in the school context but are moving towards psychological wholeness.

IMAGINATIVE REHEARSAL

This is a technique which has been widely borrowed and translated into behaviourist language for use in 'stress management' and 'desensitization'.

Use Your Imagination

Students about to sit an examination, attend a job interview or face a confrontation can be taught to visualize the scene, play it out fully in imagination, confront its horrors calmly in imagination, and experience dealing with it excellently. The effectiveness of the technique has been well demonstrated.

It has also been demonstrated that athletes can improve their performance by visualising themselves performing their routines perfectly. It is a lot easier to get hard research data on improved sporting performance than on improved interpersonal skills or study habits, but the technique appears to be effective in these areas too. Assagioli did not express much interest in the physiological consequences of imagining, but he knew from his experience that vividly imagining an action performed successfully trains our brain and our body to perform it.

The evidence from sports psychology is a little ambiguous. It seems that not everyone can improve their swimming or skiing through mental practice.[77] It's obvious that we don't all become brilliant athletes by watching the experts on television, no matter how closely we identify with them. The evidence indicates that those with well-developed skills gain more benefit from the technique than beginners.[78] The effectiveness of the technique depends on our ability to imagine the movements vividly and in detail. Nevertheless, there seems to be no reason why what has worked for Tiger Woods and Roger Federer should not work for the teaching of skills in the classroom.

Occasional sessions of mental practice seem to have a place in the teaching of handwriting, crafts, typing and instrumental music. Even if the value of the technique had not been adequately demonstrated, the procedure would still be worth suggesting for its likely placebo effect.

The extensive literature on healing through visualization leads us in the same direction. Image-healing has thousands of years of successful practice to legitimize it. If this is not enough, it has been regularly demonstrated in laboratory studies that imagery can substantially affect blood flow, heart rate, skin temperature, brain waves, gastric secretions, sensitivity to pain and the immune response. Claims to heal cancer or arthritis through imagery are disputed, but evidence is growing.[79]

Writers on self-healing through visualization usually suggest imagining the malfunctioning limb or organ operating at its very best, holding this image in the mind's eye and perhaps also directly addressing the unconscious, asking it to continue the healing process. Tissue repair and regeneration are processes which the body does for itself anyway. Visualization can apparently enhance these processes. Another recommended technique is to visualize (either naturistically or symbolically) the healing process, for example a bone mending, an infection being fought, a blockage being removed.

Techniques that can help mend a broken bone or diminish pain or bleeding are obviously worth learning for their own sake. Moreover, the same principles can be applied to dealing with the problems of being a student. Students can deal with learning difficulties by imagining themselves able to handle the task with ease. They can deal with fatigue and boredom by a visualization in which they are refreshed and energized. They can deal with depression and frustration by a fantasy in which these emotions are symbolically transformed into their opposites. These skills are fairly easily acquired.[80]

While psychosynthesis exercises are designed to be performed in the normal waking state, the imagining and the accompanying suggestions sometimes have the effect of inducing a trance-like state. This is nothing to be concerned about. Some children go into trance very easily and can be brought out of it just as easily. In conducting visualizations, it is a good idea to have a ritual way of completing the exercise, which will have the effect of bringing all the children back to their normal state of consciousness. Here is an example:

> As I count to five you will gradually come back to this classroom and open your eyes. As you do so you will feel refreshed and alert and ready to work.

This is not meant to be a complete catalogue of imaginative techniques derived from Assagioli's work and applicable to the classroom. There are excellent sources available in which teachers may pursue the subject, both in search of techniques and for a development of the theories of education of which these techniques are a reflection.[81]

Use Your Imagination

In the development of psychosynthesis, Assagioli acknowledged his debt to therapists such as Jung, Désoillé and Leuner, whose ideas and techniques he adapted.[82] Since his death his techniques in their turn have been borrowed by other approaches to therapy and the psychosynthesis method has incorporated techniques developed within other frameworks.

FOCUSING

Gendlin's technique of 'experiential focusing' has been found particularly appropriate for use in psychosynthesis.[83] It is aimed at our whole 'felt sense' of our world, or of a particular aspect of our world, at this precise moment. If I ask simply: 'How do you feel about X?', you will reply in words which reflect some of that feeling but are quite unable to handle its complexity. Indeed, you may have ready-made labels for your feelings about X and you may apply them automatically, thus shutting off your awareness of the subtlety and complexity of your feeling. If, on the other hand, you quietly let yourself become aware of the response of your whole organism to X, without letting yourself put labels on that response, you will find that it is extremely vague and fuzzy. Yet, at the same time, it is somehow precise and distinctive, as you find when you compare your felt-sense of X with your felt-sense of Y or Z. The vague feeling in your belly, or wherever you like to locate the centre of your feelings, is in each case unique, yet the differences may be too subtle for our limited vocabulary to handle.

Gendlin, therefore, invites the organism to express the personal meaning of X through an image, to allow the image to change until it 'clicks' with your sense of X, and you can say: 'Yes! That's it!' Because the image contains a great deal more information than a verbal label you can go on to further focus and refine your experience of X until you have brought into awareness something of the subtlety and complexity of your relationship to X. This subtlety, complexity and clarity is entirely missed by such how-do-you-feel labels as 'affectionate' or 'contemptuous' or 'curious'.

The class is confused by a poem, a mathematical concept, a social issue, a recent experience. Perhaps they are suffering information or emotion overload. The teacher suggests they pause, let themselves rest in silence, then reflect on the poem (concept, issue, experience) for a few moments.

> Now go down into that part of you where you feel joy and anger and such things and get in touch with the way your body responds to the WHOLE of this poem (concept, issue, experience) ... a sort of vague, fuzzy feeling ...
>
> Don't do anything with that feeling just let it be and stay with it ... the WHOLE of it ... for a few moments without giving it a name ...
>
> Now, if you wait quietly you will find that a picture will emerge from that vague fuzzy feeling ... a picture which somehow or other represents something about that feelin...
>
> Don't be in a hurry ... It will come if you wait patiently ... When you've got a picture just rest with it for a moment... Now go back and forth between that picture and that feeling to check whether they fit perfectly together ... If it doesn't quite fit, keep going between the feeling and the picture ... When it fits perfectly you'll get a sort of a mental click and you'll know you've got it just right ...
>
> If you don't get a click this time, don't worry. You may get it next time ...
>
> Now, let's examine the images you got out of your response to that poem (concept, issue, experience) and see if they help us understand.

The expression of experiential focusing is not restricted to visualization and the subsequent verbal processing. The felt sense can be expressed directly in mime, dance, painting, clay. The limiting factor is the teacher's success in unfreezing the students' conservative assumptions about what sort of activities are appropriate in the classroom and in persuading them to take images as seriously as words.

SCANNING

Through laboratory research on imagery it has become clear that we remember images better than we do words. Some psychologists argue that we have two distinct coding, storing and retrieval systems, one for images and the other for words, and that the image-system is somehow more

Use Your Imagination

efficient. (Possibly this is because the word-system has been developed only recently and is still being tuned.) If I ask you how many windows there are in your house you are unlikely to be able to answer immediately. You 'know' the answer, but you do not have immediate access to it. So you visualize your house as vividly as you can, walk through or around it, and count the windows just as accurately as you would if you were really in the house. The information is stored efficiently, but it is stored as image, not as a word. Of course, if you now store it as a word as well as image, you will be able to access it much more quickly next time I ask.

We believe we have very poor memories of our childhood. This belief may be based on an error in accessing. Our memories of childhood are stored as images. When we try to access them we tend to look for them as words, and can find very little. However, if we simply use a stimulus-word to evoke images, and allow the images to come without evaluation or censorship, we will find that we can actually recall a great deal about our childhood. This technique is called scanning.

> Sit quietly. Relax. Let your mind go blank.
>
> Now repeat the stimulus-words 'my childhood' a few times ... wait and see what images come up ... Describe them briefly out loud as they come ...
>
> If no image comes, just keep repeating 'my childhood'.
>
> Be passive. Don't go digging for images. Don't TRY. Above all, don't THINK.

This technique will be most effective if you do it with a companion, so that your acknowledgement of the images is communicated to someone. Your companion should listen with full attention and encouragement, but say nothing. You will discover that you have recalled far more of your childhood than you could have by our usual concentrated trying-to-remember process.

This is a technique that can be taught to quite small children as well as to adolescents. It is a very primitive form of thinking and students have to be persuaded to give up their usual thinking habits in order to do it – no words, no ideas, no analysis, no evaluation, only pictures. However it is an extremely useful tool for finding a starting point in a new topic (e.g., in social studies), for recapitulating what has been learned, or for breaking through mental blocks in writing or during examinations.

Scanning is an example of *receptive* visualization, as opposed to *programmed* visualization. In receptive visualization we consciously prepare to access the unconscious, make ourselves open to whatever message the unconscious has for us. This does not necessarily mean that we are completely passive, that we give over control altogether (as with psychotropic drugs). Jung's own experience of being overwhelmed by images flooding out of his unconscious was a disturbing one and he actually recommended others not to seek it. Like Jung, we can take an active role in receptive visualization, through dialogue (as in active imagination), through refinement of the images (as in experiential focusing) or through narrowing the range of images to fit our immediate concern (as in scanning). We can even, it is claimed, take an active role in our dreams.[84]

Programmed visualizations, on the other hand, attempt to put input into the unconscious through imagery. This is the case with healing visualizations and those methods such as psychocybernetics which attempt to achieve 'success goals' by reprogramming the unconscious through imagery. To the Jungian purist this is ego-stuff, subject to all the wrong-headedness and self-seeking to which the ego is prone. It is somehow unworthy to attempt to manipulate the unconscious in this way. After all, our unconscious knows better than our ego what is good for us.

RELAX AND REMEMBER

Whatever the merits of this argument, the two orientations share a common premise. As far as the unconscious is concerned, both 'input mode' and 'output mode' are facilitated by deep relaxation. This has been demonstrated in laboratory studies as well as by thousands of years of experience.

How specific we can be about the nature of this relaxed state is not yet clear. Assagioli did not think it necessary or desirable to go into a special state of consciousness before engaging in psychosynthesis. Simple relaxation is enough. On the other hand religious and occult traditions have elaborate rituals and exercises designed to produce an altered state of consciousness in which the unconscious is accessible. Some proponents of visualization techniques have given a great deal of attention to discovering an optimal state of consciousness in which images will be most vivid and suggestions to the unconscious will be most effective. In Schultz's *autogenic training* a specific state of consciousness is produced by suggesting bodily heaviness and warmth. In Leuner's method of *guided affective imagery* it is achieved through progressive relaxation. In yoga it comes about through specific breathing techniques.

Since the invention of biofeedback technology, it has become possible to influence the brain directly, to approximate the 'hypnogogic' and 'hypnopompic' states, the twilight region between sleep and waking, when we are likely to experience images which are peculiarly vivid and 'real'. In this state the brain produces a pattern of brainwaves in which there is a predominance of low-frequency Alpha and Theta waves, without completely inhibiting Beta waves which characterize the 'thinking' state.[85] The state of consciousness which Jose Silva discovered through experience and experimentation and made the basis of his *mind control* is an approximation to this. It has the peculiar feature of combining deep relaxation and receptivity with mental alertness and control.

The training which enables one to control one's brain waves to the point of being able to go to one's 'level' at will is the essential element of the Silva method. The techniques which follow this are in many respects similar to those of psychosynthesis. Among them are a number of visualization techniques. One of these involves the visualization of an internal screen on which images can be projected, either to change something in ourselves or the external world, or to assist the recall of information. Another technique is the visualized internal 'laboratory' which enables experiments and investigations for greater understanding or for transformation. In the Alpha-Theta state there is immediate access to the resources of the unconscious mind. By receiving and manipulating images we speak its language.

Silva developed his techniques in the first place to assist his own children in their education. The method has proved to be readily teachable to children and adaptable to the classroom setting. When people learn to function at this level of relaxation and control, memory is improved, creativity is enhanced and they are better able to solve problems. At least people who have experienced the training claim this to be so. Even if Silva has not discovered a unique secret of accessing the unconscious, his technique seems to be a powerful placebo. The Silva graduate employing the magic three-finger trick to help him or her learn something or recall something has a mental set which, if it does not guarantee success, at least makes it much more likely.[86]

The Silva method makes some use of visual mnemonics in teaching people to remember information accurately. Visualization has been used in memory systems for thousands of years. Cicero describes the 'place method' which he attributes to the Greek poet Simonides (c. 500 BC). Roman orators used this method for remembering long lists of items or the sequence of ideas and illustrations in a major oration. They converted these items or ideas into concrete images and located them in sequence within a familiar scene (e.g., a street, a house). To recall the items they only had to mentally walk along the street or through the house.

Silva recommends a more modern version of this idea called the 'peg method'. Easily visualized words are memorized to represent numbers (e.g. bun = 1, shoe = 2, tree = 3, door = 4, etc.) and these 'pegs' can then replace the numbers when remembering a long list in order. The person forms a mental image linking the peg word with the item to be memorized. When he or she wants to recall the items, it is only a matter of running through the list of peg images to 'see' the items to be memorized.

Perhaps such skills have been made redundant by the printing press and subsequent technology. Nevertheless we know that they work, and we have a fairly good idea of why they work. These and similar techniques have been developed over centuries through an ongoing experience of how we most efficiently store and access information from the external world.

This same experience has taught good teachers to ensure that wherever possible all the students' senses, real and imaginal, are involved in the perception, processing and storing of new information. All the senses, not just sight and hearing but taste and smell and touch and movement. What is often forgotten is that, after the information is stored, the students may need to be taught how to use their imaginal senses to get in out again.

What is rarely considered at all is that they can be taught to use their imagination as a tool in their attempt to understand, control and change their worlds.

The image world is the natural realm of Psyche and her lover, Eros. The indirections and multiple references of the image are the stuff of poetry rather than of science, and they are the key to creating new meanings rather than of manifesting facts. With Eros' help we create reality from moment to moment through our imagining. However, there are other gods with something to say about images.

When we choose to probe the nature of images through research or attempt to explain it in abstract language we are under the influence of Apollo. When we try to develop a technology of imagining as Silva does we are governed by the perspective of Prometheus. We may find it more nurturing to listen to music or read poetry, but Apollo and Prometheus demand our attention as well.

First, Apollo. Pure science had little interest in imagery for most of the last century but in the past two decades this situation has changed markedly. Unfortunately, little of this research and speculation has had relevance for teachers. However, two apparently unrelated fields of research have recently come together in a way which seems to have implications for teaching. These fields are brain lateralization and biological rhythms.

LEFT-BRAIN, RIGHT-BRAIN

The language of right-brain and left-brain functioning has trickled down from research laboratories to popular use over the past twenty years and, naturally, there has been a lot of distortion and oversimplification of the findings of this research. Nevertheless, it does appear to be valid to say that the two hemispheres of the brain act more or less independently (and can function quite independently when surgically separated); that in most people the left hemisphere specialises in mathematical and verbal operations, logic, detail, digital thinking; that the right hemisphere specialises in spatial operations, feelings, images, wholes and analogic thinking; that women's brains show less hemispheric specialisation than men's; that in infancy we depend on our right hemisphere and only develop the use of our left as we grow older.[87]

On the other hand it is nonsense to say that intuition and creativity are lodged in the right brain; intuition and creativity demand both kinds of process. It is nonsense to say that women are left-brained (because they are alleged to have better verbal skills) while men are right-brained (because they are more comfortable with machines) or that women are right-brained (because they have better sense of colour and design) while men are left-brained (because they are better at maths). Such differences, if they exist, are the product of culture rather than biology. We have no physiological bases for labelling a person right-brained or left-brained. The preference for one kind of mental activity or another is learned rather than given. Most of us learn to value and develop one way of thinking as appropriate and useful for us, and devalue and neglect the other. Meanwhile our brain appears to shift from right-hemisphere activity to left-hemisphere activity in tune with our natural biological rhythms.

The same twenty-four hour and ninety-minute cycles that control our fluctuations between alertness and drowsiness govern our shift from left to right-brain dominance. Every ninety minutes or so, in the 'trance' phase of the cycle, our ability and tendency to fantasize reach their peak, as activity is concentrated in the right hemisphere of the brain.[88]

Allowing that we are talking about a shift in the balance of activity in the brain rather than a complete neutralization of one hemisphere, allowing that each hemisphere can take on the functions of the other to some extent, and allowing that we have ways of controlling the process rather than letting it control us, the implications for teaching are still considerable. In any class period of forty minutes a student may have a tendency to process information predominantly in a right-brain mode or predominantly in a left-brain mode. The phenomenon of lapsing into day-dream from time to time has a physiological basis. The decision to teach a student or class through fantasy rather than structural thinking can have the same physiological basis. Research in this area has hardly touched on education, yet we can speculate that there is a fundamental biological need for fantasy as well as logical thought and that constantly overriding this biological rhythm in the interests of a standard style of teaching is a source of stress.[89] We can speculate also that teaching would be more effective if it adapted to these rhythms instead of ignoring them.

Mapping the electrical activity in the student's brain is one way of determining what part of the cycle he or she is in but we are not likely to have the technology available. Fortunately there are a number of more obvious indicators such as drowsiness, staring out of windows, daydreaming and many more subtle ones that can be detected with a little attention. One indicator which is almost bizarre in its simplicity is nasal dominance. When the right cerebral hemisphere is dominant we breathe mainly through the left nostril; when the left-brain is dominant we breathe mainly through the right. It is easy enough to detect nasal dominance. It may be obvious in testing each nostril in turn. If there is no obvious difference in feeling, it may he possible to detect by sound: the relatively closed nostril will make a higher pitched sound than the relatively open one. Failing this, a mirror placed under the nose will show more condensation under the more open nostril.[90]

The teacher who wants to take seriously the evidence of alternating ways of thinking can use students' noses as a 'window' on their brains. She can check whether they are mostly in the same phase and what phase it is. She can verify that 2.00 pm is a bad time for her maths class (if she teaches maths in the conventional way). The early afternoon does not have to be wasted as it often is on inappropriate and frustrating attempts to teach. There are subjects and ways of teaching which can engage the children at this time of day, when their fantasy life is vivid, their ability to visualize is high, their feelings are easily touched, and their ears are attuned to the rhythm and intonation of speech rather than its ideas.

Our biological rhythms do not control us completely. For better or worse we manage to ignore and override them a good deal of the time. We can even consciously control them to a greater extent than we once thought possible, by biofeedback, by self-suggestion or by deliberately changing one element in the equation.

Teachers who want to use visualization techniques know that they often need to prepare their students for it by a brief period of silence and relaxation. This has the effect of shifting the body into the right-brain modality where visualization is easier. Many yogic meditation techniques use breathing to alter one's state of consciousness. Simply closing the right nostril and breathing only through the left shifts the brain into right hemisphere dominance, which for most people means shifting consciousness into 'fantasy mode'. Breathing only through the right nostril engineers a shift into 'thinking mode'.[91] While setting out with curiosity to explore, to gather evidence and to make sense out of our observations represents the perspective of Apollonic science, our inclination to make a technology out of nose control in order to be more productive shows the hand of Prometheus. An even more Promethean approach to the use of imagination in teaching comes out of neurolinguistic programming (NLP).[92]

A TECHNOLOGY OF COMMUNICATION

When we talk about using our imaginations in teaching or teaching children to 'use their imaginations' we tend to set this aside as a special activity in contrast to the times we want them to 'use their memory' or even 'use their brains'. NLP reminds us that our communication is permeated with images from start to finish and that skilful teachers may simply use images more effectively than their colleagues. The development of NLP in the past twenty years has generated a lot of information about images and the way we use them and a set of definable skills to make our communication more efficient.

We do not all think and image in the same way. It is commonplace that some people are more 'visual', others more 'auditory', and others more 'kinesthetic'. While there may be some yet-to-be explained genetic factor in this, it is more likely that such differences are the result of habit. Early in our lives we find that one way of getting sensory information works for us, so we make a habit of getting our information in this way. The more we do this, the more we are likely to do it again, as specific neural pathways are established and reinforced. We may develop strong preference for taking in information in one way or another. This observation is supported by NLP, which provides a number of techniques for working out and utilizing students' preferred ways of handling information. The simplest NLP tool is conscious attention to the language that students use. A brief conversation may demonstrate that a student habitually processes information visually ('I see what you mean', 'I get the picture'), or auditorily ('That sounds OK', 'That rings a bell'), or kinesthetically ('I can't grasp it', 'It feels all right'). If a student does not appear to be using images at all, which is unlikely, questions such as 'What exactly do you mean?' will get him or her reaching for an image. What NLP practitioners point out is that people have a consistent preference for one sort of imagery rather than another.[93]

Detecting preference in a student may be of great practical value. Inability to get a child's attention and interest may be due to nothing more than a clash between the child's preference and the teacher's. It is easy enough to test this. If a teacher has a student with whom she has trouble communicating, she can try to establish whether the child's preferred mode is visual, auditory or kinesthetic. She can then consciously and deliberately use this mode in talking to the child. This sounds like an extraordinarily crass simplification of the complex business of communication, but the results are often magical, and not only with individuals. It is likely enough that a teacher who has successfully completed a degree in mathematics or literature has an auditory preference that has made the hours of lectures a tolerable means of learning. It is likely enough that many of the children in her middle school class are 'kinesthetics'. She wonders why it is impossible to engage their interest and concludes that they are stupid. Or she starts to use the language of *soft-smooth-heavy-cool-feel-kick-twist* instead of the language of *quiet-loud-listen-shout-song-buzz-tell* and they become intelligent.

Besides this, she can use teaching techniques appropriate to them. If they are predominantly kinesthetic in their way of taking in information and processing it, she knows that hands-on activities, games or role-play will get them most engaged. She knows she can attract the attention of visuals with pictures, films and posters. She knows that those with an auditory preference will respond best to an explanation, a story or a class discussion. More significantly, she knows that while most of her students can manage to take in information through all three modes, there are likely to be one or two whose information processing is limited to one mode. If this mode is kinesthetic they are likely to be already labelled as trouble-makers or diagnosed with Attention Deficit Hyperactivity Disorder, because of their inability to sit still and listen.

The matching of the teacher's sensory system to the student's is particularly critical in establishing rapport. Before a teacher is in a position to significantly influence a child, he or she must understand the way that the child perceives the world. Matching the child's way of processing information is one way to do this. Matching the child's intonation, speech tempo, posture and breathing pattern or reflecting back the content of what the child says, are other ways to rapport. However, once rapport is established the teacher is able to influence the child's sensory system. In NLP training one learns to test rapport by 'leading' another person. First one 'plugs into' the other person's world through mirroring their sensory system, gestures or voice patterns, then one makes subtle changes to test whether the other will follow. If a teacher is matching a child's auditory images he may test rapport by switching to visual images. If a high level of rapport has been established the child also will begin to use visual images.

According to NLP theory it is possible to judge what mode people are in even when we cannot hear their language. Eye movements, skin colour, breathing patterns and posture change according to the sensory system they are using to process information.

For example, most right-handed people glance up to the left when recalling a visual image (V^R) and up to the right when constructing a new one (V^C). They glance across to the left when recalling words or sounds (A^R) and across to the right when they imagine saying something (A^C). They glance down to the left when engaged in interior dialogue (A^{ID}) and down to the right when experiencing feelings (K).[94] These glances, which may be very quick, are known in NLP jargon as entry cues, as they signify that the person is moving into a specific mode. People who do not follow the above pattern (for example, many left-handers) will have a consistent pattern of their own.

Besides adding a new and fascinating dimension to every conversation, this information is actually of practical use. If a child has a learning problem it may be possible to work out what the student is doing wrong and remedy it. A student, for instance, has trouble with spelling. After establishing rapport the teacher talks to the child for a little while, asking questions which will discover what eye movements the child makes in remembering and constructing visual, auditory and kinesthetic images (NLP calls this 'calibrating sensory modalities'). Then the teacher watches the child as the latter tries to learn to spell a word. The teacher can now observe that the only processing involved is that the child is thinking to himself. Visual processing is completely missing.

Since good spellers (and good rememberers in general) are good visualizers, the teacher teaches the child to visualize. She asks the child to imagine seeing the word in his favourite colour, to copy it down, to imagine it again in colour, to write it down from memory. As the child works through the list of words, the teacher sees him look at the word, look up right, copy the word, glance up left, write it down again. The teacher knows the child has learned the pattern. If the teacher wants to extend this lesson she can introduce auditory or kinesthetic imagery or she can have the child imagine the word in several different colours or imagine reading the letters backwards. (This ensures that the child is actually visualising and not merely saying the word internally.)

NLP asserts that our imaging becomes more vivid when we consciously turn our eyes in the appropriate direction. Cleveland's *learning pattern for writing creatively* is based on this understanding.

> Writing creatively can be a fun and reasonably simple process when this learning pattern is employed:
>
> $V^C - A^C - K^I - A^{ID} - K^E -$ Exit.
>
> V^C – The student places his eyes in his V^C context and thinks about what responses he would like to have from his reader(s). Then he determines what images would get that response.
>
> A^C – The student shifts his eyes to his A^C position and listens for any sounds or noises connected with the response that he wishes his reader(s) to have. He examines the different aspects of the experience in an effort to hear some meaningful sounds and noises that can generate the desired response.
>
> K^I – The student shifts his eyes in his K position to sift through the

various feelings associated with the experiences, so that he can select the most powerful ones to elicit the responses that he seeks from his reader(s).

A^{ID} – The student places his eyes in his A^{ID} position and talks to himself about what words can best get his desired reader responses. He can ask himself what different people and/or characters would say about his topic. He can ask himself if his examination of what to say about the topic gives him any ideas of other ways to talk about his topic.

K^E – The student writes his topic.[95]

When 'trying to think of something' children will naturally look up towards the ceiling. NLP suggests that they should be encouraged to do so. Certainly there seems to be little gained by insisting that they 'keep their heads down' to concentrate on their work.

Used in therapy, NLP links imaging with various hypnotic techniques to change people's attitudes and behaviour in quite specific ways. Searching in this complex technology for elements that are appropriate for classroom use can be a pretty tedious business because of NLP's technical language and delight in the minutiae of communication. However, the literature applying NLP to education is growing dramatically, and is likely to continue to do so.

Some teachers will find NLP distasteful. They may feel the techniques intervene in significant areas of life without any interest in questions of meaning or concern for the subtleties of ethics. They find its mass of technical detail to be a poor substitute for wisdom. They find it arrogant in its dismissal of any perspective but its own. They find it frightening in its potential for manipulation, and narrow in its reduction of communication to technique. They find it has no soul.

TOOLS OF CREATIVE THINKING

All these attributes are attributes of Prometheus, the technocrat god, and Prometheus is evidently alive and well in society and schooling at the moment. It may yet be some time before the Promethean arrogance which has taken humanity to a hundred different kinds of destruction yields to a wiser god. Prometheus, however, like the other gods, can be nice as well as nasty. It was Prometheus who, some say, crafted humankind from earth and water in the first place, who stole technology from the gods and by giving it to man destroyed the gods' total domination. Without the Promethean instinct to craft and manipulate our environment we would still be lost in darkness, at the mercy of forces we cannot understand. We ought to appreciate this freedom Prometheus bought for us so dearly.[96]

If a technology of communication can help us to intervene in so personal a thing as our inner imaginings we ought to take this opportunity to assume some control. The danger is that we exchange the domination of Zeus (or Apollo, or Eros) for possession by Prometheus and end up, like him, with our entrails being eternally devoured as a punishment for being too clever.

Both Prometheus and Psyche begin their myths outside the circle of the gods but eventually gain divine immortality after a time in hell. However, Psyche's suffering and her journey to the Underworld are voluntarily undergone out of love. Prometheus is tied to his rock screaming defiance at Zeus. We may have to wait for the technocrat to be forced to learn wisdom through the failure of his technology to solve the problems it creates.

Jung has been presented as someone who was faced with the need to understand and control a personal and professional world that was falling apart, and did so by training his imagination. His decision to do so rather than let himself be drawn in a flood of emotions and images set him on a path towards a creative solution for himself and many others. The inventor Nicola Tesla responded to a similar need in a similar way.

As a child, Tesla was afflicted by a vivid and uncontrollable imagination. He seemed to live in two worlds, the 'real' one and a world of startling memories and images which persistently broke in upon it. Often these images were frightening and he had to learn to break their control of him in order to maintain his sanity. While still a child, he found that he could get rid of an unpleasant image by deliberately visualising a pleasant memory. Having got this much control he found that he was not limited to recalling memories, but that he could visualize places, people and things he had never seen. He found pleasure and excitement in the fantasy world he invented (or discovered) within himself.

In his teens he became interested in invention and tried using his skills to 'imagine up' new inventions. He found that he was able to do so easily and in great detail. He could visualize a machine with all its component parts, and even test it out under various conditions, before constructing it in his workshop.

> It is absolutely immaterial to me whether I run my turbine in thought or test it in my shop. I even note if it is out of balance. There is no difference whatever; the results are the same. In this way I am able to rapidly develop and perfect a conception without touching anything. When I have gone so far as to embody in the invention every possible improvement I can think of and see no fault anywhere, I put into concrete form this final product of my brain. Invariably my device works as I conceived that it should, and the experiment comes out exactly as I planned it. In twenty years there has not been a single exception ...[97]

Tesla's contributions in the field of electrical engineering were extraordinary and enduring. His demonstration of the potential and educability of our image-making faculty ought to have some comparable influence.

Jung and Tesla discovered how to use their imagination during their fight for psychological survival. They maintained and refined their technique to make it the basic tool of their creative thinking. Our students may lack their intense motivation, but they may well have some of their capacity, if only they are taught how to use it.

NOTES Chapter 4. Use Your Imagination

[70] C. G. Jung, cited in R. Papadopoulos and G. Saaynam, *Jung in Modern Perspective*, p. 90.

[71] C. G. Jung, 'A Letter to M.O.' in G. Adler, *The Letters of C. G. Jung*, pp. 459-60.

The technique of active imagination is described fully in M. Watkins, *Waking Dreams* and R. Johnson, *Inner Work*.

For Jung, active imagination was a significant activity, not to be undertaken frivolously. His cautious attitude is reflected in comment of Cecil Burney:

Use Your Imagination

The decision to begin active imagination must be the patient's; it is not something to be imposed. It should be undertaken only when the patient is willing and when there is an adequate place for the sharing of what is produced with another person. Active imagination often needs the confidentiality and protection of the analytical or therapeutic relationship to be fully contained. Because this process can release strong forces of psychic energy that can overwhelm the patient, the therapist must always ask himself or herself in good conscience whether the time is right to begin (C. Burney, 'Jung's active imagination' in S. Grof, *Ancient Wisdom and Modern Science*).

Teachers using visualization techniques with their students are not employing 'active imagination' as Jung conceived it. They are not facilitating the emergence of archetypal images from the deep unconscious of emotionally disturbed people. Their goals are rather more limited. On the other hand, such techniques occasionally stimulate disturbing images in students, and teachers need to be ready with attention and support.

[72] R. Désoillé, *Le Rêve Eveillé en Psychotherapie*.
[73] Assagioli's ideas and techniques are contained in his *Psychosynthesis and Act of Will*. Other useful books on psychosynthesis are P. Ferrucci, *What We May Be*, D. Whitmore, *Psychosynthesis in Education* and M. Brown, *The Unfolding Self*.
[74] Ferruci, p. 63.
[75] ibid., p. 67.
[76] Useful books on creative visualization are S. Gawain, *Creative Visualization*, and A. Bry, *Visualizations*.
[77] For a review of studies of visualization in sport, see P. Suinn, 'Imagery and Sport' in A. A. Sheikh, *Imagery: Current Theory, Research and Application*.
[78] Jean Houston and Robert Masters describe a number of techniques for improving physical skills through imagining. See J. Houston, *The Possible Human* and R. Masters and J. Houston, *Listening to the Body*.
[79] Many people have no problem accepting that negative visualizations (brooding on the past or anxiety about the future) affect our health, but resist the idea that positive visualizations are equally powerful. A relatively non-technical neurophysiological explanation of how the mechanism works is given by Elmer Green in 'Science and Psychobiology, Psychophysics and Mythology' in S. Grof, *Ancient Wisdom and Modern Science*, pp. 240-253. But Green admits that we are a long way from knowing how the body, in response to our visualization, is able to convert an idea into an enzyme.

On healing through visualization, see also K. Pelletier, *Mind as Healer, Mind as Slayer*, and O. Simonton et al., *Becoming Well Again*.
[80] We might note here Schultz's remark on teaching autogenic training: that teachers and academics often cannot learn in two years a simple skill like raising skin temperature which children can learn in a few minutes.

[81] As well as Assagioli's own books and those of Ferrucci, Whitmont and Brown, workshops in psychosynthesis training are available in many places.

[82] C. Leuner, 'Principles and Therapeutic Efficiency of Guided Affective Imagery' in J. Singer and K. Pope, *The Power of Human Imagination*.

For another approach to visualization in therapy see A. Shorr, *Psychotherapy Through Imagery*.

[83] E. Gendlin, *Focusing*.

[84] The phenomenon of lucid dreaming has received a lot of attention in recent years. For an account of the research and the techniques for learning to enter and control lucid dreams, see S. LaBerge, *Lucid Dreaming*. Other useful books are W. Dement, *Some Must Watch While Some Must Sleep* and G. Delaney, *Living Your Dreams*.

[85] It was formerly thought that hypnogogic imagery came only in the state preceding deep sleep, but E. and A. Green, in their early research on biofeedback, discovered that vivid hypnogogic images came spontaneously to their research subjects when they were producing Theta and low frequency Alpha waves. When they researched this phenomenon directly, they found that continued practice in Alpha-Theta production was associated with increased recall and vividness of dreams, recall of forgotten childhood experiences, the experience of archetypal images (such as floating in space, climbing a mountain, gazing into a single eye, meeting a wise old man), and the spontaneous 'intuitive' solution of problems which had been bothering the subjects (see E. and A. Green, *Beyond Biofeedback*).

[86] See Chapter 2 above.

[87] It is conventional, if somewhat misleading, to speak of the left hemisphere as 'dominant' and the right hemisphere as 'minor'. This differentiation holds for most right-handed people and some left-handed people.

[88] It appears that the ultradian (approximately ninety minute) cycle continues through both sleep and waking. In sleep we move between a state of profound unconsciousness and a state of almost waking (in which we sometimes actually awake). In our waking life we move between Beta and Alpha and occasionally into Theta. In each ninety minute waking cycle there is likely to be a brief period when we are, as far as our brains indicate, asleep. This movement between faster and slower wave rhythms is associated with a shift from a concentration of electrical activity in the left cerebral hemisphere to a concentration in the right.

For a discussion of ultradian rhythms and brain lateralization, see E. Rossi, 'Altered States of Consciousness in Everyday Life', in B. Wolman and M. Ullman, *Handbook of States of Consciousness*, pp. 97-132.

[89] Friedman proposed in 1987 that behaviour patterns out of synchronization with psychophysical rhythms are a precondition of psychomatic illness, and that getting behaviour back in phase with these rhythms would lead to improvement. This proposition has been strongly supported by Friedman's

own research and that of other medical researchers, notably Ernest Rossi:

> Individuals who override or disrupt their own ultradian cycles (by ignoring the natural periodic needs for rest in any extended performance situation for example) are thereby setting in motion the basic physiological mechanisms of psychosomatic illness. Most of this self-induced stress could be conceptualized as left-hemispheric processes overriding their natural balance with right-hemispheric processes and associated parasympathetic functions ('Hypnosis and Ultradian Cycles, a New State(s) Theory of Hypnosis', *The American Journal of Clinical Hypnosis*, 1982, 1, p. 26).

Generations of schooling experience have formalized the provision of rest periods at roughly ninety minute intervals. There is at least some recognition of a natural rest and activity cycle. Teachers, on the other hand, are often obliged to pursue intensely 'left-brain' activities (e.g., meetings, organizational tasks, preparation of teaching materials) during the children's rest periods. If Friedman and Rossi are right, this pattern would be source enough of the high level of teacher stress. If we look at students under the pressure of preparing for examinations, we would expect to find a higher level of stress in those students who are studying a narrow range of subjects that demand the constant exercise of left-brain skills. Students whose range of subjects is more diverse are able to mix or alternate left and right brain activity.

[90] A review of research on the nasal cycle and nasal dominance will be found in E. Rossi, *Altered States* pp. 113f. See also F. Brown and R. Graeber, *Rhythmic Aspects of Behaviour*.

[91] The study of the nasal cycle is not new, but the connection between this cycle and hemispheric dominance has only recently been established. Research in a schooling context has not even begun. Rossi looks at the nasal cycle, the basic rest-activity cycle and hemispheric dominance and finds 'sixty-four research projects in search of a graduate student' (*Altered States.*, p. 121). Teachers interested in applying such knowledge to their teaching can easily find another sixty-four, many of which can be performed in the classroom with no equipment more sophisticated than a clock. Our Promethean spirit may yet lead us to a nostril-led revolution in education and the efficiencies of nostril-centred teaching!

[92] See particularly R. Bandler, *Using Your Brain for a Change*, and B. Cleveland, *Master Teaching Techniques*.

[93] Howard Gardner looks at the same phenomena in a rather different way in his theory of multiple intelligences. Gardner proposes that we have a cluster of distinct 'intelligences': linguistic, musical, logical-mathematical, spatial, kinaesthetic-bodily, interpersonal, intrapersonal, naturalist. These intelligences are based in different structures of the brain. The intelligences

that schools value most (linguistic and logical-mathematical) rely largely on visual information and words and symbols processed auditorily (i.e., by 'talking to ourselves'). In most schools the students' capacity to take in and process information visually and kinesthetically and the intelligences which rely on this sort of process are neglected or marginalized. See H. Gardner, *Frames of Mind*; C. Corell, *Multiple Intelligences*; H. Silver et al., *So Each May Learn*.

[94] These directions are written here from the point of view of the subject. From the observer's point of view they are reversed.

[95] Cleveland, op. cit., p.172. K^E symbolizes external kinesthetic behaviour.

[96] The discomfort some people have with NLP can be conceptualized in terms of Jung's functions of the psyche. NLP is based on the functions of sensing and thinking. Teachers whose personal style reflects a preference for these functions will be comfortable with NLP. Teachers who are intuitive-feeling are likely to find NLP 'unnatural'. The Jungian 'functions of the psyche' are discussed in Chapter 6, below.

[97] Cited in W. Harman and R. Rheingold, *Higher Creativity*, p. 57.

THE HIGH, THE DEEP AND THE ORDINARY

The unconscious is not just evil by nature, it is also the source of the highest good: not only dark but also light, not only bestial, semihuman and demonic but also superhuman, spiritual and, in the classical sense of the word, 'divine'.

Carl Jung

SOME PEOPLE SAY THAT THEY DON'T BELIEVE in the unconscious. In one respect this is an absurd proposition – to maintain that nothing goes on in their organism, that no information is gained and stored, without their being aware of it. In another sense, their proposition is quite plausible. Plenty of psychologists have managed to explain human behaviour without including anything called the unconscious in the explanation.[98]

I have no desire to argue that a thing called the unconscious exists. However, I find it very reasonable, on the evidence, to say that human beings behave *as though* they have two minds, one where consciousness resides and one where it is absent – or use any of the other images which depth psychologists use when they are trying to put this experience into words. Unfortunately we have a tendency to turn metaphors like 'God', 'soul' and 'the unconscious' into things. We would understand more about the reality behind such words if we let them remain metaphors.

Freud began this discussion when he tried to express the idea that we sense ourselves to have two components, a conscious with which we identify, and another part which is somehow 'other'.

> Aside from the 'I', we perceive another region of the soul, much more extensive, much more impressive, and much more obscure that the 'I', which we designate the 'It' ... To all extents and purposes, the 'I', is actually the front layer, the obvious, whereas the 'It' is the inner layer, the hidden. To make it even more plain: 'I' is inserted between the reality of the outer world and the 'It', the latter constituting the soul proper, the essence of the soul, as it were.[99]

Freud is here calling on several images to explain his meaning: the 'It' is a 'region of the soul', 'the essence of the soul', 'the soul proper'. He is at the same time imagining the unconscious as a place, a thing, and a quality. In other places he envisages the 'It' as an energy source, and as a container of repressed experience. Freud and later writers have played around with many images and labels in an attempt to give clarity to the insight that not all our mental operations are conscious: primary and secondary process; autistic and reality-adjusted thinking; id, ego and superego; gestalt-free and articulating tendencies; subconscious, preconscious or paraconscious mental activity; the prepersonal, personal and transpersonal self. And so

The High, the Deep and the Ordinary

on through assorted overlapping images. Freud himself was unable to pin down a terminology which fully satisfied him, even for his own rather narrow view of the unconscious.

Discussion of the unconscious swings from the very ordinary observation that we are mentally aware of only a fragment of our experience, through romantic and pessimistic notions of a powerful force within us, to the profound or outlandish hypothesis that our individuality is only an illusion, that we are but momentary projections of Mind at Large. The shifting and overlapping images of the unconscious make coherent discussion difficult. Poetry handles this sort of thing rather better.

There are a number of schools of thought in depth psychology, not all of them derived from Freud but all at least partially shaped by his influence. Freud did not discover the unconscious or invent its name, but he did articulate the basic insight towards which a number of his contemporaries had been feeling their way. When he decided that there are processes taking place beneath the surface of the mind he set out to investigate them, convinced that they were as subject to law and as ultimately comprehensible as the processes of the body. His own investigations led him to a view which readily translates into metaphors of a garbage can or a chained beast. Yet even while Freud was writing, there were other depth psychologists such as the hypnotists Coué and Baudouin who imagined the unconscious in a wholly positive way; it was rather an inner light, an unfolding rose, a spring of wisdom, health and power.

The image of personality which Freud eventually arrived at is a vertical one in which three kinds of consciousness are layered on top of each other: conscious (I know I am reading this), preconscious (I can think of your phone number if I need to) and unconscious (something happened on my third birthday but I don't know what!). Discussing unconscious consciousness makes us aware of the limitations of language. It has been remarked that the unconscious cannot be unconscious. Only the conscious can be unconscious of what the unconscious is conscious of!

The conscious and preconscious states flow into each other but between them and what is unconscious is a barrier. In scientific language this barrier is one of Freud's key discoveries. In psyche-language it is one of his most fruitful images. This barrier is active, manifesting itself in what Freud called defence-mechanisms (repression, denial, projection, transference, displacement, reaction formation, sublimation) which work constantly to separate the two regions of personality. Below this barrier is the id-system, the reservoir of the instinctual drives of aggressiveness and sexuality, which manifests itself psychologically through what Freud called primary process thinking (wish-fulfilling fantasy, illogical associations). Supported by the id-system is the ego-system, which functions through consciousness and secondary process (rational, logical thinking) but is also partly unconscious. The super-ego (conscience) is also partly conscious and partly unconscious. Driving the whole system is the basic sexual energy (libido) which Freud eventually saw to have two antithetical manifestations, a life-energy (eros) and a death-energy (thanatos).

The aim of Freud's work was: 'where id was, there ego shall be'. He wanted to extend the control of the ego over the id through bringing the unconscious drives through the defence barrier into consciousness.

Freud's ideas began to reach a popular audience after he published *The Interpretation of Dreams* at the beginning of the twentieth century. They have had immense influence ever since. This influence has come in part through the orthodox psychoanalysis which inherited Freud's name and the purity of his doctrine. It has also come, increasingly, from those who, while convinced of the reality of unconscious processes, became disenchanted with Freud's idea of them and went off, like Jung, Adler, Rank, Reich, Horney, Moreno and Assagioli, to develop ideas and a following of their own.

Analysing the similarities and differences between the various varieties of depth psychology would take us a long way from the classroom. It will he more useful, for the moment, to concentrate on the most significant of these heretics, Carl Gustav Jung.

Jung's break with Freud in 1913 was traumatic. He had written extensively on psychoanalysis and made a substantial contribution to theory and practice. Freud had groomed him as his successor in leadership of the movement. However, when it came to the point, Jung rebelled against both Freud's ideas and his rigidity.

In the picture of the mind which Jung developed, consciousness and

The High, the Deep and the Ordinary

unconsciousness are differentiated, as in Freud's image, but both are more complex than Freud would make them. In the regions of the unconscious Jung saw a personal and a collective element, both grounded in a vast and deep collective unconsciousness which can never be made conscious. He differentiated the persona from the ego and the ego from the self. On the one hand, the ego or self-image functions through a social face (persona) through which it meets the world and with which it is tempted to identify. On the other hand, it is in constant interaction with the self, the integrative centre within the personality, which emerges as one becomes truly adult.

In the emergence of the self (a process which Jung calls individuation) there is a progressive working through of one's relationship to the shadow and the animus or anima. (The shadow is the other side of the ego, all the qualities – positive as well as negative – which are denied expression in the persona. The animus and anima refer to one's encounter with the soul image of male and female as part of one's own psyche.) In his writings, Jung struggled with the Apollonic fantasy that reality is static, that it consists of things which can be named. Yet he does try to convey something of the elusiveness of these images (persona, shadow, anima, animus, self) as they merge into one another and cross the boundaries between conscious and unconscious, personal and collective. Looked at logically, Jung's concepts are sometimes vague and confusing, but his images, like Freud's, have a great deal of power.

Jung's unconscious is much 'bigger' than Freud's. It appears that Freud only noticed what Jung calls the personal unconscious. This contains everything in our experience that has been either not attended to, forgotten or repressed.

> The personal unconscious ... includes all those psychic contents which have been forgotten in the course of a person's life. Traces of them are still preserved in the unconscious, even if all conscious memory of them has been lost. In addition, it contains all subliminal impressions or perceptions which have too little energy to reach consciousness. To these we must add unconscious combinations of ideas that are still too feeble and too indistinct to cross over the threshold. Finally, the personal unconscious contains all psychic contents that are incompatible with the conscious attitude.[100]

Freud was not interested in subliminal perceptions or simple forgetting. He was interested in the forcible repression in which we are engaged from our earliest childhood. The contents of his unconscious and that of his patients were essentially nasty. Jung was interested in rather more, and when he includes 'all the psychic contents which are incompatible with the conscious attitude' he is ready to move into the consideration that the unconscious may contain contents which are too 'good' for consciousness to tolerate as well as those which are too unpleasant. It is an idea taken up by Assagioli and Désoillé, who coined the phrase 'the repression of the sublime'.[101]

Freud was originally convinced that all of the unconscious is repressed personal experience but gradually accepted the evidence that some of the unconscious is unconscious from the start. In his study of dreams he found it impossible to sustain his hypothesis that all the symbols in dreams are generated by personal experience. He found himself concluding, somewhat reluctantly, that they are expressions in the individual of the experience of past ages. This was an idea that Jung was already developing with some enthusiasm. He became convinced that the personal unconscious with which he and Freud had been so far concerned was a very superficial layer of the unconscious. There is a deeper layer which is impersonal, universal, collective, and common to all humanity. The collective unconscious, which he eventually called the 'objective psyche', is a common psyche of a suprapersonal kind whose contents are not acquired during the individual's lifetime. It is the ground from which individual consciousness has evolved.

> Consciousness grows out of the unconscious psyche, which is older than it, and which goes on functioning together with it, and even in spite of it.[102]

Freud thought this sort of conclusion was taking Jung far beyond the facts. Jung maintained that his theory of the collective unconscious was based on solid evidence, from dream imagery, from mythology, from psychotic hallucinations. From his observations it was obvious that, just as a bird inherits a predisposition to build a particular kind of nest, human beings inherit predispositions for experiencing and responding to the world in the same ways as their ancestors. There seems to exist in the uncon-

The High, the Deep and the Ordinary

scious a tendency to produce again and again the same primordial ideas and images. Jung calls these the archetypes. They are the stuff of mythology which Freud, always more eloquent than Jung, called 'the age-long dreams of young humanity'. They also constantly fashion the perception and behaviour of modern human beings. They are personalized and worshipped as gods, projected on to ordinary human beings who are then obsessively admired, loved or hated, or they are reduced to their biological manifestations and categorized as drives or instincts.

While this archaic inheritance is both individual and collective, it is the collective which is all important for Jung. In his view, consciousness is but an island in the vast ocean of the collective unconscious. The personal unconscious is just the wetness in the sand between high and low tide.

When the archetypes break through into consciousness, the consequences can be significant: religious conversion, psychotic episodes, major works of art, mass hysteria, new scientific paradigms.

For Plato, archetypes were ideas or forms of natural objects held to have been present in the divine mind prior to creation. For St Augustine they were 'principle ideas' which are themselves not formed, but contained in the divine understanding. In the Buddhist-Hindu systems, they are the first forms of manifestation that emerge from Void Spirit in the course of creation. Kant and Schopenhauer were more immediate precursors of Jung in dealing with this idea.

For Jung, archetypes are typical and universal 'modes of apprehension' which appear as images charged with great meaning and power, images which exert a great influence on our individual and collective behaviour.

Jung agreed with his critics that archetypes do not actually 'exist'.

> Of course they do not exist, any more than a botanical system exists in nature. But will anyone deny the occurrence and continual repetition of certain morphological and functional similarities? It is much the same in principle with typical figures of the unconscious. They are forms existing a priori, or biological norms of psychic activity.[103]

Jung compared them to 'the axial system of a crystal which, as it were, performs the crystalline structure in the mother liquid, although it has no material existence of its own'.[104]

Archetypes are bipolar.

> Just as they have a positive, favourable, bright side that points upwards, so also they have one that points downwards, partly negative and unfavourable, partly chthonic, but for the most part merely neutral. They can be expressed in the constructive side of the personality as well as the destructive, in a person's highest achievements as well as in pathology or vicious behaviour.[105]

Jung was interested in archetypes as the primary forms which govern the psyche, but we can look for their manifestations much more widely than that: in political systems, philosophical and scientific theories, 'movements' in music, art and architecture, language structures, religious doctrines, social customs, physical or emotional epidemics, and theories of education.[106]

By far the easiest way to talk about archetypes is through metaphor, which can draw its language from thousands of years of mythologising. When we describe a teacher's classroom personality in images like 'guru', 'earth mother', 'sex goddess', 'macho man' or 'victim', we are discerning patterns which belong not only to our profession and our time and culture but are universal. The ancient Greeks would immediately recognize the gods at work: Apollo, Demeter, Aphrodite, Ares, Sysiphus.

Under this perspective, two mutually antagonistic educational philosophies – the essentialist, content-centred, value-closed, hierarchically organized on the one hand, and the non-essentialist, person-centred, value-open, egalitarian on the other – can be personified in Senex (the old man) and Puer (the child). We can find some understanding of these patterns in examining the mythology of Senex-figures like Zeus and Kronos and Puer-figures like Eros and Dionysos.

If we look at Jung's own psychology through the archetypal lens we will find his thinking revolving around two archetypal images: the image of unfolding (evolution) and the image of unity. These images have had a powerful hold on human thinking over the centuries, and they have been templates for much of our exploration of our concrete experience and of ultimate reality. Jung's variation on a theme from Darwin is expressed in his vision of the unfolding self, a vision shared with other post-Freudians like Progoff and Assagioli and in stark contrast with Freud's vision of the person

The High, the Deep and the Ordinary

as a psychic battlefield. Our inclination to see reality as unitary, to pursue a higher synthesis which will contain apparently conflicting ideas and evidence, to see the goal of human growth as 'wholeness', to believe (or disbelieve) in one God, are reflections of the archetypal image of 'The One'.

Jung's thinking is obviously in this mode. For him the several archetypes of the collective unconscious are diverse expressions of deeper unity. The various humanistic psychologies also reflect this archetypal image of unity through their language of wholeness, integration, self-realization, self-actualization and so on. The image of unity forms our view not only of the ideal individual but of the ideal society. In education it is reflected in the assumptions made about the proper behaviour of children, the nature of curriculum, and the goals of the whole process.

The language of unity does not reflect 'facts' about human nature, but a particular way of looking at it. There is an alternative way of looking at reality which has its own long and respectable intellectual history. The archetype of 'The Many' is reflected in belief in many gods, in seeing the personality in terms of many selves, in science's tendency to see the detail rather than the whole, and its ability to hold conflicting paradigms in balance, in styles of teaching which promote diversity rather than conformity, in the appreciation of difference, multiculturalism, plurality. 'Archetypal' psychologists choose this perspective, which involves seeing even their own perspective as only one perspective among many.[107]

In developing this fantasy of the many, archetypal psychology adopts the language of classical Greek mythology. James Hillman chooses the Greco-Roman pantheon rather than one of the other pantheons available because the images of the Greek gods are inextricably woven into European culture. He avoids the Christian pantheon of the Trinity, the angels, devils and saints so as not to confound metaphor and belief. However, archetypal psychology can find its images in this or other religious systems, or in astrology, the Tarot or the I Ching.

Our arguments about the nature and purpose of schooling may seem to be anchored firmly in our own time and place, but they represent the conflict between ancient and universal 'modes of apprehension'. In our arguments the immortal gods battle for supremacy. It is no wonder that such arguments are never finally won. The ancient Greeks could have warned us of the dangers of worshipping only one god. The modern educational monotheist who adopts exclusively the 'mode of apprehension' of Senex or Apollo, or Eros or Prometheus, is stuck with that god's worst qualities as well as the best.

Apollo, Senex, Prometheus and Eros are images; so are the philosophies of education and the psychological theories attached to them. The perspectives they represent are relative. It is difficult for a teacher who is completely locked into the Senex image, unreflectively comfortable in a bureaucratized system dominated by men in dark suits who directly or indirectly control what is to be taught and when and how, who is unreflectively comfortable with a classroom architecture which emphasizes the authority and expertise of the teacher, whose visions of excellence are shaped by the good old days, who sees professionalism in terms of expertise and organization, to accept that these values are not absolute. It is just as hard for the teacher whose philosophy and teaching style are formed by the Eros archetype to acknowledge that the Eros-values are relative. For him or her it is terribly important symbolically not to dress formally, not to stand at the front of the class with the children sitting in rows facing you, not to prepare and teach systematically, not to intimidate the children by your expertise, not to be addressed as 'Sir' or 'Miss', not to demand conformity. The Senex-inflated teacher can see clearly why his or her position is right while the teacher in charge of the chaos in the next room is unprofessional and irresponsible. Eros-inflated teachers see their own creativity and concern and look with amusement or disdain at the stupidity, rigidity and dogmatism of some of their colleagues.

An Eros philosophy, like a Senex-philosophy, can be elegant and logically consistent, but it is only a partial vision. To accept it as a total vision is to be blind to much that is significant in human living, and to teach in a way that impoverishes children rather than enriches them. To be locked into one archetypal perspective is to be locked into its negative as well as its positive aspects. A consistently 'traditional' education has the potential to narrow, distort and suppress the children's personalities. So does a consistently 'free' education.

The High, the Deep and the Ordinary

It is conventional to set 'traditional' and 'free' or 'humanistic' education against each other as if experience can be located on a single continuum. Life is more complex than that. There are more than two gods in the pantheon. On Mt Olympus there are twelve great gods and a lot of lesser ones. Apollo shares certain obsessions with Senex, and the pursuit of knowledge in our culture is very much entangled in Senex-type institutions and bureaucracies, but while the Apollo image overlaps the Senex image in some respects, the two are by no means identical. Apollo and Prometheus are both engaged in scientific pursuit of knowledge, but their purposes are very different. Each god can provide a coherent rationale for schooling: Hera (the function of schooling is to teach social responsibility, to confirm the ultimate importance of the bonds between human beings); Aphrodite (the function of schooling is to enable children to experience the pleasure of life, beauty, the joy of human contact); Ares (the function of schooling is to teach the manly virtues – courage, loyalty, resourcefulness); Hephaistos (the function of schooling is to teach children to find the resources within themselves, to learn the satisfaction of crafting); Demeter (the function of schooling is to nurture and protect the growing child). And so on. Each god can give us a theory of education which seems plausible and logically consistent, but push the theory to its logical limits and it collapses into absurdity. However, the theories are not often pushed to their logical limits. Teachers do not teach from speculation but from images, and if there is a single archetypal image which dominates our approach to teaching it is likely to be expressed not only in our thinking about teaching but in our whole personality. Like the fish in water we live in it without perceiving it. We look through a coloured lens and what we see is not a lens but a monochromatic reality.

To apply the archetypal lens to the classroom at the present time is to see Prometheus apparently competing with Apollo and Eros for control of the curriculum. Ares, god of war, is still worshipped in many places (courage, conquest, and buffoonery in the locker-room). Exclusive rights to the education of girls are contested by Hera (competence, social stability, devotion to husband and family), Athena (the superlatively successful woman-in-a-man's-world) and Artemis-Diana (independence, self-reliance, sisterhood). Aphrodite, though she does not receive official worship in the classroom, manages to keep a good hold on the media. Even Dionysos manages to keep a few devotees in the non-profit areas of the curriculum. For the archetypal psychologist, following Jung, such patterns of attitude, belief and behaviour are not just the peculiar idiosyncracies of particular teachers or school policy-makers. These recurring patterns are not individual, nor even entirely culture-bound. They belong to the species, to the collective psyche. The personality of the individual teacher is just one of the points through which they are expressed. In the individual where this archetypal image and energy is unconscious and controlling, we are faced with what Jung calls a complex.

The teacher standing before the class is not, for Jung, a simple organism nor even, in a sense, a single person. What confronts and interacts with the children is first of all a public personality, what Jung calls a persona. The teacher has, from infancy been learning a way of being with other people, of pleasing her parents, of adapting to the expectations of society. All the experiences she has absorbed, from significant adults initially and then from a broader culture, have been processed into a way of seeing herself and the world and a way of behaving in it. The finished product represents only a fraction of what that infant might have become, with a quite narrow range of behaviours, attitudes, interests, prejudices and developed talents. Yet the children may not even get to meet the whole of this limited, inhibited persona. Many aspects of the teacher's personality are likely to be reserved for friends, colleagues, family; the children may only get a tightly scripted classroom performance.

Yet there is another side of the teacher's personality which also confronts and interacts with the children. To pursue Jung's metaphor, the teacher's personality contains another person, called the shadow, who is the polar opposite of the persona.

In learning how to be acceptable to parents and society, or at least how to defend themselves against them, children must inhibit a great deal of their spontaneous activity. All of these repressed possibilities (including potentials which have never reached consciousness at all) are contained in the shadow, not only the violent, sadistic, anti-social characteristics which parents would not tolerate, but also, in many cases, the creativity, excitement,

The High, the Deep and the Ordinary

intelligence, spirituality, and assorted talents which were not thought appropriate for little boys or little girls, as the case might be.

For Jung, all human beings are androgynous. The persona, however, identifies itself as either male or female and develops either a masculine or feminine consciousness. The contrasexual aspect of the personality is repressed. Repression, however, is a matter of degree. Some people accept their contrasexuality and are comfortable with the special consciousness that goes with it. It is those who strongly repress it who are controlled by it. Behind the male teacher's macho persona is a repressed woman, the anima, whom he does not acknowledge but who controls much of his behaviour, generating the same moodiness and irrationality which he finds ridiculous in women. Likewise, the radical feminist teacher who enthusiastically and uncritically proclaims her feminine consciousness may be unaware of how in her interaction with children and colleagues she manifests the very worst aspects of the masculine consciousness she despises. Her awareness is feminine, but a dogmatic, exploitative animus controls her unconscious.[108]

Persona, shadow, animus and anima are what Jung calls complexes, that is, each is an interrelated cluster of unconscious contents which is 'strongly accentuated emotionally and is ... incompatible with the habitual attitude of consciousness'.[109] This cluster of ideas, feelings, attitudes, and values can be centred around many sorts of content: a sex complex, an inferiority complex, a saviour complex, an achievement complex, a criticism complex. Anyone who has been obsessively and uncontrollably in love knows how powerful a complex can be.

One feature of the complex is its emotionality. Another is its autonomy. We don't 'have' complexes. They 'have' us, and appear as and when they please. They behave like distinct persons.

> They slip just the wrong word into one's mouth, they make one forget the name of the person one is about to introduce, they cause a tickle in the throat just when the softest passage is being played on the piano at a concert, they make the tiptoeing newcomer trip over a chair with a resounding crash. They bid us congratulate the mourners at a burial instead of consoling them ... these impish complexes are untouchable.[110]

A complex may arise from a traumatic event or by gradual accretion. Repeated criticism from parents may have given a child a 'criticism complex', so that whatever the teacher says to the child will be heard as criticism. A teacher may have very rational and liberal ideas about sex at the conscious level, yet a sudden, direct question from a pupil may cause him or her to blush or stammer, revealing a complex of unresolved ideas, feelings and attitudes. The teacher may recognize this pattern recurring and even understand it. Unfortunately, being conscious of a complex does not give one full control of it. Occasional embarrassment may be assured.

Complexes often show up in dreams. Apart from this, there are two peculiar mechanisms by which complexes are inclined to make themselves known. One of these Jung called inflation, the other he called projection. Inflation occurs when one is possessed by a complex, so that it dominates one's consciousness. Most people have the occasional experience of being taken over momentarily by a complex when their guard is down. In inflation, however, the ego identifies with the complex. I become convinced that I am a great artist, or the saviour of humankind or the world's greatest lover and don't need any evidence to justify this obsession. Projection, on the other hand, involves attaching my complexes to someone else. If I have a deep but unacknowledged sense of inferiority I find an appropriate person to despise, and so maintain my illusory self-esteem.

There seems to be a limited number of complexes. We see the same behaviour patterns occurring again and again in our culture. For Jung, this suggested that the complexes are collective rather than individual, that they have the source in the energy-centres of the objective psyche – the archetypes or, in mythological language, the gods. Occasionally we find a teacher so firmly in the grip of a 'mother-complex', an 'authority complex', a 'saviour complex' or a 'victim complex' that the ancient Greeks would have had no hesitation in diagnosing possession by a god.

For the remainder of teachers, whose pathology remains at the normal level, complexes are not much more than a nuisance. They cause occasional embarrassments, and wreck a relationship here and there, but a certain degree of watchfulness can prevent them from dominating our lives. If we are attentive we can even learn what our complexes are and do something

The High, the Deep and the Ordinary

about them. One way of dealing with them is through what Freud called sublimation, letting the energy of the complex express itself through some kind of creative work. If I find myself inhabited by an irrational tyrant, who breaks out from time to time to the horror of myself and my class, I can get some control by painting or writing or acting out my authority-complex. Another way of dealing with it can be called transformation, in which 'the drive itself becomes changed and ceases to trouble us, because it has turned its other face, has been made into a constructive and helpful impulse'.[111]

We must remember that complexes have a positive side as well as a negative one. If I examine my authority-complex I may find that I am repressing or denying not only my desire to control others but also my need to take control of my own life. If I acknowledge this need and do something to satisfy it I may find that the negative energy of the complex has disappeared and I am no longer taken over unpredictably by the tyrannical stranger.

The 'I' who does all this examining and acknowledging is called, in the accepted jargon, the ego. This ego is the centre of consciousness, the sense of I-ness, the point of reference for one's conscious experiences.

Freud actually did not mean to write about the 'ego'. He wrote in German *das Ich*, which means the 'I', which he contrasted with *das Es*, the 'It'. It was his English translators who turned the 'I and It' into things, the 'Ego and Id'. It is difficult to define ego, but we think we know exactly what we mean by 'I'.[112]

Jung's concept of the ego is almost identical with Freud's. However, while Freud's ego is wrapped up in the conflict between id (instinct) and superego (conscience), Jung's appears to be relatively free. Its behaviour is purposive, not simply reactive. It is characterized by one of the dominant attitudes (introversion or extraversion) and one or two of the dominant functions (sensing, intuiting, thinking, feeling).

In early infancy there does not appear to be any sense of 'I' as distinct from the mother. There is a gradual differentiation of 'I' from 'other' and the child begins to identify with his or her body. There follows a differentiation of I from the body so that the child experiences himself or herself as having a body rather than being a body. In late childhood identification is collective, that is, the children learn from others who they are, and what they value. The ego is almost contained in the persona, which is unconscious. In adolescence it begins to be possible to differentiate the 'I' from the persona, though some people never accomplish this task.

Jung was less interested in the development of the ego than in the integration of ego and unconscious which ought to follow it. However, he does point out the importance of teachers in helping children free themselves from unconscious identification with the family. Teachers are clearly involved in this task in providing a safe and resource-rich environment where the children are free to find out who they are, to try out new roles and behaviours and develop an identity which is not entirely bound by the family context. They are involved for better or for worse in the child's development of a public self, a persona. As the children's development of discrimination and logical skills allows it, the teacher can intervene through a socially critical curriculum to enable the adolescent to discriminate between the environmental persona and the ego, to distinguish between behaviours, beliefs and values which are merely conventional and those which are consciously and rationally chosen.

The everyday use of the word ego subverts Freud's and Jung's idea of a strong ego. The 'big ego' is actually a weak ego; narcissism, inflation and dogmatism are signs that the ego is being dominated by the contents of the unconscious (i.e. the complexes). The strong ego is a free ego.

The ego has an archetypal core which is often represented by the image of the hero. Many cultures have initiation rituals which enable children to pass from childhood to adulthood through the experience of an heroic journey or struggle. Some Jungians suggest that if the adolescent is provided with no culturally approved way of being a hero, he or she is likely to act out the hero-myth through violence or anti-social behaviour. Alternatively, a repressed hero-complex will be projected on to a pop star or someone more sinister. Many adolescent girls in particular, perhaps because they have been offered fewer invitations than boys to excel, cling to a weak ego as they project all their resourcefulness on to a succession of admired males. It is only later in life, when their final heroic projection has collapsed, that they find in themselves the resources to make their own 'heroic voyage'. In the meantime, they resist all attempts by teachers and others to convince them that they have talent of any kind.

An ideal schooling would, of course, ensure that every adolescent has the opportunity to excel in some way and be applauded for it.[113] The adolescent's heroic activity may conform to the school's and parents' declared values or may defy them. The latter case may be a little harder to cope with from the school's point of view, but from the adolescent's point of view some sort of delinquency may sometimes be the only way to find identity.

Ego-psychology, which deals with such matters with some sophistication, is a development of Freud's thinking. Jung did not have the same interest in the ego. There are many modern Jungians and transpersonal psychologists of other hues who maintain that the ego is greatly over-valued in Western psychology. Some see emergence of a strong ego as no more than a half-way mark in the individuals development. Full potential emerges only through transcending the ego. Others emphasize that the individual has many selves, actual and potential. For them, the concentration on a single identity and self-image is a denial of most of the things a person is and can be.

In discussing this question there is often a confusion of language. The 'I', the 'ego', the 'self' and the 'persona' slip around and exchange meanings according to who is speaking and when. It is necessary to remind ourselves that the ego, or whatever we call it, is a metaphor, not a fact. Metaphors do not have clear boundaries; to try to impose such limitations on them is to restrict their power to enlighten us.

In Jungian terminology, the centre of the whole personality, which includes both conscious and unconscious, is not the ego but the self. The self combines (potentially at least) all the mental contents, all the psychic opposites – constructive and destructive, positive and negative – as part of a pattern for the development of the whole person. The self is purposeful, it has direction, it knows what it is doing. Jung suggested that the self guides the individuation process, shaping the relation of the various parts of the personality to each other.

For Freud, the ego was the centre of the personality. The drives which make up the unconscious were irrational, senseless, chaotic, anti-social, attempting to rush off in many different directions at once. The unconscious was attached to the ego as a sort of vast garbage bin to contain whatever the ego must repress because it is socially or personally unacceptable. Jung, however, was impressed by the evidence he found that the unconscious is not chaotic and directionless. While the ego seems to be an important element, organising the way we behave in a purposeful manner, our personality seems to be a lot bigger than the part we are conscious of.

The archetype of the self was, for Jung, the most important element of the unconscious. It is the idea and image of human wholeness. The striving of the individual psyche for wholeness is generated by the archetype of wholeness or unity which belongs to the objective psyche. It is an archetypal idea which can be detected in specific images: the mandala, the square, the number four, the figure of Christ. Jung suggests that, psychologically, the symbol of self is indistinguishable from the image of God.

Jung's key images of evolution and unity come together in what he called the process of individuation. This is a process which begins after one reaches adulthood, a process which leads to both wholeness and uniqueness. Individuation is both collective and individual. It is collective because it is impelled by an archetype of the collective unconscious – the self. (Jung considered individuation to be a drive as compelling as hunger or sex.) It is not initiated and controlled by the ego, that is, it is not something we do. It is rather something that happens to us, like adolescence.[114] The archetype of the self, or wholeness, guides the evolution of the species as it does the emergence of the individual. Yet, at the level of individual psychology, its effects are different for each person.

The necessary precondition for individuation in Jung's model is a robust ego. In many people this is adequately achieved in young adulthood. They have a strong sense of who they are and what they value. This strong ego has often been gained at the cost of one-sidedness, which represents in effect the denial of a great deal of a person's potential. While some Jungians assert that this one-sided development and a strong identification with a particular public self are necessary for ego-development in adolescence, it is not necessarily so. It would indeed be surprising if the culture's (and schooling's) sexual stereotyping, its valuing of extroversion over introversion, and its strongly presented models of behaviour, did not produce one-sidedness as the norm. It is a big leap from this to a position that one-sidedness is good and necessary for adolescents. Some adolescents and even children are extraordinarily diverse and flexible in their roles without losing a sense of who they are.

Assagioli's theory of psychosynthesis sees the development of diversity and flexibility of role-taking as an appropriate aim in education. Children can learn readily enough to disidentify from their roles and act 'from their centre'. This step in individuation – the assimilation of persona into consciousness – can start early. At the same time it must be acknowledged that many children and adolescents cling tightly to a very narrowly defined ego, refusing to experiment with the possibility that they may have other potentials.

For Jung, a key element in this process of becoming, in awareness and behaviour, all that we potentially are, is the withdrawal of projections. In common usage projection often refers to the defensive manoeuvre of deliberately blaming others where we feel guilty ourselves. Both Freud and Jung used the word rather differently. For them, projection was the work of the unconscious mind; consciousness, intention and choice had no part in it.

For Freud, projection was a defence mechanism by which we protect our fragile ego from the beast which lurks in our repressed unconscious. We genuinely attribute to others qualities which belong to ourselves but which we find too nasty to acknowledge. Jungian writers are inclined to use the term more positively and less narrowly. For them projection is 'the avenue by which the unconscious complex attempts to reach our consciousness'.[115] The organising energy of the self is attempting to transcend the split between conscious and unconscious in us. Projection is the means by which the ego can perceive what the non-ego part of us contains, to enable us to acknowledge our qualities which are hidden from us (though not necessarily from anyone else). 'Owning' or 'withdrawing' these projections is the next step towards integration. For Jungians, projection is less something we do than something which happens to us, since it originates in complexes which are not under the control of the ego.

We may constantly misjudge others, perceiving them as bored, angry, dishonest or resentful, and cling to such misjudgements in spite of evidence to the contrary. The teacher who sees a good-natured and energetic class as hostile may be the only person on staff unaware of his or her own hostility to children. The teacher's emotional denial that he or she feels any hostility can be taken as a sign that projection is involved. The teacher who is not dominated by an unconscious complex will be able at least to acknowledge, rationally, the possibility that he or she is hostile to children.

The teacher's denial is not an attempt to mislead. He or she is entrenched in this conviction. Yet gradually or dramatically the unconsciously hostile teacher may be forced to confront the uncomfortable reality. If the ego is strong the projection may be owned and the teacher may come to a more complete and realistic self-image and the development (either inside or outside the profession) of the positive aspects of that energy which is being repressed. On the other hand, the acknowledgement may be so much at odds with self-image that it sparks a collapse or headlong flight.

When we see something in a student or colleague which displeases us we can generally decide whether we want to do something about it. However, when we find we cannot leave it alone, when it gets under our skin and stays there, we can conclude that we are projecting. It is an invitation to search for an aspect of ourself which is not getting recognition in our self-image or adequate expression in our behaviour. Though complexes have positive as well as negative poles, it is the negative which gets under our skin the most. However, acknowledging that the cynicism, pig-headedness or wishy-washiness that drives us crazy in particular students or colleagues are really our own may give us access to the positive aspects of those energies (maybe humour, purposefulness, flexibility) which are undeveloped in us.

It is not only the nasty which is projected. We seem to prefer to project our wisdom, power and beauty on to other ordinary mortals rather than face the consequences of acknowledging them in ourselves. Film stars, gurus, political leaders, sports heroes, are manufactured by such projections. If you come across a statement in a book which strikes you as being somehow 'wise' you are projecting your wisdom on to the writer. The writer has managed to say, in language you understand, something which you knew already. Perhaps she has given you a label for something you had

The High, the Deep and the Ordinary

not previously articulated, but the wisdom you recognized is truly your own. If a teacher tells you something you do not already know you are not likely to understand it, much less be struck by its wisdom.

Projection of our wisdom on to a teacher may often be our only way of discovering it, in the same way as we often project our power to heal ourselves on to a doctor and a placebo. It is easier to say that the pill cures us than that we cure ourselves.

Very often the behaviour of the other person or persons has a 'hook' which catches our projections. The other person may really be 'wise' or 'hostile'. Often, however, the 'hook' is only indirectly associated with the quality projected. In the 'hostile' class it may be the children's energy, their physical resemblance to a previous class which gave the teacher a hard time, their social or ethnic background. But even where the class is actually 'objectively' hostile, the teacher's emotional obsession indicates that it is the teacher's unconscious hostility which is being confronted. As Whitmore says: 'If we wear red spectacles and look at a traffic light, the red that we see may be there, but it may also only be in our spectacles.'[116]

Projection has a powerful influence in interpersonal relations. If I am not trustworthy (whatever my self-image may be) I will perceive my class as untrustworthy and treat them as such. They will then justify my lack of trust by their behaviour. If I am trustworthy myself, I will attribute the same quality to my students, trust them and find my trust rewarded. Obviously, trust cannot exist without the possibility of betrayal, and it may be necessary to bestow trust in stages in order to minimize disasters. It is fairly clear, however, that projection is one mechanism by which behaviour is changed – for better as well as for worse. It is certainly one of the ways by which parents and teachers tend to mould children in their own image.

Relatively non-neurotic teachers are likely to spend more energy dealing with their students' projections than with their own. Pre-adolescents and adolescents engaged in the fairly turbulent business of developing a stable identity are particularly prone to project their undeveloped qualities on to any teacher who displays the appropriate hook. The obsessive, sexually-charged 'crush' and the obsessive irrational antipathy to a teacher are of the same nature as the hero-worship of a pop star. A key part of the adolescent's personality is being dealt with as 'out there' rather than as 'in here'.

The 'hook' by which the teacher invites such projections may be associated with parent-figures in the adolescent's past. In this case the phenomenon should be more precisely called transference. For Freud, transference was at the centre of the therapist-patient (and by implication teacher-student) relationship. Working through the transference towards insight was to take up much of the energy of the relationship. For Jung, transference was simply a particular form of projection. And it was often destructive, getting in the way of individuation.

Transference/projection is something we are engaged in all the time. We keep trying to relive old relationships, to hang on to our old script rather than notice that we are in the middle of a new play with an entirely new cast. Many new acquaintances have to carry the burden of our old well-rehearsed projections because they resemble in some way the previous recipients of these projections. They may not even share significant personal qualities with the people we confuse them with.

When an adolescent transfers to a teacher all of his or her resentment against a tyrannical father, the hook may indeed be this teacher's talent for tyranny. However, it is quite likely to be the teacher's haircut, choice of clothes, or way of speaking. It is a common experience for a teacher in a new class to be confronted with a level of hostility, contempt or resentment which seems to have no basis in his own behaviour. Even admitting the possibility that he is a thoroughly unpleasant person whom the children could reasonably resent, he knows that these particular children have not yet had time or opportunity to find out how nasty he is. Their hostility must have another source. It is useful for him to reflect that the hostility, contempt and resentment belong not to him but to someone else, perhaps to a long line of teachers and parent-figures who have manipulated, oppressed or betrayed these children. He is merely providing a hook for their projection, for the moment, at least.

A defensive reaction to this projection/transference will confirm the children in their perception of the teacher and trap class and teacher in the usual destructive pattern. On the other hand, the teacher who can reflect non-defensively and humorously on what is happening will find himself with choices open to him. He can work on making the class conscious of what they are doing:

> 'You must have had some pretty rotten teachers if you think I'm going to behave like that ...'
> 'You must be mixing me up with someone else ...'

He can attempt to work out what the hook is and change accordingly. It may not be feasible to change his gender or age, if that is where the problem lies, but sometimes quite superficial changes in appearance or mannerism can undermine a transference by removing a hook. Or he may deal with the problem by deliberately acting in ways contrary to the class's expectations. Projections are pretty resilient, but they eventually collapse when they are not consistent with the evidence.

Teachers attract projections of the 'good parent' as well as the 'bad parent'. Projections of the all-loving, all-forgiving mother or father are as common as projections of the tyrant, and rather more seductive. Freud coined the term counter-transference to refer to the way a therapist can be 'sucked in' to a patient's transference and become the patient's parent or lover. Because the relationship is dominated by the unconscious on both sides it is full of energy, anguish and ecstasy. But it is not a genuine encounter between adults, based on mutual respect and concern. The therapist must 'work through' this counter-transference while guiding the patient towards insight through the transference. Otherwise, old destructive patterns are simply confirmed.

Teachers are not immune to being 'sucked in' to a counter-transference. In some teachers, mothering has the obsessive quality which indicates its source in the unconscious. They strenuously protect 'their' class from the influence of any other teacher. The readiness of the class to be dependent on them has seduced them into defining their relationship totally in terms of parent-child, and striving to maintain it that way; they are threatened by any attempt by the children to grow up and leave them.

It is just as seductive to receive a student's projections of excellence. When faced with wide-eyed admiration from an attractive student it is more tempting to conclude that one is endowed with superhuman goodness, wisdom, strength and sensitivity than to reflect that the student is projecting his or her own unrecognized capacities and that this particular package of projections is almost certainly inherited from a parent. To be drawn into a counter-transference, e.g., to respond to an adolescent's crush by falling in love, will provide some exquisite anguish for both parties, but should not be mistaken for an adult relationship. Jung explains the phenomenon of falling in love as a special case of projection. (One projects one's anima or animus on to another then falls in love with this part of oneself. It is only as the projection is withdrawn and the real person emerges that love becomes possible. One either chooses to love this other person as distinct from one's own repressed masculinity or femininity, or one feels betrayed and rushes off to project one's animus/anima on to someone else.)

In Freudian thinking, projection is a mechanism for concealing the contents of the unconscious from the ego. In Jungian thinking, it is a mechanism for revealing them and allowing their integration. In either way of thinking, while projection may start as a wholly unconscious phenomenon, characterized by obsessive emotionality, it doesn't have to stay that way. Just as we can detect our own emerging potential in our projections and begin to own and explore it, we can assist our pupils in the same process. The student who is intellectually or emotionally dependent on a teacher is externalising a range of qualities and abilities which actually are within himself or herself. Rather than exploit this dependence or treat it as a nuisance, the teacher can take on the role of educator, and coax out of the student's unconscious and into consciousness those qualities and abilities which are being denied. The way to do this is not persuasion, which only engages resistance. It is rather to acknowledge and appreciate those glimpses of intelligence and resourcefulness which slip past the student's negative self-image, and to consolidate them by indirect suggestion. People often spend a long period of time learning that they are incompetent. It takes a very patient, indirect approach to turn this around.

Projection is not only a personal phenomenon but a collective one. Nations and whole cultures find groups and individuals on whom they can project their shadow. National pathology regularly expresses itself in

The High, the Deep and the Ordinary

hatred of an 'evil empire' without, or a treacherous minority within. The hook is regularly, but not necessarily, racial. Scapegoating is unpleasant whatever form it takes. And whatever form it takes it is resistant to rational argument.

If there is scapegoating going on in a class, the teacher's first responsibility, obviously, is not to join in. It is not altogether rare for a teacher to collude with a class in setting up one child to be the class idiot or delinquent. Even the child in question may collude in this as a way of achieving, at least, a sort of negative identity in the class. More often the whole process is unconscious. In any case, it is destructive both for the scapegoated child and for those engaged in the exercise. In spite of the nastiness of the behaviour, the teacher who can see what is going on may need to resist the urge to reprimand and punish the class. Delivering a sermon or harangue may give the teacher a pleasing sense of righteousness and some release from frustration, but may also give the class one more reason to resent the scapegoat.

A change in the system (e.g., by shifting the child to another class) may resolve the problem in the short term but withdrawal of projections is not a quick and easy process. In an ideal world it might be possible to engineer some event which transforms the scapegoat into a hero, or at least into a human being. The imaginative teacher might introduce a mythological shadow (Darth Vadar or Dr Moriarty) who is kept in a box in the corner and who gets the blame for everything, or might invent a ritual by which the role of scapegoat is rotated in the class day by day. Such methods if used lightheartedly can educate the class with regard to their own psychology without arousing hostility. If particular children need to find a scapegoat in order to protect and confirm their own sense of identity, the solution lies in building up their self-esteem rather than in attacking their behaviour. A Jungian therapist might look in the contempt-envy ambivalence that characterizes powerful projections for clues as to the undeveloped capacities which are trying to emerge in the client, and might help the client to acknowledge these capacities and seek ways to give them expression. The teacher's role may be more diffuse and she may work under greater pressure, but a similar course can be followed.

If you take a vertical cross-section of Jung's image of the psyche, you will find it layered in a manner similar to Freud's: conscious, preconscious, personal unconscious, all upheld by a vast collective unconscious (objective psyche). If you take a horizontal cross-section you will find the 'contents' of the psyche: shadow, ego, persona, anima, animus, self and other complexes, which have both conscious and unconscious aspects. Slice it again on a different plane and you will find the attitudes and functions of the psyche.

Jung's observation led him to conclude that people have a natural tendency either to move towards new experience or away from it. Of the two alternative attitudes towards the world, which he called extroversion and introversion, they have a preference for one or the other and this is expressed in their habitual behaviour. They prefer either the external world or the world of their own inner experience. They are interested in experiences and people and want to embrace them, or they feel overwhelmed by experiences and people and constantly need to retire from them. Jung was inclined to believe that the tendency to introversion or extroversion was inborn, but acknowledged that there is a great deal of learning involved. In an extroverted culture like our own, children actually learn to be extroverted in their behaviour against their natural tendency. For many parents and teachers, 'well-adjusted' children are extroverted, and children get the message and do their best to please.

Jung also observed the two distinct ways of perceiving the world which he named 'sensing' and 'intuiting'. He called these the 'irrational' functions of the psyche because they are applied to our simple perception of the world, without any element of judgement or evaluation. In judging or evaluating, the psyche has two other functions to use, the 'rational' functions which Jung called 'thinking' and 'feeling'.

According to Jung's observations, some people judge the rightness of what they see in terms of whether it is true or false, useful or useless, logical or illogical, faithful to the evidence or not. Others judge on different grounds: whether it is nice or nasty, beautiful or ugly, pleasant or unpleasant. Those who habitually prefer their thinking function will be concerned that the description of an event is objectively accurate; the 'feelers' will be more interested in whether it sounds good. The 'sensers' will be most interested in the concrete details of an experience, the 'intuiters' will give their attention to the overall impression. In Jung's view, the preference for a particular function is part of our natural endowment, but like our attitude preference is very much affected by education.

Jung's assessment of attitudes and functions is value-free. Introversion and extroversion are equally valid ways of facing the world; sensing and intuiting are equally valid ways of perceiving it; thinking is no more or less valid a way of evaluating experience than feeling, and is just as prone to make mistakes. However, society does not take the same value-free stance. In some cultures such as our own, extroversion is highly valued; our cultural heroes are people of action, people who have made an impact on the world through sport, entertainment, finance or whatever. We do not give the same adulation to the mystic, the poet, the hermit or the theoretical scientist, and people who get too involved in their interior worlds are likely to be locked up for their own good.

Our society also values sensing over intuiting. The development and maintenance of an industrial society and its associated bureaucracy has required people with a well-developed sensing function. The same people have designed and still control a schooling system in which children are taught to accumulate facts, draw conclusions from hard evidence, manipulate figures and words, operate complicated machinery. Children with an inclination to deal with information via their sensing function find their preference confirmed and they develop their skills through the tasks the school gives them. Their sensing function will get them through school because most school tasks can be handled through this function. They can keep doing what they do best.

The intuitive child has a more difficult time in most classrooms. He or she learns that being a good guesser has a limited future. Teachers don't seem to value the skill and certainly don't encourage its development. If they want to be successful they have to learn how to gather and organize the facts first, and only then to dare to reach a conclusion. If they are reluctant or unable to learn this skill they become frustrated, angry or apathetic and fall out of the system.

Schools are likewise inclined to discriminate in favour of the thinking function over the feeling function. Schools need no justification for concentrating their attention on teaching children to think. What they overlook is the large group of children for whom thinking is not the natural way of making decisions. These children miss out on two counts. First, their feeling function is not of much use to them in doing the things which schools consider important so they are at a disadvantage compared to 'thinkers'. Second, their feeling function, which they could learn to use with skill and discrimination, remains neglected and undeveloped in that large area of their life which is dominated by schooling.

It can be argued that society gives schools the specific task of dealing with children's socialization and teaching them the skills associated with what Jung called sensing and thinking. There is plenty of time outside the classroom to withdraw within oneself and meditate, to learn to follow one's hunches, to be drawn by the good and the beautiful. Some would argue that such activities are unnecessary luxuries anyway. Dickens obviously had heard the argument in an industry-obsessed nineteenth century England.

> Now, what I want is, Facts. Teach these boys and girls nothing but Facts. Facts alone are wanted in life. Plant nothing else, and root out everything else. You can only form the minds of reasoning animals upon Facts: nothing else will ever be of any service to them. This is the principle on which I bring up my own children and this is the principle on which I bring up these children. Stick to Facts, sir![117]

The words of Thomas Gradgrind ('... a man of realities. A man of fact and calculations. A man who proceeds upon the principle that two and two are four, and nothing over, and who is not to be talked into allowing anything more') may seem to overstate the case somewhat.[118] Yet the education Dickens caricatured in the 1850s was an education dominated by 'economic realities', and the same pressures are in evidence today to make education more instrumental, more 'relevant to the needs of industry', more 'accountable'. This approach does not work. The narrowing of the focus of education to eliminate the intuitive, the sensitive and the subjective is counter-productive. At the least, it is a waste of resources. Introverted intuition and feeling have produced some of the world's greatest works of science as well as the greatest works of art and architecture. Potential geniuses aside, a schooling which takes no account of the way that half the students receive and process infor-

The High, the Deep and the Ordinary

mation must be considered inefficient. Dickens made the point forcefully in *Hard Times*, as Thomas Gradgrind saw his system of rational instrumental education fail with his own children. The lesson has not been learned yet.

While we have the four functions available to us, and while perceiving (sensing or intuiting) and judging (thinking or feeling) are quite different operations, we all manage to grow up one-sided. We discover quite early in life what we do best or most easily and we get into the way of doing it even when it is inappropriate. We develop one of the functions at the expense of the other three. Jung called this our 'superior' function, and its opposite (e.g., feeling vs thinking) our 'inferior' function.

Our superior function does a lot of work for us, but it also gets us into trouble. A well-developed sensing function which gives me the eye for detail and the skill in assembling and organising facts which makes me a competent administrator may be of no help at all in a personal crisis. The person with a superior feeling function may act as inappropriately in financial dealings as a superior thinking person does in a delicate relationship. The rich fantasy and the sense of possibilities which come with a superior intuitive function may make a mess of your tax return.

While our superior and auxiliary functions control our conscious behaviour, our inferior, undeveloped, repressed function controls our unconscious. Its undeveloped state does not imply that it lacks strength, only skill. The teacher who sees herself as a rational, logical (thinking) type suddenly, under pressure, makes an emotional, impulsive, stupid decision. The feeling function is there all right, it is just not very skilful. The conscious functions and attitudes are balanced by their unconscious opposites, which are seen when defences are down. The introvert becomes extroverted when drunk, and vice versa. The intuitive person becomes dogmatic and obsessed with detail at the most inappropriate times.

Jung turned his observation of one-sidedness into a theory of personality types. People can be classified by attitude and function as introverted sensing, extroverted feeling, introverted thinking and so on. This gives us eight personality types. When we add the observation that a superior rational function will be supported by an auxiliary irrational function (and vice versa) we get sixteen.

Jung found this scheme helpful in discussing human personality and working with people as a therapist. Others, for better or worse, have developed elaborate tests for classifying people as extroverted intuiting thinking judgers and so on. Jung himself had no enthusiasm for such attempts at classifying human beings and putting labels on them. The problem is that writings on personality type are inclined to take too static a view of human nature. When I find myself classified as an extroverted intuiting feeling perceiver (ENFP), I may get some useful insight into why a particular student (immediately diagnosed as an introverted sensing thinking judger[119] gets on my nerves or why I have such a good understanding with a particular colleague (another intuitive feeler). However, if I identify with this ENFP one-sidedness as though set in concrete I will be denying the complexity of who I am.[120]

When one-sided pupils meet one-sided teachers the possibilities for teaching are limited. For example, the child who sits apart from the class like a block of wood, who shows very little response, who seems to have no imagination, who is painstakingly slow in everything he does, who gets the joke some hours after the rest of the class, may drive an extroverted intuitive teacher crazy. Or she may just think he is stupid. He may not be stupid at all. He may be an extremely introverted sensing type, who takes everything in and deals with it internally, but has no interest in moving out of himself. The subtle and detailed observations he makes may never get to be expressed if he is dismissed by the teacher as 'slow'.

The introverted thinking teacher, who values order, responsibility, dependability and hard work, may find herself surrounded by aliens in the classroom. Three-quarters of her class are extroverts, and most of the others are trying to be. The children with a dominant sensing function don't share her interest in order and hard work: those with a dominant feeling function don't share her passion for right answers: the intuitives are bored by her painstaking explanations: the extroverts want interaction. Introverted thinkers form only a tiny fraction of the population and she may literally be the only person of her personality type in the classroom – or in the staffroom for that matter. If she carries on teaching in the way she likes others to teach her, no matter how well she does it, many of her pupils will decide maths (likely to be her favourite subject) is too hard or too boring and drop the subject as soon as they can. Or she decides children are stupid and looks for another job. What she does not acknowledge is that there is more than one kind of intelligence, that many kinds of intelligence can be engaged by maths if the teacher will only find the appropriate technique to engage them.

According to Kiersey and Bates' research, most teachers (about ninety per cent) are either SJs (sensing judgers) or NFs (intuitive feelers).[121] The SJs, who value responsibility and utility, form a majority in their own right and dominate the schooling system, under the impression that theirs is the only normal way of behaving. The NFs, who value growth, integrity and relationship, occasionally seem to take control of the schools but eventually lose their momentum and yield to the SJs again. The handful of NTs (intuitive thinkers) just keep on teaching knowledge and skills without having much influence on the system. SPs (sensing perceivers) don't usually get into teaching, and if they do they resign early. Their preoccupation with free expression (artistic or otherwise) seems to make them temperamentally unsuited for the profession!

Yet in the wider community, and presumably the classroom, SPs form one of the largest groups. They are equalled only by SJs. The intuitive types, while a significant minority in the teaching profession, are considerably less numerous in the general population. It follows that the kind of teaching and learning which comes naturally for a teacher may be seriously at odds with the inclinations of a majority of his pupils. One consequence of this is that children of the SP type (what Kiersey calls the 'Dionysian temperament') may be intelligent, creative and energetic but become persistent 'troublemakers' for teachers who have no appreciation of their value system, and no tolerance of their restlessness. Many of these children drop out of school at the first opportunity. Some are lucky enough to encounter a teacher (in a technology-based subject, in drama or physical education) who can tune into their style and their energy. The rest just put up with being bored. Teachers sometimes talk about wasted talent. It may rather be a matter of wasted opportunities. If teachers were not so inclined to turn their personal preferences into absolute values they might shape their teaching methods to their students' needs instead of trying to sculpt the children according to their own image.

Teachers are presumably no more one-sided than any other group of people. It is common for people to identify with only a fraction of their personality. Even the psychologically healthy person who is able to distinguish between her social roles and her 'true self' makes narrow assumptions about the nature of this 'true self'. It is only when the concrete starts to crumble, when she becomes bored with doing what she does well and begins to acknowledge and explore the shadow side of her personality, that she starts to approach the world through her inferior functions.

Moreno and Assagioli, whose ideas are in important respects similar to Jung's, had no time for one-sidedness. They saw it as essentially neurotic. Becoming aware of and growing through all of one's latent possibilities was, in their view, not something which emerged spontaneously in one's forties but something to be consciously pursued all one's life. The techniques which they developed – Moreno's psychodrama and Assagioli's psychosynthesis– were formed by a vision of the mature, balanced child or adult in flexible, spontaneous interaction with the world through a variety of roles or subpersonalities. For Jung, a one-sided and predictable persona was a necessary means to psychological adjustment in the first half of life. For Moreno and Assagioli, a rigid identification with a single 'self' was no sort of life at all.

Both Jung and Assagioli believed that individuation or self-realization came about through the integration of the diverse aspects and functions of the personality around an organising centre – the personal self. For Moreno, the self was just one role among many. His thinking comes closer to that of James Hillman. For Hillman, the aim is to live through all of one's personalities, all of one's selves, in all their richness and diversity.

Jung devised his theory of psychological types long before brain researchers discovered hemispheric lateralization. Attempts to map the brain on the left-brain/right-brain model have gathered evidence that introversion, intuition and feeling are predominantly associated with right-brain activity, while extroversion, sensing and thinking seem to be mainly functions of the left hemisphere. Writers on cerebral dominance no longer talk much about left-brained and right-brained people but rather suggest that

The High, the Deep and the Ordinary

while people seem to habitually prefer one kind of functioning to the other, the brain is busy making both kinds of functioning available. It is the culture, rather than the individual, which has a 'dominant hemisphere', reflected in the devaluing of the introverted attitude and the neglect of the intuiting and feeling functions in our schooling.

Whichever way we look at it, treating personality type as something fixed seems something of a dead end. The ideal teacher is the one whose whole personality is available to her class, who is not limited by a narrow self-image, whose behaviour with each child at each moment is entirely appropriate to the child and the moment, who acknowledges her pupils' right not to be carbon copies of herself, who gives her pupils every opportunity to do the things they do best while leading them gently to expand their image of who they are and what they can do, whose teaching methods reflect an ability to carry through the biblical recommendation to be everything to everybody.

This means both contacting children through the attitude and function in which they are most comfortable and educating them to develop their less skilful functions. A single lesson can call on both the extroverted and the introverted attitude and give opportunity and support to the children's sensing, intuiting, thinking and feeling. If the teacher accepts and works with Jung's image of basic human motivation as a movement towards wholeness, she will have patience with the sometimes disconcerting behaviour of her pupils as they oscillate between the extremes of their personality.[122]

Jung often proclaimed that he was not a Jungian, nor should anyone else be. He gave up his early attempts to categorize and label aspects of the human personality, as he realized that for him the perspective of Psyche was more fruitful than that of Apollo, that he was less interested in the scientific examination of human beings as objects than in the exploration of humanity as a process. His early preference for his sensing function yielded to a delight in intuition. He found it less enlightening to proclaim facts about the psyche than to construct images of it. He came to see himself as a creator of reality as well as a manifestation of it.

Furthermore, the reality that was simultaneously manifested in him and created by him was not simply a personal one. When Jung looked at the individual and saw the total, integrated self attempting to emerge through the encrustations of self-image and social expectations, he observed the selfhood of the universe emerging. It is not a concept which conventional Western psychology is inclined to take very seriously, though Hindu and Buddhist psychology is largely devoted to it.

It may not seem to have much practical application for the common or garden teacher to envision her pupils as the critical point in the universe where evolution is in process, where matter is evolving into consciousness, where universal mind is emerging, but it certainly gives her activity some significance.

NOTES Chapter 5. The High, the Deep and the Ordinary

[98] On the other hand, some very hard-headed brain researchers have claimed to have located the unconscious in various parts of the brain. MacLean distinguishes our human, conscious brain from our older and relatively unconscious mammalian brain (the limbic system) and reptilian brain (the brain stem). Winson locates 'the psyche' (by which he means the Freudian unconscious) in the hippocampus. Eccles, Jaynes and Galin argue that the unconscious is situated in the right cerebral hemisphere. See R. M. Restak, *The Brain*; J. Eccles, 'Brain and Free Will' in G. Globus et al., *Consciousness and the Brain*; G. Galin 'Implications for Psychiatry of Left and Right Cerebral Specializations', *Archives of General Psychiatry*, 1974, 31, pp. 572-593; J. Jaynes, *The Origin of Consciousness in the Breakdown of the Bicameral Mind*; J. Winson, *Brain and Psyche*; P. MacLean, *The Triune Brain in Evolution*; A. Damasio, *Self Comes to Mind*.

[99] S. Freud, *The Problem of Lay-Analysis*, p. 53.

[100] C. G. Jung, *Collected Works* 6, pp. 712-14.

[101] If repression is unconscious, who is the 'I' who represses? Freud decided that part of the 'I' must itself be unconscious. This part, itself unconscious but doing all the repressing, he called the super-ego. It contains our basic assumptions, our meanings, our values, our attitudes, our moral standards, our prejudices, our frames of reference, our mental sets, insofar as all of these are unconscious. Our 'I' largely identifies with this super-ego and lets it distort our experience to maintain itself. Jung sees it as an aspect of what he called the persona, the public self. It contains the unconscious contents with which the 'I' is completely and unreflectively comfortable. Since it obviously did not repress itself, it must have another source than repression. We can trace its contents to the forgotten and subliminal. All the experiences we have absorbed from infancy, from significant adults initially and then from a broader culture, have been processed into a way

of seeing ourselves and the world and a way of behaving in it. We can even entertain the idea, as Jung did, that some at least of these embedded patterns come to us by biological inheritance.

[102] C. G. Jung, Collected Works 9, 1, p. 281.
[103] C. G. Jung, Collected Works 1, 1, p. 309.
[104] C. G. Jung, Collected Works 9, 1, p.155.
[105] ibid., p. 413.
[106] James Hillman uses the word archetype a little differently from Jung. Jung represents the archetypes as forms without substance, expressing themselves through archetypal images and being themselves the expression of a deeper, underlying unity. Hillman refuses to speculate on the existence of any level of reality more basic than these images. Psychologically, the images are all we can know. Jung himself said that 'everything of which we are conscious is an image' (*Collected Works* 11, p. 889). What we take for reality is a world of images. And every image to the degree that it has universal implications is archetypal. See J. Hillman, *Archetypal Psychology*.
[107] Archetypal psychology is a distinct branch of neo-Jungian psychology, which owes as much to the thinking of Henri Corbin as it does to that of Jung. It is represented in the writings of James Hillman: e.g., *Revisioning Psychology*; *Archetypal Psychology*; *Kinds of Power*. Other books that reflect the archetypal perspective are R. Avens, *Imagination is Reality*, and D. Miller, *The New Polytheism*.
[108] Often enough a man will identify with a feminine consciousness and repress the animus or a woman will adopt masculine consciousness and repress the anima.
[109] C. G. Jung, *Collected Works* 8, p. 201.
[110] C. G. Jung, *Collected Works* 9, p. 202.
[111] E. Whitmont, *The Symbolic Quest*, p. 123.
[112] It is possible to conceptualize the ego in process terms, e.g., as 'the process of organising experience around a point of identity', but it is certainly easier to discuss it in thing-language.
[113] It would also provide opportunities to engage in activities that are difficult and even dangerous.
[114] Jung's notion of individuation belongs within the image of an unfolding universe. The unfolding of the individual's personality and life are part of a cosmic process.

The intrinsically goal-like quality of the self and the urge to realize this goal are not dependent on the participation of consciousness. They cannot be denied any more than one can deny one's ego consciousness. C. G. Jung, *Psychology and Religion*, p. 960.

Jung's theory of individuation makes one simple yet very significant point, which has immense implications for the education of adults. Developmental psychologists, with a couple of notable exceptions, have assumed that psychological growth ends with the end of adolescence. In Jung's theory, psychological development is just starting at that point. The first twenty years of adulthood are occupied with differentiating our ego from the persona we have painstakingly built during childhood and adolescence. For Jung, the really interesting phase of growth does not even begin until the age of forty or thereabouts, when the repressed and unacknowledged aspects of personality begin to emerge, and to be acknowledged and appreciated.

Ken Wilber places the development of a strong ego at the midpoint of individual development. Rational, egoic adulthood is the readiness for a further stage of development, potential from the beginning but only becoming possible with the unfolding of what he calls the emergent unconscious.

> The transpersonal realms are not yet repressed – they are not screened out of awareness, they are not filtered out – they simply have not yet had the opportunity to emerge. We do not say of a two-year-old that he or she is resisting the learning of geometry, because the child's mind has not yet developed and unfolded to the degree that he or she could even begin to learn mathematics. Just as we do not accuse the child of repressing mathematics, we do not accuse him of repressing the transpersonal ... not yet, that is (K. Wilber, *Eye to Eye*, p. 113).

[115] Whitmont, op. cit., p. 60.
[116] ibid., p. 63.
[117] C. Dickens, *Hard Times*, p. 47.
[118] ibid., p. 48.
[119] We have a conventional shorthand language for indicating personality type according to Jung's typology. E signifies extroverted, I = introverted, S = sensing, N = intuiting, T = thinking, F = feeling, P = perceiving, J = judging. The latter two categories indicate whether a person's superior function is one of the perceiving (sensing – intuiting) pair or one of the judging (feeling – thinking) pair. Thus a person categorized as ENFP has a superior intuiting function; the ENFJ has a superior feeling function. See I. B. Myers, *Gifts Differing*, and D. Kiersey and M. Bates, *Please Understand Me*. A useful application of typology theory to a discussion of learning styles will be found in H. Silver et al., *That They May Learn*.
[120] Jung developed his theory of the functions and attitudes of the psyche quite early in his career and then went on to explore matters that were of more intense interest to him – the unfolding of the self and the religious or transpersonal dimension in human experience. There is some excellent Jungian writing on the typology, but the model has been taken up by psychologists with little interest in Jung's thought, to the point that it is probably, in a distorted form, the best known of Jung's theories. A whole

technology and organization has been built around the assessment of people's personality types and the training of experts to do this assessing. The usefulness of the schema has become more important than the power of Jung's image to enliven and enlighten us. Typology assessment is commonly carried out within a static model of personality, so that people can be categorized and then advised what kind of occupation or lover they should pursue. Often, the initiative for assessment is taken by an organization so that its employees can be slotted into the tasks where their talents can be most efficiently used. This is no doubt a legitimate expression of the Promethean spirit of our age, and has positive as well as negative consequences, but it has little to do with Jung.

[121] Kiersey and Bates use the Jungian categories to develop a theory of four basic temperaments, which they call Apollonian, Promethean, Epimethean and Dionysian. Their book contains an instrument which is a simple and useful way for teachers to investigate their own personality according to the Jungian typology. The figures cited here are based on their research on teachers in California.

[122] Oscillation between extremes of behaviour is common in adolescents as they strive to develop a functional persona

> In our attempt to fathom the learner's motives, we should recognize the function of movement towards extremes and its frequent necessity. Students' behaviour could be better understood, and their erratic inclinations harnessed to educational aims, if their behavioural excesses could be read for meaning rather than scorned. If there exists highly motivated movement in some direction, the educator should wonder from where is the movement travelling? In the continuing pursuit of realization which sortie is being redirected? The point is not conversion into the opposite but conservation of precious values together with recognition of their opposites. The educator should be able to identify the values referred to, but the knowledge is not commonly sought. If known, such values can be accounted for in the educational environment! (P. Shaker, 'The Application of Jung's Analytical Psychology to Education', *Journal of Curriculum Studies*, 1982, 14, 3, p. 247).

6

CATCHING THE LIGHT

The truth not sought for comes forth to the light.

Menander

Educating Psyche

IN 1908 THE MATHEMATICIAN Henri Poincaré wrote an essay in which he explored the nature of mathematical creativity. He used his own experience as the raw material for his analysis. Poincaré related how he had been working fruitlessly and with great frustration on a mathematical problem with which he was obsessed — trying to prove the non-existence of what he later called Fuchsian functions.

> One evening, contrary to my custom, I drank black coffee and could not sleep. Ideas rose in clouds; I felt them collide until airs interlocked, so to speak, making a stable combination. By the next morning I had established the existence of a class of Fuchsian functions ... I had only to write out the results, which took but a few hours.[123]

The following day he had to travel, and forgot his mathematical work. At one of his stopovers he boarded a bus.

> At the moment when I put my foot on the step the idea came to me, without anything in my former thoughts seeming to have paved the way for it, that the transformations I had used to define the Fuchsian functions were identical with those of non-Euclidian geometry. I did not verify the idea; I should not have had the time, as, on taking my seat in the omnibus, I went on with a conversation already commenced, but I felt a perfect certainty. On my return to Caen, for conscience' sake I verified the result at my leisure.[124]

So Poincaré casually went about his business in the perfect confidence that the solution which had come to him was correct. He got on with his work and eventually came up against another difficulty which he found impossible to solve.

> Disgusted with my failure, I went to spend a few days at the seaside, and thought of something else. One morning while walking on the bluff, with just the same characteristics of brevity, suddenness and immediate certainty, I saw that the arithmetic transformations of indeterminate ternary quadratic forms were identical with those of non-Euclidian geometry.[125]

He went back to work, to deduce in systematic fashion all Fuchsian functions. But there was one piece in the puzzle that he could not deduce. His work was then interrupted by his military service. He had no leisure in which to think of mathematics.

> One day going along the street the solution suddenly appeared to me. I did not try to go deep into it immediately, and only after my service did I take up the question. I had all the elements and had only to arrange them and put them together. So I wrote out my final memoir at a single stroke and without difficulty.[126]

THE CREATIVE PROCESS

When Poincaré came to analyse his experience he found that this creative act could be broken down into four stages: an initial investigation which works on the problem until it can go no further; a period of rest; the occurrence of a sudden and unexpected solution; conscious, rational work to validate this insight. He found that other thinkers in maths and sciences had described the process in similar terms. These four stages in the creative process were later labelled by the psychologist Graham Wallas as preparation, incubation, illumination and verification.[127]

One question that puzzled Poincaré was how some combinations of ideas led to 'illumination', how, during the incubation period, the best combination formed and became ready to emerge. He decided that the emergence of good combinations is not due to chance, but that the unconscious mind really does know what it is doing. In the first place, the material it is dealing with is not random. The period of preparation has mobilized the ideas from which the solution is going to be formed even if, as in Poincaré's case, the conscious mind is relentlessly pursuing the wrong solution and is getting frustrated with the task.

> These efforts, then, have not been as sterile as one thinks: they have set going the unconscious machine and without them it would not have moved and would have produced nothing.[128]

In the second place Poincaré suggests that the solutions which the unconscious puts up and which are seized on eagerly by the conscious mind are those which are beautiful or elegant. The most useful combinations are precisely the most beautiful.[129]

Poincaré's experience of arriving at the beautiful in a moment of relaxation after 'real, hard thinking' has apparently failed is replicated again and again in the history and mythology of science. The stories of Archimedes, Galileo, Newton, Darwin, Kekule, Mendeleev and numerous others reinforce the importance of an incubation period as a prelude to scientific insight.[130] It might mean taking a bath, or sitting under a tree, or going to bed, but in one form or another it turns up in case after case. Einstein remarked on how many scientists have had major flashes of insight while shaving.

FLASHES OF INSIGHT

The anecdotes do not come only from the sciences. Unusually creative people in every field have described how inspiration or insight came to them at a moment when they were not consciously working on their problem.

In the midst of his mid-life crisis, with his inspiration apparently drying up and his energy for life leaving him, Richard Wagner decided to travel. Travel exhausted and depressed him. He was still unable to compose, though he tried desperately to do so. At length he stopped trying.

> After a night spent in fever and sleeplessness I forced myself to take a long walk in the country. It looked dreary and desolate. Upon my return I lay down on a hard couch. Sleep would not come, but I sank into a kind of somnolence, in which I suddenly felt as though I was sinking in swiftly flowing water. The rushing noise formed itself into a musical sound, the chord of E flat major, whence developed melodic passages of increasing motion. I awoke in sudden terror, recognising that the orchestral prelude to *Das Rheingold*, which must have long laid latent within me, had at last been revealed to me.[131]

Wagner's inspiration came to him through hypnogogic imagery. The insight which led Einstein to the theory of relativity came to him in a daydream. Mozart claimed that his music came to him freely: 'when I am, as it were, completely myself, entirely alone, and of good cheer – say, travelling in a carriage, or walking after a good meal, or during the night when I cannot sleep.'[132] Kipling would let himself drift off into reverie, in which state his 'daemon' would guide his writing. 'When your Daemon is in charge, do not try to think consciously. Drift, wait and obey ...'[133]

Inspiration has often come through dreams. James Watt struggled to find an economic way to manufacture gunshot. He dreamed that he was in a rainstorm in which the rain drops were made of lead. When he awoke he conceived the idea of the shot-tower. Mendeleev saw the Periodic Table of the Elements in a dream. Mozart, Schumann, Beethoven, Saint-Saens and Tartini reported that they sometimes dreamed their music. R. L. Stevenson claimed that he had learned to control his dreams and used them to invent stories.

Brahms said that 'I have to be in a semi-trance condition to get such results – a condition when the conscious mind is in temporary obeyance and the subconscious mind is in control ...'[134] At one period in his life Wordsworth used to fall into a trancelike state in which poetry would come to him. Goethe and Milton both claimed that on occasions they had the sense that their poetry was being dictated to them while they were in a half-conscious state.

While such accounts are very numerous it is not to our purpose to deal with them at greater length here. There is only a limited number of Goethes and Einsteins in the normal classroom and the Goethes and Einsteins seem to be able to transcend the limitations of their teachers and environment anyway. The manufacture of great works of art or profound and beautiful scientific theories is not one of the primary concerns of the classroom. Understanding and getting some control over the processes that lead to creative expression or creative insight is, or ought to be.

DEVELOPING CREATIVITY

Curricula are not usually written with the development of 'creativity', 'insight' and 'intuition' set out as explicit goals. Teachers are commissioned by the culture to transmit information, skills and attitudes. While the leading edge of the scientific and business world may value insight, intuition and innovation, and while the artistic world is inclined to reward spontaneity and originality, the school system as a whole does not. The ideal product is not conceived in such terms and the public examination system generally leaves such qualities alone. Certainly individual schools and individual classrooms may go counter to this trend, and teachers in infant and primary classes are often much freer and more active in this regard than are secondary teachers. However, it remains true that in the socialization of children in our culture the balance leans heavily towards convergence and conformity.

It is not necessary here to tease out the differences in meaning between creativity, insight, originality, intuition, divergent thinking. While conceptually different, they have a great deal in common both in their psychological origins and in the conditions that facilitate them. As far as the goals and methods of teaching are concerned, what serves one of these skills seems to serve them all.

The categorization of the stages of the creative process – preparation, incubation, illumination, verification – makes some immediate sense. It provides a useful framework for looking at the teacher's task and possibilities in developing 'creativity' in the classroom. More than that, it provides a framework for looking at the whole process of teaching and learning in a way that takes account of more of the mind's abilities than are conventionally acknowledged. What appears extraordinary in Brahms and Poincaré may not be extraordinary at all. It may be a fairly spectacular instance of a process which regularly occurs in all of us, an ordinary process whose presence and potential tend to be overlooked in many classrooms.

Most of what passes for thinking in classrooms is not thinking but remembering; either the teacher remembers something and tells the children or the child remembers and tells the teacher. We need not belittle the importance of remembering in schooling, but we ought to acknowledge that memory is only one of the functions of the brain. An approach to teaching which is in tune with the creative process as manifested spectacularly in Brahms and others may engage some of the other functions without displacing memory. Such an approach may even allow rational-critical thinking a bigger share of the action than it tends to get in conventional teaching.

Catching the Light

PREPARATION

Preparation is something that conventional teaching does well. It involves the presentation of information and the establishment of connections through discussion. It involves indirect and subliminal transmission of information as well as direct: charts or pictures on the classroom wall, teachers' non-verbal behaviour, messages inherent in the particular medium of teaching. If the content is presented with an awareness of the critical importance of the sensory input, if the children can see and hear and touch and set out and visualize the information being presented, so much the better.

Seeing all this classroom activity as preparatory to the real business of learning requires a change in perspective for some teachers. They have to shift their focus from their own teaching to the children's learning (which is, after all, the raison d'être of the classroom). They have to learn to present the content in such a way that the end of their class presentation is the beginning of the 'real work', not the end of it. In practice this means presenting material in a way that raises questions rather than answers them, conducting classroom discussion in a way which leads to possibilities rather than reinforces 'the facts'. It means restraining the desire to show the students that you 'know all about it'. In short it means deliberately avoiding premature closure, and maybe avoiding closure altogether.

This sort of teaching ought to have two outcomes. One is that the students are stimulated and consciously motivated to go and find the answers for themselves. The other is that processes are set in motion in the unconscious mind, which like a computer begins to scan all the data looking for connections. So that between today's class and tomorrow's the learning proceeds quietly and efficiently even if the students pay no attention to the process.

So much is potential. In practice, the result may be frustration rather than excitement. The students may be habituated to quite a different mode of teaching where the facts are presented learned and forgotten, and where classroom discussion means joining in the teacher's game of 'Guess What's In My Mind'. If such is the children's expectation, the teacher may have to begin by meeting their needs, establishing credibility, before setting out to introduce them to the satisfaction and excitement of thinking, and the euphoria that comes with a flash of insight.

Educating Psyche

When the teacher adopts a problem-solving style of teaching, these operations can be made much more explicit. Though the unconscious will work on an unsolved problem anyway, its efficiency will be affected by the way the problem is presented. The more clearly, precisely and purposefully the problem is presented, the more thoroughly the information is assembled, the easier the task of the unconscious. To take up the computer analogy again, the unconscious is very sensitive both to the nature and structure of the input and to the program it is instructed to follow. Not only should the input be sufficient to generate a solution (and input includes not only facts, but images, analogies, metaphors and fantasized solutions), but the operation should be purposive. The computer must be instructed to find a solution. This means combining a strong motivation with the technique, apparently essential in working with the unconscious, of not trying too hard. And above all, as people who talk to computers often say, 'Garbage in, garbage out!'

We need to step back from these very sensible statements about clarity, precision and purposefulness, and acknowledge that they express only one perspective on the methodology of preparation. This rational perspective, which comfortably uses the analogy of computer input and processing, reflects what has been called 'digital', 'linear', 'left-brain' thinking. Many teachers who adopt a problem-solving approach do so in this mode and do so brilliantly. They know that if students are to make the associations that will give them the thrill of insight, the information must be presented in a way which makes this possible. They know there is a straight line from information to insight. They regularly have the satisfaction of seeing their work rewarded as their students' faces light up with the excitement of discovery.

Other teachers handle this preparation phase rather differently. They do not give the same priority to the systematic organization of information. They take their students towards understanding by an indirect route, picking up a topic briefly, raising questions or demonstrating skills, then moving on to something else, leaving the questions unanswered and the skills unpractised. They have no wish to restrict themselves to teaching one thing at a time, or teaching topics in logical order. They do not think it matters whether the children understand immediately what they are teaching; they are quite happy to leave the children a bit frustrated and perplexed. They know they will understand it better and practise their skills more purposefully when they circle round to it again. Understanding is only relative anyway, and teaching is just a preparatory contribution to the understanding which the children will construct for themselves when they are ready for it. So they circle, more or less, through the curriculum, adding bits of information and hints of solutions as it seems relevant, rarely giving a definitive lesson and sometimes avoiding a final statement altogether. When impelled by their student's need for clarity and closure, or by the imperative of an examination system to 'finish off' a topic, they feel it is 'a bit of a cheat'.

The phase of preparation has two distinct aspects. One is to establish a ground of data that can be processed consciously and unconsciously and out of which, it is hoped, an insight will emerge. Another is to establish an appropriate mental set. However we describe that mental set, one aspect of it will be a clutch of unanswered questions. There will be no experience of a solution without at least a vague consciousness of a problem.

Teachers can establish this database and mental set through orderliness and precision or through randomness and ambiguity. Good teachers will not disdain either approach, or turn their personal preferences into absolute values. They will be flexible enough to teach either way, to meet the needs and preferences of their students and not only their own.

INCUBATION

Incubation often means 'sleeping on it'. If we look at the history of science, art or literature, incubation sometimes means 'sleeping on it' for years. The physiologist Otto Loewi woke up one night with the design for a critical experiment seventeen years after he had his original wild idea that nerve impulses might be both chemical and electrical. Teachers are not dealing with that sort of time-scale.

Fortunately, experience and research, especially biofeedback research, have shown that the qualities that make sleep an efficient incubator can be approximated in other states of consciousness. The computer can be put into 'processing mode', through relaxation, day-dreaming or meditation, or simply by forgetting all about the task and doing something else.

On occasions we reach our insights while working on the problem, apparently without any pause for incubation. Psychologists persuaded that incubation is essential would argue that we are constantly slipping in and out of trance, that these moments of trance (which, of course, we don't notice ourselves having) are essential to enable us to synthesize the information we receive. It does appear that our brains regularly switch their activity between left and right hemispheres. It may be that our left brain collects and orders the verbal information and our right brain works at synthesising it.

Whether the incubation period is essential or not, there is plenty of evidence that people can make themselves more open to insights by putting themselves into an altered state of consciousness, whether we call it daydream or meditation. Aldous Huxley, for instance, used to go into what he called 'deep reflection'. This was a sort of meditation in which he became very relaxed, oblivious to everything around him and narrowly focused on the problem occupying him. He did not think in this state, but simply let ideas 'happen' to him. He was able to write in this state, if he desired, just as Brahms could in his self-induced trance.

If incubation does not have to be a lengthy process, it is feasible to fit it into the structure of a lesson. The few minutes silence in the middle of a suggestopedia session comes out of Lozanov's experience that this pause makes learning the material more efficient. Unfortunately, even teachers who value meditation may be unwilling to devote a few minutes to the practice during a lesson, because it might be considered a waste of time. Lozanov's experience is that the time is more likely to be wasted by pressing on in an effort to get through the material. Many teachers have learned the value of a pause and a brief change of activity (physical exercise, deep breathing, a quick game of some kind) in the middle of a lesson. The argument here is that such a pause does more than relieve boredom; revive energy, increase involvement or whatever. It is a critical element in the learning process. The brain makes use of this pause to get on with the task of synthesising.

There is reason to believe that the Alpha-Theta state arrived at through meditation is particularly effective in facilitating the synthesis of ideas, the development of the 'combinations' referred to by Poincaré.[135] If biofeedback were generally available in classrooms it could be used to develop exactly the same state of consciousness in which to incubate ideas and the whole process would be legitimated as scientific instead of being 'tainted by mysticism'.

Another perspective on what is occurring in this incubation period is offered by Arieti's concept of the endocept.[136] The endocept is the sort of 'vague sense' which is attended to in Gendlin's technique of experiential focusing, described in chapter four.

The endocept is an organization of past experiences and perceptions, images, unconscious feelings, physical state and immediate stimulation. It is an amorphous, dim and faint kind of knowing. Indeed it may be so faint and dim that we are not aware of it at all. It is a disposition to feel, think and act, but it is too vague and uncertain to be called either a thought or a feeling. It is global and diffuse. It cannot be directly communicated; it has to be translated first into words, music, pictures, action. It is an intermediate construct of the brain, between perception and processing on the one hand and clearly thought ideas and clearly felt emotions on the other.

In the stage of incubation there is a lot of endoceptual activity. The preparation stage, which is characterized by a conscious effort to master a subject, is followed by this period in which what used to be clear becomes less distinct and confused with other things. It regresses to the more primitive endoceptual level (pre-word, pre-thought). Anyone who has taken time over writing an essay will recognize the phase. There appears to be nothing left but a confused feeling that defies any attempt to give it shape.

This phase may be accompanied by a level of frustration or apathy which will inhibit the emergence of a solution. If time allows, we can turn off our frustration or boredom by attending to something else. Or we can teach ourselves and our students to do so quickly and efficiently through brief and deep relaxation. Then something new will emerge, the translation of the endocept into a concept or a product that is somehow adequately satisfying to us and can be communicated to others.

ILLUMINATION

Deep relaxation not only allows for more efficient processing and synthesising of information. As a state midway between waking and sleeping it shares some of the features of both and provides a way of opening up the unconscious to the conscious mind.

One of the characteristics of the mind's activity in this state is the availability and vividness of images. At the same time, unlike dreaming which is not normally under the control of the conscious mind, this state allows the mind to choose and control images as well as simply to be receptive to them or to inhibit them altogether. Imagery is closely connected with both creative insight and creative expression. It is not surprising to find creative artists confirming the importance of images in their thinking. Yet this confirmation comes also from scientists and mathematicians. Einstein, for instance:

> When I examine myself and my methods of thought, I come to the conclusion that the gift of fantasy has meant more to me than my talent for absorbing knowledge.[137]

And again:

> The words or the language, as they are written or spoken, do not seem to play any role in my mechanism of thought: the physical entities which seem to serve as elements of thought are certain signs and more or less clear images which can be voluntarily reproduced and combined ... The above-mentioned elements are, in my case, of visual and some of muscular type. Conventional words or other signs have to be sought for laboriously only in a secondary stage.[138]

No wonder Einstein's mathematics teacher thought he was stupid. His amorphous, endoceptual understanding had to be translated into images and then translated a second time into words. Presumably this second translation was only undertaken in order to communicate with others. His own knowing was satisfactorily achieved through images. Einstein's teachers shared the common irritation of teachers with students who come up with the 'right answer' but are quite unable to verbalize the logical-rational-sequential steps that they ought to have gone through to reach it. Such irritation is not confined to mathematics teachers. Teachers who are humbly serving a school culture and an examination system which overvalues the analytic at the expense of the intuitive will react in the same way to the child who claims to understand a poem, a painting or a piece of music but is inept at verbalising this understanding.

This analysis and verbalization is often necessary for communication. It is certainly necessary for passing examinations. However, it is often counter-productive to attempt to push the student directly from input to verbalized insight. Where they cannot make the jump, pressure only generates resistance and frustration. What often happens, of course, is that the teacher gives up waiting for the student to get an illumination and simply hands over a pre-packaged interpretation, the product of someone else's insight. Thinking is completely abandoned in favour of remembering.

Instead of this essentially sterile activity, a teacher can guide students on a path from information to insight which is easier than the direct one, and much more likely to arrive at its destination. The existence of the endocept (amorphous cognition, the vague sense) can be taken seriously and attended to. And it can be allowed translation into images, at least as a stage on the way to clearly expressed ideas.

Experiential focusing[139] is one technique which is appropriate for this purpose. Another is scanning.[140] The teacher can set out to establish an understanding that communication through images is a legitimate way of dealing with ideas. The teacher's own free use of metaphor and analogy will provide a model and the students will be encouraged and invited to use images in their own attempts to express ideas ... What does it remind you of? What sort of picture do you get? If X was a colour, what colour would it be? One discovery the teacher will make is that image is associated with a much higher level of energy than abstraction. Another is that faces occasionally light up with the pleasure of understanding.

If imagery is the first characteristic of illumination, the second is the flash-of-lightning effect. Insight is sudden and often unexpected. One moment one is confused, the next moment one is saying 'Aha!' as the solution is delivered ready made from the unconscious. Kekule described his visualization of the structure of the benzene molecule:

> I turned my chair to the fire and dozed. Again the atoms were gambolling before my eyes. This time the smaller groups kept modestly in the background. My mental eye, rendered more acute by visions of this kind, could not distinguish larger structures, of manifold conformation; long rows, sometimes more closely fitted together; all twining and twisting in snakelike motion. But look! What was that? One of the snakes had seized hold of its own tail, and the form whirled mockingly before my eyes. As if by a flash of lightening I awoke ... Let us learn to dream, gentlemen.[141]

The 'Aha' comes not only in major scientific or artistic breakthroughs, but also in our experience in solving the very ordinary problems of life when our reasoning has failed to deliver an answer. The fact that our students do not leap from their chairs shouting *Eureka*, or collapse trembling under the weight of the chord of E-flat major, does not mean that illumination is unknown in classrooms. The process which is written large in the lives of geniuses is usefully seen as a style of thinking different from the rational-logical mode which is the standard in the culture of schooling, but just as legitimate and just as useful. For some people 'thinking' means sitting with one's mind more or less blank, waiting for an idea to arrive. Indeed, it may sometimes be the only style of thinking that works. Jungian psychology suggests that preference for one or the other style is a matter of personality type. Whatever their preferences, children and adolescents are capable of both kinds of thinking, and schooling ought to provide the opportunity to practise both.

Creative illumination may sometimes be exciting and spectacular, but our usual experience of it has little to do with the agony and the ecstasy. Intuitive thinking is a very ordinary and undervalued operation. Most of what we learn in childhood we 'pick up' intuitively. We collect sense impressions and bits of information, often subliminally; our unconscious stores, selects and synthesizes; and suddenly we 'know' something. As we grow older we continue to learn in the same way; only occasionally do we learn by being 'told' or 'shown', or by thinking something out for ourselves. Except in school, that is. In school, our ability to think intuitively and learn indirectly is largely ignored, at least in the formal business of the classroom. On the other hand, intuitive thinking remains our way of dealing with the hidden curriculum of assumptions and attitudes, the things we 'just know' because that is the way things are. A result of this undervaluing and neglect is that our intuitive skills remain underdeveloped. Yet intuitive thinking is at least as teachable as the skills of logic and analysis.

One striking characteristic of illumination is the sense of certainty which accompanies it. When the one illuminated is Einstein or Beethoven, this sense of rightness seems admirable. Unfortunately, it also accompanies the 'knowing' that emerges when the unconscious has been processing incorrect or incomplete information. We find it in the conversion of a non-believer to an absurd cult (religious, political or psychological), in a teenager's stubbornly held, bizarre misinterpretation of *Hamlet*, in deeply held prejudices.

EMERGING KNOWLEDGE

Another common characteristic of illumination is the sense that it has been 'given', that it comes from somewhere (or someone) else. When this is combined with a sense of certainty the result can be powerful. Human history has been significantly influenced for better and for worse by such revelations.

How a person attributes this inspiration obviously depends on a belief system. It was natural for nineteenth century Christian Romantics like Brahms and Beethoven to experience their music as part of God's revelation. The extraordinary Indian mathematician Ramaniyan received his insights in dreams or visions from the goddess Namagiri. Kipling attributed his inspirations to his personal daemon. George Eliot said that when she was inspired she felt that her personality was 'merely the instrument through which this spirit, as it were, was acting'.[142] Strauss was 'conscious of being aided by more than an earthly power'.[143] Blake wrote, on occasion, 'from immediate dictation ... without premeditation and even against my will'.[144] And so on through countless examples.

Such testimony is not confined to the nineteenth century. We ought to assume that the habit of writers in classical times of attributing inspiration to the gods or the muses was more than a poetic convention: it most probably had a basis in experience. Many cultures have a prophetic literature, delivered to a chosen human instrument in a trance or vision. Occult societies and charismatic religious sects have largely depended for their influence on messages from 'the other side' or the direct inspirations of the Holy Ghost. Some of these phenomena involve full conscious insight, in some of them the human instrument's involvement is totally robotic. In either case the product, wise or banal or toxic as it may be, is experienced as coming from outside the self.

The physicist Pauli, who was an associate of both Einstein and Jung, argued that scientific inspiration is an example of the breakthrough into consciousness of an archetype of the collective unconscious. For Jungians, Ramaniyan's image of Namagiri and Mozart's image of the Holy Ghost are archetypes of the collective unconscious which are experienced as 'other' though they are most deeply 'self'. Although this attribution of inspiration to the collective unconscious is a satisfying theory in cases where the scientist or prophet or creative artist has a revelation whose contents could not have been already potentially available (and this may prove to be all the cases), the theory is probably unnecessary. We can as readily say that subliminal or forgotten perception provides the information, the personal unconscious provides the illumination and the mechanism of projection ensures that it is attributed to some being worthy of it.

Sudden, brilliant illumination may be a feature of the events which creative artists and thinkers (and their biographers) single out as worth reporting. Most intuitive thinking is somewhat less spectacular. Intuition sometimes emerges as 'knowledge', without any sense of process at all. Sometimes it gradually reaches full awareness, as when we start a poem, a painting or an essay with only a vague feeling of what it is we want to express; we work on it till the painting, poem or idea that was latent in that vague felt sense is suddenly complete on canvas or paper, and we recognize that it is exactly what we wanted to say. Or we write six drafts of an essay or story while the idea that was in us all the time gradually takes the form that we can recognize as 'right'.[145]

This kind of illumination is not only extremely common, it has been the basis of inestimable works of art and major advances in science. For many people it is the preferred way of 'thinking'. 'How can I know what I think until I hear what I say?' For others it is an underdeveloped skill that could be developed through encouragement and practice. Unfortunately, it remains underdeveloped in many because the school culture undervalues it, and many teachers have learned to deal even with 'creative' work through secondary process alone. They teach their students to 'create' through getting their ideas clear, and carefully structuring the product. Such skills are certainly useful and rightly valued. However, those pupils whose natural processes are different are inclined to resist this sort of teaching.

EDUCATING INTUITION

At the other pole is a minority of teachers who see creativity as an uninhibited outpouring of the soul. Their teaching suits some pupils perfectly and frustrates and irritates others. As a view of creativity it is just as narrow and wrongheaded as the other. As an approach to teaching it is just as remiss in ignoring personality differences and attempting to push square children through round holes. Some students get frustrated with teachers who insist that they 'plan' their piece of creative writing. Others get frustrated with teachers who insist they don't.

Jung observed that some people gain information about the world with an eye for the specific and concrete. They collect details and add them up to form conclusions. Other people go straight for the conclusion without being aware of the precise information which might be leading to those conclusions. They see the situation as a whole without any sense of the details. Jung concluded that 'sensing' and 'intuiting' were two distinct functions of the psyche and that people tended to have a clear preference for one or the other.

Whether or not we accept the logic of Jung's distinction between sensing and intuiting functions, it is clear that there are real differences of attitude and behaviour here, in both the teachers and the children, which ought to be acknowledged in teaching practice. The child in school has already developed a preference for one function over the other, as a way of dealing with the confusion of living and developing a stable personality. The teacher's task ought to be to value the child's 'natural' way of thinking and help the child to use it more skilfully – not to attack the child's developing sense of identity by labelling his or her thinking as wrong.

While the developed function in both sensing and intuiting children needs to be supported and trained, teachers also have an obligation to coax their pupils' undeveloped function into use. The problem is that although, through training and experience, they have a sense of how to develop the children's logical and analytical skills, they are likely to be at a loss when it comes to developing intuitive skills.

Nevertheless, the complete person uses both functions with skill; the complete creative product demands the use of both.

Experiential focusing, scanning, psychosynthesis, relaxation, meditation and psychodramatic techniques that are described elsewhere in this book are ways of learning in the intuitive mode. Any mode of teaching which works through concrete images and materials facilitates intuitive thinking. 'Active' methods, such as dramatic improvization or certain games and simulations, which push the children to make quick responses and decisions, can develop their intuitive skills. Unfortunately, many teachers do not recognize the learnings gained in this way, which are often stuck at the level of endoceptual cognition, and do not know how to guide their students to translate their vague feelings into communicable symbols.

BRAINSTORMING

Some useful techniques for developing intuitive thinking have come out of problem-solving. Brainstorming is one well-known and well-tried method of problem-solving, where the group interaction enables one person's ideas to spark ideas in others. There are four formal rules.

- Quantity is desirable; the more ideas the better.
- There is to be no criticism or judgement of any ideas presented. Evaluation is done in a subsequent session.
- No idea is too bizarre, too wild or too irrelevant. The purpose

is not to be correct but to stimulate the process of generating imaginative alternatives.
- Combinations, modifications and improvements on previously mentioned ideas are encouraged.

Many teachers feel they have 'done brainstorming' in some workshop or other. It didn't excite them then, and they have no reason to believe it will be a useful technique in their classroom. It's likely that they haven't 'done' it at all. Education professionals are trained and practised in evaluating, and have great difficulty in inhibiting their urge to evaluate, even when they are doing something called 'brainstorming'.

Brainstorming was developed by Osborn in the 1940s as a means of dealing with such momentous issues as discovering two hundred new ways of marketing blankets.[146] This does not invalidate it as a classroom technique applicable to many areas of curriculum. It is invaluable as an introduction to classroom discussion on almost any subject. To be effective, it needs to be taught and used as a formal technique and distinguished from other form of discussion. Learning to speak and listen without evaluation is a skill that does not come easily after a few years of schooling. Indeed, the idea of listening without evaluation is often strongly resisted by students, as those teachers who attempt to use the technique soon discover.

The strength of the technique is in the formality of the rules, which work to overcome this resistance. The rules, if imposed absolutely and authoritatively, give the students permission to defy logic, to abandon conventional modes of thought, to express 'crazy' intuitions. Whether the class is exploring a theorem, theory, historical problem or work of art, the technique enables the development of skills and the accessing of knowledge that could be neglected in conventional consensus-dominated discussion. Osborn's discovery of a means to postpone evaluation is critical. Evaluation inhibits the illuminative phase.

INVITING ILLUMINATION

Another useful aid to intuitive thinking is the 'right-brain diagram' described by Buzan in *Using Both Sides of Your Brain* and Rico in *Writing the*

Natural Way.[147] A topic word is written in a circle and then words associated with it are written down quickly, each in its own circle, radiating out from the nucleus. Each word or phrase is connected by a line to the preceding circle, and to any others with which it might be connected. Each circle may become a secondary nucleus in itself. As this proceeds a pattern often emerges, showing connections not previously thought of. The technique not only 'loosens up' the mind to acknowledge the diversity of information it contains, but leads to the perception of patterns of ideas, and consequently to new insights. Like brainstorming, the technique breaks the conventions of critical thinking and allows connections to be made in non-logical, non-sequential ways. By setting out ideas spatially rather than sequentially it calls on the capacities of 'right-brain functioning'. Planning an essay or revising a course of work by this method is quite a different experience from the conventional method of writing down a list of topics or ideas. It is well worth using frequently as a class exercise and teaching to students at any level as a study skill.

In his writing on lateral thinking, De Bono describes a number of exercises which can be used for training intuition.[148] Some of them can be adapted to exploring content issues. One such technique is the use of random stimuli to generate ideas. A word is chosen at random (e.g., the first word on a randomly chosen page of a book) and is used to generate ideas on a particular topic. Anything about the stimulus word can be associated to the topic – its properties, uses, opposites, puns, rhymes. As a group exercise it can generate chains of associations, unblocking thinking and leading to new ways of perceiving an issue or problem. Like brainstorming, it depends on keeping one's thinking uncritical, postponing evaluation of the ideas.

Another way of stimulating intuitive thinking is to seek solutions and perspectives through metaphor and analogy. Understanding of a historical, chemical or political process can be greatly enhanced by drawing diverse responses to the question, 'What is it *like?*' Not only does this have the effect of bringing primary process under conscious control to address an issue, but the metaphor often contains information and understanding which could have been verbally stated only with difficulty. Translating from the image into words is often easier than attempting to express something in words in the first place. Besides, translation is not always necessary or appropriate. To draw, dance or sculpt an answer to the question may be even more productive than a verbal metaphor. Such activities are usually seen as purely expressive; while they might be conceded a place in the 'artistic' curriculum, they are thought to have no role in the teaching of the 'hard' subjects. On the contrary, they can be applied very productively to the teaching of specific content. They are energising, they are involving, they stimulate intuitive thinking, they call on capacities of the brain neglected in conventional teaching.

The unconscious can work a great deal faster than the conscious mind, and deal with more complex information, much of it subliminal to our awareness. In mathematics in particular, it has been well demonstrated that the human brain can process information much faster than we usually allow it to. There have been many studies of people with spectacular ability to do complex calculations almost instantaneously. Lozanov argues that the main inhibition to us all being able to do such things is our unwillingness to believe that we can. Even without going so far, it is clear that we have unused capacity to reach solutions by intuition rather than by procedures in which all the steps are conscious.

One way of 'forcing' such intuitive thinking is by giving pupils a difficult task within a ridiculously short time limit. Give them thirty seconds to write a poem, do a mathematical problem or compose a melody. Give a group three minutes to summarize the consequences of the Thirty Years War. This procedure not only energizes the class, it can also produce results of remarkable quality. Lozanov found in suggestopedic language teaching that if students were given the expectation that they would learn a hundred new words in a session they were unlikely to reach the target. If they were told that students usually learned a thousand words in the session their progress was often spectacular. If we ask students to do a difficult task in a time span which is slightly shorter than usual, they will attempt it by their usual mode of thinking. If we insist that they do it in a ridiculously brief time, their usual mode of thinking cannot cope with it. They are forced to reach a solution by another means.

Training children in intuitive thinking means teaching them to seek answers within themselves as an alternative to seeking them in external evidence. The psychosynthesis meditation on 'I know' will do something to teach this.[149] Some will perceive this meditation as a way of tapping into the collective unconscious for some transcendent unarticulated knowledge, but that is not the point here. It is enough to see it as a way of getting in touch directly with the products of subliminal perception and unconscious processing. Perkins, in his book *The Mind's Best Work*, discusses what he calls 'the art of introspection' and presents exercises designed to make the practice of introspection more skilful and more precise. The following exercise is worth trying in the classroom as a way of getting students to discover what they actually are thinking or feeling about a topic or experience at the present moment. The children can work in pairs, one being designated talker and the other listener. The talker talks according to the following rules. The listener listens without responding, except to intervene when the talker needs to be reminded of the rules.

> Say whatever's on your mind. Don't hold back hunches, guesses, wild ideas, images, intentions.
>
> Speak as continuously as possible. Say something at least once every five seconds, even if only 'I'm drawing a blank.'
>
> Speak audibly. Watch out for your voice dropping as you become involved.
>
> Speak as telegraphically as you please. Don't worry about complete sentences and eloquence.
>
> Don't overexplain or justify. Analyse no more than you would normally.
>
> Don't elaborate past events. Get into the pattern of saying what you're thinking now, not of thinking for a while, and then describing your thoughts.[150]

Training in intuitive thinking means more than simply encouraging guessing. It means taking the randomness out of guessing, helping students develop an awareness of the subtle physical sensations that accompany a 'good hunch'. In particular it means teaching students to value both the uncritical frame of mind in which illumination is possible and the critical frame of mind in which it must be evaluated.

VERIFICATION

In his presentation of brainstorming Osborn emphasizes the critical importance of separating the generation of new ideas from their evaluation. The evaluation session should take place some hours after the brainstorming. It is only then that we can step in with logic and commonsense to eliminate the absurd and unpractical. This is true not only for the products of 'cold' creativity, of which brainstorming is an example, but also for the products of 'hot' creativity like Wagner's *Das Rheingold*.

When Poincaré had his moment of illumination in the act of stepping on a bus, he felt such complete assurance that he did not even interrupt the conversation he was engaged in. Later, when he had a convenient opportunity, he verified the results 'for conscience sake'. He knew the process was not complete until he had done so. Like Wagner and Einstein, he had to translate his images into marks on paper which would be intelligible to others.

The unconscious is an inexhaustible source of content. Sometimes it comes into our awareness suddenly and unpredictably. Sometimes it comes by invitation. Whichever way it comes, it comes uncritically. The sudden illuminations of 'hot' creativity, in particular, are likely to come with a sense of certainty. Freud observed that there is no 'no' in primary process. The possibility of a critical 'no' does not exist until the contents emerge into awareness.

The mythology of the artist or creative thinker tends to overlook the significance of verification. Any teacher who has tried to teach 'creative writing' is likely to have come across students who believe that what emerges 'spontaneously' when they sit down to write is somehow sacred. They may be aware of Coleridge composing *Kubla Khan* while 'stoned' or of Van Gogh producing his sunflowers 'in a dream'. They ignore both the preparatory phase and the verification phase. Coleridge and Van Gogh spent years acquiring the skills and understanding manifested in any of their major works. Coleridge sweated over *Kubla Khan* until it had a form he could be content with; Van Gogh hated to let his paintings out of his hands because he was never satisfied that they were finished.

When Jung took to painting as a means of dealing with his inner conflict after his break with Freud, he found himself tempted to view his productions as great art, because to him the process of painting them in emotional intensity felt like great art. Fortunately he was clever enough to recognize what was happening to him – a phenomenon that he called 'inflation by the anima'. He took a cool, critical look at his masterpieces out of the heat of creation, and formed a more realistic assessment of their value. 'Inflation by the anima' may be an exhilarating experience, but it does not make for great art. Only the conscious and unconscious working in cooperation can produce a truly worthwhile creative product. That cooperation involves the conscious mind's ability to evaluate.

In discussing the functions of the psyche, Jung distinguishes between two 'judging' functions. He suggests that each person has a preference for one function over the other as a means of evaluating what is perceived through sensing or intuiting. The 'thinking' person asks questions like: 'Is it true?' 'Does it work?' 'Is it consistent?' 'Is it useful?' 'Does it make sense?' The 'feeling' person asks: 'Is it beautiful?' 'Do I like it?' 'Is it exciting?' 'Does it feel right?' Poincaré was inclined to evaluate mathematical concepts on the basis of their beauty. The inventor Tesla, by contrast, evaluated his ideas by their practical utility.[151]

Students are engaged not only in the verification of their own insights and creative products but also in judging the work of others. The way they are shown how to evaluate the work of others provides a model for their evaluation of what they produce themselves. It provides an opportunity to develop both their thinking function and their feeling function.

The schooling culture has a clear preference for the thinking function. Even in areas of curriculum where the feeling function has obvious relevance, as in the 'appreciation' of the great works of art, the accepted mode of evaluation is critical analysis. The use of the critical mode in evaluating aesthetic products is obviously important. Its monopoly of the process is disastrous.

For many people the feeling function plays a major part not only in evaluating music, painting and literature, but also in evaluating ideas. The feeling function serves them adequately in 'real life'. It is only in the classroom that it is neglected and devalued. It is not surprising that many of them have little energy for what they are asked to do in school.

There is no need to argue for or against the training of the thinking function. What has to be argued is the importance of allowing both functions to be exercised. This serves the needs not only of those for whom feeling is the 'natural' way of dealing with things, but also helps correct the imbalance in those whose thinking has developed at the expense of their feeling. For Jung, both functions are 'rational' (that is, they involve a consistent method of ordering things), both are legitimate, and both are liable to make mistakes. The teacher who calls attention to both kinds of criteria in evaluating ideas and images may do a great deal to help pupils learn how to choose confidently and well.

Learning to choose confidently and well by trusting their intuiting and their feeling may help fit students for many careers, as well as for fulfilling lives. However, it is less likely to fit them for getting the qualifications which lead to those careers. Many correct conclusions in business, medicine, research, interpersonal relations and everyday living are made intuitively and feelingly. However, it is often insufficient to say 'I know' or 'I understand'. One must also be able to explain 'rationally' how and why one knows or understands. One must be able to trace the knowledge back to the evidence. Poincaré went through this exercise 'for conscience' sake. We all must learn to do it if we wish to persuade others of the rightness of our conclusions.

The scientific method, which has been of such critical importance in our culture, is usually presented as hard-headed, critical-logical thought – pure secondary process. This is nonsense. There is a great deal of primary thinking involved: imaging, analogy, unconscious processing, hunches. Scientific thinking constantly swings between intuition and validation, between hypothesis and measurement. This blending of mind and matter, of the rational and irrational, is what Arieti calls the 'tertiary process', which is for him the basis of creativity.

> Instead of rejecting the primitive (or whatever is archaic, obsolete or off the beaten path) the creative mind integrates it with normal logical processes in what seems a 'magic' synthesis from which the new, the unexpected and the desirable emerge.[152]

It is only when the research report comes to be written that the scientist pretends that conclusions are reached carefully and logically only after the evidence is collected. The conventions of academic writing do not deal very easily with primitive notions like inspiration, except in the case of acknowledged genius. Gauss, who was notoriously careful to justify his mathematical insights logically before publishing them, admitted in a journal in 1886:

> Finally, two days ago, I succeeded, not on account of my painful efforts, but by the grace of God. Like a sudden flash of lightening, the riddle happened to be solved. I myself cannot say what was the conducting thread which connected what I previously knew with what made my success possible.[153]

Usually, scientists leave such accounts for their autobiography or relate them in their later years, from the security of an entrenched reputation. Creative artists, on the other hand, have often promoted the mythology of romantic inspiration, underestimating the logical component of the 'magic synthesis' which makes great art. The balance in this primary-secondary synthesis shifts according to the content, the cultural climate and the mode of expression, not to mention the personal obsessions of the artist. In the visual arts the product can emerge as image, without the added sophistication of verbal or numerical processing by which the writer and mathematician communicate their images. The judgement whether the painting is true, good and beautiful must largely be left to posterity.

FINDING AN AUTHENTIC RESPONSE

The evaluation, interpretation and appreciation of significant works of art and literature used to be thought an essential part of schooling. It still has some importance, though in many places relevance and accessibility seem to have displaced quality as criteria of significance. Be that as it may, the task of interpreting works of art is rightly seen as involving the use of analytical skills, and desirably helps children to develop them. But this is not all there is to it. For many students such analysis is an unnatural and uncomfortable way of confronting a work of art. They would learn to analyse more effectively if their need to respond intuitively and feelingly was first acknowledged and respected. Arieti suggests that interpretation is illumination in reverse. In producing the painting (or the poem or sonata) the artist gathered impressions both consciously and subliminally, processed them, often unconsciously, became aware of a vague feeling and the urge to communicate it through an image. The image eventually took a concrete form, after a major illumination or a series of minor ones. When we perceive the completed image it arouses in us a vague feeling that cannot be communicated directly. If the work is successful, our vague sense will approximate in some way to that of the artist. To communicate this to others we can trace it back to the artist's seed impressions, or we can allow our own symbols to emerge to express the meaning it has for us.

We can do this well or badly. To do this well we will have to become aware of fairly subtle signals in the response that our whole organism, not just our intellect, makes to the work of art. Such an awareness can be developed through a technique like experiential focusing.

This ability to detect our authentic response is critical to accurate intuition. Knowing what we really feel does not come too easily to us. Carl Rogers in his writings on therapy makes much of the concept of congruence, the match between what I say and what I do, between what I think and how I feel, between my words and my non-verbal expression. For instance, I believe that I like my job; my body knows that I don't. I believe that I am relaxed or content; my body knows I am tense or angry. If someone asks me how I feel, I reply in clichés and easy labels, because I have got used to a convenient way of identifying myself, because I have no skill in detecting and articulating my real feelings, or because I wish to avoid doing so. My body (my unconscious) has to symbolize what it knows through tension, sickness, emotional outbursts, irrational decisions, unpredictable and impulsive behaviour.

For Rogers, full 'organismic experiencing' is the only authentic way of responding to the world. This represents his perspective on growing up, the getting together of mind and body, conscious and unconscious, which Jung calls 'individuation', Maslow calls 'self-actualization' and Assagioli and Horney call 'self-realization.'

Full 'organismic experiencing' involves acknowledging our total experiencing of the world, including all the experience which is subliminal. We are directly aware of only a fraction of this experience. As for the rest of it, we can learn to detect the synthesis which our unconscious makes from all of these impressions: the endocept (Arieti), the vague, felt sense (Gendlin), our tacit knowledge (Polanyi), our somatic knowing (Egan) Teaching children to recognize what they really feel may be as essential a goal of education as teaching them to 'think' and teaching them the skills they need to act in the world. The evaluation of art and literature is presently the only place in the curriculum where teaching young people to discriminate between feelings has any legitimacy at all. Unfortunately the opportunity is often squandered through an obsession with critical analysis.

REMEDIAL VERIFICATION

It is a relatively simple matter for teachers to deal with the verification of ideas and the evaluation of art and literature. However, much of the verification in which teachers must intervene is remedial. It is unverified intuitive thinking which brings people to their self-evident truths. Socialization and enculturation depend on unconscious processing. The agents of propaganda (cultural, political and consumerist) deliberately use messages that avoid critical thinking and aim directly from image to conclusion. Racism, sexism and assorted other prejudices become established as 'truths' without being subject to any process of verification. They do, of course, have rationalizations whose faulty logic and blindness to the facts are obvious to all but the believer. Using the procedures of rational verification to point out errors in the evidence and inconsistencies in the argument has no affect at all on the true believer. When the leader of a religious cult announces with absolute certainty that the world will end on Tuesday, the faith of the disciples is in no way diminished by Wednesday's evidence that the world is still with us. Their faith may even be strengthened by the new demand on it. Critical and logical verification is likely to be just as unsuccessful when applied to racism, sexism, fundamentalist creationism and Darwinian economics.

Adolescents may happily engage in a critical evaluation of what seem to be the basic assumptions of our culture, yet become emotionally and dogmatically resistant to any challenge to some belief which from their teacher's perspective is pernicious, antisocial or simply stupid. The beliefs by which we identify ourselves tend to be non-negotiable.

If sweet reason fails, the attempt to displace one intuitively reached conclusion by another is just as difficult. Visual images, films and stories are effective in broadening the information on which intuitive conclusions are based, but they are not half as effective in modifying such conclusions once they are entrenched. Teachers in junior classes can have considerable impact on the development of attitudes. In the senior school they have more success in reinforcing the attitudes they share with their students than in demolishing attitudes which they consider wrong-headed.

Teachers are not usually inclined to see themselves as being in the business of personality change, yet change in any of the self-evident truths around which a student's identity is built involves just that. A change in one element of our self-identification upsets the whole jigsaw puzzle so that all the other pieces have to be reshaped and rearranged till the whole thing fits together again. An adequate treatment of the conditions for personality and attitude change would take us too far from our discussion of intuitive thinking. Nevertheless, such a study gives teachers some leads worth following.

For instance, we know that significant changes in people generally take place in the context of a supportive and trusting relationship. In the absence of such a relationship change is possible but often traumatic. We know that change in beliefs is often an intensely emotional experience. We know that for many, but not all, people the consensus of their peers is all-important in deciding what they believe. We know that beliefs and attitudes are largely role-bound. A person will act out of one belief in one role and out of a conflicting belief in another role, without noticing the inconsistency. We know that increasing pressure only increases resistance; the quicker way to change is to find a means to lower the resistance. A boy's sexist attitudes are only likely to be increased by vigorous arguments; it is more productive to look at the needs or fears that generate these attitudes and find a means to minimize them.

THE ESSENCE OF CREATIVITY

It is difficult to see the common ground between an adolescent acceptance of the ideology of Rambo and the creative intuitions of Einstein and Beethoven. Nevertheless, both depend on the more primitive mechanisms of the brain, which are in many respects more powerful and more generally useful than the more recently developed operations of secondary process. The unconscious, through the primary process, delivers messages which range from the gloriously transforming to the toxic and banal. Einstein and Beethoven knew how to 'gentle' the unconscious into delivering its product to a refined and skilful consciousness. As in Jung's active imagination 'the conscious and unconscious personality of the subject flow together into a product in which both are united'.[154] For Jung, as for Arieti, this union was the essence of creativity.

Whatever teachers do or say in class, their pupils are busy unconsciously processing the images they receive. 'Proper rational thinking' will go into idle often enough but the unconscious will continue its processing. Good teaching involves neither ignoring this unconscious activity nor in devaluing it in a pretence that only logical and sequential thinking can gain us understanding. Good teaching involves respecting both processes.

Poincaré and Wallas were thinking of exceptional creativity when they outlined the phases of the creative process: preparation, incubation, illumination, verification. I have suggested that this process is not confined to the spectacular insights of notoriously creative people, but is a natural way of learning which teachers ought to be aware of and exploit. We might go further and suggest that all cognitive learning is part of such a process, that learning is most effective where the process is completed and least effective where it is not, and that even learning which is anti-social or self-destructive goes through these same phases of what Wallas called the creative process.

The accumulation of bits of information has a place in this model. So has testing and repetitive practice. The accumulation of bits of information is not, however, the goal of teaching and learning; it plays an essential part in achieving a goal beyond itself. Teachers are well aware of the impossibility of imparting information to pupils for whom the information has no purpose. However, when the information-giving is part of a process which goes through insight and evaluation to a need-satisfying end teachers are able to stop inventing bribes and punishments to persuade their students to learn. What the students' end-goals are will vary immensely in specifics, but they can be generalized as making sense of the world and getting some power over it. They can be expressed more portentously as the creation of meaning.

We do not expect scientific theories to confirm myths, or vice versa. Yet when we look at the way Poincaré describes the operations of the psyche in the act of creation, and compare it with the way the Greek, Roman and renaissance psychologists expressed them poetically in the myth of Psyche and Eros, we find a remarkably similar picture.

Psyche yearns for marriage and prepares herself assiduously for it. She stands on the mountain-top, not knowing what god, or monster, or demon, or human is going to carry her off. In one version of the myth she is there by her own choice. In another she is placed there by her father on instructions from Apollo. In any case she is prepared.

The next phase of her learning takes place in darkness. She is in contact with the god but does not know it. She does not even try to find out who her lover is. She sleeps on it. Incubation.

Then, in the light of her lamp, she knows Eros. Yet this illumination is by its nature a momentary experience. She must go through the difficult and sometimes tedious process of discovering him again. Verification.

Much writing about insight takes a view that there are two distinct kinds of discovery, which we might call 'insight learning' and 'accumulative learning'. It makes more sense to see these as elements of a single process which is, unfortunately, often not completed. I am inclined to argue that the accumulation of facts gets its justification and direction from the insight that it prepares for, and that critical and enquiring thought is shaped and directed by what is already known intuitively at least at the endoceptual level. I would argue, furthermore, that information-gathering in some form is an essential prelude for insight, and that insight when it comes, is incomplete without analysis and testing.

One psychologist who understood this was George Kelly who, in his psychology of personal constructs, refers to what he calls the 'creativity cycle'.[155] His observations led him to conclude that our learning goes through two alternating phases. First, we accumulate bits of information which we try to make sense of by fitting them into some sort of pattern. Second, the bits of information that don't seem to fit frustrate us to the point where we have to let go of this pattern and (hopefully) set about constructing a new one which can accommodate them all. This leads us to accumulate more bits of information and the sequence of impasse, letting go and reconstructing is repeated. With an ear for jargon, Kelly called the two phases of the process 'accumulative fragmentalism' and 'constructive alternativism'. When Thomas Kuhn wrote *The Structure of Scientific Revolutions* he used basically the same idea to explain how scientific ideas change over the centuries.[156]

We can usefully see teaching as a continuing intervention in some such creativity cycle, in which the accumulation of information leads into an impasse and a consequent leap to insight (whether this insight is something that 'happens' to us or something we consciously create or construct) and then on to a testing and grounding in 'real life' which generates new questions and new information. We can blame the sterility of much teaching on the abortion of insight, through providing ready-made answers, and with it the abortion of meaning.

In out-of-school learning the process is permitted to work itself through. There is both random and purposive information-gathering, there is unconscious processing, understanding is accepted as it comes and is tested in experience. In school learning, however, the process is often thwarted by the needs and limitations of the teacher and the constraints of curriculum and timetable. Questions are answered which have never been asked; facts are divorced from meaning; accepting and repeating the solutions of others is rewarded; creating temporary approximate solutions is not.

This short circuiting of the process makes learning less effective than it ought to be. Moreover, if teaching is given over completely to information-giving and reflective analysis it may actually be frustrating specific biological needs.

THE RHYTHM OF LEARNING

Our patterns of sleeping and waking, our ninety-minute rest and activity cycle, our monthly mood cycles, our connectedness to the change of seasons, even our breathing in and breathing out, all reflect a pulsating organism, which alternates between two contrasting modalities: a passive-receptive-letting-go and an active-assertive-taking-hold. A yin and a yang. The phenomenon of alternating hemispheric dominance has been reported elsewhere in this book. It is worth referring to it again in the context of the suggestion that there is a natural learning cycle that is associated with biological rhythms. The cycle may be conceptualized in Wallas' language of the creative process: a movement from preparation to incubation to illumination to verification and back to preparation. Or as an alternation of right-brain, receptive, incubative, intuitive processes with the left-brain processes of information-collecting and critical analysis.

If we look at the evidence that the overriding of biological rhythms is harmful to health,[157] we are faced with the implication that teaching which directs children into unrelenting left-brain activity is actually harmful. A similar argument can obviously be made against a monopoly of right-brain functioning, but it is hardly necessary to argue it here. Good teachers know that learning calls on both sorts of function. They do not need to be informed by scientists that the twenty-five or so little organisms in front of them go into a 'dip' in the early afternoon, or that they have to vary their manner of teaching according to the fluctuating mental states of their pupils. However, it may be useful for them to consider the possibility that their pupils' switching on and switching off is not random, unpredictable and a frustration of their own best attempts to teach, but rather the reflection of biological rhythms which make the different capacities of the brain available in turn in a natural learning cycle.

There are a lot of gaps in our knowledge here. Researchers have not yet started looking at the implications of ultradian rhythms for education. However, even if it is too fanciful to imagine a schooling organized to take full advantage of these rhythms rather than working against them, we can at least imagine teachers being perceptive enough to notice when their students are moving into the slightly 'trancy' state which characterizes right-brain dominance, and having the flexibility to adjust their teaching methods accordingly. There have always been teachers who do this intuitively. There is enough information available now to enable us to do it rationally and systematically as well.

Truly efficient teaching demands the demolition of the superstition that there is a direct and simple relationship between the amount of time teachers spend dispensing information and answers and the amount their pupils learn. The psyche's modes of apprehending reality are subtle and complex, and a teaching which ignores them in Apollonic or Promethean arrogance is wasteful and ultimately harmful. Moreover, a teaching which ignores the evidence that many students actually have a strong preference for right-hemispheric modes of apprehension is oppressive. When we consider that such students are more likely to be girls we are confronted with the argument that schooling generates and reinforces toxic imbalances in the social organism.

For the psyche (as for Psyche), information is but a means to an end, and that end is the creation of meaning. If teachers wish to intervene in their pupils' creation of meaning they have to teach without the arrogant belief that it is what they tell their pupils that matters. In the creation of meaning their contribution may often be helpful, but it may be neither necessary nor sufficient.

NOTES Chapter 6. Catching the Light

[123] H. Poincaré, 'Mathematical Creation' in B. Ghiselin, *The Creative Process*, p. 25.
[124] ibid., p. 26.
[125] ibid.
[126] ibid.
[127] G. Wallas, *The Art of Thought*.
[128] Poincaré, op. cit., p. 27.
[129] ibid., p. 29.
[130] For further examples, see B. Ghiselin, op. cit.
[131] Cited in W. Harman and R. Rheingold, *Higher Creativity*, p. 32.
[132] Cited in P. Vernon, *Creativity: Selected Readings*.
[133] R. Kipling, *Something of Myself*, p. 262.

[134] Cited in A. Abell, *Talks with Great Composers*.
[135] See A. Green, 'Psychophysiology and Health: Personal and Transpersonal' in S. Grof, *Ancient Wisdom*.
[136] S. Arieti, *Creativity: The Magic Synthesis*.
[137] Cited in Arieti, op. cit., p.181.
[138] A. Einstein, 'Letter to Jaques Hadamard', in Ghiselin, op.cit., p. 32.
[139] See Chapter 4, above.
[140] See chapter 4, above.
[141] See O. Benfey, 'August Kekule and the Birth of the Structural Theory of Organic Chemistry in 1858', *Journal of Chemical Education*, 1958, 1, pp. 21-23.
[142] Cited in Harman, op. cit., p. 24.
[143] ibid., p. 17.
[144] ibid., p. 46.
[145] Geniuses are not exempted from going through the same process.

> When I have a model who is quiet and steady and with whom I am acquainted, then I draw repeatedly till there is one drawing that is different from the rest, which does not look like an ordinary study, but more typical and with more feeling ... How does it happen that I can express something of that kind? Because the thing has already taken form in my mind before I start on it. The first attempts are absolutely unbearable (Vincent Van Gogh, 'Letter to Ridder Van Rapport', cited in Ghiselin, op. cit., p.46).

> I keep the subject constantly before me and wait till the first glimmer of light begins to dawn slowly and gradually, and changes into full light and clarity (Isaac Newton, cited in P. Duhen, *The Aim and Structure of Physical Theory*, p. 256).

[146] A. F. Osborn, *Applied Imagination: Principles and Practice of Creative Problem-Solving*.
[147] T. Buzan, *Use Both Sides of Your Brain*, and G. Rico, *Writing in the Natural Way*.
[148] De Bono's theory and techniques are elaborated in a number of books. See *New Think*, *The Mechanism of Mind* and *Lateral Thinking*.
[149] See Chapter 4, above.
[150] D. N. Perkins, *The Mind's Best Work*, p. 33.
[151] Poincaré writes of the need for a 'sieve' to sort out good 'combinations' from bad. For him the sieve was an 'aesthetic sensibility'.

> Thus it is this special aesthetic sensibility which plays the role of the delicate sieve of which I spoke, and that sufficiently explains why the one lacking it will never be a real creator (Poincaré, op. cit, p. 29).

[152] Arieti, op. cit., p.13.
[153] Cited in J. Hadamard, *An Essay on the Psychology of Invention in the Mathematical Field*, p. 15.

[154] Cited in R. Papadopoulos and G. Saayman, *Jung in Modern Perspective*, p. 90.
[155] G. Kelly, *The Psychology of Personal Constructs*.
[156] T. Kuhn, *The Structure of Scientific Revolutions*.
[157] Tolaas comes to a similar conclusion by somewhat different arguments.

> In technological societies we may have been neglecting this 'inefficient' image-language until whole generations have come to suffer from the deficiency disease I have called metaphor blindness. The fact that dreaming is a universal phenomenon and an involuntary act points to its basic biological significance. Perhaps nature also wants us to 'stand and stare' and 'go off into a reverie' at certain intervals during the day because we need to probe into the invisible emotional field linking us to others (J. Tolass, 'Transformatory Framework: Pictorial to Verbal', in Wolman and Ullman, *Handbook*, p. 62).

7

THE SEARCH FOR SPONTANEITY

How can we know the dancer from the dance?

William Butler Yeats

JACOB MORENO GREW UP IN VIENNA at the time when Freud and his friends were engaged in the great work of uncovering the mysteries of the unconscious mind, when psychoanalysis was radical, controversial and subversive. As a young doctor he entered into the controversies with enthusiasm. But, though Freud's ideas were rich and exciting, Moreno, not being given to excessive modesty, preferred his own.

In personality, he could hardly have made a sharper contrast with Freud. Freud was a very proper gentleman. Moreno was manic, narcissistic, impulsive, exhibitionist. So was his psychology. Besides, psychoanalytic theory seemed to say that heroes and geniuses are neurotic or insane, and Moreno had a strong intuition that he was a hero and a genius.

> I wanted to show that here is a man who has all the signs of paranoia and megalomania, exhibitionism and social maladjustment, and who can still be fairly well controlled and healthy and, indeed, apparently of greater productivity by acting them out than if we would have tried to constrain his symptoms.[158]

Moreno saw himself as the protagonist in his own drama, like Oedipus or Medea or Herakles in Greek tragedy, playing a repertoire of roles and creating at each moment a world around himself through the roles he projected onto others. He disdained Freud's 'talking cure' and invented a form of therapy in which the patient could recreate the key moments in his or her personal drama and act them through again with an enriched awareness of their meaning. He called his therapy psychodrama.

Like Jung and Assagioli, Moreno was repelled by Freud's narrow image of the unconscious and by his narrow image of sanity. He did not share Freud's obsession with control and adjustment. His own obsession was with the uninhibited flow of experience, with the coming together of body, mind and emotions in spontaneous action. The energy of the unconscious was something to be expressed directly, not something to be repressed or sublimated. Freud, he sensed, wanted everyone to be the same; Moreno wanted everyone to be unique.

> Psychoanalysis – if one looks at it from a high, historical plane – is the vengeance of mediocrity. As everyone has complexes and as

creativity consists of complexes, every man is a genius. There are only geniuses.[159]

Moreno saw psychodrama as an extension of childhood play and play-acting. His recollections of his own dramatic play as a child were significant to him, as was his experience, as a boy of sixteen, of telling stories to children, and of finding how much more fun it was to help them act the stories out. His interest in healing was matched by his interest in theatre. He developed his psychodramatic techniques side by side with innovations in improvizational theatre. His work with professional actors and his therapy with disturbed adults fed into each other in a peculiarly productive way.

When Moreno first began to realize that his work in theatre had direct implications for therapy, he gave his attention to applying the techniques to his work with seriously disturbed patients. Nevertheless such is the flexibility of the psychodramatic approach that it was very quickly adapted to more broadly educational purposes. It is not uncommon now to find psychodramatic techniques in use in schools and preschools, by teachers who claim no competence as 'therapists' but who nevertheless find psychodramatic techniques a valuable means of assisting the learning and emotional growth of their students.

Psychodrama involves the 'acting out' of emotionally charged situations (real or imaginary) under the direction of a teacher or therapist, and with the involvement and assistance of a group of peers. Some writers insist on referring to all educational psychodrama as role-playing (perhaps to evade the charge that teachers might trespass on the territory of the psychotherapist), but there is little point in avoiding Moreno's original term. It adequately covers work with children who are emotionally disturbed, as well as children who are emotionally balanced, and dramatizations that demand either much or little emotional involvement. As long as children are acting out situations in which they have some personal, emotional involvement, they are engaged in psychodrama.

Moreno's writings may be sometimes confusing, but his techniques are simple enough to be learned by young children. They are also sophisticated enough to engage the attention of analytically minded adults. They do not depend on sharing Moreno's firm conviction that psychodrama can save the world.

It must be admitted that it is easier to demonstrate Moreno's ideas than to describe them adequately. The essential rules can be reduced to two: that the subject (patient, client, protagonist) acts out his or her conflicts instead of talking about them, and that the subject acts in the here and now. These essential rules are operationalized in a number of more or less standard forms and techniques.

The Director

This is the person who guides the psychodrama. The role demands a degree of confidence, authority, sensitivity and creativity, but neither mystical insight nor magical powers.

The Stage

This is the area set aside for the enactment. In 'classical' psychodrama, this is a tiered platform with spotlighting and such effects. In the classroom it is usually just a cleared space. Those who find a degree of ritual productive may have a square of carpet set aside for such occasions.

The Protagonist

This is the child who is the central actor in the psychodrama, and whose experiences (or conflicts, or problems) are to be acted out.

Director: Who's got a play for us today?

Billy: My dog went into Mrs David's place and he wouldn't come out, so I went in to get him. And Mrs David ...

Director: OK Billy. This can be Mrs David's place. How did you get in?

Billy: Through the gate.

Director: Well, then, show us the gate. (Billy indicates the gate and fence.) Now you can go in.

The Auxiliaries

These are members of the group who play minor parts in the psychodrama. In Moreno's theatre they are professionals. Here they are children chosen by the protagonist at the suggestion of the director.

Billy: Mrs David was cross because ...

Director: We need someone to be Mrs David. Who do you think, Billy?

The Search for Spontaneity

Billy: Janie.
Director: You try being Mrs David, Janie. (Janie takes up a position on 'stage'.) What does she say, Billy?

Role reversal

This is a technique by which the protagonist and auxiliary change roles. The protagonist may feel that the auxiliary is not playing the part accurately, and the director suggests the protagonist demonstrate it. Alternatively, the director may decide to use the technique because she feels that the protagonist could profit from seeing the situation from another point of view.

Janie (as Mrs David): You're a very naughty boy.
Billy: But she didn't say that.
Director: You try being Mrs David, Billy, and show us what she said. Janie, you be Billy. Go on, Billy, what did she say?

The Mirror Technique

This is a technique by which the protagonist sees his or her behaviour imitated by an auxiliary.

Billy: Yes, Mrs David. (He goes out and shuts the gate.)
Director: Will someone do what Billy just did? Sam?
(Sam repeats the performance, exaggerating Billy's look of defiance as he slams the gate.)
Director: Did Billy really look like that? ... What do you think, Billy?

Doubling

An auxiliary stands behind, or at the side of the protagonist and serves as an 'alter ego'.

(Billy slams the gate.)
Director (to group): How do you think Billy felt when he did that? (The children start to speak up.)
Director: Yvonne, you stand beside Billy, and when he slams the gate, you slam the gate and say what you think Billy wants to say, but doesn't.
(Billy and Yvonne slam the gate.)
Yvonne: I hate you and I wish you'd die!

The Empty Chair

The director places an empty chair on stage. She says that the chair represents Mrs David and invites the children to approach it and speak to it any way they wish. Out of this may come the opportunity for further exploration, perhaps through giving the children the opportunity to express their frustration at the unreasonable behaviour of adults.

INVOLVEMENT AND INSIGHT

It is unlikely that any teacher will need to, or want to, use all of these techniques in the same classroom psychodrama, unless, of course, the teacher is more concerned with demonstrating her own virtuosity than with serving the needs of the children. There is always this possibility, for while the protagonist's concern is the starting point of the psychodrama, its form and direction are very much the creation of the director. In the above episode the director has decided that the exploration of Billy's feelings, and the other children's sharing them, is likely to be productive. She could as easily have used the occasion to direct the children towards an understanding, or, at least, acceptance of Mrs David's horror of children and concern for her rose bushes; or, indeed, the teacher could have explored the children's relationships with their pets. In any case, while taking responsibility for directive decisions, she has to remember that the immediate aim is involvement and insight, not performance, and certainly not her own performance. The more skilful her direction the more control Billy will have over his drama.

Involvement is more important than either the quality of the production or the accuracy of the representation. There may be value on occasion in trying to determine 'what really happened'. For example, a conflict between two children can be re-enacted and explored through role reversal to identify its causes and perhaps to affect its consequences. Usually, however, it is the child's present perception of, and attitudes towards, an episode and the persons involved in it that are the stuff of the psychodrama. If these perceptions and attitudes change in the course of the enactment, the focus of the drama will shift with them. The incident is just a starting point. The point of the psychodrama is not to reproduce the incident but to explore the reactions, the feelings and the attitudes that are made concrete in this incident and which, it is assumed, the director, the actors and the audience have all at some time experienced.

The gap between Billy's drama and a serious therapeutic psychodrama with adults is not very wide. For children, an activity like this is very natural, not far removed from their spontaneous play. Moreno perceived that it was natural for adults, and adolescents also, that self-consciousness and inhibition about acting out are learned, and that the formal structures of psychodrama can give people permission to do something that they not only unconsciously yearn to do but actually have a psychological and maybe a biological need to do.

Although psychodrama began as a technique, it soon became a way of life for Moreno and his disciples. Moreno eventually offered it as a means of salvation for our universe:

> Psychodrama is a way to change the world in the HERE and NOW, using the fundamental rules of the imagination without falling into the abyss of illusion, hallucination or delusion ... By means of these methods a healthy person may live more efficiently, a sick person may learn to bear his misery, and the dead may continue to play a part in our lives. Fear is dispelled and human limitations are stretched. The astronaut becomes a psychonaut exploring the spaces of the mind.[160]

Most teachers who are using psychodramatic techniques with children have goals that are rather more modest than these. They believe that the education of children's emotions comes within their professional scope and competence. They further believe that children can be – and need to be – educated in an awareness of, and sensitivity to, their own and other's emotional and interpersonal processes. They find psychodrama a ready instrument for building a child's sense of worth and competence.

The theory of psychodrama developed by Moreno is an energetic and enthusiastic mixture of sociology, psychology, theology, anthropology, mythology and philosophy, as well as assorted ideas which defy classification. If genius is in our complexes, as Moreno claimed, it is not hard to see which complex was the source of his own. His preoccupation with both raw energy and high culture, his constant injunction to 'go with the flow', his charismatic personality, his paranoia, his brilliance, his craziness, his carelessness of logic, his religiosity, his tendency to confuse enthusiasm with truth, mark him as a devotee of Dionysos.

DIONYSOS

Where Apollo is light and clarity of thought, his brother Dionysos is darkness and intensity of feelings. The key images of his myth echo those of the Psyche story, but whereas Psyche is hated and persecuted by Aphrodite, Dionysos is hounded by Hera, Queen of the Gods. Hera manifests herself in a concern for social stability and harmony, and Dionysos is clearly subversive and not easily controlled. When he disguises himself as a man he is thrown into prison by the forces of law and order. He is full of contradictions. He is a young god and an old god. He is ecstasy, excess, intoxication and madness, a god of the present moment. Yet he is also a god of civilization. He is a vegetation god, the force which through the green fuse drives the flower, yet he was worshipped through one of the most complex and stylised expressions of European culture – the Greek theatre.

Moreno had a taste for big and unconventional ideas. Much of his writing concerns the clash between Dionysos and Hera, the conflict between spontaneity and what he called the cultural conserve. He pursued spontaneity with great enthusiasm, valuing it as the only truly god-like experience, yet he maintained that human beings as a species fear spontaneity and try to suppress it. We prefer the security of the cultural conserve – a term which includes the whole of our culture, all the fixed and stereotyped ways of perceiving and ways of behaving, all works of art and social structures, which are actually the dead residues of moments of spontaneity.

Moreno discovered in his Theatre of Spontaneity that a spontaneous act is a political act. His experience in Vienna in the 1920s persuaded him that the destiny of humankind depends on the successful unfolding of our relationship to spontaneity. He discovered also that it was a healing act and he invented specific techniques by which he could, in full awareness of the paradox, 'train spontaneity'.

Moreno set out to transform the world by teaching people to respond to each situation in their lives in a manner that is immediate and appropriate. He was persuaded that most of our behaviour is fixated or 'conserved', that we are stuck in frozen patterns of behaviour that we have learned in other contexts and which only occasionally fit the present moment. Much of our anxiety comes from our murky awareness that there is a tension between the needs of the situation we are in and the fixated behaviour with which we respond to it. There is in us the constant but unacknowledged pressure of contained energy, wanting to bubble up in truly spontaneous activity, if only we will raise the lid. Moreno believed that if only we can be taught to give up the security of our frozen roles we will feel our energy flowing out into behaviour which is new and adaptable and creative.

Drama and psychodrama break down conserved behaviour by putting actors and students into roles which go counter to their self-image, enabling them to discover in these roles the parts of themselves which they have disowned and projected on to others. In therapeutic psychodrama the director often encourages the patient to regress to a child-state so that she can relive a scene from childhood in which a particular attitude and pattern of behaviour was frozen. In reliving the event as a child, with roles unfrozen and with her adult understanding and experience available to her, she can make the choices that will unfreeze her adult behaviour. For Moreno, childhood represents the flow of energy uninhibited by the expectations and limitations of the culture, and the function of psychodrama is to take us back to a child-state so that we can carry the aliveness of childhood into our adult life. There is here an idea of childhood as a state of natural wisdom in which the world is experienced directly and freshly and action is not contaminated by the cultural conserve of roles and taboos. Moreno's fantasy of the Kingdom is entered only by those who become as little children, who die a sort of a death in psychodrama and are born anew. This central image of the child in his psychology and his technique points directly at the myth of Dionysos, the Divine Child.

THE DIVINE CHILD

Keith Johnstone, whose brilliant book *Impro*, while ostensibly concerned with the training of actors, is full of insights and techniques that can transform any kind of teaching, also writes in Dionysos language.[161] In 'Notes on Myself' he talks about his own pursuit of spontaneity. Like Moreno he found it in training actors to be spontaneous, but in the meantime he became convinced that 'most people lose their talent at puberty' and 'began to think of children not as immature adults but of adults as atrophied children'.[162] So, like Moreno, he teaches adults to play games again, to wear strange faces and unaccustomed roles, to stop being clever and original and to trust what comes when habitual roles are disrupted. What comes may be comic or romantic or tragic but, if it is really allowed to flow, it is never trivial.

It ought not be necessary to teach children and adolescents to be children again, but for some children and most adolescents schooling puts a considerable distance between them and the spontaneous play that is their natural way of relating to the world. Besides, many teenagers live in a prison of other people's expectations, their behaviour is every moment shaped (willingly or resentfully) by their fantasies of what peers, school, parents and the larger society demand of them. A Dionysian schooling would not only keep the child alive in them, but nourish it through play, dance and drama; conventional schooling seems more intent on killing it.

Dionysos was for the Greeks a god of ecstasy, a god of emotional release, whose presence could be sought in alcohol or dancing, but he was above all a god of civilization, of emotional release crafted with intelligence and sensitivity into a work of art which would engage and entrance and transport an audience.

The enduring link between Dionysos and the theatre is more than a literary convention. The Greeks thought it perfectly natural that a god who personified the animal flow of life should be celebrated through the formal archetypal dramas of the tragedians as well as the subversive energy of the comedians. It is more than a convention that the word 'play' (a superlatively Dionysian activity) should be applied to the most serious of dramas. The notion of 'play', the experience of 'flow', the romanticization of childhood, the masks and roles and scripts of the theatre, the phenomenon of charisma, the multiplicity of personality, seem to have little logical connection. Yet we find them linked again and again in writings on the theatre, in the enactments of psychodrama, in the lives and

The Search for Spontaneity

personalities of Moreno and of countless stars of stage and screen, and, most especially, in the myth of Dionysos.

Looking at Moreno's own personality, it is tempting to suggest that his obsession with spontaneity came from his own difficulty in being spontaneous. Many people spend their lives trying to extend those magic moments when they feel the Dionysian 'flow', when body and intellect and emotions seem to be one and the boundary between self and the rest of the universe seems to have dissolved. Such moments can be found in surfing or skiing or singing or making love or looking at a work of art. There are even magic moments in teaching when everything comes together, spontaneously and perfectly. The flow is difficult to describe and impossible to engineer, but we know when we are experiencing it. Being something of an adrenalin junkie, Moreno sought it in moments of excitement. He could well have devoted his life to climbing dangerous mountains or jumping out of aeroplanes. Instead, he got his high from being on centre stage, with no script and no resources but what he found within himself, and the challenge of finding the flow not only within himself but also in the sometimes frightened and inarticulate patient who was working with him.

WARMING UP

While Moreno could not turn his spontaneity on at will, he discovered that he could create conditions in which he was more likely to find it. He found he could 'warm himself up' to spontaneity. What worked for him he made into an essential part of the psychodramatic method, which he called the warm-up. He had found, like Coué and Lozanov, that the success of any learning experience depends largely on the presence of a mental set. However, where Coué and Lozanov were interested in establishing a set of appropriate expectations that would make their clients or students more receptive to suggestion, Moreno wanted to establish an emotional and intellectual readiness for action.

Preparation for classroom psychodrama, then, involves the development of an environment in which the children feel comfortable enough with each other and the teacher to act spontaneously and naturally. Beyond this, the immediate warm-up for a class is goal-oriented and specific. If the teacher wishes to explore a particular issue or event psychodramatically, she can warm the class to the topic through story, information or questions. If she is really clever, she may be able to find in the students' intellectual and emotional residue from their preceding activity (a rest break, another lesson) a pointer to the issue she wishes to deal with. We can make a distinction between warming a class up to content and warming them up to an activity or a particular way of teaching. Children can be warmed up to doing something exciting, something collaborative, something imaginative, something introspective, something challenging. Most successful teachers do this sort of thing naturally and intuitively and only become aware of the process when they unexpectedly encounter resistance and realize that they have tried to lead their class into an activity without warming them up first.[163]

The various ends of warm-up can be met by such means as having a picture or object in the classroom that will provide a focus for the children's attention, a brief discussion in which questions are raised or experiences shared, a few minutes of meditation or at least of silence after a direct or indirect reference to the topic, a game of some kind. When Lozanov describes the state of mind he wants his students to have if they are to get the full benefits of the suggestopedic method, he uses the word 'infantilism'. The word is not very satisfactory, but the meaning is clear enough. He wants his students in a state of mind in which they are childlike, that is, receptive, alive, uninhibited, ready for anything, imaginative. He wants to get them out of their 'grown-up' frame of mind in which they know their limitations and have set ideas on how they can learn and how teachers should behave. Infantilism is a state of mind we sometimes arrive at through enjoying a game. Many teachers know the benefits of starting or interrupting a class with an absurdly infantile game which leaves the children (or adolescents, or adults) laughing, alert and receptive, temporarily freed from the prison of their inhibitions and ready to deal with anything.

Whereas the psychotherapist using psychodramatic techniques may actually use the context and the warm-up to generate anxiety – on the grounds that the anxious protagonist will be less controlled and less inhibited by rationality, and will be consequently more likely to achieve a catharsis – the teacher will aim at reducing anxiety and encouraging the kind of spontaneity that comes from being at ease with oneself and one's surroundings. For Moreno, psychodrama is basically a cathartic process, in which the individual 'exhales' problems through the reliving of past experiences, or the acting out of a desire or fear. Teachers using the same basic techniques can give the psychodrama a play orientation or perhaps a problem-solving orientation. In neither case will catharsis be a very significant element.

This is not to say that psychodramatic techniques used with education rather than therapy in mind will not generate strong emotions. Any form of drama, scripted or improvised, can do that as the actors find themselves confronting their own conscious and unconscious roles, and the audience identifies with them. Neither is it to say that strong emotions do not have a place in education. For Moreno, or anyone who adopts the Dionysian viewpoint, the expression of intense feelings, including painful ones, is a superlatively healthy activity, but this viewpoint is not widely shared in the schooling system. It is, of course, possible to envision a schooling based entirely on a Dionysian understanding of the world. Rousseau's vision of education comes from such an understanding. But such a vision, in which the emotions are cultivated and their artistic expression highly valued, sits rather uncomfortably in a culture like our own which actually seems to be afraid of intense emotional expression. There are certainly situations in which the release of intense emotions is tolerated but the classroom is not generally one of them, certainly not when the emotions are generated by teachers 'messing about with people's minds'.

CLASSROOM AS THEATRE

Moreno's impromptu theatre began with actors playing out not their personal conflicts but contemporary political events. It was when Moreno pushed them to explore the depth in these events that they found they were exploring the depth in themselves.

Psychodrama in the classroom will often start, like Moreno's theatre, with the exploration of a designated issue, event or idea. Whether this exploration remains mainly in the universe of ideas or moves deep into the universe of feelings depends on the skills of the teacher-director, and on the particular techniques she uses. More than either, it depends on the needs of the students and their readiness to deal with them.

A teacher taking a social studies class and wishing to deal with the topic of (say) discrimination may start by trying to find a contact point in the children's own experience. A useful warm-up might be to have the children, in small groups, telling each other stories about times when they have felt or witnessed discrimination. (There may be some resistance to simply telling stories instead of doing real school work like discussing and giving opinions, but it is worth the trouble to keep reminding them not to do these things but to confine themselves to telling stories.) Then the teacher can call on a volunteer to act out the scene she has described, while the members of her group assist by playing the other roles. A number of such scenes can be played to provide the stuff on which the subsequent discussion can build, or the teacher can use some of the psychodramatic techniques to expand one of these episodes into a major drama.

In psychodrama proper, the protagonist provides the script for all the characters in her story.

> *Rebecca* (ignored at checkout counter): Could you please ... (pause)
> *Teacher-Director*: Reverse roles.
> *Rebecca* (as cashier): Wait your turn, you little tart!

The teacher now directs Robin (Rebecca's chosen auxiliary) to take over the role of cashier and repeat Rebecca's response, and the drama then proceeds with Rebecca reversing roles with the cashier to provide each new line of script.

For Moreno, the most important work in psychodrama is done through the experience of what he calls 'surplus reality', that is, the levels of reality that were not in Rebecca's consciousness during the original event. For example, she might explore 'What if?' fantasies, try out different ways of behaving, or explore feelings she did not acknowledge at the time but which emerge in her re-living of the event. The most significant aspects of this surplus reality are likely to be found in the role reversals with other characters, as Rebecca imagines what they were thinking or feeling about her. One of the simplest and most productive ways of exploring the event and the issue is through interviewing Rebecca in the role of the cashier and other characters in her story.

Teacher (directly to Rebecca as cashier): Why are you ignoring the girl?
Rebecca (as cashier): What does she expect if she comes in here dressed like that?
Teacher: What's wrong with it?

Psychodrama is not usually concerned with re-enacting events with objective accuracy. All we can know is Rebecca's perception at this moment of what happened some weeks ago. We do not have the cashier present; we only know the thoughts and feelings that Rebecca projects on to him. Psychodrama will intensify and expand Rebecca's perception of the incident by engaging her in the exploration of surplus reality. Yet here we encounter the paradox that the more deeply and uninhibitedly she explores and the more uniquely personal her feelings and their expression are, the closer she comes to what is universally human and the more her audience identifies with and shares her emotion and insight. However, for all its demonstrated value, this is unlikely to be the regular mode of dramatising personal and social issues in the regular classroom. Quite apart from the institutional pressures that make it difficult to find a suitable context and environment, there are skills involved which, while not magic or mystical, are not learned in a hurry and not readily learned out of books.

It is often easier and more appropriate to play the scene with the protagonist as witness and commentator. Rebecca does not star in her drama but directs a group of her classmates in a performance of the incident for the rest of the class. Alternatively, the enactment is developed sociodramatically, taking Rebecca's incident as a starting point and developing it as a dramatization of the way some adults discriminate against some teenagers. The same psychodramatic techniques can be used (doubling of roles, role reversal, interviewing, soliloquies, asides, mirroring) to develop the sub-text of the drama. Sociodrama does not need a protagonist; all roles can take on a life of their own as different children take turns to play them, and,

Educating Psyche

as each view of the situation and the world is developed in its own right, the children discover that they know far more about the way society works than they have ever managed to put into words.

A step further from classical psychodrama is playback.[164] Rebecca tells her story and a group of students immediately act it out, without rehearsal and after only a few moments of preparation. If Rebecca finds that the performance does not give an accurate picture of her experience she can explain what is lacking and the actors can repeat the performance. Playback is an ideal instrument for developing intuition and spontaneity while focusing on a task.

Or the teacher can set aside psychodramatic techniques altogether and present the first two lines of the exchange between Rebecca and the cashier and an unfinished script, asking the students in pairs to play it through to a conclusion.

Teachers of drama obviously have a lot more opportunity to use such techniques to explore whatever theme they will. Likewise, primary teachers seem to have more opportunity and flexibility of role than secondary teachers, though they don't always take advantage of it. Yet even in the content-dominated high school classroom there is plenty of room for dramatic and psychodramatic techniques.

There is no question of the effectiveness of such techniques in dealing with the content of school-learning. We know enough about how our brains work to explain the efficacy of a technique which turns abstract notions into concrete challenges, which involves purposeful activity, which deals with issues from the inside rather than the outside, which engages the senses and the emotions, which calls on right-brain as well as left-brain functions, which allows non-verbal expression of endoceptual knowledge, which needs no extrinsic motivation, which unites understanding and action. It is not the problem of efficacy that bars drama from most history and science classrooms. It is the problem of imagination and the problem of enjoyment. It is lack of imagination that limits teachers' visions of who they are and what teaching can be. It is the presence of enjoyment that makes dramatic methods suspect.

The Search for Spontaneity

TEACHING AS ADVENTURE

There is a deep and widespread prejudice against schoolwork being too enjoyable. Work and play have been seen as opposites for so long in our culture that classrooms where the students are obviously enjoying themselves are widely assumed to be classrooms where no work is being done. Yet we readily accept that the surgeons, the actors, the financiers, the filmmakers, the farmers (and the teachers) who really get a 'kick' out of their work, who get completely lost in it during magic moments of 'flow', can find this enjoyment through calling on all of their resources to meet a challenging task, through responding to pressure by performing at their peak, through putting all their energies into the task for the reward of doing it well, and forgetting for the time being the money or status that might be attached to it. Mihaly Czikszentmihalyi, who investigated the experience of enjoyment in a variety of occupations, suggests that anything (including schooling) can be made enjoyable as long as certain structural conditions are observed.

> If educators were to start with the questions 'How can learning be made more enjoyable?' the students' gains in performance should increase tremendously. It is crucial to remember, however, that one does not make learning enjoyable by trivialising it – by making it easy, or pleasant, or 'fun'. The hardships and dangers of rock climbing are probably a better model for enjoyment in learning than the gussied-up educational techniques based on a hedonistic escapist notion of what enjoyment is.[165]

For Czikszentmihalyi, the 'flow' comes when the challenge of the task is matched by the skills we bring to it. The rock climber stuck on a rock-face which is far beyond her skill experiences not exhilaration but anxiety. The same climber on too easy a rock-face experiences not enjoyment but boredom. If she wants to experience enjoyment she can do so by making the task more difficult (for example, by climbing with one hand or blindfolded) or she can try to do it more simply and elegantly, or she can find enjoyment in things other than the task – the scenery or the presence of her companions.

While good teachers do not need to be told that the same principle applies to the child learning to operate a computer or write an essay, they may be less likely to reflect on how it applies to their own teaching. The schooling system is full of bored and anxious teachers: anxious teachers who cannot find in themselves the resources to cope with an overwhelming task; bored teachers who have spent years repeating the same lessons to (it seems) the same students. Anxiety can become completely crippling or it can turn into excitement if the teacher becomes aware of untapped skills, gains new ones, or learns to see the task in a different way. Boredom can turn to excitement too if the vision of the task is expanded or new challenges invented. Unfortunately boredom is not so strong a stimulus to change as anxiety is. Many teachers are content to accept boredom as a way of life, to measure out their teaching career in coffee spoons. Unfortunately they inflict the same blight on their students.

Moreno sought 'the flow' with enthusiasm, and by inventing psychodrama he constructed for himself a career in which his skills always faced a challenge which extended them to the full. Though common themes emerge again and again in psychodrama, no moment of any person's experience is repeatable, and the dramatic and purposive expansion of that moment calls on all the skill and elegance the psychodramatist can command.

Milton Erickson enjoyed immensely his work as a therapist and made major contributions to theory and technique. However, those who wanted to catalogue his techniques found that he constantly lost interest in them and set about finding a new, better, simpler, more beautiful way of solving that problem. Carl Rogers developed a technique he called 'client-centred therapy', then had to spend the rest of his life explaining that it was not really a technique at all. What worked in his therapy was being truly present to the client in this moment of dialogue, responding to all of the client's being with all of his own, without a role, a technique, a script or an expectation of what ought to happen.

The three therapies have considerable contrasts between them, but they all have a touch of Dionysos. They seek the newness of experience, and they begin their impact through the therapist's own way of being. The therapist helps the client to 'spontaneity' or 'organismic experiencing' or 'congruence' through pursuing this experience for himself.

The Search for Spontaneity

If we shift our focus from therapy to teaching we see the Dionysian teacher who asks not only, 'How can I make this learning enjoyable for the students?' but also, 'How can I teach this lesson in a way which is an adventure for me? How can I engage in this topic in a way which calls on all of my imagination, skills, and quick-wittedness, as well as those of my students? How can I craft this lesson into an original work of art? How can I be with my students so completely in this lesson that we really experience something new together?'

Magic moments don't last forever, even for spontaneity addicts like Moreno. Dionysos comes and goes. In his myth he suddenly enters the lives of men and women, drives them into a divine frenzy, then just as suddenly disappears and leaves them floundering.

The Greek tragedies warn us of the perils of worshipping a single god too obsessively. When that god is Dionysos, we may find not only spontaneity, creativity, flexibility, vitality, civilization and the joy of performing, but also self-obsession, uncontrolled emotionality, paranoia, narcissism and a craving for adulation. Dionysos has his own pathology no less than Apollo and Prometheus.

Dionysos has always been under attack from the forces of respectability. Teachers whose work bears the Dionysian stamp are bound to be thought a bit disreputable. This goes without saying for art, drama and dance teachers, but they are not taken very seriously in any case. It is likely to apply to any teachers who meddle with the conventions of mainstream teaching. Either they are supposed to be indulging their pupils in some touchy-feely orgiastic experience or they are trivializing the curriculum through games and play-acting. Their pupils are even alleged to be having 'fun'. Actually, the Dionysian teacher may get some satisfaction out of being marginalized or persecuted. Paranoia belongs to the complex. Dionysos-figures in our culture – Jesus, Moreno, the leaders of religious cults – have always been persecuted.

There is no denying that a good deal of trivialization goes on in classrooms. Much of it occurs in the standard lesson of the bored and boring teacher, who can reduce an event of immense passions and massive significance, such as the French Revolution, to a list of dates, a list of causes and a list of consequences. It is certainly not trivialization to invite the children to enter the event and experience some of those passions and sense some of that significance by following Moreno's psychodramatic rules: *Do it, don't talk about it*, and *Do it in present time*.

A DRAMATIC CURRICULUM

In the lesson on the French Revolution and the Terror a student may take on the role of Marie Antoinette in her attempted flight from France while the rest of the class interviews her, asking her not only about the 'facts' but also about her hopes, fears and fantasies; or rather than designate a single student to take the role, the teacher may place an empty chair facing the class and the students address their questions to the chair, then take turns to sit in the chair to answer them; or she places two chairs face to face to represent the conflict between Robespierre and Danton and the students take turns to sit in the chairs and argue the points of view they represent; or the whole class take on roles to enact the whole complex event from start to finish.

The English lesson involves the class in interviewing the author of a novel, or one of its characters. The role may be played by one student, or by several in sequence, or by several simultaneously, who are free to give conflicting answers to the same question. Or the students use the empty chair technique, asking Anna Karenina why she is unhappy, reversing roles with her to answer their own question, reversing again to continue the interview. Or the teacher introduces the study of a novel by dividing the class into groups and giving each group a couple of photocopied pages to dramatize without prior knowledge and without context. At the end of these dramatizations (which can be amplified through doubling and interviews) the students are ready to read the novel with curiosity, attention and perhaps some sense of what the novelist's craft involves.

The social studies or science teacher introduces a new topic or recapitulates an old one by designating a key word and asking the children in small groups to mime its meaning. The mimed understandings of osmosis, nationalism, erosion, photosynthesis, multiculturalism or reproduction will provide a substantial basis for discussion. Apart from the obvious desirabil-

The Search for Spontaneity

ity of finding out what the students know and how they perceive the topic, and the value of presenting the children with a task which requires them to share their knowledge with each other, the mime enables them to express at a pre-verbal level what is known endoceptually. This visual and kinesthetic expression of what is vaguely known is sometimes a necessary step towards the kind of verbalized knowledge which is the only form of knowledge with any standing in conventional schooling. If, at the other end of the lesson, mime is used as a way of closing discussion of a topic it is a step towards the efficient storage of that information as image as well as word.

In the language class the students can learn the way infants do, using their new language in situations where they have something to communicate and some need to be understood. The teacher expands the world of the classroom through fantasy and role play and thus extends the range of situations in which the students' ideas and feelings demand accurate expression. She warms her students up to using language the way infants do, without inhibition, self-consciousness or the fear of making mistakes. She helps them to shift the identity away from the role of one who is struggling with an alien language to the role of one for whom it is a natural means of expression.

The mathematics teacher enriches the children's imagination with stories of how the great mathematicians struggled to find a language to describe the universe, and gets them to identify with our civilization's virtuoso problem-solvers. It could be the sixteen-year-old Einstein trying to visualize the face of a clock in a spaceship speeding away from earth at the speed of light, or the six-year-old Gauss asked by his teacher for the sum of $1 + 2 + 3 \ldots + 10$ and giving the answer instantly, or Archimedes watching the water lap over the sides of his bath as he wonders how to calculate whether the tyrant's supposed gold crown is really made of gold, or the ancient Polynesian who laid the foundations of trigonometry as he (or she) sat in the stem of a canoe toying with the idea that maybe from this particular position on the boat the top of the mast would be in line with that particular star at this particular time of morning only at this particular spot where the fish were biting. Through role play she can place her students in situations where it matters desperately that a solution be found or that a calculation be accurate. Or through games she can teach them how to learn in a state of serious playfulness, instead of the states of indifference or tension which make learning next to impossible.

SERIOUS PLAYFULNESS

Dionysos, the god of playfulness, is also the only god who is able to suffer like humans. When the Titans or Giants went to war with the gods to win the world for uncontrollable power, arrogance and violence, they captured Dionysos and tore him to pieces.[166] Zeus struck them with his thunderbolts and reduced them to ashes. It was from these ashes, mingled with the blood of Dionysos, that humanity was born, always in balance between a capacity for Titanic destruction and a capacity for Dionysian creation. It is the blood of Dionysos which keeps us from mindless violence, and it is in the godlike activity of play that the god's presence is most deeply felt, and in which we find the answer to our basic question: 'How shall I live?'

> Human play, especially tragic drama, is ... a way of facing finiteness without neurotic repression of losing your life in imagination in order to retain it longer in reality, and of studying the consequences of moral choices in dramatic simulation. Hence, when the real crisis comes you are inured not to scientific dispassion but to the emotional resilience and moral courage demanded by life.[167]

Dionysos is a god of the Now, of the felt truth of the present moment. He is a god who is constantly born anew. He is also a god of fragmentation and integration. His myth is full of images of dismemberment; the god himself, wild animals, his persecutors are torn limb from limb. It is also full of images of disguise, of ambiguous identity, of masks, of changing shapes and symbols. In Greece he had many names and was worshipped in many forms. It is not surprising that the craft specifically under his patronage is the craft of acting. It is not surprising either that the other side of Moreno's fascination with spontaneity is his fascination with role.

ROLE

For Moreno, role was all powerful. As a matter of fact, as far as personality structure is concerned, he saw nothing else. We are inclined to think of ourselves in terms of an ego surrounded by a number of roles into which we can more or less comfortably fit. Moreno would have none of this nonsense. What we may call our ego is merely one of our roles with which we particularly identify. Our ability to move freely and fluidly through many roles is a measure of our psychological health.

In Moreno's personality theory, there is no question of a specific ego or self acting through various roles. The roles come first. We exist as persons only in our relationships, real and imagined. Roles do not emerge from the self; a sense of self emerges from our roles. The image of a god being torn apart and put together again may appear grotesque to us, but the psychological meaning of the metaphor is fairly accessible. Our sense of who we are goes in a cycle from unity to multiplicity and back again. We become what we are capable of being only by periodically dissolving the glue that binds our parts in a single 'personality', so that we can achieve a higher integration that the next creative crisis or challenge can dissolve.

Assagioli, whose introversion contrasts with Moreno's extroversion and whose concerns and methods were different in many respects from Moreno's, comes to a similar view of personality. For him the self or 'I' is a point of pure consciousness, without content. We mistakenly give it content by identifying with a particular role or (to use Assagioli's term) a particular sub-personality.

When Moreno and Assagioli use these terms they are not just referring to ways of acting. Each of these roles (sub-personalities) is indeed expressed in its own peculiar ways of acting but it also has its own set of values and attitudes, its own self-image, its own peculiar ways of thinking and feeling. Each is fairly autonomous. What we believe and say in one role may be quite different from what we believe and say in another.

Some people identify so completely with a particular sub-personality that they are stuck in it. We are all familiar with the teacher, doctor, parent or administrator who cannot stop being a teacher, doctor, parent or administrator even with people and in situations where it is clearly inappropriate.

On the other hand, some of us can shift our identification among a number of roles. We have all experienced how, for example, we are different when we are with our parents from when we are with our own children and different again when we are with our students or colleagues. When people shift their identifications in this way, they are often reacting to the demands of the situation they are in. They are drawn, largely unaware, into the role that is expected of them. This reactive shifting of roles seems to be an advance on obsessive identification with a single role. At least it makes social functioning possible.

From this viewpoint (which in the language of archetypal psychology might be called the viewpoint of Hera, goddess of sociology), roles are unavoidable, essential to our proper functioning. From the viewpoint of Moreno (and Dionysos), our habitual roles are a prison. This tendency of ours to have a situation control our behaviour, to write scripts for ourselves or borrow them from others and then follow them slavishly, to imitate ourselves and imitate others, is something from which we must be freed. Our godlikeness is in our spontaneity, and spontaneity involves doing something new and is always opposed to the cultural conserve.

In a therapeutic psychodrama, the protagonist is commonly struck by the insight that in this situation X he is following a script that he learned long ago in situation A. He may set out to explore a present situation in which he feels anxious or uncomfortable and find himself re-enacting a long-forgotten episode in which he made decisions and established patterns of behaviour which have remained with him all his life. With the help of a skilled director he may be able to move through this insight and the emotional release that comes with it to a point where he is able to act freely, spontaneously and appropriately in the situation which has aroused his anxiety, without being constrained by any 'mind-forged manacles'.

Of course, spontaneous expression can easily be petrified and perpetuated in a role. For Moreno all roles, not just destructive ones, are part of the cultural conserve, in much the same way as *Guernica* and *The Trojan Women* are part of the cultural conserve. Though they came to us from Picasso and Euripides through the crafting of a spontaneous expression, generated by deep passion in an intensely experienced moment in history, they remain with us as objects. They are powerful objects indeed, capable of forming our understanding of war and influencing every subsequent artist's attempt to deal with the subject, but they are only objects nonetheless. It was the act of genius which fascinated Moreno, not the artefacts of genius. No matter how wonderful a painting is, the artist who imitates it, consciously or unconsciously, is avoiding his or her own genius. No matter how good and useful a particular role may be, the person who stays within its limits is extinguishing the same spark.

Assagioli was not inclined to romanticize craziness and deviance the way Moreno did, but in his explanation of how self-realization is related to role-taking he comes very close to Moreno's ideas. In Assagioli's thinking, there are four levels on the way from neurosis to self-realization:

1. Rigid identification with a particular sub-personality.
2. Reactive identification with different sub-personalities according to the situation.
3. Ability to choose and shift identification.
4. Identification with the I, the true centre of awareness, which allows for the full and spontaneous expression of the whole range of our possibilities.[168]

While the occasional crisis will throw us back to rigid behaviour (level one), and while there will be times when we are totally 'free' and 'whole' (level four), most of us seem to maintain ourselves between levels two and three.

Sometimes a principal's, colleague's or student's behaviour will draw us reactively into a particular role. We suddenly switch to whatever sub-personality this behaviour hooks onto – defiant child, or mother hen, or martyr, or bully. On the other hand we may notice what is happening, even recognize a recurring pattern, and make a conscious decision that this time we will not take the hook, choosing instead to act through a different sub-personality – reasonable adult, for instance, or laid-back cynic. The difference between two and three is in the locus of control – whether we control the role or the role controls us.

SURPLUS REALITY

One way in which Moreno freed his actors from the prison of their roles was to push them into surplus reality. As long as we can keep playing a role with which we easily identify we cannot be truly ourselves. We know the script so well that we do not even recognize that we are playing a role. Our persona – our posture, our dress, our speech patterns, our beliefs, our attitudes, our gestures, our words and ideas – is entirely borrowed from others, yet we take all this borrowed stuff and call it 'I'. When pushed in psychodrama into taking on the role of an antagonist, or playing a past scene which never happened or a future scene which never will, we may be left without a script to follow and forced to find a way to respond spontaneously. The pretence that we are someone or somewhere or some time else relieves us of the need to maintain our public face and enables us to discover whatever we are in this moment. In this discovery are all the possibilities which our narrow self-image denies us.

Assagioli states as an axiom that we can control whatever we can disidentify from. The teacher who says: 'I am the kind of person who ... 'is controlled by that particular image and that sub-personality. The teacher who can disidentify from this sub-personality (who can say, 'I have this role available ... and this other ... and this other') is in control, to a much greater extent, of her behaviour.

When the teacher/psychodramatist suggests to Rebecca that she reverse roles with the cashier, he is giving Rebecca an opportunity to detach herself from her usual role. When she speaks in the critical, judgmental voice of the cashier and allows herself to feel all the emotions attached to it, she may come in contact with a part of herself that she usually denies. It may be in this instance her own self-criticism which is being projected on to someone who provides the necessary hook, but it might just as easily be her intelligence, her strength, her sensitivity or her exuberance.

Children's imaginative play involves shifting identifications around all sorts of real and fantasy characters. Children are allowed to enjoy a multitude of personalities, to be sweet and nasty and heroic and omnipotent in their play, as they seek answers to such questions as, 'What is it like to be a daddy? How does it feel to be a doctor ... a champion athlete ... a horse ...

an astronaut?' As they grow older, the culture withdraws this permission. Play is kept within strict limits, and the adolescent has to find a way of being which stays within the fairly narrow range of what the adult culture and the peer culture will tolerate. 'Doing plays' in school has many justifications, the opportunity to expand the sense of self is one of them. In the exhilaration of a successful school production we see Dionysos at work. There is no business like show business to get the Dionysian juices flowing, as even the least demonstrative children play in the stream of their possibilities. In finding untapped areas of themselves in the characters they play, they exult in the sense that there is more to themselves than they have settled for. The exultation may not be very enduring, but the flash of insight may last a lifetime, even if it has failed to transform that lifetime.

For those working in the conventional theatre of the cultural conserve, no less than for Moreno, the relationship between role and spontaneity and the tension between them has been a constant focus of exploration and experiment, as the reality of repeating the same words and actions in performance after performance is tested against the ideal of experiencing and representing each dramatic moment again and again as though for the first time.

TRANSCENDING ROLE

Assagioli's solution to the problem, in theory and therapy, is to distinguish between two different levels of spontaneity: level three on his self-realization scale, in which spontaneity is experienced and expressed through sub-personalities, and level four in which sub-personalities are completely transcended. Human behaviour generally comes in packages and for a lot of the time the best we can do is to exercise some control over the packages through which we express who we are. The ideal, however, is to be able to act without the prop of these sub-personality structures, to have the vast array of our possibilities available to us at every moment, so that our behaviour can be at once entirely appropriate and entirely unpredictable. In practice, however, we can consider that we are doing fairly well if we can restrain our sub-personalities from fighting with each other.

Neither Moreno nor Assagioli contradict the conventional wisdom that children and adolescents must develop a stable sense of self if they are to cope in an adult world, but their idea of self is rather more expansive than that of most ego-psychologists. They are concerned that a one-sided development may leave the child's genius tied up in undeveloped roles.

A lot of writers use the word 'role' to refer to something pretty superficial – the surface behaviour as contrasted with the 'real person' beneath it. Not so Moreno. Role goes to the depths of the psyche, there is no 'real person' to compare with the roles. Our roles are the visible expression of our complexes. Assagioli's preference for the word 'sub-personality' reflects his perception that, whatever we call them, they are largely autonomous personalities with their own conscious and unconscious processes, their own values, obsessions, ideologies and ambitions, their own ways of interacting with others. We have been taught to see multiple personality as pathological, so that if we cannot sum up exactly who we are there is something wrong with us. Moreno and Assagioli, no less than Jung, see multiplicity as our proper healthy state reflecting the multiplicity of archetypes (or gods) of which each individual personality is an expression. For them it is our lack of awareness of our many personalities which is unhealthy – both the 'normal' unawareness in which we identify with one sub-personality and suppress all our other possibilities, and the 'psychotic' unawareness in which people with a condition called 'multiple personality' shift from one personality to another without the personalities knowing of each other's existence.

Multiple personality is something that fascinated the nineteenth century medical hypnotists such as Charcot, who first inspired Freud's exploration of the unconscious. They found that when they put their disturbed patients into trance they could discover other 'people' inside them – whole personalities quite distinct from the patient's conscious personality who seemed to be leading independent lives within the same person. Jung provided a way of relating multiple personality to normal behaviour when he developed his theory of complexes. Federn, a contemporary who stayed closer to Freud's thinking, called these personalities ego-states. Berne followed the same line of thought when he developed the idea that we each move between a child ego-state, an adult ego-state and a parent ego-state, in each of which we have a different way of relating to the world. Berne's reduction of the range of ego-states to variations of these three may seem altogether too narrow but, whether we follow Federn or Jung or Assagioli or Moreno, we are faced with evidence that we have available to us a range of more or less autonomous personalities which are rooted in the depths of our being. We are faced also with the suggestion that our identification with just one of our personalities is a defensive manoeuvre with its source in our fear of our own possibilities.

CONFRONTING CREATIVITY

Anyone who has participated in psychodrama or improvizational drama, or played a role in conventional drama, has some sense of how intelligence and creativity, even knowledge and ignorance, are intricately entangled in role. Moreno often dealt with a protagonist who was stuck in the slough of incomprehension by taking her out of her customary role and letting her play the role of God, or an angel, who witnesses the incomprehensible situation from above and understands it entirely. It seems very apparent in such a drama that the protagonist knows a lot more than she knows she knows. Assagioli's experience led him to develop his meditation on 'I know' and guided fantasies in which the client converses with his higher self or guru or some other inner projection of his own knowing, and hears a wisdom that in his customary identity he could not allow himself to express. Lozanov found that adult students could learn a foreign language much more quickly if they abandoned their regular identity during classes and formally took an entirely new one, which was not controlled by the same fears and inhibitions to learning. When conducting group therapy, even with seriously disturbed patients, Moreno insisted on introducing everyone by the title Doctor, in order to emphasize that every member of the group was there in the capacity of teacher and healer, and that they were to take this role and responsibility seriously. Raikov, the Soviet experimental hypnotist, found that he could increase people's ability to learn and play a musical instrument by inducing them to accept the suggestion that they were Beethoven or Paganini. After hypnosis their playing maintained an improvement, even if it did not quite approach the standards of Beethoven or Paganini.[169]

Such an experience does not depend on hypnotic trance. If children take their role-playing seriously, if they have not yet been taught that pretending is a trivial and childish activity, they will readily put on the personality of the poet to write poetry and that of the artist to paint, and will solve complex puzzles while pretending to be engineers, and speak with understanding of other times and cultures while pretending to inhabit them. If Moreno is right and the teacher knows how to use this capacity for role playing, this flexibility will extend to their 'real' roles as well as their 'pretend' ones. She will be able to persuade them to shake off their role of ignorant student or detached onlooker and take on that of curious investigator or assured expert, roles that are already familiar to them outside the classroom. And if she has a good sense of the system of roles operating in the classroom she will be able to move her students into more productive roles by changing her own.

Unfortunately, many teachers who understand this aspect of knowing and wish to exploit its possibilities run into difficulties. Role-playing is not taken seriously. It is not 'real work'. They may not themselves be sufficiently convinced of the value of serious play to take the trouble to teach their students to enter new roles and believe in them. There is little educational value in the kind of role-playing in which the students are permitted to resist the roles and where the teacher has no sense of what can be gained through complete engagement in them.

Much of what passes for role-play in classrooms and elsewhere is, unfortunately, pretty superficial. The role-players manage to trivialize both the roles and the issue to be explored. The enactment is superficial because, instead of allowing the emergence of that part of themselves demanded by the role, they spend their energy in repeated attempts to escape from the role back to their habitual identity or in thinking of clever or funny things to say. Moreno was convinced that we are afraid of our own spontaneity. Certainly adolescents or adults invited to role-play often seem to be afraid of what they might learn or disclose of themselves if they let go of their usual identity and let the role take over for a few minutes.

The Search for Spontaneity

The best way to stop people doing something badly is to give them the experience of doing it well. When the activity is role-playing the gap between badly and well is readily bridged by the teacher with a few simple techniques. It is necessary only to consider that role-play must be prepared for (in secondary school at least) and that the students must be taught to do it. In primary school, unless their experience of schooling is unusually unfortunate, they are in close enough contact with the activity called 'play' to be able to carry it into the classroom.

Be that as it may, the most obvious cause of the disappointment of a pointless, boring or chaotic role-play is the absence of warm-up. The class may need to be warmed-up to the topic, to action, to a role expressing feelings, to working as a group. They may even need to be warmed-up to talking. The specific form the warm-up takes will vary with the context, but it may be no more than some minutes of discussing and sharing feelings about the issue which provides the content of the role-play. Or it may be a series of exercises or games designed to eliminate self-consciousness and generate what Moreno would call 'act-hunger'.

A good warm-up will eliminate most problems, but some students have a way of volunteering for activities and then finding ways of avoiding them.

For example, the teacher sets up a role-play in which a girl meets her boyfriend in a coffee-shop after work because she wants to tell him that she is being sexually harassed by her boss.

> *Debbie*: I was sexually harassed at the office today. (Laughs inappropriately and looks around at class.)
> *Tim*: Who was it?
> *Debbie*: The boss. (Debbie glances at teacher as if to check that she has got the script right.)
> *Tim*: What did he do?
> *Debbie*: He ... um ... touched me ... (Giggles, addresses teacher.) This isn't realistic!

Debbie may have been warmed up to the topic and warmed up to volunteering to act it out, but she has not been warmed up to the role and the context.

Educating Psyche

The teacher could have warmed Debbie up to the point of entry of this drama. On her way to the coffee shop he could have had Debbie engaged in a soliloquy in which she explored her feelings about what happened at the office and rehearsed what she wanted to say to Tim. Or he could have interviewed Debbie sitting alone in the coffee shop, asking her first of all to describe the coffee shop in detail and then asking her about her day at the office, and getting her to describe her feelings as she sits waiting. He could have used one of these procedures also with Tim.

Before setting up this role-play he could have taught his students something about going with the flow, how to recognize when they are blocking the interaction and what they can do about it. Specifically he could have taught his students how to keep each other in role by treating all behaviour in the course of the role-play as coming from the role and not allowing escape back to the usual identity.

> *Debbie*: I was sexually harassed at the office today. (Laughs inappropriately and looks around.)
> *Tim*: Was it funny?
> *Debbie*: No. It was awful. (Looks at teacher for help.)
> *Tim*: Why do you keep looking over there?
> *Debbie*: (To teacher.) This isn't realistic!
> *Tim*: Are you hallucinating or something?

Tim may be trying a little too hard, and it may be time for the teacher to accept Debbie's message that she does not really want to do it. For all that, it is possible to teach teenagers to engage deeply in this sort of play, to take the 'as if' seriously and to be open to the experience of emerging spontaneity. The time required for this teaching is not very great, but the rewards are enormous whether we measure them by the Dionysian criteria of the cultivation of feelings, and the experience of spontaneity, or make an Apollonine judgement of the clarity of the light we throw on the murky business of human motivation, ethics and behaviour.

Teachers, since they are not employed to teach students to act, may resist this idea. If students have to be taught to role-play before role-playing is effective, why bother with it at all? Actually, the point here is not to teach

The Search for Spontaneity

students to act but to teach them how not to act, to express parts of themselves that their usual narrow persona-identification denies. The last thing effective role-playing is about is pretending, unless it is the kind of pretending little children do when they lose themselves in their play. Serious play is playful as well as serious. Losing oneself in role is liberating in the way that losing oneself in fancy dress is liberating. Effective role-playing involves the comic as well as the romantic and tragic dimensions of behaviour; it can be based on broad and biased caricature as well as subtle observation and interpretation. What makes it useful dramatically and educationally is not the genre; it is whether the energy goes into living the roles or into killing them to preserve our inhibitions.

Keith Johnstone shares Moreno's conviction that people are afraid of spontaneity, and uses his own ways of seducing them into expressing something of their own.

> I say to an actress, 'Make up a story.' She looks desperate, and says, 'I can't think of one.'
>
> 'Any story', I say. 'Make up a silly one.'
>
> 'I can't', she despairs.
>
> 'Suppose I think of one and you guess what it is.'
>
> At once she relaxes, and it's obvious how very tense she was. 'I've thought of one', I say, 'but I'll only answer 'Yes', 'No', or 'Maybe'.
>
> She likes this idea and agrees, having no idea that I'm planning to say 'Yes' to any question that ends in a vowel, 'No' to any question that ends in a consonant, and 'Maybe' to any question that ends with the letter Y.
>
> For example, should she ask me 'Is it about a horse?' I'll answer, 'Yes', since 'horse' ends in an E.
>
> 'Does the horse have a bad leg?'
>
> 'No.'
>
> 'Does it run away?'
>
> 'Maybe.'
>
> She can now invent a story easily, but she doesn't feel obliged to be 'creative', or 'sensitive' or whatever, because she believes the story is my

Educating Psyche

invention. She no longer feels wary, and open to hostile criticism, as of course we all are in this culture whenever we do anything spontaneously.

Her first question is: 'Has the story got any people in it?'

'No.'

'Has it got animals in it?'

'No.'

'Has it got any buildings in it?'

'Yes.' (I'm having to drop my rule about consonants, or she'd get too discouraged.)

'Does the building have anything to do with the story?'

'Maybe.'

'Does it have any aeroplanes in it?'

'No.'

'Fish?'

'No.'

'Insects.'

'Yes.'

'Do the insects play a large part in the story?'

'Maybe.'

'Do they live underground?'

'No.'

'Do they start out as harmless?'

'No.'

'Do the insects take over the world?'

'Yes.'

'Are they as big as elephants?'

'No.'

'Do they take any poison?'

'No.'

'Is it a gradual process, this taking over of the world?'

'No.'

'Were there many insects?'

The Search for Spontaneity

'No.'

'Do they reign utterly alone?'

'Yes.'

'Do they destroy the world in a foul manner?'

'No.'

'Does the story begin with their existing?'

'No.'

'But there aren't any people in this bloody story. So it must start with the insects. Have the insects been reigning alone in the world for a long time?'

'Yes.'

'And then they suddenly decide to destroy the world?'

'Yes.'

'And they don't die. And when they eat everything in sight they become larger.'

'Yes.'

'And then they can't fit into the building again.'

'Yes.'

'And is that the end of the story?'

'It is.'[170]

ROLE TRAINING

One of Moreno's personal projects was to develop techniques for training spontaneity. Another was to develop techniques for training role. His procedures for role training are based on his understanding that there are two kinds of memory: *content* memory is stored in the brain as thoughts, feelings and facts; *act* memory is stored not only in the brain but also in the musculature as tension, tingling, warmth, habitual movement, and so on. The psychodrama director gets the protagonist to go to a past scene and act it out, recapturing the act memory. She pays intense attention to the protagonist's physical behaviour and, if need be, directs him to amplify it, so that the thoughts and feelings attached to it come into consciousness. Moreno found that engaging one's muscles in movement intensifies recall and the feelings associated with it, and that preparation for a new behaviour is most effective when it involves physical practice instead of mere talk.

The technique of role training, in one form or another, is commonly used in the training of teachers, health professionals and managers. It is less commonly found in the education of children and adolescents, though it certainly merits a place there as long as the content of education is considered to include children's skills in dealing with interpersonal situations.

Joe brings to class his disappointment at failing in a job interview. Not only did he fail to get the job, but he sensed from the beginning that the employer was not taking him seriously as an applicant. The teacher suggests that he play out the scene for the class, choosing auxiliaries to play the other character or characters in his story. Before he begins his enactment, the teacher asks him to nominate three members of the class who will pay special attention to his behaviour in order to be able to reproduce it.

Joe and his auxiliaries play out the scene, with Joe supplying his auxiliaries' lines through role reversal. The three nominated students in turn act out the scene, imitating (mirroring) Joe to the best of their ability.

The class discusses the aspects of Joe's behaviour which the three students managed to mirror accurately. The other auxiliaries give Joe feedback on how they perceived his behaviour and how it affected them. Joe gets some insight into the effect his customary role has in this situation. He decides that he wishes to make a different sort of impression on an employer.

Joe tries out a different role. He gets some feedback from auxiliaries and audience. He is still dissatisfied. The teacher suggests that Joe asks some other students to show how they would handle the situation. As they do so Joe becomes aware that he has a number of options. He decides to try out a new role. The teacher instructs the class to watch out for what they like in Joe's new behaviour. Joe rehearses the situation again. The teacher ensures that all comments from the class are concrete and positive: 'I like the way you ...' Negative or inadequate aspects of Joe's behaviour are to be simply ignored.

This step is repeated, maybe two or three times. Joe's role is shaped by reinforcing the constructive aspects of it each time. Joe decides that he is comfortable with his new role. He has by now committed it to his body-memory as well as his content memory.

It may be that Joe will have the opportunity to try out the new role that he has been rehearsing. If not, it may be of no great consequence. His most significant learning has been the enlargement of his repertoire of roles, and even if the exact situation never presents itself again, he has gained some capacity to meet new situations freshly and spontaneously.

BEING CRAZY

As a young man, Jacob Moreno wandered around the streets of Vienna dressed in a long white robe, calling on people to be true to their own inner natures as co-creators of the universe. Wherever he went he created spontaneous street theatre in which he brought people face to face with the problems of their age.

As a maverick psychiatrist in the United States he explained how he managed to keep smiling when his ideas and methods were viciously attacked.

> First ... I know I'm right. Secondly, I may be crazy like they say, but I'm making a lot of people, like you, crazy with me; and each year, as more and more people join our movement, I will be considered less crazy.[171]

At eighty-five, after suffering a stroke, he decided to die with dignity and control. He let his friends and students know his decision and stopped taking anything but water. He said all his goodbyes and died in his own time. He managed to make even his own death an act of spontaneous will, an expression of the life-force which was the centre of his intellectual and emotional universe.

Moreno, like Freud, had seen how people are shaped and shackled by society, prohibited from seeking their own ends, seduced from their individuality. But he did not share the bitterness of Freud, who had no vision of a better society, whose own shackles made him see the id as alien and brute, and who feared the devastation that would follow if this pent-up energy were ever released without restraint. Moreno believed rather that in the release of this energy lay our only hope of change. Where Freud saw people acting because they are frustrated, Moreno saw them frustrated because they do not act. Where Freud hoped that the ego could tame the raw energy of the id by deflecting and reflecting it in thought, Moreno set out to bind thought and energy inseparably together in action.

As a young man Moreno was introduced to Freud and brashly claimed that he, Moreno, was enriching people's dreams while all that Freud could do to their dreams was kill them. It seems he never found cause to change his mind. He may have lacked the adjustment and the calm detachment which Freud pursued with great conviction, but he knew, like Dionysos, how to both suffer and enjoy.

NOTES Chapter 7. The Search for Spontaneity

[158] J. L. Moreno, *Who Shall Survive?*, p. 19.
[159] ibid., p. 34.
160 J. L. Moreno, 'The Magic Charter of Psychodrama', *Group Psychotherapy and Psychodrama*, 25, 4, 1972, p. 131.
[161] K. Johnstone, *Impro*.
[162] ibid., p. 25.
[163] For an excellent discussion of warm-up in psychodrama see A. Williams, *Forbidden Agendas*.
[164] Playback Theatre was developed by Jonathon Fox in the United States in the early 1970s. He began to use the technique as a schoolteacher working with parents who wanted to create theatre to tell their 'story' to their children. It has since become a form of professional theatre in several countries.
[165] M. Czikszentmihalyi, *Beyond Boredom and Anxiety*, p. 205.
[166] It is significant, in view of the notorious narcissism of the Dionysos-impelled 'artistic personality', that the Titans managed to catch Dionysos by surprise while he was fully occupied admiring himself in a mirror.
[167] C. Hampden-Turner, *Maps of the Mind*, p. 16.
[168] R. Assagioli, *Psychosynthesis*, p. 214.
[169] For a description of Raikov's work, see S. Krippner, *Human Possibilities*.
[170] K. Johnstone, op. cit., p. 113.
[171] L. Fine, 'Psychodrama', in Corsini R., *Current Psychotherapies*, p. 436.
For further reading on psychodrama see J. L. Moreno, *Psychodrama*; H. Blatner, *Acting In*; I. Greenberg, *Psychodrama: Theory and Therapy*; A. Williams, *The Passionate Technique*.

8

SITTING QUIETLY

*T*he most beautiful emotion we can experience is the mystical. It is the source of all true art and science.

Albert Einstein

THE DISTINCTION JUNG MADE between the extroverted and introverted attitudes is well illustrated in the contrast between the ideas and methods of Moreno and Assagioli. Both had a deep trust in the organism and its ability to find its own way to healthy living. Both sought ways to unite thought and feeling in spontaneous action. Both looked beyond ego-development to a spiritual or transpersonal dimension of living. Yet where Moreno would have us adopt an active frame of mind, to take our inner experience and place it in the external world where we can act on it energetically, amplify and intensify it, Assagioli suggests that we adopt a receptive frame of mind, that we take our external experience and turn it inward where we can deal with it in calm and detachment. Moreno turns images into objects which we can manipulate. Assagioli turns objects and persons into images which we can allow to change and which we can allow to change us.

Assagioli was one of the pioneers of psychoanalysis, but he could not tolerate for long Freud's narrow idea of the human being. As his own ideas broadened, so did his search for a range of techniques which might enable people to find in their lives the worth and meaning which they were hiding from themselves. He found such techniques in the literature of meditation.

SECULAR PRAYER

Meditation is a word that is applied to a variety of mental activities, some of which have little in common. When Assagioli started working with meditation, the word had strong religious connotations. Even today, when there is a substantial non-religious and scientific literature on meditation, people are still automatically inclined to associate meditation with religion. While there are good reasons for such an association, there is certainly no direct relationship between religious belief and the state of mind attained through meditation. Assagioli looked in Western and Eastern meditation literature for methods by which a therapist could help a client to create a unifying centre in a fragmented personality. Contemporary writers on meditation are likely to expound the same techniques as means by which we can become a more alert student, a more competitive athlete or a sounder financial manager, and can learn to conquer serious illness.

Sitting Quietly

One might ask if twentieth-century man, having secularized art, music, poetry, education and politics, has finally decided to do the job properly and secularize prayer. After all, he needs prayer no less than he needs air and water, so he might as well have it without the burdensome trappings and useless paraphernalia of Christianity, Buddhism or anything else.[172]

The scientific evidence that meditation is good for us has come fairly recently. Jewish, Christian, Sufi, Buddhist and Hindu writers on meditation have much to say about meditation being good for us, but they give their attention to such matters as unity consciousness, the quest for the Beloved, communion with the Godhead or the attainment of bliss, and they use language which means little to modern science. Science prefers to put meditation in a laboratory and study its effects, describing them in its own mystical language: perceptual sharpening and increased ability to attend to a target environmental stimulus, modification of immunity and disease susceptibility, increased cortical specificity, autonomic stability, decrease in the rate of metabolism, lowered limbic activation, equanimity in responding to emotionally loaded and threatening stimuli, trophotropic arousal, EEG synchronization, increase in Alpha-rhythm amplitude and decrease in frequency, decline in blood lactate levels.[173]

Of course, much of the traditional mystical literature contains science at its best, with centuries of continually refined observations on the experience and effects of meditation. It is fascinating to find experts from a wide range of times and cultures coming to identical conclusions when they speak of the kinds and stages of meditative experience and the variety of techniques that lead to them.

The way in which a teacher argues for the teaching of meditation to a group of children or adolescents in an extroverted culture like our own is likely to vary somewhat with the context. In some classrooms meditation has a place in a professed religious tradition; in others the association of meditation with religion is an obstacle to be climbed over or circumambulated. In either case, there are strong educational reasons for teachers to do some meditating themselves and to teach their students to meditate.

When we try to define what meditation is, we find the term used to denote a number of quite different activities, which do not all produce the same mental state. However, what they have in common is more significant than what distinguishes them. They all involve a turning from the outer world to the inner, a stifling of the mind's activity and a receptive rather than assertive engagement with reality. There are similarities between meditation and sleep and between meditation and trance. Physiologically, the meditative state is characterized by relaxation of the body and an increase of Alpha and Theta wave activity in the brain. Meditation is not the only way of producing this state. Hypnosis and self-hypnosis can produce a similar state of deep quiet. So can biofeedback.

TOUCHING ULTIMATE REALITY

There are many arguments for spending part of our waking life in such a state. Some of them concern our relationship with 'ultimate reality', however this is named. Some of them concern the efficient functioning of our organism.

We do not have to go to the writings of the great religious mystics to find the first kind of argument. Many scientists have sought through meditation a direct experience of reality that their science was unable to give them, and in the classroom their arguments may be more plausible than those of the mystics. Sir James Jeans, one of the founders of modern physics, uses Plato's image of the cave to illustrate the inadequate reach of science.

> The essential fact is simply that all the pictures which science now draws of nature, and which alone seem capable of according with observational fact, are mathematical pictures ... They are nothing more than pictures – fictions if you like, if by fiction you mean that science is not yet in contact with ultimate reality. Many would hold that, from the broad philosophical standpoint, the outstanding achievement of twentieth-century physics is not the theory of relativity with its welding together of space and time, or the theory of quanta with its present apparent negation of the laws of causation, or the dissection of the atom with the resultant discovery that things are

not what they seem; it is the general recognition that we are not yet in contact with ultimate reality. We are still imprisoned in our cave, with our backs to the light, and can only watch the shadows on the wall.[174]

Jeans found himself drawn to the conclusion that, while science can explore the shadows and the shadows of the shadows, the reality which casts the shadows has to be sought in another way – through meditation. Eddington, another physicist, came to a mystical view of the world through a similar realization that science deals in shadows, not in reality itself.

> Briefly the position is this. We have learnt that the exploration of the external world by the method of physical science leads not to a concrete reality but to a shadow world of symbols, beneath which those methods are unadapted for penetrating. Feeling that there must be more behind, we return to our starting point in human consciousness – the one centre where more might become known. There (in immediate inward consciousness) we might find other stirrings, other revelations than those conditioned by the world of symbols ... Physics most strongly insists that its methods do not penetrate behind the symbolism. Surely then that mental and spiritual nature of ourselves, known in our minds by an intimate contact transcending the methods of physics, supplies just that ... which science is admittedly unable to give.[175]

The sense of being somehow in direct imageless contact with the ground of our being is something which comes slowly or suddenly to many meditators, religious or agnostic. Whether this experience represents something 'real' (whatever that means) or is just a trick of our brain chemistry, it is an experience that has profoundly changed many lives.

Another kind of 'ultimate reality' argument comes from Ken Wilber. He finds in meditation a way of entering into the evolutionary process. It is 'a sustained instrumental path of transcendence ... a sustained development of growth'.[176] It is an activity that involves us in the evolution of the universe, 'the natural and orderly unfolding of higher-order unities, until there is only Unity, until all potential is actual'.[177]

EFFICIENT FUNCTIONING

Other arguments for meditation are based on notions of the efficient functioning of the organism. Some use the image of balance or that of pulsation, arguing that we must regularly switch from the extraverted to the introverted attitude, or from left-brain to right-brain activity, or from assertive to receptive modes of functioning for our physical and psychological health. Yehudi Menuhin puts it in this way:

> We believe in the exertion of the most and have lost the understanding of the power and the subtlety of the least. It is only in going back repeatedly, every day, to a neutral point, to a meditative instance of balance, silence and emptiness, can we find the sources and the ways of strength.[178]

The medical meditators, Herbert Benson and Ainslie Meares, argue along similar lines, that the stresses of modern life will do enormous damage to our health unless we can turn periodically to a simpler mode of consciousness in which we can repair the damage and prepare to re-enter the toxic environment in which we live out our lives.[179]

Benson, a cardiologist, and Meares, a psychiatrist, each developed a specific technique of meditation which they taught to their patients. They were not motivated by any quest for mystical experience but by the clear evidence that meditation practised regularly according to their method made many sick people well and kept them well. What is more, they were able to explain in the language of neuroimmunology how meditation has this effect.

Meditation has other demonstrated effects besides the more spectacular medical ones. The serious meditator may find them fairly trivial, but in the context of an attempt to find meditation a place in schooling, they are quite significant. There is not a great deal of research evidence available on the effects of meditation. Because 'advanced' meditators are somewhat difficult to find living close to laboratories and, when found, are somewhat reluctant to be wired up and measured for fairly trivial purposes, most of the research has been done on inexperienced meditators. This actually makes the results more useful for teachers interested in justifying the teaching of meditation in schools. Most such data comes from studies of Zen in Japan and studies on Transcendental Meditation in the USA, but there is no reason to suppose that the meditative state of consciousness has other effects when produced by other techniques.

The most outstanding and consistent conclusion of such research concerns the effect of meditation on anxiety. The reduction of anxiety seems to follow almost immediately on learning to meditate. There is evidence that not only does meditation reduce present anxiety but it reduces also the susceptibility to become anxious in threatening situations. There are also clear physiological effects like the slowing of respiration and the lowering of blood pressure that are closely associated with stress reduction.

According to some studies, meditation increases energy and alertness and reduces the need for sleep. It lessens dependence on addictive drugs, including alcohol and nicotine. Meditators tend to become more tolerant and accepting of themselves and others, and generally easier to get on with. There is also evidence that they become more assertive and decisive, and experience a greater sense of well being.

A lot of research has been carried out on the effect of meditating on people's skills. Meditation seems to develop a faster reaction time, the ability to better discriminate between sounds, to perceive things more accurately and to perform manual tasks more efficiently. All of these skills are related to learning. We ought to anticipate that children who are taught to meditate will find an improvement in their ability to learn.

While it is legitimate to talk of meditation as a single, definable activity, it is useful also to consider the variety of forms that meditation can take. In introducing meditation to adolescents and children this variety may be used to advantage to teach something of the culture in which these techniques arose and in which they are still significant, and to point to the common humanity and the common quest behind this multiplicity. It also enables the students to choose a way that is comfortable for them, free of the dogmatic one-way-one-truth assumptions originally attached to them. In a pragmatic approach to meditation in education, techniques are just techniques, and biofeedback is no less sacred than contemplation of a mandala.

PSYCHOSYNTHESIS

A wide range of meditation techniques can be found in the exercises Assagioli developed or borrowed for psychosynthesis. They include gentle speculation on an idea, the deeply felt contemplation of an image, autogenic training, focus on a phrase or mantra, repose in a state of deep quiet without thoughts or images, guided and spontaneous fantasies. Some of these exercises represent notions which are central to psychosynthesis. The meditation on the words 'I know' is one instance. The 'disidentification exercise' is another.

The exercise can be done as follows (when it is performed by a group, the one who directs the exercise naturally speaks in the first person, but each participant can apply to themselves what is said):

I put my body into a comfortable and relaxed position with closed eyes. This done, I affirm:

'I have a body but I am not my body. My body may find itself in different conditions of health or sickness, it may be rested or tired, but that has nothing to do with my self, my real "I". My body is my precious instrument of experience and of action in the outer world, but it is only an instrument. I treat it well, I seek to keep it in good health, but it is not myself. I have a body, but I am not my body.

'I have emotions, but I am not my emotions. These emotions are countless, contradictory, changing, and yet I know that I always remain I, myself, in times of hope or of despair, in joy or of irritation or of calm. Since I can observe, understand and judge my emotions, and then increasingly dominate, direct and utilize them, it is evident that they are not myself. I have emotions, but I am not my emotions.

'I have desires, but I am not my desires, aroused by drives, physical and emotional, and by outer influences. Desires too are changeable and contradictory, with alterations of attraction and repulsion. I have desires but they are not myself.

'I have an intellect, but I am not my intellect. It is more or less developed and active; it is undisciplined but teachable; it is an organ of knowledge in regard to the outer world as well as the inner, but it is not myself. I have an intellect, but I am not my intellect.'

After this disidentification of the 'I' from its contents of consciousness (sensations, emotions, desires and thoughts) I recognize and affirm

Sitting Quietly

that I am a Centre of pure self-consciousness. I am a Centre of Will capable of mastering, directing and using all my psychological processes and my physical body.[180]

Reciting or hearing these words does not necessarily involve meditation. There is a peculiar kind of mental activity that is essential to meditation, whether it be a reflective meditation like this exercise, attention to an image, chanting a mantra, or what the Christian mystics called *silentium mysticum*. It is a kind of effortless attention. Schultz, when he developed autogenic training, used the term 'passive concentration' to describe the necessary state of mind. Acquiring skill in the technique, or in any other meditative technique, demands disciplined practice, but one must practise through quiet detachment, not manic striving. Assagioli speaks of this kind of activity specifically when he distinguishes two different operations of the will in his instructions for activating intuition.

> The first step is of a negative character – the temporary checking or elimination from the field of consciousness of other functions which generally have a spontaneous and uninterrupted activity. Constantly sensations from the outer world or from the body intrude into the field of consciousness; emotional reactions do the same, and often the mind is over-active and undisciplined. All this obstructs, fills the field of consciousness, and makes either the entrance or the recognition of intuitions impossible or difficult. Therefore, it is necessary to carry out what we might call a psychological cleansing of the field of consciousness; metaphorically, to ensure that the projection screen is clear and white. This permits in the subject a sympathetic opening of the consciousness towards, or a reaching actively for, that truth or section of reality with which he seeks to come into contact for the solution of a human or an impersonal cognitive problem.
>
> The second stage is then possible, in which he quietly waits for the result of the approach, this nearing, which in successful cases becomes a contact with and even an identification of the subject with the looked-for experience of reality or truth.
>
> In this process we emphasize the necessary co-operation of the will (in every technique there is the god behind the machine – *deus ex machina* – which is the will). Just as in the first part of the procedure, of the stilling or clearing of consciousness, there is a conscious and

active action of the will, so also in the second part, that of relaxation and quiet waiting, the will continues to function, although in a subtler way, and as it were, remaining in the background. This is so because in order to maintain an attitude of relaxation and quietness – and one which is not purely passive – the will is still required to act metaphorically, as the watchman at the door of consciousness to exclude intruders.

To further clarify the difference between the action of the will in the first and second stages, we could say that in the former the will actively ejects the occupants of the 'room of consciousness' and in the second stage the will merely watches at the door so that no unwanted intruder can enter.[181]

Assagioli applies the same quiet attention in his meditations on symbols, as in his exercise of the *Blossoming of the Rose*.

> Let us imagine we are looking at a rosebush. Let us visualize one stem with leaves and rosebud. The bud appears green because the sepals are closed, but at the very top a rose-coloured point can be seen. Let us visualize this vividly, holding the image in the centre of our consciousness.
>
> Now begins a slow movement: the sepals start to separate little by little, turning their points outward and revealing the rose-hued petals, which are still closed. The sepals continue to open until we can see the whole of the tender bud.
>
> The petals follow suit and slowly separate, until a perfect fully-opened rose is seen.
>
> At this stage let us try to smell the perfume of this rose, inhaling its characteristic and unmistakable scent; so delicate, sweet and delicious. Let us smell it with delight. (It may be recalled that religious language has frequently employed perfume as a symbol, e.g., 'the odour of sanctity'; and incense is also used in many religious ceremonies.)
>
> Let us now expand our visualization to include the whole rosebush, and imagine the life force that arises from the roots to the flower and originates the process of opening.
>
> Finally let us identify ourselves with the rose itself or, more precisely, let us 'introject' it into ourselves. Symbolically we are this flower, this rose. The same life that animates the universe and has created the miracle of the rose is producing in us a like, even greater,

miracle – the awakening and development of our spiritual being and that which radiates from it.

Through this exercise we can effectively foster the inner 'flowering'.[182]

It is clear that for Assagioli this is not just an aesthetic experience. He points out that the rose has in many cultures been regarded and used as a symbol of the soul. For him the dynamic visualization of the opening flower not only represents psychospiritual growth, but actually stimulates it, for the symbol corresponds to a profound reality, to a fundamental law of life that governs the functions of the human mind as well as the processes of nature. Growth is achieved through 'the wonderful and mysterious action of the intrinsic 'livingness' which works with irresistible pressure from within'.[183]

Assagioli was persuaded that the visualization of particular symbols sets in motion unconscious psychological processes. The symbol is chosen as a way of addressing the unconscious directly. Since Assagioli's primary interest was in therapy with disturbed people, he tried to select a symbol which would have integrating value for a particular patient at a particular time. Very often he would find such symbols in the patient's conversation or dreams.

The same quiet attention that can be given to the image of a rose, a jewel, a bird or whatever can be given to a feeling. Assagioli recommends the practice to cultivate a desirable feeling or state of mind, as in his *exercise for evoking serenity*.

> Assume a physical attitude of serenity; relax all muscular and nervous tension; breathe slowly and rhythmically; express serenity on your face with a smile. (You can help yourself in this either by looking at yourself in a mirror or by visualising yourself with that expression.)
>
> Think about serenity; realize its value, its use, especially in our agitated modern life. Praise serenity in your mind, desire it.
>
> Evoke serenity directly; try to feel it; with the help either of the repetition of the word or by reading some appropriate sentence, or by repeating many times a suggestive phrase or motto. For example: 'Both action and inaction may find room in thee; thy body agitated, thy mind tranquil, thy soul limpid as a mountain lake.'

> Imagine yourself in circumstances which would tend to agitate or irritate you; for instance, being in the midst of an excited crowd – or in the presence of a hostile person – or confronted by a difficult problem – or obliged to do many things rapidly – or in danger – and see and feel yourself calm and serene.
>
> Pledge yourself to remain serene throughout the day whatever happens; to be a living example of serenity; to radiate serenity.[184]

This is the kind of exercise that Christian writers on meditation have traditionally recommended for beginners. The mind, while quiet and controlled in comparison with its usual frantic activity, is nevertheless still busy compared with the 'simple attention' or 'prayer of silence' which is the aim of more experienced meditators. We might argue that quiet attention to a feeling or quiet contemplation of an idea or image, which has been a valued exercise in the education of children and adults in many cultures, ought to have a valued place also in our own. Our cult of analytic thought is also in a sense a cult of violence. Knowing something analytically is to grab it, take possession of it, tear it to bits. No matter how alive, how subtle and complex that something may be, we manage to reduce it to an object. Contemplation on the other hand allows the being of a poem, a painting, a person or an idea to simply be, and examines it without killing it.

CATCHING THE FLOW

In many cultures the practice of quiet attention has been associated with physical movement. Yoga, Tai Chi, Aikido and the Zen walking meditation are examples, as are Balinese and Sufi dancing. Middle class Western culture has recently developed a form of ritualized movement meditation known as jogging. There is a growing literature on athletics which proclaims the benefits of playing or performing in the state of passive concentration characteristic of meditation or certain martial arts rather than the assertive, controlling attitude which tends in our culture to be associated with the attainment of skills.[185] Now we find meditation being acknowledged as an appropriate activity for the ski slope or golf course. Much of the delight of such activities is in the sense of 'flow' which comes as one becomes skilled enough to perform them with passive concentration rather than active effort.

> In the flow state, action follows upon action according to an internal logic that seems to need no conscious intervention by the actor. He experiences it as a unified flowing from one moment to the rest, in which he is in control of his actions, and in which there is little distinction between self and environment, between stimulus and response, or between past, present, and future.[186]

Meditation techniques are sometimes seen simply as systematic ways of pursuing this experience of flow (to which different traditions give quite different names and which also comes to people suddenly and unpredictably in all sorts of situations — listening to music, surfing, making love, travelling in the desert). In some forms of yoga, posture and breathing are used systematically for this purpose. Other traditions rely on a rhythmic repetitive movement. A common, but not universal, feature of meditation techniques is the narrowing of one's focus of attention.

> One of the simplest kinds of focusing in meditation is breath-counting. You start by placing yourself in a comfortable position so that you will get as few distracting signals from your body as possible. This may be either sitting, lying on the floor, or standing, depending on your particular wishes. Set an alarm or timer for fifteen minutes, or if this is not available, place a clock face where you can see it without moving your head. If you use an alarm clock or timer, use one with a gentle sound or muffle it with a pillow.
>
> Now simply count silently each time you breathe out. Count 'one' for the first breath, 'two' for the second, 'three' for the third, 'four' for the fourth, and then start with 'one' again. Keep repeating this procedure until the fifteen minutes are up.
>
> The goal is to be doing simply that and nothing more. If other thoughts come in (and they will) simply accept the fact that you are straying from the instructions and bring yourself gently and firmly back to the counting. No matter what other thoughts, feelings or perceptions come during the fifteen minutes, your task is simply to keep counting your breaths, so keep trying to be doing only that. Doing or being conscious of anything else during this period is wandering away from the task.

Do not expect to do well at it, to be able to succeed for more than a couple of seconds at a time in being aware only of your counting. That takes long practice. Simply do your best.[187]

If we can successfully shut out external stimuli in this way, and shut down our thinking processes at the same time, we will experience a state of deep quiet. The same experience can be gained through repeating a word or phrase (mantra) over and over again. This is the way of Transcendental Meditation (TM) and of the technique that Herbert Benson, whose interests are medical rather than mystical, uses to elicit what he calls the relaxation response. This method has four simple elements: a quiet environment; a word or phrase to be repeated over and over again; a passive attitude; a comfortable position.[188]

STILLING THE MIND

Transcendental Meditation is a form of mantra meditation taught in the West by Mahareshi Maresh Yogi. For Mahareshi, meditation means 'turning the attention inwards towards the subtle levels of thought until the mind transcends the experience of the subtlest state of thought at the source of thought'.[189] This is achieved through daily repetition by the meditator of a mantra given him by a teacher trained by Mahareshi. It does not involve special postures or breathing, or forced concentration. The special, secret mantra is repeated inwardly for twenty minutes, morning and evening. In this school the meaning and even the sound of the mantra are critical, but as far as the physical effects are concerned it does not seem to matter what the phrase is. As far as our measuring devices can tell, the brain responds in the same way to nonsense syllables as it does to *om mani padme hum*, *Allah hu* or *kyrie eleison*. It is the passive concentration and the repetition that produce the effect on the brain, and the sense of deep quiet, not the content of the phrase.

Of course the effects of meditation go far beyond decrease in the rate of metabolism and the frequency of our brainwaves. After Benson had published the research which led him to the conclusion that the relaxation response was an effective remedy against atherosclerosis he became aware that there was something else involved. This he called the faith factor. Practice of the relaxation response proved to be more effective if associated with faith. It did not seem to matter what or who the object of that faith was. It might be belief in the power of the mantra or the doctor to heal, or it might be a religious faith.

> The relaxation-response state is fairly well defined. The question now is how to use this state. If you couple belief with the relaxation response, the results are sometimes remarkable. A technique for evoking the response is to focus the attention on a word, prayer, sound or phrase and passively disregard intrusive thoughts. When you choose a word, sound, prayer or phrase that conforms to a person's belief system, you enhance the effectiveness of the response. We frequently use prayer to accomplish this. This is nothing new – it has been going on for thousands of years.[190]

If we like we can reduce the healing power of prayer to the placebo effect, but where meditation is concerned there is another aspect to consider. For most people who meditate the practice has, or acquires, a dimension of meaning. It is more nurturing for them to chant a phrase which has meaning (even in a language they do not understand) than a group of nonsense syllables, more healing to give passive attention to 'peace' or the image of a child or lover than to repeat the words 'coca cola' over and over, more satisfying to gaze for fifteen minutes at a flower than at a fly-spot on the wall. However, those who choose to gaze at the fly-spot may actually reach the state of deep quiet faster, since it is easier to still the mind for a fly-spot than for an image with strong emotional associations.

Stilling the mind is not easy in either case. One of the first things a meditator learns is how little control she has over her mind. As Le Shan points out, 'after fifteen minutes of attempting to count our breaths and not be thinking of anything else, we realize that if our bodies were half as unresponsive to our will as our minds are, we would never get across the street alive.'[191] Yet with regular and disciplined practice we can learn to focus our minds steadily when we wish to. If meditation had no other function than this, we would still have a strong argument for including it in the curriculum.

While some techniques of meditation achieve stillness by blocking out external stimuli, others do it by heightening awareness of whatever is going on around the meditator and within her. One such technique is Gurdjieff's 'self-remembering'. Another is the Zen practice of 'open-meditation'. Zen meditators seek to be aware of each here and now moment, through what they call 'bare attention', without holding on to any sensation or thought or being distracted by them. The eyes and ears are open and objects are seen and heard in their suchness without judgements such as beautiful, ugly, nice, nasty, good, bad, useful, useless.

The Tibetan teacher Chogyam Trungpa describes this technique:

> In this kind of meditation practice the concept of nowness plays an important part. In fact, it is the essence of meditation. Whatever one does, whatever one tries to practice, is not aimed at achieving a higher state or at following some theory or ideal, but simply without any object or ambition, trying to see what is here and now. One has to become aware of the present moment through such means as concentrating on the breathing, a practice which has been developed in the Buddhist tradition. This is based on developing the knowledge of nowness, for each respiration is unique, it is an expression of now. Each breath is separate from the next and is fully seen and fully felt, not as a visualized form nor simply as an aid to concentration, but it should be fully and properly dealt with.[192]

Zen meditators call their practice zazen or 'just sitting'. Stopping the incessant chatter of the mind either through bare attention to sensation or by occupying the mind totally with a koan brings a more profound stillness than any amount of sitting and daydreaming. Not only is total passive concentration paradoxically restful; it is often intensely pleasurable.

One Western version of 'just sitting' is 'mental ataraxis', a technique developed by the Australian psychiatrist Ainslie Meares. What he learned about healing from his experience as a medical hypnotist and what he learned from his observations and conversations with holy men in India and Nepal came together as a method of meditation which he claimed could heal both physical and mental illnesses. So convinced was he of what he was doing that he abandoned his lucrative medical practice and became a teacher of meditation.

Meares' method of meditation is utterly simple. There is no attempt to reach an altered state of consciousness, no ritual, no internal or external object on which to focus. 'In the meditation I would advise you to practise there is no striving, no activity or brain function, just stillness, a stillness of effortless tranquillity.'[193] There is simply a 'letting go'.

> No forcing ourself.
> No striving to do it. No contemplation of any image. No awareness of our breathing. No repetition of a mantra.
> No forcing ourselves to maintain a posture.[194]

Meares' only instruction on posture is that there should be an element of slight discomfort to keep us awake and to ensure that the sense of profound calm comes not from the ease of our bodies but from the way we use our minds. In essence, to move into the state of mental ataraxis we simply sit and stop all mental activity. If thoughts and images enter consciousness we do nothing with them and they move away. Eventually they cease to bother us and we move into a state of profound calm.

In his earlier career as an experimental hypnotist Meares developed the atavistic theory of hypnosis. According to this theory the basic factor in hypnotic trance is a regression to a more primitive mode of mental functioning.

> In auto-hypnosis the individual learns to let his mind regress, and it comes to function in this more primitive way. This accounts for the absence of anxiety, and the feeling of calm and ease which we experience in auto-hypnosis. A very similar state of affairs occurs in deep meditation. There is a great feeling of calm; logical critical thinking is suspended and the individual ceases to be aware of his physical environment.[195]

When he taught his own patients to meditate by 'just sitting' he found that it did not take weeks or years of practice to learn how to go into this 'primitive' state. We have a natural tendency to move from our active state to an interior and 'regressed' one from time to time during the day. The ten minutes spent in meditation each morning and evening simply allows us to go more fully into this state and experience its benefits.

Not all writers on meditation would be happy with Meares' assessment of the meditation state as a regressed one. Most prefer to regard it as more advanced than our normal state. They believe that the abandonment of the logical egoic thinking which is the great achievement of our normal consciousness allows us to perceive reality with a new intensity and richness. The simplicity of the meditation state is a transcendence of our rationality, not a regression to a more primitive way of being.[196]

The argument is interesting but it does not need to bother the meditator. It is based on a linear image of the universe in which up and down, forwards and backwards, better and worse, are in opposite directions. Such an image serves us well in our day-to-day living but it is not necessarily useful when we try to explain our relation to 'ultimate reality'.

Meares' writings are full of case studies of healing achieved through mental ataraxis. When he began teaching the technique to his patients he expected that it would be useful only for psychological and psychosomatic problems. He discovered that it was effective also in cases of organic illness and in his later years his name was most closely associated with the treatment of cancer.

MEDITATION IN THE CLASSROOM

Teaching is not generally regarded as a healing profession. The growing evidence of the power of deep relaxation for healing is not much help to the teacher who wants to argue for its place in the classroom. All the same, teachers are involved, for better or worse, in the health of their students. The anxious classroom is toxic; the relaxed and caring classroom is a centre of wellness. It certainly comes within the ambit of the teacher's activity to deal with the anxieties of a class or a student. The usual way for a concerned teacher to do this is to attempt a little counselling. Meditation provides an alternative approach, or, better still, a complementary one.

The impact of meditation on anxiety levels hardly needs comment. It has been confirmed again and again in both laboratory studies and clinical observations, and the most casual and irregular meditator has evidence of it. Meditation has demonstrated physiological effects which reduce stress.

Sitting Quietly

Not only is there an immediate effect during the practice of meditation, but the effect can last for some time afterwards, and if meditation is regular the lower stress levels become habitual. When children learn to meditate they show less overt anxiety, more tolerance for frustration, less restlessness, greater ability to attend to a task. They have fewer headaches; their sleep improves. If the source of their anxiety is specific they become able to talk about it without distress. In short, they are happier.

The state of consciousness we call meditation or mindfulness seems to have a balancing or organising function. It allows the psyche to reorganize or reintegrate itself, just as trance does. As a result, children or adolescents can be taught to meditate as a way of improving their self-image, increasing their energy, overcoming their depression, developing their sense of identity, becoming more assertive, lessening their tendencies to blame self and others. The studies of Transcendental Meditation in particular claim solid research evidence of its value for students: enhancing creativity, overcoming writer's block, improving memory, increasing students' ability to deal with complex tasks, sharpening their powers of observation, enabling them to concentrate on a task for a long time without exhaustion.[197]

Sometimes all this seems a little too much, but it ought to be taken seriously. The neglect of such a powerful instrument for education would be puzzling if it was not so obviously out of harmony with the extroverted, instrumental nature of our schooling system. 'Just sitting' has no status at all in our society. The situation seems to be changing, partly because the collapse of consensus Christianity is inducing people to seek the benefits of contemplation without the doctrine, and partly because 'just sitting' is now claimed to have some instrumental value. As the business sector catches on to the idea that training executives in Transcendental Meditation or the relaxation response (assisted by biofeedback) may make them better at handling stress, money and people, and that giving a similar (but less expensive) training to process workers may enable them to stay contented in a boring job, the schooling system may pick up meditation as a legitimate school activity. For the present, teachers who try to meddle in such things are likely to be thought dangerous or deviant.

There is some prejudice against introducing children to meditation.

Prayer is OK in the right place, but meditation could be dangerous. This fear can dress itself up in logical arguments but it is basically irrational. What is more, it is culturally specific. There are plenty of times and places, such as in Balinese or traditional Aboriginal cultures, where trance or 'just sitting' or dancing meditation is regarded as a normal and unremarkable feature of a child's education.

AUNTIE HESTIA

The gods that have dominated our intellectual culture in recent times – Apollo and Prometheus – are gods who hate the darkness. Not so Psyche, who finds Love and Beauty in the darkness. Not so Hephaistos who dwells under the mountain quietly crafting delicate and powerful instruments for the other gods to use. Not so Hestia (or Vesta) the goddess of the hearth (*focus*, in Latin) whose warm glow is the centre of the family, the centre of the city, the centre of the world, the centre of the individual, who was seen, in ancient Greece, in a heap of glowing coals in a shrine in Delphi, the 'navel of the earth'. All our language of centring and focusing and navel-gazing takes us back to her myth. There we find that, unlike most Greek and Roman gods, she hardly seems to be personified at all. She is rather a place than a person, a point to gather round or return to, a point of balance, a point of stillness in a turning world, a point where one can just be without worrying about achieving or struggling, or even about being good at things. When the madly energetic Dionysos gains membership of the company of twelve Olympian gods, it is Hestia who steps aside and gives up her place for him.

The images of Hestia's myth enrich greatly our sense of what meditation is and does. There is an image of circularity. She is the oldest of the Olympians and the youngest (the first to be swallowed by her father, Kronos, and the last to be regurgitated); every feast must begin and end with an offering and invocation to her; the domed ceiling of her circular shrine reflects the roundness of the earth. There is an image of detachment. She takes no part in the quarrels of the gods or the wars of humankind; she dwells far removed from violence, and even excitement. There is the image of the virgin

Sitting Quietly

goddess, the maiden aunt of all the younger gods, immune (as few gods and mortals are) to the power of Aphrodite. There is the image of contained fire, the glow of coals on the hearth, with its associations of warm inner glow, the brightness of inner illumination, the trance-inducing and comforting experience of sitting quietly in silence, staring into the flames, while beasts and enemies prowl in the darkness outside. There is the image of 'home', of stable foundations, of ceasing from wandering and coming back where one belongs. There is the image of the focus, the hearth, the gathering place, the point where light and warmth are concentrated. There is the image of Hestia the weaver, quietly gathering threads of different textures and colours into a pattern which is both beautiful and warm. And there is the image of the stillness of Hestia giving way to the ecstasy of Dionysos.

Hestia is not the only god we find in meditation. Dionysos has an obvious connection, and Apollo gives us spiritual enlightenment. Yet Hestia is assuredly the god of 'just sitting'.

The stillness and centredness of Hestia is something that children and adolescents seem to appreciate and return to eagerly when given the chance. Teachers who introduce their classes to meditation, either through simple centring techniques or through guided visualization, are apt to find in their students a remarkable readiness for sitting quietly. The children quickly learn to find the practice satisfying. They do not demand to be persuaded of the instrumental value of meditation. Such arguments can be reserved for countering the objections of colleagues.

A NECESSARY ECSTASY

Our mainstream culture has a deep suspicion of meditation. Some of this suspicion has its source in ignorance and superstition: some of it derives from the multiple uses of the word 'meditation'. Actually, many writers on meditation, especially from the great traditions, would argue that the kinds of meditative activities that are practicable in the classroom should not be called 'meditation' at all. They would reserve the word to refer to the end-state, not the means of getting there.

In the spiritual traditions, meditation is used as a way of becoming aware of one's contact with 'ultimate reality'. It is seen as one element in a total way of life, in which a lifetime's practice is required to attain unity with the godhead (however imagined), the highest state of consciousness we can attain or be blessed with. It involves discipline, a skilled teacher, hours of daily practice. The concentration on chanting, breathing or other forms of focusing is something which beginners do, a warm-up to the real business of meditation – the attainment of ecstasy or bliss.

'Ecstasy' and 'bliss' are not words we use very often in writing about education. Neither is 'joy', for that matter. Even if we can dismiss the religious associations of ecstasy, our conventional fantasies of education do not easily accommodate the idea of teaching children to transcend their ordinary mental states. Nevertheless, the experience of being caught up in a state of *samadhi*, of deep peace, of unity, of flow, of exceptional clarity, is a fairly common one and can be triggered off by all sorts of events, pleasant or traumatic.

In many cultures the structured and acknowledged experience of ecstasy has been an important rite of passage for adolescents. Not so in our own. Rituals like baptism, confirmation, barmitzvah and the like, which once had the power to provide this experience, have largely lost it. Conventional Christianity, like the wider conventional culture, does not now promote an unforgettable ecstatic adolescent experience as the irrevocable step into maturity. It is only in fringe groups, religious and secular, that ecstatic initiation is valued – being 'filled with the Holy Ghost' in a fundamentalist sect, experiencing *shaktipat* in the presence of the guru, gaining membership of a drug subculture with one's first mind-exploding hallucinogenic experience.

Willard Johnson asserts that the absence of a ritual of ecstatic illumination in adolescence is a significant factor behind the self-indulgent infantilism of our culture, which steadfastly refuses to develop 'safe, institutionalized means for reaching ecstatic states'.[198]

> Unfortunately, we achieve ecstasy these days in the worst of ways; as by-products of accidents and near-death experiences, through hallucinogenic 'trips', through borderline cult experiences directed at times by near psychopathic personalities, or through such

uncontrollable media as alcohol and drug abuse, UFOs and snake-handling cults or rock and roll concerts, to name a few of the many ways by which this deepest of human experiences can sometimes be produced.[199]

Johnson argues that there are safe and tried means of reaching ecstatic states and that they ought to be taught. Adolescents of all ages need ecstatic experience to become adult, and if the culture does not provide it they will seek it in any case, often in ways which do them harm.

Even if we strongly support Johnson's argument, we have to acknowledge that meditation in this sense – as goal rather than method – does not come within the agreed social purposes of most schools. If we want to introduce our students to the benefits of meditation it is not productive to talk too much about ecstasy and enlightenment, nor about transformative states of consciousness, nor spiritual commitment. In any case, meditation in its early stages is not about these things. It is about training the mind. It is also about making life more pleasant, effective, healthy and enjoyable. It may be better for teachers to avoid using the term at all, but to teach 'centring' and 'relaxation' techniques.[200] This is not deceitful. Rather, it makes explicit the necessary distinction between the state of 'meditation' which the meditation schools see as the end product of their training, and the techniques which may not only lead to this state, but also produce many other effects which are much more readily acknowledged as goals of schooling.

DEVELOPING SERENITY

It is one thing to make a clear distinction like this in writing and another to find things so clearly distinguished in practice. Sometimes a profound and life-changing experience comes out of using a simple centring technique. Occasionally a teacher may come across a child who is spiritually precocious. Alternatively, a centring technique may be the context for a disturbing experience, just as a child's sleep may be the context for a nightmare. Such experiences, though not common, are sometimes adduced as evidence that 'meditation is dangerous'. Such statements reflect the quite irrational belief that what happens in meditation is out of the meditator's control. Actually, if a meditator, even a child, is truly troubled by an image that emerges in meditation, all he or she has to do is stop meditating.

One rational and non-superstitious way of dealing with a child's disturbed imagination is to take the position, developed in psychosynthesis, that no matter how frightening images may appear to be they are actually friendly and can be approached without fear. If a child is deeply disturbed and keeps experiencing frightening or violent images, a teacher can purposely use meditation techniques designed to develop a sense of serenity. Psychosynthesis provides many such exercises. Alternatively, we can teach a technique like Ainslie Meares' mental ataraxis, in which all images including pleasant or enlightening ones, are set aside as distractions, as the meditator quietly returns to 'just sitting'. In this, Meares is in tune with the Buddhist attitude, which ignores all images, however wonderful, that might appear during meditation.

There is a Zen teaching story about a monk who came in some excitement to his teacher to tell him that as he sat in meditation the Buddha himself had appeared in a vision surrounded by light. 'Don't worry', said the teacher. 'If you keep your attention fixed on your breathing it will go away!'

Meares, dealing with patients in a psychiatric setting, found that while they were engaged in mental ataraxis they might have spontaneous images (for example, long-forgotten images from childhood) that had obvious relevance to their present anxieties. Yet he remained convinced that no matter how useful the cultivation, examination and analysis of these images might be, it was never as useful as simply ignoring the images and spending the time 'just sitting'. He found, as Coué, Erickson and many others have found, that 'just sitting' is healing of itself.

MEDITATION AND TRANCE

Meares, Coué and Erickson seem to talk about the same physiological state, though we may wish to argue about what it should be called. The argument as to whether meditation can be distinguished from trance or hypnotic states is not one that can be resolved simply. It depends entirely on what sort of meditation we are talking about on the one hand and what sort of trance we are talking about on the other.

If we use brainwaves and other physiological indicators as our means of making the distinction we find that advanced meditators produce quite different patterns from beginners or the merely competent, that 'focused' meditation produces different wave patterns from 'open' or 'insight' meditation. Whereas focused meditation may make one 'trancy', open meditation (and some other kinds of meditation) keep the meditator exceptionally alert. If we examine hypnotic and trance states on the same criteria, we find that hypnosis and auto-hypnosis can produce patterns identical with those achieved through meditation (lowered metabolism, slower wave patterns), states that are physiologically identical with normal wakefulness, and states (for example in the hypnotically 'psyched-up' athlete) in which metabolism is raised and brainwaves are accelerated.

Within this range of possibilities is a state or states which we can call 'centred', which can be achieved in a number of different ways: through autogenic training, breathing techniques, focused attention, certain kinds of visualization, repetitive movement, listening to music, contemplating nature, sensory deprivation, sensory overload, Silva mind control, dance, chanting, biofeedback and prayer. There seems little point in trying to make fine distinctions between Huxley's 'deep reflection', Silva's 'going to one's level', Romen's 'self-submergence', Coué's 'healing trance', Benson's 'relaxation response', biofeedback's 'programmed Alpha-Theta state', Meares' 'mental ataraxis' and even the mystic's 'prayer of quiet'.

We can, however, distinguish trance states from meditation by our means of entering them. Trance is something that can 'just happen' to us, can be induced by another person, or can even be generated mechanically. Meditation (centring), on the other hand, is something we have control over, something we do. We can acknowledge also that meditation techniques provide something more than the end product; much of their value lies in the doing. They involve learning a mental discipline and a skill that can be applied to many different goals.

'USING' MEDITATION

If we cannot distinguish unambiguously between a centred state and a state of trance, we can at least distinguish a number of different ways of 'using' such a state. It can be a way of training consciousness, of developing concentration, of inhibiting rational functioning so that the unconscious mind can do its work. It may be a preparation for *samadhi*. It may be a state of peculiar receptiveness to suggestions from oneself or from others, a means of enabling the operation of intuitive, right-brain modes of experiencing reality, a means of relaxing and of enhancing our health and our feeling of well-being. It may give us a sense of contact with the divine. It may be a means of deepening our sexual experience or of becoming accessible to extrasensory communication. It can be a way of reducing stress, of making our immune system more efficient. It can be a way of unblocking our thinking and preparing ourselves for creative activity.

Perhaps not all of these uses are particularly relevant to the classroom, but many of them are. Quite apart from the established benefits to physical and mental health of spending a few minutes each day in meditation of some kind, there are specific situations in which meditative practices can be a valuable aid in our teaching.

If, in teaching a particular class, we intend to use a method of teaching which requires the students to be in a quiet and receptive state of mind, a few minutes of centring meditation is an excellent warm-up to such a state. If we are attempting to teach, and find the children are too scatty and distracted to get any benefit from our efforts, we can use a meditation technique to 'settle them down'. In handling a particular unit of work we can design a teaching strategy around Wallas' preparation-incubation-illumination-verification sequence and utilize a brief period of 'just sitting' as a controlled incubation phase.

We can accept the arguments of the experts in the great meditative traditions, such as Patanjali (c. 200 BC) and St Bonaventure (c. 1250 AD), that truth comes not only through the senses or through intellectual striving but also from a non-sensory inner calm, and conclude that if we want to truly understand something we might, instead of worrying about it or trying to 'work it out', just be still for a while, not thinking at all but simply experiencing calm. Aldous Huxley felt that such an exercise, which he called 'deep reflection" was essential to his attempts to understand or communicate anything. Whatever it is which inhibits teachers from encouraging such behaviour in their classrooms ('We'll stop now and meditate for a couple of minutes, then we can attempt the problem again!' 'We are having some trouble getting a starting point for our story. Let's meditate for a couple of minutes and then see if we can do better'), it is certainly not some intrinsic absurdity in the approach, or evidence of its ineffectiveness.

It is not unusual for athletes, musicians, actors, public speakers and others who have to perform under pressure to establish a personal ritual in which they prepare for a performance by stopping mental activity altogether and 'just sitting' for a while. Teachers who have discovered for themselves the value of such an exercise may go through it before a difficult or challenging class. With practice they can go into this state very quickly. A brief dip into Alpha can restore their energy, if they are feeling rattled or exhausted, can get them orientated to a task, can give them a sense of being clear, competent and spontaneous. They find the same sort of exercise an excellent preparation for other tasks which are specifically intellectual (taking an exam or writing a paper), aesthetically creative (writing a love-letter), life-threatening (getting back into the traffic after a pause at the lights) or potentially conflictful (attending a staff meeting). They can teach their students to do as much for themselves.

One of the clearly demonstrated physiological effects of meditation is what researchers in TM call 'hypersynchrony' of the brain waves. Not only does the density of Alpha waves increase markedly, but it increases in both hemispheres, not simply in the hemisphere which is dominant. The two hemispheres get into harmony. This sort of thing usually only happens when we are asleep or in the process of falling asleep. In some forms of meditation we can have this synchrony between the two halves of the brain without losing our clarity and alertness. Exactly how this phenomenon affects our thinking is not yet clear, but it is reasonable to guess that it enables left and right hemispheres to work simultaneously and co-operatively on whatever bit of reality presents itself. Meditation may encourage the integration of our analytic mode of thinking and our synthesising and intuitive mode.[201]

One of the things we learn very quickly when we start to practice meditation, whether concentrative meditation or insight meditation, is just how uncontrolled our mental processes are. This is reflected in the brain wave patterns characteristic of our 'normal' waking and thinking state. The great meditative traditions like Zen set out to teach people to gain control of this uncontrollable mind. One of the thrusts of contemporary meditation research, especially biofeedback research, is in exactly this direction: to learn what sort of wave patterns are associated with truly productive thinking and to teach people how to switch them on and keep them under voluntary control. Such research has a long way to go, but it is confirming the value of techniques already developed through rigorously examined experience over hundreds, or even thousands, of years. It has also demonstrated that such techniques do not cease to be effective when detached from their religious associations. A 'secular' and instrumental approach to meditation can actually produce useful results very quickly, often more quickly than meditative practice in a religious tradition, which has other purposes and other expectations. We can quite quickly teach ourselves and our students new ways of using our minds.

THE RECEPTIVE MODE

We can also teach ourselves and our students ways of 'unfreezing' our perception and thinking. One of the experimentally demonstrated effects of meditation is what Arthur Deikman calls 'deautomatization of the brain's structures'.[202] A great deal of our living is automatic, robotic. This applies even to our way of perceiving the world. There are a number of ways of shaking our learned, rigid, patterns of perceiving; some of them are traumatic. One non-traumatic way is meditation.

If, following Deikman's research, we focus intently on a particular object for a number of meditation sessions, perceiving it simply as it is, without thoughts, values or associations, we will find that it changes. It may become larger, smaller, rougher, smoother, may move or change colour. Immediately after this experience we will find that other things look different, that the learned patterns we constantly apply to what we perceive are not operating any more, that we are seeing as if for the first time. Clearly the intense focus triggers the same sort of mechanism as is sometimes triggered by hallucinogenic drugs. The specific visual effect does not last for long, but feelings of newness, aliveness and intensity of experience (seeing colours and hearing sounds more clearly) persist. For Deikman deautomatization is not just an interesting experience, it is an experience that allows a reorganization within the personality, that allows us to let go of rigid ways of perceiving and reacting and behaving. This experience comes to some extent with all levels of meditation, not just with the more spectacular ones. If there is any validity in this kind of speculation we might see it as a way of explaining how an apparently unsolvable problem sometimes becomes solvable after it has been interrupted by a period of meditation (a trance, or even sleep). It might encourage us also to try the same approach when we find our students stuck in a set of frozen ideas, feelings and values (e.g., racist or sexist bigotry) that we wish to unfreeze. Even successfully teaching children to move into the 'receptive mode' basic to meditation may be a big step in this direction. Rigidity and bigotry are not really compatible with the receptive mode.

This statement should not lead us into the nonsense of declaring that habitual meditators are never rigid, bigoted or dogmatic. Jung warns us often enough that the more we are committed in our consciousness to one mode of perceiving and behaving the more we are vulnerable to control by the repressed but powerful opposite – the shadow. We are familiar with, and amused or irritated by, the 'meditation fascist' who wants to impose on us a doctrine of inner freedom, peace, openness and receptivity which comes from the narrowest of doctrinal perspectives, and who is innocently unconscious of his own dogmatism.

Hestia, like all the gods, has her own pathology. Those who worship her obsessively and neglect the other gods have a tendency to mistake the certainty of their own inner illumination for *The Truth*, to sit warming themselves in their own enlightenment and to leave to others the contemptible business of hunting and gathering, to become so centred and stable and immovable that they are immune to any influence, so self-preoccupied that they are insensitive to others, so 'spiritual' that they lose contact with reality, so contemptuous of egoic striving that they are controlled by their unconscious drives. The great meditative traditions have a different vision of how the search for enlightenment (or for the divine) ought to affect us. We are hewers of wood and drawers of water before enlightenment and hewers of wood and drawers of water thereafter.[203]

TOWARDS MYSTICAL EXPERIENCE

Hestia-inflation is not likely to be a source of much concern in the classroom. Hestia will be lucky to get any acknowledgement at all. Nevertheless, even the secular, instrumental, scientific approach to meditation, which sees useful techniques rather than potential for enlightenment, and which seems to be the most appropriate approach to meditation in the classroom, has to be seen in a context in which ecstasy and enlightenment are important. Hestia does seem to give way to Dionysos. If we read Ainslie Meares' writings from beginning to end we will see a shift from a consideration of meditation as a means of voluntarily entering a regressive hypnotic trance for medical purposes to a conviction that samadhi is somehow what life is all about, that through meditation we come into direct contact with the ground of our being. His hard-headed science led him straight into mysticism. In this he is not unusual.

William Johnston, commenting on 'secular meditation' remarks:

> Even as I write I am aware that much of the seemingly agnostic meditation is not agnostic at all. Frequently the self-styled agnostic who meditates is searching for something ultimate. And the person who searches believes, or hopes, that an answer exists somewhere. In this sense he is not agnostic. Many meditators are in quest of truth, wisdom, ultimate values – things they have failed to find within their own religious tradition. It could be plausibly argued that secular meditation has arisen partly because traditional and established religion has ceased to give people, particularly young people, the religious experience for which they are craving. So they look elsewhere ... Anyhow, experience of meditation gives people a sense of being on a way that goes somewhere; and this is what they want.[204]

Sitting Quietly

We can say a great deal about meditation in the language of science, and no doubt we will find satisfactory ways of reducing mystical experience to chemistry and electricity. Satisfactory, that is, if we know how to value our scientific fantasies for the power of their images rather than mistake them for ultimate reality, if we keep reminding ourselves like Plato that we are in a cave, with our backs to the light, and can only see the shadows on the wall.

No matter how energetically we argue the instrumental case for meditation, we are forced to acknowledge that there is another dimension to the experience of meditation that we cannot avoid. Even those of us who are reluctant to use the words 'religious' and 'mystical' must accept that meditation is more than technique, that even when we are concentrating on technique meditation provides a way of looking at the universe which is paradoxically very different from the universe of technique. The universe of Hestia is one where we know we are at home, at peace, where all things come back to their beginnings, where we are united with the centre of things, at one with the rounded earth, where we know not the parts but the whole. All the traditions, primitive and sophisticated, ancient and contemporary, Eastern and Western, religious and scientific, speak a common language. It is very tempting to weigh in our own experience with the mystical consensus of the ages and declare that here at last we have found The Truth. It may be wiser to acknowledge the possibility that The Truth is beyond us, and that even Hestia's illumination can only show us shadows on the wall.

The truth of Hestia is no less true for being different from the truths of the other gods. Apollo, for instance, tells us to search for truth in the clear light of the intellect as it investigates more and more thoroughly the intricate order of the universe. Prometheus suggests that all we need to know is how things work. Dionysos would have us seek truth in the dance, the flow, the unpredictability, the many-shapedness of things. Hestia tells us the truth is within, in stillness, in one-pointedness. Eros gives us a very different image of ultimate reality. The meaning of life is not to be found within ourselves but in relationship. God, according to Eros, is love.

NOTES Chapter 8. Sitting Quietly

[172] W. Johnson, *Silent Music*, p. 18.
[173] An excellent account of scientific research in meditation will be found in Patricia Carrington, *Freedom in Meditation*.
[174] J. Jeans, cited in K. Wilber, 'Of Shadows and Symbols: Physics and Mysticism', *Revision*, 7, 1, 1984, p. 4.
[175] A. S. Eddington, cited in K. Wilber, *Eye to Eye*, p. 5.
[176] K. Wilber, op. cit., p. 115.
[177] ibid., p. 116.
[178] Cited in L. Freeman, *Light Within*, p.27.
179 Herbert Benson, a distinguished medical researcher, has outlined his conclusions in a simple and accessible form in *The Relaxation Response*. Ainslie Meares' technique of meditation will be found in *Relief Without Drugs*. For a popular account, see P. McKinnon, *Living Calm in a Busy World: Stillness Meditation in the Meares Tradition*.
[180] R. Assagioli, *Psychosynthesis*, p. 118.
[181] ibid., p. 220.
[182] ibid., p. 214.
[183] ibid.
[184] ibid., p. 223.
[185] See M. Murphy, *Golf in the Kingdom*; W. T. Gallwey, *The Inner Game of Tennis*; W. T. Gallwey, *Inner Skiing*; P. Payne, *Martial Arts: The Spiritual Dimension*.
[186] M. Csikszentmihaly, *Beyond Boredom and Anxiety*.
[187] L. Le Shan, *How to Meditate*, p. 11.
[188] H. Benson, 'Looking Beyond the Relaxation Response', *Revision*, 7, 1, 1984, p. 51.
[189] Mahareshi Maresh Yogi, *The Science of Being and the Art of Living*.
[190] H. Benson, op. cit., p. 51.
[191] Le Shan, op. cit., p. 14.
[192] C. Trungpa, *Meditation in Action*, p. 52.
[193] A. Meares, *The World Within*, p. 113.
[194] A. Meares, *Relief Without Drugs*, p. 18.
[195] A. Meares, *Strange Places, Simple Truths*, p. 37.
[196] If we adopt a 'structures of consciousness' model such as that of Jean Gebser, the argument becomes fairly meaningless. In Gebser's theory both the primitive 'archaic' structure and the more complex 'integral' structure are capable of experiencing 'the origin' or 'ultimate reality'. The difference is that our archaic consciousness has only a dim awareness, whereas our integral consciousness transcends mental clarity without suppressing it. We can argue that the various techniques of meditation activate different structures of consciousness (or different parts of our brain). In Meares' mental ataraxis we may fall back on our archaic structure. The power of rituals and incantations comes from the magic structure. The

mythical structure enables visualization and other imaginative techniques. Deautomization and other techniques of switching off 'the robot' become possible through the mental structure. Advanced meditators will exercise their skills through the integral structure. See J. Gebser, *The Ever-Present Origin*.

[197] A summary of the findings of education-related studies of TM will be found in F. Griffith, 'Meditation Research: Its Personal and Social Implications', in J. White, *Frontiers of Consciousness*, pp. 119-137.

[198] W. Johnson, *Riding the Ox Home*, p. 93.

[199] ibid., p.92.

[200] A simple and useful approach to introducing meditation to children will be found in G. Hendricks and R. Wills, *The Centering Book*.

[201] The recently established connection between nasal cycle and hemispheric dominance may give us a way of explaining the efficacy of some yogic breathing techniques in altering one's state of consciousness. The well-established technique of breathing through alternating nostrils (Block the left nostril; breathe in through the right. Block the right nostril; breathe out through the left; breathe in through the left ...) is an example of a technique which slows and amplifies brain waves while maintaining mental clarity. Another is Jack Schwarz' yoga-inspired technique of 'paradoxical breathing' in which an abdominal pattern of breathing is generated by paradoxically pulling in the abdomen with each sharp intake of breath. EEG monitoring has demonstrated that the deep abdominal breathing developed in this way (with brief inhalation and extended exhalation) is associated with Theta activity in the whole brain. Yet rather than inducing drowsiness it makes the mind exceptionally alert. See J. Schwarz, *Voluntary Controls*.

[202] A. Deikman, 'Deautomatization and the Mystic Experience', in C. Tart, *Altered States of Consciousness*.

[203] 'Illumination' is not necessarily associated with moral excellence.

> I have witnessed with much initial dismay, that some of the best mystics were the greatest stinkers among men. Self-righteous, smug, anti-women, anti-men, politically fascist, stubborn, irrational ...
> The naïve assumption is that yogic vision, the zero experience, also brings about knowledge of all things to be known. This is nonsense!
> (A. Bharati, *The Light at the Centre: Context and the Pretext of Modern Mysticism*, p. 91).

[204] W. Johnson, op. cit., p. 19.

9

EROS AND ASSOCIATES

And there shall be for
thee all soft delight
That shadowy thought can win,
A bright torch, and a casement ope at night,
To let the warm Love in.

                              John Keats

Educating Psyche

WHEN WE THINK OF SOUL, if we think of soul at all, we are likely to be stuck in a medieval fantasy of something immaterial which is contained, for the time being at least, in the vessel of our body. The ancient Greek fantasy of the psyche was quite different. For them, Psyche was rather the relationship between humans, gods and nature. Individual soul was not individual at all but was an expression of the soul of the world, the universal pattern that binds us to spirit and matter. Her myth was essentially a myth of relationship. We see this fairly obviously in her unswerving commitment to her unseen, discovered and vanished lover, her service to the gods (even to Aphrodite who hates her) and the involvement of plants and animals in her story. We see it also in the identity of her lover, Aphrodite's child, Eros. Psyche and Eros desperately want each other. When, after surviving all her trials and returning from the Underworld, Psyche opens her casket to see the beauty of Death and falls into an eternal sleep, Eros defies his mother once more by flying to where Psyche lies and awakening her with the touch of his arrow. He then persuades Zeus to make their love eternal and we reach what is literally the archetypal romantic ending.

We recognize Eros fairly easily as the god of Love, and we know that he is distinct from his mother, the goddess of Beauty and Sensuality, and that it is somehow his love for Soul which separates him from Aphrodite We find him in mythology as an adolescent, inclined to shoot his arrows somewhat irresponsibly at gods and humans alike and to get some amusement from the consequences. We also find that he is a mighty and powerful god who demands to be taken very seriously indeed. In Greek mythology there seem to have been two gods called Eros, one of them the child of Aphrodite and the other an ancient god of Unity and Harmony, the force which draws things together, more ancient than Zeus himself. The Greeks themselves were inclined to assimilate the two. Eros is firmly established in classical mythology and the European imagination as both the oldest of the gods and the youngest, as a god of union and communion, relationship, newness and process, romance and delusion, procreative power.

We know Eros most of all as a god of emotional attachment. Eros is at work in sexual involvement, in family relationship and in simple friendships.[205] It is from Eros that we get the joy of being comfortably close to someone, of working side by side with someone, of being 'connected'. He is at work in the bonding between people who confront a problem together, or who play as a team. He is present in the love that binds musicians to their music, mathematicians to their mathematics, teachers to their teaching. Without Eros, music, mathematics and teaching are dead and deadly. It is through Eros, also, that the gods themselves come together and through him that they are loving and creative.

Thinking about Eros mythologically helps us to be aware that love is not personal. The delusion that my loving is uniquely mine, that no one has ever felt like this before, is part of love's craziness, but love is not really something we own. It is certainly not something that we have much control of, something that we can 'do' by summoning up all our strength and determination. It is something that happens to us, something that we allow, something that we 'fall' into. At least, this is what the Eros myths tell us and, if we look at life from an Eros-perspective, this is what we see.

Freud looked at life from an Eros-perspective and saw, for a time at least, only one instinct, a unidimensional and unidirectional sexual instinct which he called 'libido'. His influence on our thinking is felt every time we use the word 'erotic' to denote the sexual in both its narrowest and broadest senses. He saw creativity and relationship as one, just as the Eros myths do. The drive towards life is a drive towards unity. This seems true enough on the level of biological reproduction, but we need to carry the metaphor to other levels as well. It is in the coming together of two (or more) elements, two personalities, two ideas, two cultures, that something new comes into being. When we turn the Eros-perspective on to education we find both knowledge and personal growth created in the encounter of two minds.

PASSIONS OF THE SOUL

Yet Eros is not the only god with a high profile in the classroom. There is always Apollo and Prometheus to consider. There is also another figure whom we are inclined to see as the very opposite of Eros — power opposed to love, distance opposed to closeness, coldness opposed to warmth, wisdom opposed to naivety, state opposed to process, position opposed to momentum, pessimism opposed to optimism, work opposed to play, maturity (or stagnation) opposed to growth, oppression opposed to freedom. When Freud came to the reluctant conclusion that Eros (libido) was not the only god (instinct) involved in human behaviour, he imagined that there was another which he called Thanatos, the death-instinct, which contradicted the life-instinct in every way. In archetypal psychology this constellation of values, images and drives is often personified as Senex (the old man), who is manifested in such old gods as Uranus (father of the gods), Kronos (who devours his children, and is still represented as Old Father Time with his death-dealing scythe), Saturn (who sits brooding, cold and remote from humanity) and Zeus (who sees everything, knows everything, and maintains his power with thunderbolts). Eros is one of a group of gods who personify the Puer (youth) archetype – the polar opposite of Senex. Dionysos, Narcissus, Hermes and Icarus personify other aspects of this archetype, one that brings together a constellation of themes that seem to dwell together in our experience and philosophies: change, unfolding, self-discovery, life-force, process, relationship, creativity, dialogue, freedom, authenticity, romance, optimism, self-obsession, irresponsibility, love, inspiration, effeminacy, beauty, spontaneity, spiritual striving. The specific Eros-dimension in all this is relationship.[206]

Our ways of thinking and talking are formed according to such archetypal perspectives. Teachers who think of their teaching essentially in terms of passing on established information to their pupils are likely also to be convinced of the importance of 'keeping one's distance', of avoiding 'innovation for innovation's sake', of having rigorous standards, of teaching respect for authority, of keeping in touch with 'hard reality', of maintaining a sense of order and stability. They are inclined to confuse thinking with remembering. They are even inclined to develop a fantasy of 'the good old days' which bears little relation to reality. All of these notions are found imagined in the myths of the Senex gods – Uranus, Kronos, Saturn and Zeus.

Teachers who think of their teaching in terms of the primacy of relationship are likely also to put a high value on creativity, growth and enthusiasm (which belong to Dionysos, the vegetation god who is constantly reborn), self-discovery and a sense of wonder (Narcissus, who turns into a flower while admiring his own reflection), dialogue, process and relevance (Hermes, the winged messenger of the gods, the awakener) freedom from the constraints of 'hard reality' (Icarus, who dons wings and flies towards the Sun), and emotional engagement (Eros again).

It has been common enough for people who think and write about education to make a bipolar distinction between a schooling dominated by a Senex perspective and one dominated by Puer. Carl Rogers distinguishes between 'traditional' education (which is nasty) and 'facilitative' education (which is nice); others contrast 'conservative' and 'progressive' education. The Brazilian educator, Paolo Freire, in looking at the ways in which schooling can be an instrument of either oppression or liberation, places what he calls 'banking' education at one pole and 'problem-posing' education (which is pursued through dialogue) at the other.[207] This polarization has proved very useful in clarifying what teachers do, but every simplification has its dangers.

Martin Buber warns us that neither Eros nor the 'will to power' is in itself a principle of education.

> But Eros and the will to power are alike passions of the soul for whose real elaboration a place is prepared elsewhere. Education can supply for them only an incidental realm and moreover one which sets a limit to their elaboration; nor can this limit be infringed without the realm itself being destroyed.[208]

Such passions of the soul give education its vitality, but we are well advised not to hand over ourselves and our classrooms to either of them exclusively. Nevertheless, whether or not the classroom is only an 'incidental realm' for Senex and Eros, it seems that at the present time it is a realm where they are in conflict.

TEACHER-STUDENT RELATIONSHIPS

People have been trying for a long time, at least since Socrates and Lao Tse, to say something definitive about the connection between learning and relationship, but it seems to have assumed a particular significance in recent times. Some of this thinking considers relationship simply as a context in which learning occurs. Some of it goes further and sees relationship as essential to the process of learning. Whatever we might say about learning we have to acknowledge that teaching, at least, is possible only through relationship. No one can claim to be teaching unless someone is learning. It is not what I do which entitles me to call myself a teacher, no matter how skilfully I do it; it is the fact that others interact with what I do and say that in such a way they learn something. Even when the contact between teacher and learner is filtered by time, distance and information technology, the teaching is in the interaction.

We do not have to sentimentalize teacher-student relationships to argue for their importance. Many teacher-student relationships are merely instrumental and some are destructive or manipulative. Relationship, in teaching as elsewhere, can be for better or worse. Eros, like all the other gods, has his pathological side, and romance regularly leads into spitefulness, delusion and hurt. We can nevertheless start with the erotic premise that relationship is central and concern ourself with what makes for better and worse relationships in the classroom and how the better and worse in relationship is reflected in the better or worse in teaching.

The question of what sort of relationship is most appropriate in the classroom is not one that can be easily resolved by a casual survey of teachers.

> 'Kids have to know they can trust you.'
>
> 'Let up on them for an instant and they'll tear you to pieces.'
>
> 'The girls and I are really good friends.'
>
> 'The last thing they want is a friend. They want somebody to tell them what is what.'
>
> 'The important thing is to accept them as they are.'
>
> 'You mustn't take any nonsense from them.'
>
> 'A little fear doesn't do them any harm.'
>
> 'Children won't learn when they are being threatened.'
>
> 'Sometimes you have to mother them.'
>
> 'They're not here to be cuddled. They're here to learn to read and write.'

'We have a lot of fun together.'
'The kids in this school need firm direction.'
'They know what they want. It's my job to help them get it.'
'I'm the authority here. They know where they stand.'
'You have to work hard to get their respect.'
'I really love these kids.'
'You've got to keep your distance.'

If we are looking at these teachers solely from the viewpoint of Eros we are likely to have already sorted out the nice ones from the nasty. Yet there are other perspectives on relationship, other gods involved. We can certainly detect here Eros seeking growth through intimacy, but we can also hear Demeter insisting that relationship is motherhood, Saturn proclaiming the hierarchy at the heart of things, Zeus waving his eternal thunderbolts, Dionysos leading the dance, Artemis announcing the miracle of sisterhood. We must remember that all the eternally arguing gods must be honoured. To be nothing but a mother to one's students may be as destructive as being nothing but their manager. An unwanted lover may be as heavy a burden to them as an unwanted tyrant. It is easy to see only the positive in those perspectives that are most compatible with our conscious personality and most strongly confirmed by our experience, and to see only the negative elsewhere.

There are, no doubt, teachers who are neurotically fixed in a single perspective and the needs, attitudes and behaviour which go with it, inflated by a complex and the archetype behind it. There are certainly many whose behaviour moves over a narrow range, who have, essentially, only one way of relating to children but who are able to respond at least minimally to the needs of different children. But there are many, too, who would readily own to making many of the quoted statements, at different times, in different places, to different audiences, in reference to different children. They may be bemused by their own inconsistency, but they know that there is no single way of behaving which always and unambiguously represents the best kind of relationship to have with their students.

If we try to make simple generalizations about student-teacher relationships which make sense of this we are likely to fall into an either-or position and lose the multi-perspectivism which is archetypal psychology's distinctive achievement. Freud and Jung are not much help to us. They both tell us a lot about Eros in different ways, but they both had a fairly negative view of him. In the end each became a wise old man who founded a school of psychology, with its own dogma, orthodoxy, institutional forms, hierarchy, accreditation procedures, morality. This is the stuff of Senex, who has no real interest in connectedness. Neither had Freud or Jung. Though the language of repression, denial, transference, reaction formation, sublimation, complex, introjection and projection enables us to talk in clever and complicated ways about relationship, it says nothing about our experience of intimacy. Neo-Freudians and the neo-Jungians, humanistic and existentialist psychologists, have rather more to say about what relationship means to us. However, many of them talk only in Puer-speak: intimacy, growth, wholeness, process, creativity and the immediacy of experience. Their frame of reference often does not allow them to deal with the obsessions of the Senex: power, traditional values, absolute morality, and (when schooling is spoken of) the essentialist curriculum.

There are a lot of gods with something to say about relationship, but Eros has special rights here. The other gods, while jealously guarding their own specializations, acknowledge that relationship is pre-eminently his domain. It is only the presence of Eros in the relationship of mother to child, boss to worker, guru to disciple, master to apprentice, healer to patient, teacher to student that can make such relationships fruitful. If such a notion appears romantic, so be it. Romanticism is an essential dimension of the Eros-perspective. If we want to be cynical or critical, we must abandon Eros for the time being and take the view of Senex or Apollo.

ROGERS' RELATIONSHIP THEORY

Senex-consciousness or Eros-consciousness is not attached to age. When Carl Rogers died (in 1987) in his mid-eighties he was, he believed, in the most creative and productive period of his life. He had spent sixty years developing and applying an Eros-theory based on his experience that people have an innate and powerful tendency to become most fully themselves, and that they do this in and through relationship. He had translated this principle into the practice of client-centred therapy and student-centred teaching. He had set out to demonstrate that the technique of client-centred therapy was more effective than other techniques and discovered instead that the magic of therapeutic effectiveness came not from Prometheus, the technician, but from Eros, the one who joins together. He had found that it was not technique which made the difference between helpful and unhelpful therapy, but the quality of the relationship between therapist and client. He had distinguished what it was in the relationship that gave the client the freedom to be healed: the realness or genuineness of the therapist, her acceptance of and trust in the client, her ability to enter the client's world and understand it from the inside. He had made the leap again from therapy to education and argued that these three qualities are the essential qualities of the good teacher. Rogers applied his theory to groups and systems and found that it worked there also. Finally, in his eighth decade, he was using all his skill and experience to demonstrate that relationship was the key to international and intercultural peace, helping the antagonists to talk and listen to each other in Central America, Northern Ireland and South Africa and taking his own initiatives to promote dialogue between the USA and USSR.

Rogers' development of the idea of the 'facilitative' teacher has been profoundly influential even among those who have a horror of the word and even in the schools where the loudest voices heard are Senex ones: back to basics, law and order, corporate planning, greater output for smaller investment. Rogers was certainly not alone in developing the twentieth-century version of Eros-consciousness, but he was one of the most persuasive in applying it to education.

> It would be most unlikely that one could hold the three attitudes I have described, or commit herself to being a facilitator of learning unless she has come to have a profound trust in the human organism and its potentialities. If I distrust the human being, then I must cram her with information of my own choosing lest she go her own mistaken way. But if I trust her capacity for developing her own potentiality, then I can provide her with many opportunities and

permit her to choose her own way and her own direction in her learning.

It is clear, I believe, that [such teachers] rely basically upon the tendency toward fulfilment, toward actualization, in their students. They are basing their work on the hypothesis that students who are in real contact with problems that are relevant to them wish to learn, want to grow, seek to discover, endeavour to master, desire to create, move toward self discipline. The teacher is attempting to develop a quality of climate in the classroom and a quality of personal relationship with students that will permit these natal tendencies to come to their fruition.[209]

Rogers has often been criticized for being soft-headed and naive in expressing such an optimistic view of human nature. He is optimistic indeed, but he is neither soft-headed nor naive. The simple lucidity of his later writings was a matter of choice; in his earlier writing he had adequately demonstrated his ability to develop complex intellectual structures and express them in turgid pose. He wished to be read, and he wished to be understood. (Jung, on the other hand, seems to have deliberately written in an obscure style in order to give his ideas credibility.) His theories, including his theories on facilitative teaching, have been corroborated again and again in research. Even Eros manages to adapt his rhetoric to a scientific age. The Eros perspective expresses a truth, a limited truth indeed but a powerful and important limited truth, and in Rogers' work it has the essential twentieth century adornments of truth – systematic theory and scientific corroboration!

A theory of education which focuses on the teacher-student relationship, which castigates the teacher who crams a child with 'information not of her choosing', which underlines the importance of 'real content with problems that are relevant to them' which emphasizes seeking, discovering and creating is in danger of forgetting a few things. Rogers may have been too subtle and sensitive (and too conservative) a person to forget that the new and the now only exist in the context of the old and the then, or to discount the importance of traditions, established wisdoms, the structures that give us stability, but unfortunately the past few decades are littered with the debris of Eros-fantasies that went wrong, 'free' schools, 'alternative' schools, 'community' schools and 'open classrooms' that came to grief in the same way that political Eros-fantasies like romantic socialism have come to grief. Some, indeed, were destroyed when they came into conflict with Senex in his nasty aspect: institutional power, hard reality, political repression, intolerance, soulless bureaucracy, economic rationalism. Yet others destroyed themselves through an inflated Eros which used intimacy as a substitute for ideas, refused to value the positive aspects of Senex (work, limits, knowledge, history, order, endurance), and slid into delusion, disillusion and chaos.

Rogers himself tried to heal the split between Eros and Senex when he wrote *On Personal Power*. Unfortunately, unlike his other books it sold very poorly. Presumably, people interested in power did not want to read a book by Carl Rogers and people interested in Rogers did not want to read a book about power. We do not seem to be very interested in developing double-vision, yet single vision leads us into nonsense or pathology and may be positively dangerous. Senex intolerance and blindness is presently destroying the earth; Eros intolerance and blindness will not save it.

GIBB'S TRUST THEORY

Rogers was supported in his development of the Eros-perspective by other humanistic psychologists such as Rollo May, Sydney Jourard, Arthur Combs and Abraham Maslow. Out of the same humanistic framework the organizational psychologist, Jack Gibb, has developed a theory which, while basically an Eros-fantasy, does attempt to maintain double vision. Gibb's theory emerges from the field of business-management, which accounts for its acknowledgement of the Senex perspective, but it has, by implication, a great deal to say about what goes on in classrooms.[210] Though Gibb developed his theory as a way of looking at corporations, he argues very plausibly that it applies to every kind of group: a friendship, a partnership, a marriage, a family, a club, a class, a school, a school system, a nation-state. The application to education is worth exploring.

Gibb's theory attempts to link relationship, work and the satisfaction of basic human needs. When we place it in the context of the classroom we find that it has no place for the assumption that genuine caring is incompatible with firm direction or for the equally absurd assumption that the more attention teachers give to relationship the less attention they give to thinking.

Gibb sees trust and fear as the key to understanding persons and social systems. When trust is high relative to fear, people and people-systems function well. When fear is high relative to trust, they break down. He summarizes the process central to personal and organizational growth by the acronym TORI: trusting, opening, realising, interdepending.

The language with which Gibb describes these processes is charged with Puer-images.

> Trust is the process of discovering.
> To trust with fullness means that I discover and create my own life. The trusting life is an inter-flowing and interweaving of the processes of discovery and creation. These processes have four primary and highly interrelated elements:
> — Discovering and creating who I am, tuning into my own uniqueness, being aware of my own essence, trusting me – being who I am. (T)
> — Discovering and creating ways of opening and revealing myself to myself and others, disclosing my essence, discovering yours, communing with you – showing me. (O)
> — Discovering and creating my own paths, flows, and rhythms, creating my emerging and organic nature, and becoming, actualising, or realising this nature – doing what I want. (R)
> — Discovering and creating with you our interbeing, the ways we can live together in interdepending community, in freedom and intimacy – being with you. (I)
>
> Use of such words as 'discovering' and 'creating' may suggest to some that I am talking here of largely cognitive and conscious process. I do not mean to imply this at all. I am referring to organic, holistic, bodymind, total-person processes that have the quality of an intuitive or instinctive quest about them. Each process is both a discovering and a creating – indistinguishable in fusion. I think of the person, the group, and the organization as total organisms that develop these processes, especially under climates of high trust.[211]

Gibb suggests that we can focus on these processes to distinguish between systems that function well and those that function badly and that by giving attention to these processes we can change a group from one characterized by defensiveness, constraint and ill-feeling to one characterized by trust, high self-esteem and high productivity.

In a classroom where there is little mutual acceptance (trust) between teacher and student and student and student, communication and the flow of information (openness) is likely to be poor. Productivity (realization) will be low and there will be little mutual assistance (interdependence). In a classroom where there is high trust, teacher and students can be open to each other, information can flow freely and accurately, the shared task of the group can be accomplished efficiently, and in the sharing of the task and the satisfaction of achievement everyone in the class will become both teacher and learner.

For Gibb, trust is the catalyst in an evolutionary process (another Puer image): trust begets openness, openness begets realization, realization begets interdependence, interdependence begets trust, in an upward spiral. Or a downward spiral can be generated by fear: fear begets defensiveness, defensiveness begets passivity and resistance, passivity begets imposition and dependence, which confirms and increases fear. Gibb suggests that we can distinguish several levels in this upward or downward movement and uses a ten-point scale of 'environmental quality' to do so.

FROM CHAOS TO CARING

At the bottom of the scale is chaos, a state dominated by fear, in which authority, consensus, respect for the rights of others, do not exist. The first step out of chaos is the punitive environment, in which the group is dominated by a leader who controls through punishment. A further step up the ladder is the autocratic environment in which the leader controls not by the threat of punishment but by the force of authority and the group's readiness to obey. Higher again is the benevolent environment, where the leader's relationship to the group is that of a caring, nurturing, protecting parent.

Gibb's scale describes an evolution. There is a natural movement from punitive to autocratic to benevolent, as each level carries in itself the beginnings of the next. The leader who successfully establishes a stable punitive environment as the only apparent alternative to chaos, establishes with it the habit of obedience so that the constant use of punishment becomes unnecessary. The autocratic leader, who maintains order through the simple force of his or her authority, can eventually afford to smile benevolently, and care for the group like a good father or mother. From the point of view of group members, the establishment of an efficiently punitive regime may be welcomed if it ends the fear of chaos, but the certainty that one can at least survive by following a set of rules allows them to experience the need for mental and physical safety of a higher order. Respect and unquestioning obedience are then willingly given in exchange for a stable environment without the threat of punishment. Once this is established they become aware of other needs: to be dependent, to belong, to be cared for. The move from ruthless power to benign administration is not unknown in politics at the macro and micro level. It is not unknown in schools and classrooms either, though it may be less manifestly bloody in its origins.

At its worst the punitive class will be teetering on the brink of that state of deep chaos in which humanity must perforce prey on itself like monsters of the deep. At its best (and it has a best) it will be accepted as a place to meet a group of students who have learned to expect no more of school than this, to give them an experience of order and stability, through which they can be taught that other ways of relating to teachers are possible and rather more satisfying. What distinguishes the best from the worst is the presence of Eros. Love has many manifestations, and punishment can occasionally be one of them, as every loving parent is aware.

There is a distinct difference between an environment in which the teacher says: 'Do this or I'll punish you', and one in which the message is 'Do this because I say so'. In the autocratic environment there is less fear, paranoia, cynicism, hostility, resistance, deceit; more energy, acceptance, directness, fluidity, frankness. Whereas in the punitive environment the children will learn only what is necessary to avoid being punished, in the autocratic classroom they cease to be dominated by fear. They will learn what is necessary to get the teacher's approval and meet society's expectations. When writing from the Eros perspective it is easy to see the inadequacy, narrowness and destructiveness of the punitive and autocratic environments and neglect their positive aspects. Yet the instinctual pattern in human behaviour which in archetypal language is personified in Senex or Saturn is just as important a part of us as Eros. The needs the autocratic environment sets out to satisfy are genuine ones: we have a need for order, for continuity, for criteria of right and wrong, for endurance, for tradition, for limits, for work. Society has good reasons for approving the Senex-values which the autocratic teacher promulgates: obedience, respect for one's elders, discipline, perseverance and conformity.

Yet, if we look at what human beings are capable of, we see much that the autocratic environment can do nothing to develop. At worst autocracy produces students who are passive, or who put their energy into actively resisting learning and avoiding trouble. At best the kind of motivation and behaviour it encourages enable an efficient learning of skills over the narrow range that corresponds with the teacher's interests and the curriculum's demands. Development of what we commonly call creativity – in the sciences, the humanities or the expressive arts – has no place in it. Knowledge in the autocratic environment is always given, never created. So is meaning. There is no place in 'banking education' for ambiguity and little place for subtlety.

Obviously these environments are not 'pure'. The autocratic teacher's behaviour will have elements of the punitive and the benevolent in it. If there are a number of independent-minded yet non-threatening students in the class the teacher may even withdraw her power occasionally to move into an advisory mode. Moving from one level up to another, however, presents both teacher and children with an impasse. They must give up one sort of satisfaction (in this case the joys of power and obedience) without the certainty of finding another.

Moving from a master-slave relationship to a parent-child one may seem particularly risky, and some teachers are not prepared to try it at all. Those who do find the satisfaction well worth the risk.

The language Gibb uses to describe the benevolent environment (level three) is the language of Demeter, the Mother-Goddess. The teacher is 'nurturing and caring'; he or she 'provides security and affection'. The environment satisfies the teacher's need to protect, to help and rescue, and the children's need to be protected, to be cared for, to be dependent, to be nourished.

The climate of the benevolent classroom is very different from that of the autocratic, and the child's experience of learning is very different. Instead of, 'Do this because I say so', the child hears something like, 'Do this because I love you. Do this because it will please me.' There may be occasional punishment but the teacher prefers to reward rather than to punish. Anyway the child's greatest punishment is to acknowledge that he has disappointed the teacher. Learning is no longer motivated by fear or the desire for power and status but by genuine desire to please the teacher. And since the teacher genuinely and manifestly likes and values the children, they know that there are many different ways of pleasing her. They may even please her by showing resourcefulness and initiative. Benevolence removes many inhibitions to learning, and creative behaviour begins to be possible. There is trust enough here to allow teacher and students to be open to each other. The children get the affection and acknowledgement they need if they are to grow.

The behaviour which we call 'fathering' in our culture has strong associations of authority, morality and limit-setting; the behaviour we call 'mothering' is characterized by warmth, nourishment and possessiveness. It may be a woman doing the fathering (either absolutist, punitive Kronos-fathering, or cold, remote Saturn-fathering or benevolent-yet-autocratic Zeus-fathering) or a man doing the mothering. In any case the mature, self-actualising, self-realising, integrated, individuated personality will encompass both. We need to acknowledge what is constructive in both ways of relating to children and also what is potentially damaging. The benevolent relationship satisfies emotional needs, but it also produces dependence. Warmth, acceptance and the teacher's pleasure can be powerfully manipulative. Maternal possessiveness is no great promoter of growth. Possessiveness has more to do with power than with love.

A teacher may clearly see the limitations of the benevolent relationship and be uncomfortable with it. Her ideology may demand that students be treated as free, decision-making agents for whom learning is a natural, intrinsically-rewarding process. On the other hand the students (including adult students) may demand security, warmth and reassurance. It does them no great service to attempt to force them to be independent learners when they are desperate to find the all-knowing, all-caring teacher who will gently deal with all their problems. The teacher must meet them where they are, give them some of the knowing and caring they are asking for, and help them develop the confidence to trust in their own resources.

The punitive, autocratic and benevolent environments, which we can see as phases in the evolution of a group, are all characterized by an obviously vertical power relationship. As fear diminishes and trust increases, the leader can afford to share some power with the group.

SHARING POWER

If the teacher truly trusts her students' competence she can pass over some of her power to them by moving into an advisory or consultative relationship with them, which involves caring for them in a way which diminishes their dependence on her. She will then find herself confronted by a whole new set of truths, a new set of values, a new set of needs and a new set of satisfactions.

In the advisory-consultative environment (Gibb's level four) it is no longer true that children want to be told what to do, that teacher status depends on authority, that children 'have to be motivated', that teachers must lay down firm demands. The students set out to learn because they are curious, and they perceive the teacher as a resource in the pursuit of their own goals, not as someone to be feared, pleased, avoided or resisted. They are interested in understanding and being understood, aware of their own needs and their own resources.

Power relations are still top-down, of course. Even though the teacher's status depends on expertise rather than authority, the teacher is still very much in control. The teacher whose self-esteem is entangled in the need to control others can still feel comfortable enough. The advisory environment presents a different and better form of management than the punitive or benevolent one. Energy need no longer be wasted in coercion, dependence or resistance. The students have a sense of owning what they are doing, are free to be creative and use their talents, are genuinely interested in the quality of what they produce, are invited to enjoy their work. However, they have this freedom within a structure provided by the teacher-manager-expert, who makes the major decisions, sets goals and poses problems or, as often as not, passes down these decisions and goals from a higher authority.

In the classroom functioning at this level the children will often be engaged in working on their own projects, alone or in small groups, calling on the teacher for advice and information when it is needed. Ideas of reward and punishment seem irrelevant in this context. The children find their satisfaction in successfully pursuing their goals and the teacher finds his satisfaction in supporting them and watching their skills grow. When we look at the potential for oppression and emotional overdependence in the environments lower on Gibb's scale, the advisory-consultative classroom represents a major advance. For some educational theorists it approaches the ideal learning situation. It is the level at which the teacher begins to be 'facilitative', as Rogers uses the word. Knowles' self-directed learning model[212] and Graves' process-writing[213] seem to be based on this notion of the teacher as expert advisor-consultant-facilitator and the notion of the student as someone who will find in herself the motivation and resources to carry out a learning task effectively as long as she finds a task which has some meaning. Yet for Gibb this level of environmental quality only hits number four on a scale of ten. Unless such a classroom is enlivened by Eros, the energies of children and teacher may be channelled into a soulless collection of data on the one hand or manipulative management on the other.

One further turn up the trust-openness-realization-interdependence spiral we find the participative environment (level five). The focus shifts from individual task to shared task and from supportive teacher-pupil relationship to participation, choice and consensual decision-making. The teacher gives the students more power, allows them the same right to be in charge of themselves as she maintains for herself. Participating in group decision-making comes to be seen as an end in itself. The teacher enters into this process herself, providing a model of the way the children should relate to each other: listening, respecting differences, being courteous, ensuring that the strongest opinions and the loudest voices do not always prevail. It becomes terribly important that all the class are involved in the process in some way. The dialogue between children and the conflict or consensus that ensue are seen to be the ground of the children's learning: the teacher's input as expert appears much less significant, and the teacher can even tolerate her expertise being overlooked. Involvement, loyalty, community and the capacity for choice have completely replaced obedience, status and the ability to assimilate information at the centre of the educational process. The satisfactions of avoiding punishment and gaining approval have given way to the much more erotic satisfactions of intimacy, dialogue, cooperation and shared discovery and achievement.

The facilitative teacher working in this environment is concerned not so much with what information she can pass on the children but with what structures and experiences she can design and initiate (and help the children design and initiate) to ensure that the children are engaged and challenged, that they ask themselves and each other questions that are important to them, that they do not inhibit each other's learning , that they listen to each other, that they become aware of the resources available to them. Where the effective autocratic teacher gets satisfaction out of a lesson where information has been successfully transmitted to the students, and the effective benevolent teacher gets satisfaction in meeting 'her' children's need to know, the effective participative teacher is most delighted when, after all her work, the children really perceive that they have done it all themselves. Where the autocratic teacher follows the barrister's rule of never asking a question unless she knows the answer, and where the benevolent teacher gently guides the children towards the answer she wants, the participative teacher consciously avoids asking questions to which she knows the answer. Dialogue is too valuable to be contaminated by tricks like that.[214]

The teacher's role in the participative group is always somewhat ambiguous. She may join in group discussion and decision-making, taking pains to keep her participation low-key so as not to shape the process too strongly. She may exact neither obedience nor status, yet her role is distinctly and significantly different from that of her students. The participative decision-making and co-operative learning are possible only because she allows and encourages them. The thirty children or adolescents engaged in enthusiastically solving a problem, making a play or discovering ancient Mesopotamia are not doing so because this is the 'natural' thing for children of this age to be doing at this time of day. And they did not find the enthusiasm and involvement by chance. The choices they have made and are making are indeed genuine choices, but they have been shaped by the direct and indirect suggestions of the teacher. The belief that children have a natural curiosity and a natural desire to learn and a natural preference for cooperative activity may be necessary for the development of a successful participative group, but it is certainly not sufficient. The teacher, and perhaps her predecessors in this class, have worked hard and skilfully to construct an environment in which power can be shared, where interpersonal trust is high, where children feel the freedom to make choices and make mistakes. The children may have consciously chosen the topic they are studying and a way to go about it, but the idea of what it is appropriate to study is one that they have received, formally or informally from the teacher. The teacher herself, while genuinely respecting the competence of her students to choose what is best for themselves, has to make sure that the choices they make are consistent with what the school, the school system and the wider society take to be the aims of education. In any guided democracy the guidance and the democracy dwell uneasily together.

Some of this ambiguity vanishes at the next level of environmental quality. If teacher and students can trust themselves and each other enough to make a break with the procedures of a participatory democracy based on firm leadership, they may find themselves working from a new set of assumptions in what Gibb calls the emergent environment (level six). The teacher ceases to assume that she must maintain the role of expert and facilitator and enters the teaching-learning process as a learner. The students cease to assume that the teacher has an altogether unique role in the group and come to accept the teacher's knowledge or organizational skills as a contribution to the group's work alongside one member's contribution of enthusiasm and another's contribution of a critical mind. They cease to assume that, even when they work with other students, their learning task is essentially worked out in a relationship with the teacher, and they begin to see the task as a common one, to be worked through in relationship with all members of the group. In the participative group the teacher is using her leadership skills in the service of the children. In the emergent group she dispenses with the status of leader altogether. She and her students move from the understanding that leadership is attached to a single person to the understanding that leadership is something shared by all members of the group.[215]

For the first time the teacher and students enter the realm of what Martin Buber calls the 'interhuman'.[216] For Buber, there are three things that impede the growth of dialogue between human beings: the tendency towards 'seeming' rather than 'being': our difficulty in freely perceiving another person, and the tendency towards imposition rather than unfolding. For the interhuman to occur there must be no seeming, there must be genuine perceiving of the other, there must be no imposition. The interhuman becomes possible only when teacher and students can leave their social roles, a process that must begin with the teacher. As Gibb says:

> The teacher is no longer the 'facilitator', motivator, model, or person responsible for the standards of the class; not the method-provider, character example, target, the one responsible for helping students clarify their values or negotiate the contracts, or to rewrite their life-scripts. The teacher simply joins the group, learns and struggles, has fun and pain, tries to make sense out of the world, appreciates the universe, assimilates the traditions of our forefathers, or builds a new world. Or tries, along with the others, to do these things.[217]

Every shift from one level of environmental quality to a higher one involves risk and requires an injection of trust. Abandoning one's view that the class is a collection of people for whom one has responsibility and for whom one performs certain functions, and genuinely joining the class as a learner is a frightening prospect for some teachers. There is a lot of satisfaction in being a leader, controlling, manipulating benevolently, being needed. Unfortunately we have to jettison some of these satisfactions if we want to experience the new satisfactions which come with being part of an emergent group engaged in the process of enquiry. The students also have to abandon the satisfactions of being looked after, of giving someone else responsibility, of just 'going along', before they can experience the quite different satisfactions of being self-determining, of creating with others, of sharing a focus and an energy.

Paolo Freire's vision of problem-posing education can be lodged comfortably with Gibb's fantasy of the emergent group. Problem-posing education 'regards dialogue as indispensable to the act of cognition which unveils reality ... bases itself upon creativity and stimulates true reflection and action upon reality ... affirms men as beings in the process of becoming – as unfinished, uncompleted beings in and with a likewise unfinished reality.'[218]

Freire made his contrast between banking education and problem-posing education with adult students in mind, yet we are as likely to find the genuinely 'dialogical' teacher in the infant school as in the university. For Freire, education must begin with the solution of the teacher-student contradiction, by reconciling the poles of the contradiction so that both are simultaneously teachers and students.

> Through dialogue, the teacher-of-the-students and the students-of-the-teacher cease to exist and a new term emerges: teacher-student with students-teachers. The teacher is no longer merely the-one-who-teaches, but one who is himself taught in dialogue with the students, who in their turn while being taught also teach. They become jointly responsible for a process in which all grow. In this process, arguments based on 'authority' are no longer valid; in order to function, authority must be on the side of freedom, not against it. Here, no one teaches another, nor is anyone self-taught.[219]

Environmental quality is symbolized in the way teachers use the language of ownership. The punitive or autocratic teacher will say such things as, 'I will not tolerate that sort of behaviour in my classroom', 'If you want to be in my class, you'll have to work', to imply that he, not the children, owns the space. The benevolent teacher will refer to the space as 'our classroom' yet talk of the children as 'my class' in tones of affection or frustration, like any parent speaking of 'my family' and 'our home'. Both ways of talking are out of place in the emergent group. It is genuinely 'us' and 'our space' and 'our project', without condescension or pretence.

It is symbolized also in the way the curriculum is perceived and handled. At the punitive and autocratic levels, which are dominated by Senex, there is a strong sense of right and wrong answers. The curriculum is a body of public knowledge, which the teacher receives from those who have the authority to dispense it and which he deals out in his turn to his pupils. It is something to be remembered, applied and tested. As we move through the advisory and participative levels, the curriculum becomes something to be negotiated between teacher and pupils. The children's sense of their own needs and interests begins to be taken into account. The teacher brings to that negotiation his sense of what is central to the culture and his sense of what society expects children to learn at school. What emerges, hopefully, in the emergent group is a knowledge that is both public and personal, a learning which is, by Carl Rogers' definition, 'significant'.

> It has a quality of personal involvement – the whole person in
> both feeling and cognitive aspects being in the learning event. It is
> self-initiated. Even when the impetus or stimulus comes from the
> outside, the sense of discovery, of reaching out, of grasping and
> comprehending, comes from within. It is persuasive. It makes a
> difference in the behaviour, the attitudes, perhaps even the personality
> of the learner. It is evaluated by the learner. She knows whether it is
> meeting her need, whether it leads towards what she wants to know,
> whether it illuminates the dark area of ignorance she is experiencing
> ... Its essence is meaning.[220]

Gibb reiterates that the level of environmental quality attainable by a group depends on the needs of all the group members. Children with a strong need for direction or reassurance, or who are accustomed to finding their own sense of identity through resisting their teachers, may be unable to function in an emergent group. Nor will teachers with strong need to control their students, or who are addicted to the delights of being mummy or daddy or nurse to their class, or who are uncomfortable without a fan club. Assuming that the teacher is prepared to let go of these satisfactions, she may still find that the children's needs and expectations will define the level at which she can meet them. Even one student who cannot cope with trust or independence (and who gets less and less comfortable as the group moves up the spiral) can frustrate the teacher's best efforts. The vision of a group in which she and the class share a purpose and a commitment, a deep trust in themselves and each other, a delight in working together and a readiness to be fully available to each other may need to remain a vision while she meets the children's (or adults') need for security, dependence and direction.

The emergent group, standing at level six on the scale, has within it the beginnings of something better. The spiral of trust-openness-realization-interdependence can take a few turns yet. The nature of schools and schooling places some limits on how far up the scale a classroom group may go, but Gibb assures us that we have not peaked at level six.

BECOMING HOLISTIC

Phases seven to ten represent the organic, holistic, transcendent and cosmic levels of environmental quality. In the organic phase the nature of communication changes from the verbal and logical to the empathic and intuitive. The holistic group integrates unconscious, archetypal and latent processes. In the transcendent phase we are ego-less, need-free, as we tap into non-sensory sources of being and energy. The cosmic phase focuses on cosmic, universal and nirvanic states of community and being.

The organic environment (level seven) is part of people's occasional experience outside the classroom and is not unknown within it. It may be easier to find the characteristics of the organic group – mutual transparency, genuine dialogue, spontaneity, unselfconscious physical touching, total engagement, intuitive communication – in a pair of lovers, a group of children playing, an organization coping successfully with an emergency. Yet we can be lucky enough to experience it occasionally as teachers at any level, from infant school to university, if we can abandon for the moment our sense of ourselves as teachers, if we can stop doing things to the children (punitive-autocratic) or for the children (benevolent-advisory-participative) and truly start to do things with the children.

In the autocratic classroom we gave up the right to use force in getting the students to do what we wanted; in the benevolent phase we stopped being the single, absolute, unchallengeable authority; in the advisory phase we stopped trying to impose knowledge on our students; in the participative phase we let go of the full responsibility for providing the structures through which they might learn; in the emergent phase we found we no longer even had to 'facilitate'. In the organic phase there is no room for a 'teacher' at all. If we want to be a member of the group we must enter it on the same terms as the (other) students. This may be a little further than we want to go, but we know that education does not stop where people stop 'teaching' each other.

In the organic group, Senex values are very much in the background. The 'realization' of the TORI cycle is just as essential a part of the cycle as before, but its nature has changed. What was realized at the lower levels was a product. What is realized at the higher levels according to Gibb is 'my emerging and organic nature'. The purpose of the group is found in becoming, actualising or realising this nature – doing what I want. There is no sense that 'I am learning this because I have to' or even that 'I am learning this because it is useful'. In the Eros-dominated, organic group, learning does not count unless it is 'significant'. It may in fact be very appropriate and very useful to society, but its essence is personal knowledge and personal commitment.

Most of us can follow Gibb as far as level seven (organic) but find that his descriptions of the last three stages have few points of contacts with our experience. Certainly they don't say much about our experience of teaching. It is fairly apparent that the larger the group and the more diverse the needs and aims of its members the more difficult it will be for it to reach the higher levels of environmental quality. A large and complex system like a modern state cannot move very far from the punitive level, no matter how benevolent its leadership may wish to be. A simpler system such as a sexual relationship may certainly be stuck at the punitive or benevolent level, but it does have some chance of reaching the holistic level, at least sometimes. A basketball team or a string quartet may function quite well under autocratic leadership, but after months or years of playing together leadership may be fully shared. The members of the group develop an interdependence, a mutual understanding, an ability to communicate intuitively, which enable them to play in complete unity of purpose and action. It may well be impossible to do as much in a classroom where one adult and twenty-five children with diverse wants have been randomly allotted to each other for the purpose of studying a subject in which many of them have no interest. It is not surprising that most classrooms illustrate the lower points on the scale.

The shift from the organic to the holistic environment (level eight) involves abandoning the dependence on rational processes and verbal communications. Conscious and unconscious processes are integrated. What we do together intuitively is far more appropriate and creative than what is produced by our usual rational modes of thinking. For illustration we might imagine a pair of mountain-climbers hanging over an abyss, where their lives depend on having absolute trust in each other even if they do not particularly like each other, where they must communicate with absolute accuracy by the subtlest of signals, must share exactly the same vision of what they are trying to do, must be totally engaged in the task, take complete responsibility for each other and yet depend completely on each other. Or we might imagine the consummate jazz ensemble where each member of the group 'knows' without reflection what others are doing and about to do, where communication is entirely non-verbal and largely subliminal, where the individual's spontaneous and original contribution finds meaning in the beauty of the total sound When the equivalent experience happens in the classroom, whether in a group of infants painting a mural, a group of graduate students engaged in a research project or a group of adolescents solving a problem or exploring a poem, the experience is magical. Unfortunately, the experience is not something we can easily manufacture in the classroom. The intense focus, the heightened awareness, the sensitivity to each others' inner worlds, the experience of 'flow', are more likely to take us by surprise.

It may be inevitable that such magical experiences are somewhat unusual in the classroom. When children have spent years learning to do what they are told at school, learning to compete with each other, learning to perceive schooling as meeting teachers' needs and interests rather than their own, it may be altogether too much to expect this sort of magic.

BETWEEN TRUST AND FEAR

Besides, the school has Senex values to uphold and the teacher, as an accredited, responsible, accountable, paid professional, is expected to have a commitment to them. There are things to be learned, structures to be maintained, a culture to be transmitted, standards to be enforced, adults to be respected and obeyed. Some would argue that such things define the nature and purpose of schooling. In such schooling there is not much value attached to the kind of learning that takes place in the Eros-dominated organic or holistic group, where everything is open to questioning and exploration and where a reliance on process has taken the place of the security of static knowledge. Moreover, the transcendent and cosmic levels in Gibb's model – the experience of pure process, of self-transcendence, of psychic communion, of cosmic harmony – would be thought bizarre in most classrooms, if not positively dangerous.

A teacher may believe, with Rogers, that 'the basic nature of the human being, when functioning freely, is constructive and trustworthy'[221] yet find that external pressures and her own lack of confidence and skill have her limiting her students' freedom rather than increasing it. On the one hand she cannot impose freedom on them; on the other she finds that leaving them to find their own way does not seem to make them any more free. From Eros' point of view, 'all you need is love', and this is what Gibb and Rogers seem to be asserting when they talk of the power of trust and the quality of relationships. Ironically, however, they make it clear that creative love and its rewards come not from simply feeling nice and doing nothing in particular, but through the qualities of Senex – work, commitment, purpose and, above all, time. Rogers' 'freedom to learn' is certainly not the product of *laissez faire*. It comes rather from a teacher's skilled and focused commitment to the quality of her relationship with her students. The acceptance, empathy and genuineness which define for Rogers a relationship in which freedom is possible may be common human qualities (more or less) but they are also skills to be acquired and applied through patient and purposeful practice. They are also skills to be taught in one way or another to one's students.

No matter how benevolent a teacher is, no matter how much she respects the potential of her pupils to make mature decisions, she may be drawn by them into a punitive relationship. Obviously a teacher who is a sadistic monster may find a satisfying career in punishing and humiliating children. Unfortunately, even a sane and balanced teacher may sometimes find herself forced to the conclusion that the children are unwilling to behave productively unless they are bullied into it. She may eventually be convinced that if she is not prepared to take on the role of punisher she will herself be ruthlessly punished by her students.

It is certainly too much to expect a teacher to come into a group of children whose schooling has been carried out in a punitive environment and teach them in a few days, or even a few weeks, to share and dialogue and create in the ways that an organic or holistic group can do these things. For a teacher to enter a punitive group and treat it as an organic group is a strategy for chaos. For a teacher to enter an organic group and treat it as a punitive or even benevolent group is another strategy for chaos. Teachers make both kinds of mistake, allowing their needs or their ideology to divert them from the obvious entry point to a relationship with any class, an understanding of the class's experience of the world.

The teacher who is touched by Eros will want her class to change: to become closer, more emotionally involved in the work, more free, more self-initiating, more trusting, more creative and productive. But she will find that she cannot bring about this change by thrusting children into situations they cannot handle. She may, for example, be committed to a view of education as an apprenticeship for democracy. Yet when she tries to arrange her classroom and her teaching strategies on participative lines she finds the students apathetic or resentful. They do not want to waste their time in long discussions about what they want to learn or how they want to learn it. They do not want to have choices or make decisions. They want the teacher to have the responsibility for all that, so that they are left with the much simpler task of doing what they are told, either gladly or resentfully. All her attempts to set up democratic structures in the classroom are frustrated. Democracy collapses around her and she reverts to autocracy or worse. Participative democracy in the classroom becomes a hopeless and slightly ridiculous ideal.

The teacher in the next room is also interested in establishing some participative decision-making in his class, not because he has a deep commitment to the democratic ideal but because he has been influenced, by curriculum documents or colleagues or the need to impress the principal, to believe that he ought to do so. Following his habitual autocratic mode of dealing with children he sets out to impose democracy on them. The children are firmly instructed in what is expected of them, they are punished or humiliated in the usual ways if their behaviour does not come up to expectation. They learn the forms of participatory democracy and follow them with little enthusiasm and with one eye on the teacher. The experiment does not work, and class and teachers settle back into the autocratic mode, having satisfactorily enforced the teacher's belief that kids in Year 3 (or Year 6, or Year 12) or working class kids, or middle class kids, or kids in this kind of school, or kids from this particular ethnic group, don't want this sort of thing and can't handle it.

In another class the attempt to establish guided democracy may meet with resistance for quite different reasons. It may be one of the classes where the children have already experienced the satisfactions of shared enquiry and shared leadership. They have become a close-knit group, comfortable with each other, sharing responsibility, communicating well, taking it for granted that they can and will make whatever decisions are necessary, committed to a learning task which makes sense to them. They have developed ways of making decisions informally and without insoluble conflict. When a teacher who has not shared this experience tries to introduce the group to the procedures of participative decision-making, insisting on meetings, debate, agendas, voting, specifying and defining rights and responsibilities, the children may resent the intrusion of excessive guidance into their democracy. Unfortunately, all too often an insecure teacher perceives this resistance as malicious, becomes more insistent, meets more resistance, and eventually resorts to punishment in an attempt to save the system from chaos.

On the other hand, when a group is attempting to operate at the emergent or organic level but not succeeding because, for instance, individuals in the group are demanding power or refusing responsibility, or because communication is distorted by a lack of trust or mutual respect, a shift back to the participative or consultative phase may be an appropriate way of preventing a collapse into tyranny or chaos.

Shifting a class up the spiral from the submission, resistance and dependence of the lower levels to the self-reliance and self-motivated behaviour of the consultative and participative levels is a major preoccupation for teachers who are not hooked on power or parenthood. They wish children to learn something about democracy through experience and they are persuaded that in a participative group children will learn more and learn better. They are often frustrated in their attempts to raise the quality of the environment, and frustration may make them punitive.

It is not possible, however, to achieve level five ends by level one means. History has demonstrated thoroughly enough that the Terror does not produce liberty, equality and fraternity (a level six fantasy); purges, executions and the Gulag do not create a classless society (level seven); an Inquisition does not generate a genuine spiritual revival (level nine). Neither does a punitive society in Egypt or Tunisia transform instantly, through idealism and a people's revolution, into a democratic or socialist paradise. If Gibb's theory is any guide, classrooms are no different in this from nation states and families. To get from level one to level five it may be necessary to touch all bases, at least lightly.

The key to movement, as Gibb reiterates, is the level of trust relative to fear. Both trust and fear are contagious and, things being what they are, the defensive teacher is likely to infect the children with his own fears. Research on group climate has shown how critical the teacher's behaviour is in influencing the quality of interaction in the classroom. Where a teacher is manipulative, exploitative or defensive, the children tend to treat each other in the same way. Where the teacher respects his pupils, appreciates them, listens to them, the children tend to do as much for each other. Of course the influence also runs the other way. The class whose experience of each other and of previous teachers is non-defensive may be able to infect a fearful teacher with trust, but they generally have a harder time of it. The level of trust has to be negotiated, consciously or unconsciously, by the teacher and class together. It is not just the teacher's trustworthiness and capacity to trust which is critical here. In a hostile class, too much trust may be more threatening than too little and may simply give the class another means of punishing the teacher. He does not need to withhold his concern for the class, his genuineness, his desire to understand them, his acknowledgement of their worth, but he may need to hold his trust in them at a level which they can accept and match, and adapt his teaching strategies accordingly.

Punishment may be counter-productive in the emergent group, but in a punitive environment it is an effective way of achieving some of the school's and teacher's aims. Strategies to encourage self-discipline will work in the participative environment but not in the autocratic. In the autocratic or benevolent classroom it is productive for the teacher to single out a child for praise or reward; in the punitive classroom on the one hand and the emergent on the other, a child may find the same reward or praise an embarrassment. It may be appropriate in the emergent or organic group to expect students to feel comfortable with physical contact; in the punitive environment physical contact may be associated with violence. An assertive approach to classroom management may be effective in the consultative or participative environments yet ineffectual in the punitive environment and irrelevant or destructive at the higher levels.

Once a benevolent environment has been established, a teacher may usefully invite a class to discuss what is deeply significant to them; such an overture may die with a whimper at lower levels. Conversely, an autocratic teacher may successfully engage the class productively in rote learning; a class which is hooked on co-operative learning may strongly resist this. Techniques like visualization and role playing may simply fail in the punitive group because the group does not provide a climate in which the children are prepared to engage in them. In a high-trust classroom, the teacher and children may together work out strategies for dealing with the violent or disruptive behaviour of a particular child; in a low-trust classroom the attempt can be disastrous.

Process writing and process mathematics flourish in a facilitative environment (advisory and above), but in a punitive class the children do not have the psychological freedom that the process approach demands. On the other hand, the receptive phase of suggestopedia depends on accepted authority; unless the teacher is prepared to teach with the full assurance of authority the technique does not seem to work. Likewise, an autocratic approach may be very appropriate when a class is learning to use dangerous materials; encouraging inexperienced students to experiment creatively with an electric saw or a cabinet full of chemicals is hardly in their best interests. Yet while an autocratic classroom may be a suitable place to learn specific skills, there are other things that will not be learned there. If we want children to discover how to write the story, play the melody, make the chair or solve the problem with subtlety. excitement and a sense of beauty, we need to give Eros a share in the action. It is Eros who awakens soul.

AN EROS FANTASY

It is not belittling Gibb's theory to call it an Eros-fantasy, just as we might call Moreno's theory a Dionysos-fantasy. Behind the precise classifications and systematic distinctions is a belief that connectedness is central, that love conquers all, that communion and creativity are intimately related, that becoming is more important than being, that the future is more important than the past, that the romantic is more human than the pragmatic, that goodness is not imposed but grows from within, that there is no such thing as a bad child. We find a similar fantasy in Carl Rogers' vision of facilitative teaching. To call it a fantasy is not to suggest that it is somehow untrue, but to remind ourselves that it is but one image of the truth.

Gibb's and Rogers' theories are certainly 'true' enough, in the way images are 'true'. Besides, they have been tried out in experience and investigated rigorously enough by research. We can gather plenty of evidence to support the proposition that children learn more and learn better in a class where there is a good relationship between teacher and student and between student and student, where there is trust.[222] However, an Eros-fantasy provides only one perspective. It has its blind spots. It sees only the positive qualities in Eros and the negative qualities in Senex.

Gibb's view of the Senex-dominated environments at the bottom of his scale is essentially negative. He sees the oppression, manipulation, rigidity, depression and apathy without much acknowledgement that there are positive qualities that belong to the same syndrome: tradition, standards, responsibility, industry, stability, wisdom, realism, order. He acknowledges that the punitive and autocratic environments meet real needs, like dependence and the need for structure, but for Gibb these are needs which we are supposed to grow out of as we become self-realising, grown-up people.

When Rogers talks about 'traditional' education (which he contrasts with student-centred education) his language is entirely pejorative: 'the teacher is the possessor of knowledge, the student the recipient ... the teacher is the possessor of power, the student the one who obeys ... authoritarian rule is the accepted policy in the classroom ... trust is at a minimum ... the subjects (the students) are best governed by being kept in an intermittent or constant state of fear ... democracy and its values are ignored and scorned in practice ... there is no place for the whole person in the educational system, only for the intellect.'[223] He clearly disapproves, and rightly so, for he disapproves of the negative aspects of Senex. However, a conservative educational theorist writing about the same classrooms might be referring to other aspects of Senex: the sense of order, the respect for duly constituted authority, the efficient teaching of basic skills, the inculcation of correct moral values, the transmission of the culture, the learning of rights and duties and responsibilities. The Eros-inflated teacher can make light of such values, but he can only afford to do so because there are other teachers who take them seriously.

Gibb and Rogers reserve all of their enthusiasm for Eros-values. When Rogers writes of person-centred education he sees only the positive: 'The facilitative person shares with the others the responsibility for the learning process ... The facilitator provides learning resources from within himself and his own experiences ... the focus is primarily on fostering the continuing process of learning ... the discipline necessary to reach the students' goals is a self-discipline ... In this growth-promoting climate, the learning is deeper, proceeds at a more rapid rate, and is more pervasive in the life and behaviour of the student than learning acquired in the traditional classroom.'[224] Where experiments in person-centred education have failed he attributes the failure to attacks by a negative Senex (rigid and uncaring bureaucracies, power-hungry principals, insecure and unimaginative school boards) and he does not see what the

Senex-perspective can see only too clearly: that Eros-inflation carries in itself its own destruction.

There are classes where closeness completely displaces thought, where teacher and students are so busy being nice to each other that they do nothing else and eventually lose even the energy to be nice to each other, groups where relationships move from being delightfully warm to being obsessively intense to being spitefully malicious, where intimacy turns into manipulation. Neither does Rogers acknowledge what happens when we are inflated by the other Puer figures who are never far from Eros. Where there is inflation the shadow is not far away. The Dionysian teacher generates great energy, creativity and playfulness, yet there is a point at which charisma turns to fascism and spontaneity turns to fanaticism. Narcissus in the classroom impels the excitement and beauty of self-discovery. Yet this can easily tip over into self-obsession and an incapacity for action. Hermes, the messenger of the gods, has no obsessions of his own, but personifies the interaction of ideas. For him process and dialogue are ends in themselves. But process can turn to groundlessness, and dialogue without content has a way of turning into its opposite – dogma without dialogue. Icarus drives us to reach beyond our grasp, yet if we reach too far we lose all contact with reality until we crash fatally into it.

It is not surprising that Senex-values keep reasserting their dominance in schools, as in politics, in spite of the occasional revolution of process, relevance, creativity and relationship. It is in the nature of Senex to endure relentlessly, and it is in the nature of Puer to give up easily. The myths show us Puer imagined in the germinating seed (Dionysos) and Senex imagined in the harvest (Saturn). People whose energy and ideas come out of a Puer-complex are very good at starting things but have little stomach for following them through. Senex-compelled people are inclined to knock new ideas on the head just as Kronos waits for infants to be born so that he can devour them; all their energy is in getting results, in harvesting, hoarding and selling.

In the rhetoric of Rogers and Gibb, and of most humanistic educators, positive Eros is set against negative Senex. In the rhetoric of the New Right (and the Old Right) positive Senex is contrasted with negative Eros. We somehow have to keep the consciousness of both sides, to avoid simplifications, to accept complexity and ambivalence as essential to our experience and not as something to be reduced or avoided.

When we are engaged in rhetoric, that is, when we are busy persuading others to our views, we are much inclined to singleness of vision. Gibb and Rogers are no exception. Yet Gibb shapes his Eros-rhetoric to be heard in the Senex-culture of the corporation, where there is no chance that the Senex-obsessions of organization, industry and profit will be abandoned for the joyous pursuit of togetherness. His rhetoric points to ways in which the toxic environment produced by the concentration of power and the depersonalization of relationships may be transformed into a life-supporting environment, where the empowerment of employees and the development of genuine dialogue may lead to more efficient organization, more productive industry and higher profit.

Rogers' theory of facilitative teaching grows out of his attempts to deal with the pain of his clients in therapy. He did not see his relationship with his clients as an end in itself but as an instrument to enable them to leave their pain and lead effective lives. The teacher-student relationship which provides psychological freedom is not one where closeness is sought in order to satisfy the teacher's or student's need for it, but one in which good relationship allows the student's purposive learning to proceed uninhibited by fear of punishment or fear of displeasing. For all its Puer-rhetoric it is essentially a Senex relationship, in which the facilitative teacher is wiser, more knowing, more powerful (and usually older) than the student, where freedom is something granted by the teacher, where the ever-changing newness of experience paradoxically expresses basic human values, and where the Eros of emotional engagement must inevitably turn into the Thanatos of divorce and separation

Teachers are not teachers in order to like children. Certainly, when one is impelled by Eros, love, closeness, trust and the buzz of emotional engagement are inclined to become ends in themselves, but they should not be ends in themselves in the context of the classroom which, as Buber says, provides for them only an 'incidental realm'. Eros in the classroom is about something: about realization, about generativity, about gaining skills, about the painting in which a child is intently involved, about the problem which the group is solving, about mathematics, about Shakespeare.

FIGURE AND GROUND

James Hillman, who has done a great deal to tease out the implications of Senex-consciousness and Puer-consciousness in our culture, suggests that setting up Senex and Puer as polar opposites may not be the best way of understanding them. He suggests rather that we think in terms of a single Puer/Senex archetype, imagining Puer and Senex coexisting as figure and ground. When we focus on Puer, Senex becomes the background; when we bring Senex into focus, Puer fades into background. What we experience is a constantly shifting balance.

Jung, whose psychology is largely built around images of polar opposites (conscious/unconscious, anima/animus, introversion/extroversion, thinking/feeling, persona/shadow and so on) insisted that one of a pair of opposites cannot exist on its own. When we identify consciously with one of a pair, its opposite lies dormant and undeveloped (but nevertheless powerful) in the background. Introversion and extroversion, anima and animus, Senex and Puer should, in this way of thinking, coexist in a rhythm of alternating dominance, a rhythm characterized by both harmony and tension. If we consciously identify with one perspective only, we allow ourselves to be unconsciously controlled by the other, instead of drawing delight from the harmony and energy from the tension.

Jung himself did not have much time for the Puer perspective. This is not surprising in someone who spent most of his life being a 'wise old man'. In writing about individuation he actually develops the unromantic idea that becoming most fully oneself depends not on love but on 'hatred'.

> Hatred is the thing that divides, the force which discriminates. That is to be seen when two people fall in love. They are at first almost identical. There is a great deal of participation mystique, so they need hatred in order to separate themselves. After a while the whole thing turns into wild hatred; they get resistances against one another in order to force each other off – otherwise they would remain in a common unconsciousness which they simply could not stand.[225]

Jung goes on to illustrate his point by pointing to the experience of transference in therapy. The client's exaggerated attraction towards the therapist turns into exaggerated repulsion or resistance as the hatred that was unconscious in the relationship bursts into consciousness. Teachers may be able to draw similar illustrations from their experience of the occasional adolescent crush. We can find illustrations also in our experience of groups of all kinds, which get hooked on Eros and repress their hatred. They develop the utter conviction that this is the most wonderful group of people in the world. Because intimacy is good, more and more intimacy must be better and better, so they pursue closeness and communion until suddenly everything seems to go bad. This is, suddenly, the nastiest, most hateful, most manipulative group of people in the world. Hatred refuses to be repressed any longer to maintain the Eros fantasy.

The successful and enduring group is the one in which neither the need for intimacy nor the need for distance has to be repressed. Falling in love certainly has its delights, but they are brief. Worse, Eros-inflation, like any other inflation, has a tendency to turn into its opposite. Friendship, in which closeness and distance, Eros and Saturn, are held in balance, has a somewhat better record of endurance.

Just as Senex and Puer can be kept in balance in relationships, they can be kept in balance also in the curriculum – where Shakespeare is discovered to be new and relevant and exciting and the latest rock song is heard in the context of a centuries-old tradition of popular music. They are kept in balance also in a school where the freedom for students and teachers in Year 9 to become a trusting-open-productive-interdependent organic group is affirmed by a benevolent 'traditional' school ethos and administration which takes good care of Senex values.

Hillman warns us again and again against monotheism, against singleness of vision, and with good reason. Singleness of vision, even the singleness of an erotic vision, lets uncontrolled Senex in, with all his intolerance and blindness. Creative visions quickly turn into orthodoxies. Freud, Jung, Erickson, Moreno, Assagioli and Rogers have all had their ideas frozen into doctrines by single-minded disciples who, for all their rhetoric about love, sharing and freedom, seem quite prepared to burn the occasional heretic. Hillman suggests that negative Eros and negative Senex end up being identical.

Educating Psyche

As teachers or parents we have to develop multiple vision. This does not mean a muddle-headed confusion of ideas. It means accepting a reality in which truth does not lie in one orthodoxy or another but can exist in a different way in each. It means accepting ambivalence as a part of life, an ambivalence in which the vision of possibilities is always balanced by the peripheral vision of realities.

FINDING SOUL

Rogers, Gibb and Freire have an Eros-inspired vision of possibilities. They want to end oppression (psychological, organizational, political) but are only too aware that freedom cannot be manipulated or imposed. For them, freedom – in the classroom or anywhere else – grows out of dialogue, and dialogue grows out of hope. As Freire expresses it:

> Nor yet can dialogue exist without hope. Hope is rooted in men's incompleteness, from which they move out in constant search – a search which can be carried out only in communion with other men. Hopelessness is a form of silence, of denying the world and fleeing from it ... As the encounter of men seeking to be more fully human, dialogue cannot be carried on in a climate of hopelessness. If the participants expect nothing to come from their efforts, their encounter will be empty and sterile, bureaucratic and tedious.[226]

Emptiness, sterility, bureaucracy and tedium are Senex-experiences which overwhelm us when Eros is absent, when we find ourselves hemmed in or oppressed by the Senex of an institution or relationship or when we find the pathology of the Senex oppressing us from within. Hope may bring us back the Eros-magic: either the hope of Icarus who makes a brief and glorious flight out of oppression and imprisonment (a myth we regularly live out in getting new projects 'off the ground') or the hope of Psyche who, drawn by her vision of Eros, goes with courage and endurance into the depths of things and tastes the beauty of Death before being found by her lover.

Like Psyche, we sense Eros as a vision which draws us, not a drive which pushes us. Freud was mistaken when he tried to identify Eros narrowly with libido, as though Eros can be satisfied in the satisfaction of a physical need. We know well enough that in our Eros-obsessions (when we fall in love, for instance) it is an image that has power over us, not the concreteness of flesh and blood. There is no point in saying to the Eros-obsessed social, political, or educational thinker who has a vision of a society in which 'a rediscovery of the meaning and attainability of community will make possible new caring, intimacy and depth in all forms of living'[227] and in which 'a decrease in all institutions of discipline, control, "law and order", obedience, authority, rewards and punishment, will de-institutionalize fear as a primary organising and managing principle'[228] that such visions are 'unrealistic'. If it was 'realistic' it would not be a vision, would have no power to draw us to its possibilities. It is the Senex who is 'realistic' and 'concrete'. Senex has no visions, only memories.

Many of the voices which now speak loudest about schools and the curriculum are obsessed with what Hillman calls the soulless concretism of the negative Senex, the soulless concretism of 'things', 'facts', 'structures', 'procedures' and 'cost efficiencies' that Senex mistakes for wisdom.[229] We desperately need to return Soul to the classroom or, if she is still there, to encourage her to come out of hiding. To do so, we need to take Eros very seriously indeed. It is Eros who connects us and, as the myth tells us, it is Eros who finds Soul. Only Eros can arouse in us the structures of imagination. Only Eros can awaken Psyche from her sleep.

NOTES Chapter 9. Eros and Associates

[205] Eros' connection with sexuality is mythologically expressed when he is portrayed as the child of Aphrodite. However, other myths give him a different parenthood. He is, for example, the child of Chaos, the dark, empty space from which the universe emerged. He is also the child of Penia (Need), the child of Uranus (Sky) and Gaia (Earth), the child of Artemis and Hermes, of Zeus and Semele.

[206] The images of 'wise old man' and 'youth' are to be understood as forming the sensibility and behaviour of women as well as men, just as there are quite different but parallel images of 'wise old woman' (Metis, Demeter, Hecate, Magna Mater) and 'young girl' (Persephone, Ariadne, Aurora, Psyche) which shape the psychology of men as well as women.

One recognizable characteristic of many Senex figures is their hostility to women. In this they are joined by Apollo who, although always depicted as a young man, has many of the attributes of Senex. By contrast, the myths of Eros and Dionsysos show them in joyful relationship with Psyche and Ariadne. The Puer gods have a lot of 'feminine' characteristics and seem to have been most widely worshipped by women.

[207] Banking is in itself a Senex image, relating particularly to Saturn, the Roman god of agriculture who harvests and hoards and dispenses both prosperity and depression. Freire's description of 'banking education' is full of the language of Senex.

> — the teacher teaches and the students are taught;
>
> — the teacher thinks and the students are thought about;
>
> — the teacher talks and the students listen meekly;
>
> — the teacher disciplines and the students are disciplined;
>
> — the teacher chooses and enforces his choice, and the students comply;
>
> — the teacher acts and the students have the illusion of acting through the action of the teacher;
>
> — the teacher chooses the program content, and the students (who were not consulted) adapt to it;
>
> — the teacher confuses the authority of knowledge with his own professional authority, which he sets in opposition to the freedom of the students;
>
> — the teacher is the subject of the learning process, while the pupils are mere objects.
>
> It is not surprising that the banking concept of education regards men as adaptable, manageable beings. The more students work at storing the deposits entrusted to them, the less they develop the critical consciousness which would result from their intervention in the world as transformers of that world. The more completely they accept the passive role imposed on them, the more they tend simply to adapt to the world as it is and to the fragmented view of reality deposited in them! (P. Freire, *Pedagogy of the Oppressed*, pp. 46f).

[208] M. Buber, *Between Man and Man*, p. 120.

[209] C. R. Rogers, *Freedom to Learn for the Eighties*, p. 127. See also Cornelius-White, 'A Meta-Analysis', 2007.

[210] J. R. Gibb, *Trust: A New View of Personal and Organizational Development*.

[211] ibid., p. 20.

[212] M. Knowles, *Self-Directed Learning*.

[213] D. Graves, *Children Writing*.

[214] There is a significant difference between a guess-what's-in-my-mind question such as 'What year did people first land on the moon?' and an authentic question like 'Does anyone know what year people first landed on the moon?'

[215] Lao-Tse's description of leadership is relevant here

> A leader is best
> when people barely know he exists.
> Not so good when people obey and acclaim him.
> Worst when they despise him.
> But of a good leader who talks little,
> when his own work is done, his aim fulfilled,
> they will all say, 'We did this ourselves'.
>
> (Lao-Tse, cited in W. Bynne, *From the Way of Life According to Lao-Tse*.)

[216] M. Buber, *The Knowledge of Man*, pp. 72f.
[217] Gibb, op. cit. p. 179.
[218] Freire, op. cit. p. 56.
[219] ibid., p. 53.
[220] Rogers, *Freedom*, p. 20.
[221] ibid., p. 292.

Rogers was persuaded that we all, children and adults, are essentially drawn towards the fulfilment of our potential by an 'actualizing tendency'. The task of the teacher or counsellor being to remove the barriers (e.g., fear, defensiveness, the need to meet the expectations of others) which are impeding this growth.

[222] Some of this research is described in A. Aspy and F. Roebuck, *Kids Don't Learn from Teachers They Don't Like* and J. Cornelius-White, 'Learner-Centred Teacher-Student Relationships Are Effective: A Meta-Analysis'.
[223] Rogers, *On Personal Power*, pp. 69f.
[224] ibid., pp. 72f.
[225] C. G. Jung, 'Psychological Commentary on Kundalini Yoga', *Spring*, 1975, pp. 3ff.
[226] Freire, op. cit., p. 64.
[227] Gibb, op. cit., p. 282.
[228] ibid., p. 283.
[229] Hillman and other archetypal psychologist argue that imaginal reality must be taken seriously.

> The senex ... is fixated literally on the concrete – economics, power politics, energy, whatever – without any psychological, without any anima overtones. The world for the senex ... is not an expression of soul; it is the countervalence of soul. And this soulless concretism dominates both the N-bomb project and the terrorist attitude, and this shows that they share the same archetypal reality, the same insanity. Both think what is most real are the physical and external structures. Soulless concretism. I think what's most real are the structures of consciousness, of imagination, so that when ideas move, when the mind moves, when the images move, then the other things also move. (J. Hillman, *Inter Views*, p. 122).

10

BEING ALIVE

*T*here is only one subject-matter for education, and that is Life in all its manifestations.

      Alfred North Whitehead

WHAT WHITEHEAD SAYS ABOUT EDUCATION in *The Aims of Education*,[230] first published in 1929, does not sound very radical to present day educators who are sensitive to the limitations of conventional education. We have heard and made these sorts of statements many times. They might be radical if they were applied, but they are rarely applied consistently in spite of being constantly reiterated.

For instance, Whitehead attacks examinations as anti-educational, because they force teachers to teach only what is known already, and they can make no account of the unique, creative relationship between a particular teacher and a particular student. He proposes that education is essentially an aesthetic activity. He opposes the aimless accumulation of 'inert knowledge'. He argues that imagination is central to the educative process, and that imagination is not taught but caught. He asserts that knowledge has no value in itself; it all depends on who has the knowledge and what they do with it. True learning, according to Whitehead, comes through action and experience, not through being stuffed with dead information and ideas. When he looked at what was going on in classrooms in the 1920s, the trivialization of a wonderful opportunity reduced him to 'a savage rage'. Yet what still happens in a lot of classrooms in a lot of places differs little from what was happening when Whitehead was observing it.

Whitehead argued that 'education is discipline for the adventure of life' and that schools and universities 'should be homes of adventure shared in common for young and old'.[231] He was certainly adventurous in his own thinking, challenging our conventional notions of what sort of universe we inhabit. He began his academic a career as a mathematical physicist. He could see that the reality being uncovered by Einstein, Bohr and their colleagues suggested that the image of the universe as a huge machine consisting of billions of 'things' interacting with each other in cause/effect relationships no longer made any sense. There had to be a better way of thinking about it. His thinking led him to develop what he called 'the philosophy of organism' which is now more commonly called 'process philosophy'.

Whitehead sums up his notion of a good education when he says: 'The students are alive, and the purpose of education is to stimulate and guide their self-development. It follows as a corollary from this premise, that the teachers also should be alive with living thoughts.'[232] Once again, this does not seem to be a particularly radical idea. However, it becomes a little more radical when we consider what sort of universe Whitehead is imagining when he says it.

Most significantly, he proposes that the universe is alive. This is not a new idea. Our tribal ancestors seem to have taken it for granted, as do many indigenous cultures today. Yet after a few hundred years of thinking of the universe as composed of 'dead matter' it may be difficult for us to imagine molecules, for instance, as alive. Whitehead's universe is an organism, not a machine. The universe is not composed of 'things'. The stuff that makes the universe is aliveness, which for Whitehead is synonymous with creativity. Aliveness is not merely a quality which some things have and others lack. It is the essence of being. Creativity is not just a desirable mental capacity that some people possess more than others. It is not simply a talent that teachers might encourage and support in their students. It is at the very centre not only of human life but of the cosmos itself.

The notion that the universe is an organism rather than a machine has been strongly argued by a significant minority of philosophers and scientists for several decades. James Lovelock published *Gaia: A New Look at Life on Earth* in 1979, arguing that we need to stop imagining the earth as a machine and imagine it/her rather as a living body. The notion aroused a great deal of emotional opposition in scientists. Thirty years later it has become fairly conventional for scientists to accept Lovelock's image of the earth as a dynamic, self-regulating system consisting of physical, chemical, biological, social and psychological elements, and to view humans as components of the system rather than simply observers of it. Biologist Rupert Sheldrake points to the significance of this idea.

> As soon as we allow ourselves to think of the world as alive, we recognize that a part of us knew this all along. It is like emerging from winter into a new spring. We can begin to reconnect our mental life with our own direct, intuitive experiences of nature. We can participate in the spirits of sacred places and times. We can see that we have much to learn from traditional societies that have never lost their sense of connection with the living world around them. We can acknowledge the animistic traditions of our ancestors. And we can

begin to develop a richer understanding of human nature, shaped by tradition and collective memory, linked to the earth and the heavens, related to all forms of life; and consciously open to the creative power expressed in all evolution. We are reborn into a living world.[233]

In Whitehead's philosophy of organism the universe is not only alive but experiencing. He argued that if awareness exists anywhere in the universe, for example, in that part of the universe represented by human beings, it must exist in some form or other 'all the way down to quarks or quanta or whatever may lie beyond'.[234] The kind of awareness that electrons or molecules have may bear little similarity to human consciousness, but it is experience nonetheless.

WHITEHEAD'S UNIVERSE

To many of the philosophers of the ancient world it seemed fairly obvious that the universe is alive. It was clear enough to Aristotle and his contemporaries that the universe moves itself and moves purposefully. For centuries there was not much dispute about this. In the seventeenth century Newton and Descartes introduced the notion that the universe behaves like a machine, that trees and animals, and even humans, are simply complicated machines. Though many of Newton's contemporaries such as Spinoza and Leibniz argued that the cosmos is a living organism, and the romantic philosophers and poets of the eighteenth and nineteenth century kept the image alive, it was an image that was totally rejected by mainstream science.

The image of the universe as a machine has proved so useful for science that it has come to be taken by most educated people as a truth which is unchallengeable. We have learned that the universe is a vast machine consisting of a lot of separate 'things' connected by complicated cause and effect relationships. We have grown up with the taken-for-granted understanding that the world is made up of a lot of separate, solid 'things'. Some of them have an added component called 'life'. Others do not. We imagine that we consist of a physical 'thing' called a body with a not-so-physical 'thing' inside us which we call a mind or (maybe) a soul. We use all this to observe and assess other 'things', which constitute what we call reality, and we make choices about how we are going to treat them.

Since the sixteenth century European science has been devoted to discovering and presenting the truth about the universe, without acknowledging that this truth is built on an assumption. What science has presented and still presents is not 'facts' about the universe but a way of imagining it. Whitehead and his fellow physicists in the early twentieth century argued that the machine image was no longer compatible with the kind of universe they were discovering. It is an argument that has been taken up by many contemporary scientists in a wide range of disciplines from astrophysics to biology. We are forced to acknowledge that we are not on the earth but in it, sharing its life.

If we accept the notion that the universe is alive we have to accept the implication that it has some sort of experience. We know that we, individually and collectively, can have experiences without being aware of them. It is obvious that experience does not necessarily imply consciousness. We acknowledge that even single cell organisms react to their environment, and behave purposefully, which implies that they have experience. Whitehead's radical notion is that experience goes 'all the way down' to electrons and other subatomic particles. However, we should note that when we use the word 'particle' we trap ourselves once again in the machine metaphor. For Whitehead, atoms do not consist of things called 'particles'. The universe consists not of things but of events.

After a few centuries of imagining that the universe is composed of 'things' it is difficult for us to imagine, as Whitehead does, that it is composed of moments of feeling and choice. It is difficult to imagine that everything, including ourselves, is a series of 'events' or 'occasions', each of which has a moment of aliveness and then dies, that each 'thing' we experience (including ourselves) is simply an accumulation or 'society' of such past 'occasions'. At its growing tip, this 'society' is alive and experiencing, and 'prehends' not only the rest of the universe but (more or less vaguely) all its previous moments of experience. Each 'actual occasion' is a subjective experience. It immediately perishes and becomes an object. Everything we actually perceive or remember is an object that was once a subject. In this respect human beings are no different from everything else in the universe.

The entire universe is in constant process of becoming. Creativity is not an accidental extra: it is at the very centre of the universe's existence.

It is difficult for us to imagine that at each moment the universe consists of a lot of *Is*, not a lot of *Its*. Unfortunately, our focus as teachers too easily hooks into the objects and forgets the subjects. Obviously, we do this when our focus is on the content of the curriculum, which is, as Whitehead argues, nothing but 'inert knowledge'. However, we go further than this. When we focus on Suzie, Ahmed and Lou as persons to be observed and remembered, persons who can be expected to behave in predictable ways, we are focusing on them as objects. In the present moment they are subjects, as we are, but when we look at them we always see them in the past, for it takes several micro-seconds for the light reflected from them to register in our awareness. Yet in the moment of experience we share with them, whatever its quality, they are alive, self-conscious, choosing, creating, becoming. Their choices may be dominated by all the dead selves they have been in the past, but in this moment they and we have the possibility of newness. When we do manage to focus on our shared moment of experience, when we become aware of the we in our relationship, we and our students and our teaching are alive.

It is difficult also for us to imagine that the cosmos is held together by feeling, which is the best synonym we have for Whitehead's word 'prehension'. When we think about something, or imagine something, or remember something, or have a feeling about something, or are attracted to something, or grab something physically, we are 'prehending' it either consciously or unconsciously. And just as we prehend our world, so do molecules and bacteria.[235] Prehension is what holds the world together. As Robert Mesle puts it:

> The world is composed of an infinite number of individual drops of feeling, all woven together by their experiences of each other.[236]

The drops of feeling that we call molecules are woven together by their experiences of each other, but we doubt that they are aware of it. However, we have some awareness of our connectedness at the human level. In our closest relationships we are very aware of our connectedness to others, and know that their emotions and thoughts can become our emotions and thoughts without any conscious attention or intention on our part. We may be less sensitive to our connection with those further from us, and even less conscious of our connection to all organic life. We have been taught to see ourselves as separate individuals yet we are all parts of each other.

HERAKLITUS' FIRE AND INDRA'S NET

Though Whitehead may have been most immediately influenced by what physicists were discovering about the nature of the universe in the early decades of the twentieth century,[237] his philosophy comes in a direct line from the philosophy of Heraclitus in the West and Buddha in the East, and he was certainly influenced by both. He believed that 'every philosophy is tinged with the colouring of some secret imaginative background, which never emerges explicitly into its train of reasoning.'[238] The secret imaginative background to his own thinking can be found in both Western and Eastern traditions.

In the seventh century BC, Heraclitus used the image of fire to address the question of what 'stuff' the cosmos is composed of. In so doing he was coming as close as he could to our own notion of energy. Fire (or energy), he supposed, was not simply one 'thing' among others in the universe, but was what gave everything form and kept the universe in existence: 'This universe, which is the same for all, has not been made by any god or man, but it always has been, is, and will be an ever-living fire, kindling itself by regular measures and going out by regular measures.'[239] In the fragments that we have of his writing, he expands this image, pointing out the potential for everything to turn into fire, how fire is a process of continual exchange, how fire seeks satisfaction, how fire advances and withdraws, how fire catches all things by surprise. Paradoxically the everlasting fire that creates the 'flow' of the universe, also secures its stability. For the same 'measures' of fire are always being kindled and going out. There must be a continual cycle of energy exchange, for it is impossible for fire to continually consume its nourishment if it is not at the same time giving back what it has consumed already. When Heraclitus shifted his image from fire to water (another image of flowing energy) he pointed out that not only can we not step twice into the same river, but also that we are not the same person stepping into it in two successive instants.[240]

Another image, equally ancient, comes from Hua-Yen Buddhism. It is the image of Indra's net.

Far away in the heavenly dwelling of the great god Indra hangs a wonderful net which stretches out infinitely in all directions. At each node hangs a glittering jewel and since the net is infinite in size the number of jewels is infinite. In each jewel we can see the images of all the other jewels reflected. Each jewel contains an image not only of every other jewel but of itself reflected in every other jewel, and so on *ad infinitum*. Each jewel's reflections are what makes it a jewel, so that without them it would not exist. Every jewel is part of every other and contains every other. When any jewel in the net is touched, all other jewels are affected.

Whitehead's theory is a 'bootstrap' theory.[241] If you can imagine yourself holding yourself above the ground by your shoelaces, you can get a sense of what sort of universe Whitehead is suggesting we inhabit. Each of us in our moment of aliveness is connected to every other experience of aliveness in the universe. Through our connections we each contain the whole universe. And every other entity in the universe contains us. Everything we do has an impact, however slight, on the whole universe. Not only is everything connected to everything but it only exists through its connectedness. Take away the connectedness and there is nothing left.[242]

Whitehead himself contributes an image from his own childhood. When he was three years old he was taken to Paris. He was playing in the gardens of the Tuileries when a regiment of soldiers marched from the palace, passed the park, and disappeared down the road. This incident haunted his memory in later years, but he always assumed that the park was in London, and couldn't find it. Some years later he was again in Paris. He was walking in the gardens of the Tuileries, when suddenly he found himself on the very spot, the very place where the soldiers had suddenly appeared out of the mist and vanished again into the unknown. The image still haunts his philosophy.

Being Alive

THE RHYTHM OF LIFE

When we watch our students grow we are looking at much more than their individual development. Their individual growing is an element in a much larger process. 'Growing' is a cosmic process in which they participate. Until they are taught otherwise, they feel it in their bodies and express it in their rhythms. Their teachers also feel that sense, though they may block it out of their awareness. Our bodily sense of the earth and the cosmic system to which it belongs may be the source not only of our attachment to place but also of our relationships with people.[243]

Whitehead's notion that not only is the cosmos alive but that its aliveness, and ours, is not just an accidental quality but the essence of its being has practical implications. Teachers are alive. Students are alive. Education must be alive. The fragmentation of curriculum into knowledge and skills, and the fragmentation of knowledge and skills into disconnected elements, is what kills it. The experience of education, to be alive, must be organic:

> The solution which I am urging is to eradicate the fatal disconnection of subjects which kills the vitality of our modern curriculum. There is only one subject-matter for education, and that is Life in all its manifestations.[244]

Imagining the universe as a living organism rather than a lifeless machine involves the recognition that our experience of life is characterized by rhythm. As Whitehead observed,

> ... our bodily life is essentially periodic. It is dominated by the beatings of the heart, and the recurrence of breathing. The presupposition of periodicity is indeed fundamental to our very concept of life.[245]

We now know more than Whitehead did about our biological rhythms. We know that we experience an annual cycle, a monthly cycle, a daily cycle and an ultradian (ninety minute) cycle. We know that our brainwaves cycle between the high frequency Beta waves of our 'thinking' state, through Alpha and Theta to the Delta waves of deep sleep and back again. We know that in our thinking we cycle through left-brain and right-brain processing.

Whitehead understood the ongoing life of the world to consist of 'throbs of experience'.[246] Following Whitehead, Franz Riffert writes of 'pulsating micro-processes that stretch through the universe and become especially obvious in the living organism',[247] arguing that the rhythmic pulsations that characterize processes at the sub-atomic level must pervade reality at all levels, including the experience we call 'learning'.

These pulses are replicated in each experience of learning, instantly in a moment of insight which shapes our behaviour, or extended over time in life-changing events. Whitehead was convinced that there is a rhythmic dimension within each instance of learning – a movement from physical to mental to an integration of the two. In the case of 'learning events', he labelled these phases 'romance', 'precision' and 'generalization' and argued that 'education should consist in a continual repetition of such cycles'.[248] The natural rhythm of learning starts with engagement in an experience, turns to the 'facts' through attention to detail, and then makes an imaginative leap into an understanding of what it means. This takes us back to the 'romantic' engagement in experience and a new cycle. Whitehead gives us an image of cycles within cycles within cycles, or eddies within eddies within eddies, 'the whole process being dominated by a greater cycle of the same general character as the minor eddies'.[249] The natural rhythm of learning moves us always towards what is new. As George Allan puts it: 'The stages of education are *helical* in the sense that they transform as they return, spiralling into learning contexts that are always different and sometimes more adequate. Learning is an adventure down into, and therefore out beyond, the known.'[250]

Allan's image of the spiral of learning has something in common with Bandura's image of the spiral of self-efficacy.[251] The spiral notionally starts with *planning*, which begets *effort*, which leads to *assessment of one's performance*, which begets a *positive frame of mind*, which in turn begets further *planning*. If our planning is good we are ready to expend effort. We can then reflect on the outcomes of this effort and form positive intentions regarding our future behaviour. This leads to further planning and so on around the upwards spiral. If our planning is poor, we are unlikely to expend effort effectively, our self-assessment is unrealistic and hence we do not get motivated to plan better for our next effort. We are in a self-defeating, downwards spiral. If we translate this into Whitehead's language we might start with the effort phase and rename it *engagement in experience*. Engagement in experience leads to *reflection on experience* (self-assessment), which leads to *imagining* our next step (motivation and planning) and becoming engaged once more in experience. Through the rhythmic movement, through the spiral of experience and reflection and imagination – which we can observe in each learning event – we achieve what Bandura calls 'self efficacy'.

THE FLIGHT OF THE LEARNER

In Whitehead's language, every 'drop of experience' or 'actual occasion' has a physical pole and a mental pole. The cycle of learning begins in the physical pole, in the ground of concrete, physical experience.

> The true method of discovery is like the flight of an aeroplane. It starts from the ground of particular observation; it makes a flight in the thin air of imaginative generalization, and it again lands for renewed observation rendered acute by rational interpretation.[252]

We find in this image of learning a movement from the physical pole of observation to the mental pole of generalization and back to the physical pole again. Only we are now in a different airport, ready to take off again. As Heraclitus might have said: 'You cannot land twice in the same airport.'

To pursue the image a little further, it is worth noting that what we do at the top of our flight is imagine. While on the ground we can only make what Whitehead calls 'perceptive propositions'. That is, we can only describe what we observe. At the top of our flight, however, we can make 'imaginative propositions'. That is, we can suggest possibilities. When Whitehead suggests that 'It is more important that a proposition be interesting than that it be true'[253] he is underlining the importance of imagination. The 'true' statement is only concerned with what is already there to be observed. The imaginative proposition leaps towards what is possible, towards the new.

Whitehead didn't have any illusions about our capacity to find Truth. He acknowledged that our rational minds will find the cosmos to be incomprehensible. He termed the tendency of scientists to announce that they have found the truth about something the 'fallacy of dogmatic finality'. As he said: 'There are no whole truths; all truths are half-truths. It is trying to treat them as whole truths that plays the devil.'[254] This, of course, is a half-truth, though it is by no means clear which half is true! Truth, for Whitehead, is the conformity of appearance to reality – more or less!

There is a natural and ordinary way of learning which served us well as children but which a lot of our adult habits and insecurities interfere with. We get along for most of our life with this natural way of learning, just 'picking up' what we need to know as we go along. However, as soon as we get involved in the process called 'education', we forget about learning the natural way and try to learn by more sophisticated methods which are actually much less effective.

'Natural' learning starts with awareness of a feeling and an experience. A child feels the need for something and asks her parents for it. They do not understand her. Maybe that is the end of it, in which case she has learned nothing and failed to get what she wants. Maybe she just repeats her incomprehensible request over and over and drives her parents crazy, or she simply gets frustrated and throws a tantrum. However, if she is to learn from this experience, she must do something with it. She reflects in some way on what has happened and decides that there is something wrong with her request. She remembers previous experiences like this and looks for some principles to guide her. Perhaps someone gives her some help at this point. She finds another way to say it and tries again. After a couple of attempts she gets through. She has learned something she will not forget.

Her older brother wants to learn to ride a bicycle. He gets on, tries, falls off, gets on, thinks about it a bit, maybe gets some unsolicited advice, gets back on, tries again, finds out what works, gets to stay on, becomes a cyclist, remains one.

In both these experience of learning there is a movement from the physical pole of experience to the mental pole and back again. The little girl struggling to find the right words may remain close to the physical pole of the experience: she tries a word, it doesn't work; she tries another; it may or may not bring the result she wants, but she is engaged in a movement from desire to purposive action to satisfaction. Her brother's learning may involve more conscious reflection on what is going wrong and what might work. Certainly, when he is playing his sophisticated new computer game he spends a good deal of time evaluating his previous strategies and imagining new ones. This not in order to understand the game but in order to play it.

Some occasions of experiential learning are more consciously purposeful than others, as when we set out to learn to swim or ride a bicycle or use a new piece of software. We may even get a teacher to help us, but it is obvious that our learning depends a lot less on what the teacher does than on what we do. We try something, we reflect on that experience and see if it is what we want, we look for general principles to guide our next attempt, we try again. Eventually we can do it, and it has become part of our way of being. When we are in this mode of learning, there is no such thing as a mistake. When what I am doing is not working the way I want it, I get feedback about this, and I use this feedback to improve what I am doing. Trying something and getting it wrong is an essential part of this learning process. This is what makes this natural learning cycle so efficient, in contrast to much of 'school learning', where we spend a lot of our energy trying to avoid mistakes.

The movement from ineffective action to observation to generalization to effective action is often referred to as the experiential learning cycle. We can think of it in the image of Whitehead's aeroplane of discovery, beginning on the solid ground of experience, rising through observation and evaluation to imaginative generalization and descending through a new vision to a new experience, ready to take off on a new flight. We start from the physical pole of being (experienced in action and feeling), move to the mental pole (experienced in concepts and images), and move back to the physical pole (experienced in new action and new feeling.)

It is conventional to look at learning quantitatively, as the accumulation of information. If we take Whitehead seriously, we will see it rather as a succession of transformations. There is no 'content' that we somehow store in our brains. There is, rather, a shift from a subjective experience which has a certain quality to another subjective experience which is qualitatively different. The 'I' after the learning experience is a different 'I' from the 'I' before the learning experience (which has now become part of what we are experiencing). Whitehead argues that at every moment we have the choice between repeating ourselves and being new. As adults we spend a lot of time repeating ourselves. Providing children with a lot of 'inert knowledge' without engaging them physically in an experience which catches their imagination ensures that they do the same. Ignoring the natural rhythm of learning ensures that much of what we do is a waste of time and effort.

TUNING IN TO LIFE

Conventional science asserts that only one kind of data enters our minds: the data that comes through our senses, especially our sight and hearing. Whitehead insists that we perceive two kinds of data: sensory and non-sensory. Some of what we know we know through seeing and hearing. Other things we know 'in our bones' or 'in our gut' without always being able to relate them to a particular sensory experience. When we feel curiosity, anxiety, depression, excitement, apathy, exhilaration, it may indeed come from seeing or hearing something, but it often has no immediate sensory reference. We may be 'picking up' something from another person (present or absent) or something from our past – even something we've forgotten or repressed. Whitehead argues that it is these non-sensory prehensions that give life, warmth and meaning to the data from our senses. Moreover, we are not 'picking up' signals that have to pass through space to reach us. We are in direct contact with every entity in the universe because we are part of them and they are part of us. Whitehead's cosmology provides an explanation for what are conventionally referred to as 'paranormal' phenomena such as mental telepathy and extra-sensory perception. (In Whitehead's view they are perfectly 'normal'.) Where teaching and learning are concerned it provides an argument for respecting and developing our students' capacity for 'intuitive' knowing, rather than, as often happens, neglecting or belittling this capacity.

Thinking about the universe the way Whitehead does has certain implications for the way we teach. In the first place we will be conscious of the rhythms in our own and our students' experience and will give some attention to teaching in a way which does not conflict with them. Second, we will be aware of our own and our students' shared aliveness and put it at the centre of our work. Furthermore, we will appreciate in ourselves and our students the capacity we generally call intuition.

Carl Rogers was convinced that the 'next great frontier of learning' is 'the area of the intuitive, the psychic, the vast inner space that looms before us ... the area that currently seems illogical and irrational'.[255] Like Whitehead, he imagined intuition to be of the same nature as parapsychological or 'psi' phenomena, and to be most manifest when our whole organism is 'in tune with the pulse of the world'.[256] We find a similar notion in Jung.

The essence of Jung's understanding of intuition is, first, that it is one of our two ways of perceiving the world (the other being sensation) and, second, that it is an unconscious process, grounded in 'the inherited foundations of the unconscious mind'.[257] Like Whitehead, he argues that intuition does not depend on our senses, but arises from direct connection with the whole of reality. We can add to this that where sensation experiences the world's fragments intuition experiences the world as an organic whole. He suggests that intuition is the way 'archaic man' experienced the world, and is still a basic function in the way we experience the world, more basic than the conscious thinking and feeling which characterize the later development of both the individual and the species.

Whitehead took the view that all aspects of the universe are moving towards the realization of ever greater richness of experience. The same perspective is behind Rogers' notion that organismic choice is guided by the evolutionary flow. Like Whitehead, he perceived the universe as a living, evolving organism.

> Thus, when we provide a climate that permits persons to be – whether they are clients, students, workers or persons in a group – we are not involved in a chance event. We are tapping into a tendency which permeates all organic life – a tendency to become all the complexity of which the organism is capable.[258]

Growing, for both Rogers and Whitehead, is not something we do. It is not even something that happens to us. Rather, it is a cosmic event in which we participate. The choices we make are our contribution to it.

THE CREATIVE ADVANCE

Whitehead imagines the cosmos to be involved in a 'creative advance'. Rogers shares this view:

> Some of my colleagues have said that organismic choice – the nonverbal, subconscious choice of [a] way of being – is guided by the evolutionary flow. I agree: I will go one step further. I would point out that in psychotherapy we have learned something about the psychological conditions that are most conducive to this highly important self-awareness ... The greater this awareness, the more surely the person will float in a direction consonant with the directional evolutionary flow ... Consciousness is participating in this larger, creative, formative tendency.[259]

In this respect human beings are no different from everything else in the universe. The entire universe is in constant process of becoming. In your own becoming you are, in the present moment, an 'occasion' or 'drop of experience' which 'prehends' (grasps, feels) all your previous moments of experience and identifies this community of past 'occasions' as 'me'. This present moment of experience immediately 'dies' and becomes part of this remembered (or prehended) 'me'. All the past 'occasions' shape the way you respond to the world in the present moment, but they do not determine it. In the present moment of subjectivity you can choose between repeating yourself and becoming new.

According to Whitehead, this ongoing process of becoming new is directed to the production of beauty. And it is shaped by what Whitehead calls 'eternal objects', that is, possibilities waiting to be made actual. If we think of Beauty, Peace and Harmony as possibilities which attract a certain way of experiencing the world and acting in it we will come close to Whitehead's notion of an eternal object.

The way we approach our teaching makes a difference here. If our approach to teaching is shaped by 'old' gods like Zeus and Hera, it will focus on the past. We will teach what is already known. On the other hand, we may manifest the energy of the 'young' gods, Dionysos, Eros and Hermes, and open up our students' minds to new possibilities. They may get in touch with 'the hero within' and embark on intellectual discovery as an adventure. Or, even more radically, we may give Aphrodite her proper place in education and put beauty, pleasure and fun at the centre of it. If we think that knowledge is a 'thing' to be transmitted, possessed, measured and traded for a prosperous life, we may be condemned to deal in what Whitehead calls 'inert ideas', providing the kind of schooling which, according to Whitehead 'is not only useless: it is above all things, harmful – *corruptio optimi pessima*'.[260] Such schooling he argues, is harmful because teaching a lot of facts or ideas which are not utilized leads to 'mental dry rot', which kills the divine spark of learning. If we are interested in moving into the future we will support and nourish our students' imagination and creativity, which enliven their ideas and turn them into action. In providing experiences which lead to engagement and enlivened ideas teachers are assisting and supporting children and adolescents in creating themselves from moment to moment.

Unfortunately a lot of 'inert ideas' – 'ideas that are merely received into the mind without being utilized, or tested, or thrown into new combinations'[261] – are transmitted in classrooms. Teachers conventionally pass on ideas to their students, but their students may not even be interested in whether these ideas are true or not. There are many young people in our schools who are not the least interested in accumulating the facts and skills that society thinks are important. On the other hand, they are interested in experience and apt to be engaged by an education that takes their experience seriously. However, while they may not be interested in accumulating 'knowledge' that someone else has decided they require, they may be very interested in 'knowing'. And they may be interested in knowing how true their 'knowing' is. We can teach them to challenge not only the taken-for-granted truths of their society, but also their taken-for-granted truths about themselves. The way into this kind of reflection on what is true and what is false starts with experience, proceeds by imagining the principles that might explain it, and then tests these principles out through new experience. The alternative, and all too common, approach of directly teaching 'facts', generalizations and principles is likely to be counter-productive. Not only do the students not learn the 'inert ideas' but they are convinced that they have no interest in knowing them.[262] Whitehead insists that there can be no mental development without interest, for 'the natural mode by which living organisms are excited [toward] suitable self-development is enjoyment'.[263]

Whitehead insisted that what the natural rhythm of learning allows is 'the joy of discovery', a joy which the child finds in the discovery of new facts which are important of themselves, but not yet in the discovery of 'general ideas' – 'ideas that give an understanding of that stream of events which pours through his life, which is his life'.[264] He observed frequently that the central problem in education is keeping knowledge alive, for this can only be done by teachers who are themselves alive, and such teachers – as far as he could see – are not particularly numerous.

NOTES Chapter 10. Being Alive

[230] Whitehead, *The Aims of Education and Other Essays*.
[231] ibid., p. 98.
[232] ibid., p.v.
[233] R. Sheldrake, *The Rebirth of Nature*, p. 188.
[234] C. De Quincey, *Radical Knowing*, p. 301.

> This doesn't necessarily mean that rocks know what is going on but, as De Quincey points out, it is just as unscientific to assume that rocks have no awareness as it is to assume that they can think and feel. Such a belief is based entirely on an assumption about what kind of world this is. Science currently has no way of proving it to be true. See also De Quincey, *Radical Nature*.

[235] In the moment of their becoming, electrons also experience the universe, and, like us, they make choices. This is not to say that electrons are conscious. Whitehead make a distinction between conscious and non-conscious experiencing.

> Whitehead was bold enough to take on, face to face, the most difficult of intellectual problems – the fact that each one of us has a conscious experience, whereas in science we try to account for the behavior of things by means of concepts or entities – atoms, waves, fundamental particles, and so on – whose definition does not contain any reference to consciousness. Whitehead argued that this is not good enough: you have either got to have consciousness, or at least something of that

general kind, everywhere, or nowhere; and since it is obviously in us, and cannot be nowhere, it must therefore be everywhere, presumably mostly in very rudimentary form (Conrad A. Waddington, cited in John A. Jungerman, *World in Process: Creativity and Interconnection in the New Physics*, p. 86).

[236] C. R. Mesle., *Process-Relational Philosophy*, p. 27.

[237] There are strong similarities between Whitehead's idea of the process by which nature unfolds and the ideas of quantum theory. Whitehead says that the world is made of 'occasions', each of which arises from potentialities created by prior actual occasions. These occasions are 'happenings' modelled on experiential events, each of which comes into being and then perishes, only to be replaced by a successor. It is these experience-like 'happenings' that are the basic realities of nature, according to Whitehead, not the persisting physical particles that Newtonian physics took to be the basic entities.

[238] Whitehead, *Science and the Modern World*, ch. 1.

[239] Heraclitus, Fragment 30, in J. Burnet, *Early Greek Philosophers*, p. 138.

[240] The comic playwright Epicharmos already made fun of this idea by putting it as an argument into the mouth of a debtor who did not wish to pay. How could he be liable, seeing he is not man who contracted the debt?

[241] The 'bootstrap' image of a universe comes from physics. According to bootstrap theory, the so-called elementary particles such as protons, neutrons, and mesons are actually not elementary at all but rather they are composites of each other which create each other.

[242] Whitehead's way of dealing with the problem which bothered many of the Greek philosophers – 'Does the cosmos consist of one thing or many things?' – was to argue that the whole cosmos is contained in each of the many beings that comprise it. Each unit is a microcosm representing in itself the entire all-inclusive universe. The physicist David Bohm proposed that the universe is a giant hologram, an image constructed by the mind. If a holographic plate is shattered, each fragment is found to contain 'enfolded' information about the whole image. When these fragments are illuminated, every one can reproduce the whole picture, not as clearly as the intact plate did, but whole nonetheless. The total information is enfolded in every point of the plate. Bohm believed that each part of physical reality contains information about the whole. Every part of the universe 'contains' the entire universe. See D. Bohm, *Wholeness and the Implicate Order*.

243 Theodore Roczak argues that our identification with the earth is the source of 'the empathic rapport with the natural world which is reborn in every child and which survives in the work of nature poets and landscape painters. Where this sense of shared identity is experienced as we most often experience it, person to person, we call it 'love'. T. Roczac, 'Where Psyche meets Gaia', in T. Roczak et al., *Ecopsychology*, p. 16.

[244] *The Aims of Education*, p. 18.
[245] Whitehead, *An Introduction to Mathematics*, p. 122.
[246] Whitehead, *Process and Reality*, p. 190.
[247] F. Riffert. 'Whitehead's cyclic theory of learning and empirical research', in F. Riffert (ed.), *Alfred North Whitehead on Learning and Education*, p. 90.
[248] Whitehead, *The Aims of Education*, p. 19.
[249] Whitehead, *An Introduction to Mathematics*, p. 127.
[250] Allan, G., 'Helical Learning', in A. Scarfe (ed.), *The Adventure of Learning*, p. 32.
[251] A. Bandura, *Social Foundations of Thought and Action*.
[252] Whitehead, *Process and Reality*, p. 5.
[253] ibid., p. 269.
[254] L. Price, *Dialogues of Alfred North Whitehead*, p. 14.
[255] *A Way of Being*, p. 312.
[256] ibid., p. 313.
[257] ibid., p. 507.
[258] ibid., p. 134.
[259] ibid., p. 189.
[260] Whitehead, *The Aims of Education*, pp. 1-2.
[261] ibid., p. 1.
[262] In case teachers are inclined to respond to this 'rhythm of learning' argument by arguing that this model of learning is only relevant for the Humanities, Arts and Social Sciences, it should be remembered that Whitehead was a mathematical physicist whose educational writings were largely focused on the teaching of Mathematics.
[263] Whitehead, *The Aims of Education*, p. 39.
[264] ibid., p. 3.

 11

BEING IN FIVE MINDS

*W*e are a five-minded animal.
Kieran Egan

WHITEHEAD DISTINGUISHES BETWEEN three phases in the development of a mature human being, each characterized by a different mode of being. Children experience the world through the confluent mode, which is essentially physical. The adolescent phase is dominated by the discernment mode, a mode dominated by the experience of detachment, separateness and discrimination. Instead of being absorbed and controlled by the physical world like infants, adolescents are able to consciously observe it, organize their experience and make choices. The third, mature, phase is dominated by what Whitehead calls the spiritual mode of being. It is the experience of the relationship between the two other modes. As mature adults we are able to reflect on the way our sensory experiences are related to the ideas, images and meanings they trigger in us.

When Whitehead distinguishes between the kinds of experience and awareness that are dominant in childhood, adolescence and maturity he is not suggesting that we stop thinking like infants when we become adolescents and adults. We maintain the earlier ways of thinking as adults and, indeed, in our natural rhythm of learning we cycle through the three of them. His thinking matches that of developmental psychologists such as Kieran Egan and Robert Kegan, both of whom distinguish five stages of cognitive development, but reject Piaget's notion that we necessarily leave one level of consciousness behind when we become capable of another. As Egan (1997) puts it:

> We have, you might say, a fivefold mind, or, more dramatically, we are a five-minded animal in whom different kinds of understanding jostle together and fold on one another, to some degree remaining 'somewhat distinct.'[265]

A similar argument was made some decades ago by the cultural philosopher Jean Gebser.[266] His interest was in the emergence of 'structures of consciousness' in human culture rather than in individual psychology. He argued that we can find five distinct 'structures of consciousness' that are manifested in culture. They emerged in a particular sequence in the course of human evolution. There is the basic 'archaic' consciousness of our pre-human ancestors, through which the world is experienced with little or no awareness or reflection. There is the 'magic consciousness' which emerged with the first humans and their close relatives and experiences a world of 'vegetative entwinement' in which everything is connected. Then there is the 'mythical structure' through which we live our lives embedded in particular tribal narratives which give them meaning. Fourth, we have a 'mental' consciousness, which enables us to think, objectively and rationally, as individuals. Last, the 'integral' structure of consciousness, a new structure which integrates all the others, enables us to experience the universe transparently. If we look at cultures historically we are likely to find one or other of these structures dominant at particular times. Gebser was careful to point out that his theory was not framed within a fantasy of progress. Mental and integral consciousness are not better than archaic or magic consciousness. They are just more complex. Besides, all the structures of consciousness have both 'efficient' and 'deficient' manifestations.

Gebser's argued that we do not outgrow, individually or collectively, our pre-modern modes of consciousness:

> We must first of all remain cognizant that these structures are not merely past, but are in fact still present in more or less latent and acute form in each of us.[267]

Likewise, Merlin Donald,[268] writes of the evolution of consciousness going through three key phases: the mimetic, the mythic and the theoretic, and argues that modern consciousness

> still rests on the same old primate brain capacity for episodic or event knowledge. But it has three additional, uniquely human layers: a mimetic layer, an oral-linguistic layer, and an external-symbolic layer. The minds of individuals reflect these ways of representing reality.[269]

There are some interesting parallels with neurobiology. While recognizing a common tendency to prematurely seize on the findings of neuroscience to reinforce our assumptions about how we should teach,[270] we can nevertheless find some interesting points of comparison between the findings of neuroscience and the notion that we have several more or less independent minds.

Paul MacLean has argued that we have not one brain but three. This 'triune brain' is made up of our ancient reptilian brain (brainstem and cerebellum), our paleo-mammalian brain (limbic system) and our neo-mammalian brain (neo-cortex). Each of these brains has its own intelligence, its own subjectivity, its own sense of time and space, its own memory and a tendency to operate independently of the others. MacLean is at pains to point out to us that for all our illusion of cognitive sophistication, there are parts of our brains that still think like lizards and horses.[271]

Our reptilian brain doesn't have any capacity for self-awareness or abstract thought. It governs arousal, drives, instinctual impulses and raw experience. Our limbic brain processes our emotions and memory and much of our social behaviour and learning — capacities which we share with animals. Our neocortex, which includes the corpus callosum, the bridge between the left-brain and right-brain, enables self-awareness, conscious thought and information processing. Each of these brains generates a specific form of knowledge and a specific kind of understanding. Our reptilian brain gives us our basic instinctual tendencies and habits, and enables us to survive in the world, our limbic brain provides affective knowledge, subjective feelings and emotional responses to events in our world, and our neocortex generates propositional information about the world through higher cognitive functions, reasoning and logical thought (see Panksepp, 1998, p.43).

Antonio Damasio[272] has argued from the evidence of neuroscience that we have three 'selves', a primitive 'proto-self' through which we experience the world, a 'core self' through which we are aware of our experience and an 'autobiographical self' through which we know who we are. If we add to this what we have learned about brain hemisphericity and distinguish between 'right-brain', 'left-brain' and 'whole-brain' thinking in the neo-mammalian brain, we find ourselves again contemplating the notion that we have five minds, as Egan says, 'jostling together', whatever labels we choose to give to them.[273]

We should not indulge the fantasy that we can integrate these theories in a single model of the mind. They have been constructed on the basis of very different evidence from very different disciplines. It is better to acknowledge that the truth about reality cannot be reduced to a single set of 'facts' and that we are here dealing with different perspectives on the nature of mind, which may contradict each other in various ways. However, in these particular perspectives there is a suggestion of an evolution or development (both in the species and in the individual) from a physical experience of the world, with little sense of individual consciousness, to a fully conscious experience in which a sense of oneself as an individual is central.

However, this is not the end of evolution or psychological development. Gebser looked at the evolution of culture and saw the emergence of the 'integral structure of consciousness' in which the all the earlier, simpler structures are transcended in a new 'integrative' mode of experiencing the universe, a mode that connects mental consciousness with the earlier, simpler structures.[274] Egan points to the potential in each of us to exercise an ironic mode of consciousness that experiences the relationship between the individualistic, 'philosophic' consciousness characteristic of adolescence and the simpler (somatic, mythic and romantic) modes which dominated our infancy and childhood. Similarly, Kegan's fifth order consciousness[275] transcends the other orders to be conscious of its own mode of consciousness. MacLean finds in us a reptilian brain which experiences the world purely physically alongside a mammalian brain which feels and relates, a neo-mammalian brain which observes and reflects, and a limited capacity to integrate the three. We find in all of these models not only a move from collective, physical identity to individual, mental identity, but a move beyond individual identity towards greater complexity and wholeness. There is also an acknowledgement that while these different structures may represent phases in cultural history or individual cognitive development, we bring them all to our daily experience of the world.

BEING A BODY: ARCHAIC MIND

The archaic consciousness that Gebser imagines to have been dominant in the first hominids is presumed to be somewhat dim, being essentially a very physical sense of aliveness, without language or sense of self, experiencing drives and appetites but with little awareness of this experiencing. This structure still operates in us, though overlaid by more complex structures. Our primary experience of the world is physical and collective. Likewise, Kieran Egan writes of *somatic understanding*, the understanding that we feel in our bodies, an organic, pre-linguistic understanding that we cannot readily put into words. From the perspective of neuroscience, Antonio Damasio writes about 'dispositions', which is his term for basic background feelings that are located in the brainstem and basal ganglia. These dispositions generate conscious states (e.g., we are aware when our hearts race, or we begin to sweat, and we notice thought and images that seem to come into our minds spontaneously) but we do not control this process and we have no way of knowing the content of these dispositions themselves.

> Our memories of things, of properties of things, of people and places, of events and relationships, of skills, of life-management processes – in short all of our memories, inherited from evolution and available at birth or acquired through learning thereafter – exist in our brains in dispositional form, waiting to become explicit images or actions. Our knowledge base is implicit, encrypted and unconscious.[276]

The archaic consciousness centred in our reptilian brain does not have much flexibility. We have a good deal of flexibility at the higher cognitive level of abstract processing. We have somewhat less when it comes to the emotional responses processed by our limbic brains. At the sensorimotor level governed by our brainstem our behaviours are fixed and concrete. While ideally the three basic levels of our brain should work together so that our instinctual reponses are moderated and regulated by our feelings, relationships, values and beliefs, this is not always the case. This is particularly the case in what we call post-traumatic stress, where 'disregulated arousal may drive a traumatized person's emotional and cognitive processing, causing emotions to escalate, thoughts to spin, and misinterpretation of present environmental cues as those of a past trauma' (Ogden et al., 2006, p. 7)

A child or adolescent may react in an apparently irrational way to the sight of a middle aged, overweight male teacher who bears some resemblance to an uncle who has abused her. She has no idea why her body reacts in terror: her heart races, she struggles to breathe and she feels an uncontrollable urge to run away. She decides that the teacher is dangerous. The thing her teachers need to be aware of is that she has no control over her response. It is not something she chooses to do. It is something her brain does without any interference from her awareness. (Research in brain plasticity has demonstrated that it is possible to 'rewire' the brain through training, so that such extreme reactions can be avoided.)

We and our students do not need to have experienced trauma to respond to the world in this way. We are inclined to think that emotional processing is top-down, that we first have a thought and that the thought generates a feeling. More often it is the other way about. We have an experience, it generates an instinctual response which is manifested in an emotion which is then interpreted to mean something. In most of our experience and behaviour, rational thinking is an optional extra tacked on at the end.

Our past (individual and collective) continually flows into us and is sensed, however vaguely, in our bodies. Being alive for human beings is associated with the feeling that our bodies exist. This fundamental feeling is 'the primitive behind all feeling of emotion and therefore is the basis of all feelings caused by interactions between objects and organism'.[277] Damasio suggests that this primordial feeling is produced by what he calls the protoself, the self which experiences the world without any sense of individual ego.

We may imagine ourselves to be thinking beings who have bodies. It is more accurate to think of ourselves as bodies who function instinctively, with the capacity to (occasionally) be aware of our feeling states, and even to reflect on them.

Carl Jung regularly returns to the theme that, at depth, we retain the modes of experience characteristic of our remote ancestors. For Jung, we are all 'archaic' or 'primitive' at depth.

> Every civilized human being, however high his conscious development, is still an archaic man at the deeper levels of the psyche. Just as the human body connects us with the mammals and displays

numerous vestiges of early or evolutionary stages going back even to the reptilian age, so the human psyche is a product of evolution which, when followed back to its origins, shows countless archaic traits.[278]

Jung has a disconcerting tendency to use the word 'primitive' for pre-conquest cultures where we would prefer other words such as 'primal' or 'pre-scientific'. He was aware that the term was problematic and pointed out that

> I use the term 'primitive' in the sense of 'primordial' and I do not imply any kind of value judgment. Also, when I speak of a 'message' of a primitive state, I do not necessarily mean that this state will sooner or later come to an end. On the contrary, I see no reason why it should not endure as long as humanity lasts.[279]

Archaic consciousness is the very dim consciousness we share with lizards. We are simply cells of a greater organism. There is no ego, no sense of ourselves as individuals, no sense of time passing, no distinction between ourselves and our environment, no distinction between inner and outer experience. It is, in a sense, our inner Zombie, who can do all sorts of complicated things without conscious attention. This applies to a great deal of what we do, as our attention cannot hold on to many different things at the same time. Archaic consciousness is the default position we go to in deep sleep.

We have an increasing understanding that human beings are not outsiders on the planet but part of it. We no longer imagine that the planet is a lump of largely lifeless matter that we happen to inhabit. We now understand that it is a complex living system of which our species is (currently at least) an essential part. The world is not 'other'. There is no essential boundary between us and other people, between us and non-human life, between us and the greater organism. Our archaic-somatic-'primitive' minds instinctively experience life in this way yet, as Jung points out, 'we have increasingly divided off consciousness from the deeper instinctive strata of the human psyche'.[280]

We can, of course, deliberately switch off our other more complex modes of consciousness from time to time and leave our archaic consciousness in charge. We can do this through self-hypnosis, or other mind-altering techniques like drugs or repetitive drumming. Ainslie Meares taught his patients to regularly stop thinking and imagining and to regress to the state which he called 'mental ataraxis'.[281] He saw this healthy regression to a more primitive mode of experience as a way of compensating for the stress we experience in our 'normal' consciousness.

Conventional education is based on the unchallengeable assumption that human beings are essentially individuals who learn what they need to know (or society demands that they know) by passing messages between one another. How would education change if were to start from the conviction – as deep ecologists do – that we are all cells of the same living organism, that life is not something we possess as individuals but something we collectively participate in?

We still tend to see ourselves as subjects and to treat the planet, and other animals, as objects. However, if we follow thinkers like Whitehead and Sheldrake, subjectivity is not our own private possession but is the subjectivity of the cosmos in which we participate from moment to moment. If we acknowledge that we and all other entities are aspects of a single unfolding reality we might get to see our relationships with our students and our efforts to make them more conscious not as a means of better understanding the 'facts' about the world, but as an expression of the universe's evolving process. We might provide a schooling environment that allows students to *become*, acknowledging, like Carl Rogers, that in allowing children to become truly themselves, 'we are not involved in a chance event. We are tapping into a tendency which permeates all organic life – a tendency to become all the complexity of which the organism is capable.' [282]

If we and our students understood our connection to the planet in this way we would not need to be advised to be kind to the earth, respect the environment, honour plants and animals and people, because we would know that the earth and the plants and the animals and the people are us. We would know that we are not separate from the natural environment; we *are* the natural environment.

Infants are born in a state of harmony with nature, one aspect of which is their total dependence on others. Our challenge as teachers is to guide their development through increasingly complex ways of thinking without their losing their simple grounding in nature. This is made most difficult by the fact that they live in a culture that is not in harmony with Nature and belong to a species whose powerful elites have spent centuries wiping out cultures that are. Rachel Carson writes of children's 'inborn sense of wonder' and their need to have a caring adult who can rediscover with them 'the joy, excitement and mystery of the world we live in'.[283] Keeping children's grounding with Nature involves keeping them alive to the experience of Nature. There is a strong case for arguing that many children suffer from 'nature deficit disorder' and that teaching children about the natural world and their connection with it should be a priority in schools.[284] Adults' attitude towards Nature appears to be profoundly influenced by their childhood experiences.[285] For some children, the only opportunities to have a rich experience of the natural world are the ones provided by the overworked teachers in their underfunded school.

BEING CONNECTED: MAGIC MIND

Our archaic minds experience instinct and stimulus and act on them automatically. Our magic minds bring awareness and emotion to our impulses. We have no sense of individual selfhood and choice but experience what Gebser calls 'the vegetative intertwining of all living things ... in the egoless magic sphere of every human being'.[286] This sense of 'vegetative entwinement' which we share with our earliest human ancestors is spaceless, timeless and egoless. Identity belongs to the group, not the individual. Though intertwined we are no longer in a state of undifferentiated unity with nature. Rather, we are one with the clan in a world where everything is connected. We are bound to each other it by our emotions.

Magic mind, as Gebser describes it, seems to be grounded mainly in the limbic system, which MacLean has proposed is the seat of both emotion and relationship. Current neuroscience supports Maclean's argument that it can function independently of the cerebral cortex.[287] Damasio argues that it is the thalamus (a component of the limbic system) which is largely responsible for coordination of the core self, the self which not only experiences the world somatically but is aware of the emotions which are produced by the body's experience.

The world experienced by our magical minds is one in which 'things happen'. We use magic to make good things happen and protect us from bad things happening. This is most evident in our superstitions. Our stone age ancestors tried to gain some control over the transcendent power of nature through magic and sorcery, ritual, totem and taboo, experiencing this magical world through a group-ego, sustained by the clan. It is in the magical structure that empathy, considered as an experience of the primal sensing and feeling states of other members of the clan, is first a distinguishable phenomenon. We usually think of empathy as a distinctly positive experience, but we need to acknowledge that the same mechanisms which enable us to feel for and understand others are responsible for the phenomenon of mob behaviour, where the individual's capacity for thinking reasonably is overpowered by the collective energy of a group.

The conventional classroom is surrounded by rituals designed, consciously or not, to have our students share a common feeling and the thoughts that go with it. In one classroom the position of the teacher behind the desk on a raised platform is designed to embed in students' consciousness a sense of the teacher's authority, as they sit behind their desks in uniforms and straight lines. In another the teacher and students relax in casual dress in a circle of comfortable chairs and address each other by their first names. The assumption behind current architecture-driven school reform is that if teachers and pupils are located in 'flexible learning spaces' rather than traditional classrooms they will eventually feel differently about schooling and teach and learn in a different way.

We can't escape magic. We fill our lives with ritual: the morning cup of coffee, the favourite chair, the favourite jacket, the way we greet our colleagues and students, all function to keep us safe and keep the world turning smoothly. It makes sense for the teacher to decorate the classroom in a particular way, arrange the seating in a particular way, have a particular routine for telling the daily story, in the expectation that these things will automatically affect the children's feeling and attitudes. Obviously the magic doesn't always work, because there are a lot of other things going on and there are other minds jostling with our magic mind, but the automatic response to rituals, symbols and incantations is there just the same.

The anthropologist E. T. Hall writes about the phenomenon of 'syncing'. When two people talk to each other their movements are synchronized. In barely perceptible ways, their eyelids, fingers and other body parts move simultaneously with the rhythms of their conversation. Even their brain waves get 'in sync'. It is as though they are dancing together to a tune played by a third person. This phenomenon also can be observed in groups. It is most easily observed in crowds that are caught up in a tribal experience, like a rock concert or a football match, but it happens even in groups where the members are not very aware of each other. We know that our body rhythms sync with the rhythms of nature, that women who live together tend to sync their periods and patients in hospital wards tend to sync their metabolism if they are together long enough. Being in tune with each other comes to us naturally. If we are emotionally close to a partner, a friend or a sibling, we may be in tune with them much of the time, enough to sense their moods and share them. If we play team sports we may learn to be in tune with a particular group of people in a particular context. Children seem to be able to do it more readily than adults. Dogs seem to be able to do it more readily than humans.[288] However, most of us adults have learned very well how not to be in tune.[289]

The teacher facing a class is not simply facing a number of individuals who happen to be in the same place at the same time. If this group of children, adolescents or adults have spent some time together, the group itself will have become a complex organic system. The private emotions they bring into the classroom will tend to become collective emotions. Their private rhythms will tend to become collective rhythms. Adults can armour themselves somewhat against this, but where people are intimate or the emotion is intense, they tend to lose their individuality in a group emotion and rhythm. With children, the group comes first. We are inclined to think of ourselves as individuals first and members of a group second. However, group identity is more basic than personal identity. A sense of individual identity is a fairly modern phenomenon. We seem to have become able to think and feel apart from the group less than three thousand years ago.

When *homo erectus* first stood on her hind legs nearly two million years ago, she had no vocal language. Indeed her larynx had not descended to enable her to speak. She communicated through her whole body. In writing about the evolution of consciousness, Merlin Donald uses the word *mimesis* to refer to the kind of communication that preceded the development of spoken language. Children acquired the skills and rituals they needed by copying their parents and other adults. Culture was developed and maintained by everybody unconsciously copying everybody copying everybody copying everybody. Donald argues that we are still doing this, even though we have long ago found additional ways to think and communicate. He points out that there is a strong connection between our tendency to communicate through mimesis and our tendency to tune in to the rhythms that surround us.[290]

Recent research in neuroscience has confirmed the existence of 'mirror neurons' which are alleged to be the basis of the human capacity for empathy and the evolution of what we call 'culture'. It appears that if we watch someone doing something or having an experience (for example, of pain) the neurons that our brain would use to do or experience the same thing become active – just as if we were having that experience ourselves. We are biologically in tune with those around us, with an unconscious urge to copy what they do. The boundary between self and other is always blurred.[291] This is most strongly the case in infancy, before we begin to see ourselves as separate. As we grow to adulthood we continue to 'pick up' other people's sensations and emotions as our neurons mimic theirs. Of course, we don't automatically copy everything they do. The explanation for this, according to the neuroscience, is that the signals from the mid-brain are inhibited by the frontal cortex when acting on them would be inappropriate. Another way of saying this is that the impulse from our magic mind is overridden by our mythical mind and mental mind.[292]

Nevertheless magic, mimetic mind (and mirror neurons) give us a strong inclination to conform to the behaviour, attitudes and ideas of those around us. If we find ourselves thinking something which contradicts what our social group or culture is assertively proclaiming, we have a tendency to affirm our membership of the group by changing our mind – unless, of course, there is an alternative right-thinking group that we can belong to

The younger our students are the more likely they are to be dominated by a magic/mimetic consciousness. Much of the learning that goes on in classrooms is learning through mimesis. Some of this copying is intentional on the part of the teacher, student or both, but much of the time we mimic others without being aware that we are doing it. Moreover, there is another aspect to mimesis that may be even more significant. The teacher may think that she is teaching the curriculum; actually she is teaching herself.

Students, especially young students, learn their teacher. At one level (for which can use Egan's term the *philosophic* or Gebser's term the *mental*), children may be intentionally learning – or not learning – what she tells them and shows them. They look and listen, check whether it makes sense to them, and decide to take in the information. At another level, which we can call the *mythic*, they are absorbing the stories she is telling them about how the world works. However, independently of all this, they are unconsciously learning their teacher at the mimetic level, as their minds 'jostle together'. They tune in to her, see the world the way she sees it and feel the world the way she feels it. They enter her experience of this moment and accept it as their own. How powerful this connection is depends on the authenticity of the teacher's experience. If she is alive, open to the world, tuned in to the rhythms of the class and genuinely experiencing what she is communicating, her students will share in her aliveness and her becoming. (This, of course may be for better or for worse, as the children tune in to their teacher and make her fixed ideas and prejudices their own.) If she is alive in the moment and tuned into the rhythms of her students, they are engaged in a dance together which does not simply repeat old patterns but constantly creates new ones. On the other hand, if she is out of tune with her students and simply repeating what she has heard or read without engaging in it in the present moment, she is in that moment dead and giving them 'dead stuff'. They may still tune in, but it is to her and her deadness, not to the content she thinks she is transmitting. As they grow older, however, they are likely to be learning their peers as much as or more than they are learning their parents or teacher.

Being in Five Minds

Synchrony in a group is generally an indication that things are going well.[293] Lack of synchrony can be a source of tension. Good teachers learn to tune in to the rhythms of a group, across generations or across cultures, whether working with children or adults. They know how creative an environment a class can be when students are tuned into each other and the teacher. They know how to achieve this by modeling the way people can be open to each other and respect each other. Poor teachers do not.

Unconscious imitation is the way we learn when we are very young. As we gradually become aware of ourselves as separate persons the imitation becomes conscious. As teachers we are constantly involved in getting our students to imitate us. We can't avoid it. We know things that we want our students to know. We have skills that we want our students to have. We have values that we want our students to share. Even if we are committed to the idea that children should make up their own minds instead of copying others, this is a value that we'd like them to share. Schools and even universities find it convenient to take advantage of our mimetic consciousness. Conventional content-based education rewards the readiness to imitate.

Mimicry is a powerful mode of learning, but it may be for better or for worse. On the one hand we find children who have absorbed racist or sexist or anti-social attitudes through unconscious imitation of their parents. Children do not come to the conclusion that racist hatred or violence against women is normal and appropriate by thinking rationally about it and coming to a logical conclusion. They learn it the same way as other children learn to be generous or friendly – by growing up in a world that takes these things for granted. The basic assumptions we form in childhood are hard to shift. We may not even realize we make them, as magic mind, which holds these taken-for-granted assumptions, has no capacity for reflection.

Copying – whether conscious or unconscious – is an effective way of learning, but it provides few invitations to newness. It's much easier to copy than to create. Copying can be done without intention or awareness; creation demands awareness, intention and more complex ways of thinking. Fortunately, there are other kinds of learning besides imitation, and we don't all end up as clones of each other.

Gebser suggests that the subjective experience of the magic structure of consciousness is our awareness of emotion.

Emotion has not always been taken seriously in theories of learning. However, it is impossible to overlook the evidence from neuroscience that emotion provides the basis for thinking, rather than the other way round. Damasio argues that emotions are derived from bodily states. Incoming stimuli generate bodily states which are experienced unconsciously as 'dispositions'. They then have to negotiate the limbic system (MacLean's mammalian brain) where they generate emotions before they can be processed cognitively. Emotions have a much greater impact on our thoughts than our thoughts have on our emotions. Emotions motivate both our thoughts and our behaviour.

Following Damasio, Kathryn Patten distinguishes three levels of affect or emotion.[294] *Dispositions* are largely unconscious, being 'a fusion of underlying somatic states', and are by nature primitive and basic to survival. *Basic emotions* (happiness, sadness, fear, anger, disgust and surprise) primarily involve the limbic system. They are largely innate, present at birth, cross-cultural and shared with other primates. *Feelings* are more complex than this and involve the cerebral cortex and its capacity for awareness and conscious learning.[295]

This would be of minor interest to teachers were it not for the fact that a lot of learning theory assumes that learning is essentially an outcome of thinking, and ignores the role of emotion and feeling. However, what the research shows us is that our bodies register emotions before we are aware of the feelings that accompany them. Indeed, the body-states which we feel as sadness actually slow down our capacity to think. To quote Damasio, 'the fluency of ideation is reduced in sadness and increased in happiness' (Damasio, op. cit., p. 101). Given points to the research evidence that learning can likewise be shut down by fear and anxiety, whether they are aroused by immediate events or have their source in childhood trauma, regardless of whether the fear or anxiety is present in awareness. She points out that 'chronic disruptive behaviour may be symptoms of chronic stress syndrome resulting from ongoing responses to subtle fears' (Given, p. 23). Perhaps we knew this all the time.

Being in Five Minds

This certainly has implications for the classroom. There is nothing particularly new in the observation that, if the classroom environment is one of fear, the children's brains will be occupied dealing with the threat, their bodies will be tense, they will feel scared and anxious. If they are doing any thinking they are doing it as a means of survival, and are unlikely to be doing it effectively. Unfortunately, this is not obvious to all teachers, and fear remains a preferred means of management for some. Likewise the notion that a happy classroom is a place where learning is facilitated is entirely consistent with the evidence from neuroscience.

Being alive means being embedded in a repetitive cycle from dispositions to basic emotions to feelings to thinking. Our bodily experience shapes our feelings which in turn shape our awareness and thinking. This may seem obvious enough, but when we observe what is going on in many classrooms we find the bodily experience of children and adolescents to be totally at odds with the thinking that they are being asked to do. Instead of starting with a physical experience from which feeling and thoughts will emerge, many teachers ignore the physical experience of their students (and its influence on attention, memory, information processing, and wellbeing) and start at the wrong end of the natural learning process.

This is the kind of behaviour that reduced Whitehead to a 'savage rage'. He argued that unless something in the children's immediate experience excites their emotions there is little chance that they will reach a genuine conscious awareness of the subject matter and the develop the ability to reflect on it critically. Still less are they likely to gain the ability to derive general principles from this reflection and apply them to life.

Damasio notes how we keep shifting back and forwards between our *core self* and our *autobiographical self*.[296] When we are 'simply present in the moment', feeling the situation but unconcerned with thinking about it, we are experiencing our core consciousness. As soon as we start to reflect on where we are, where we have been and where we are going, (not to mention the *why* and *how* of all this) we are in what he calls our extended or autobiographical consciousness. In Gebser's language, our *mythic* and *mental* consciousness is at work.

BEING TRIBAL: MYTHIC MIND

One of the things teachers do, without always being aware that they are doing it, is tell stories. While our biological rhythms may bind us to the organism that is our species, it is our shared rituals and our shared stories that bind us to the organism that is our tribe or cultural group.

One of the minds that has unfolded in our species as it evolved, and that unfolds in each of us as we grow from infancy to adulthood, is our *mythic* mind. It was characteristic of pre-scientific people and it is characteristic of children now. It came with the capacity to talk. The development of an oral culture brought with it a new kind of knowledge. People repeated stories that told them who they were and what their place was in the world. Donald and Gebser call this kind of consciousness *mythic*. We still think in this way a good deal of the time. Though we can think abstractly, we do so within the limits of a story that we have absorbed from those around us, a story that tells us who we are and what life is about, a story that we take for granted most of the time, because the people around us take it for granted too. As adults we may be able to think in other ways, but a lot of what we call thinking is actually imagining. We imagine that we live in a particular kind of world and we imagine that we are particular kinds of people. And we repeat the stories that illustrate it.[297]

Archetypal psychologists like Jung and Hillman argue that the personal and tribal stories we tell ourselves and others are versions of the 'big stories' that are the imaginative expressions of archetypal patterns. Different tribes focus on different archetypal stories and imagine that they have some ownership of them. They may even think that they invented them. Yet the stories reside in neural pathways deep in their brain and have been there for thousands of years. They are passed on by our genes, our culture and our family because they help us survive in a world which would otherwise be meaningless.

Dominant among the tribal stories which currently shape education in many Western societies is the Promethean myth of technocratic management and technological progress. The politicians and administrators who promote Promethean values and assumptions may never have heard of Prometheus, yet they live within his story, take his values for granted and tell us that 'This is the way the world is. Get used to it.' Teachers whose experience has taught them to live in the energy of Gaia or Dionysos are also convinced that they have the truth. Like the worshippers of Prometheus they can provide evidence of the rightness of their position. Like the worshippers of Dionysos (or Zeus, or Hermes) their arguments make sense within the story that frames them. We may be capable of going to the trouble of examining the evidence objectively, but we are likely accept one worldview or another simply because 'that's just the way it is.' We give up on the evidence, make some assumptions and accept a myth. Even an inadequate myth is better than no myth at all, for without a myth our lives make no sense.

Children are happy enough in what Kegan calls their 'third order consciousness'. They have a story about the world and about who they are that has been given to them by their parents and their culture. For the most part they take this story for granted. They can think rationally and logically within the bounds of the story. (If I take the existence of Santa Claus and the Tooth Fairy for granted I can think my way around all the contradictions and impossibilities that are inherent in the notion of their existence.) As they grow there comes a time when they stop taking things for granted and start to observe the world critically and try to decide for themselves what is true. They may reject their parent's narrative and adopt another, or they may construct their own view of the world based on their 'objective' observations. But until they do, they will continue to accept the narratives of their tribe and family as simply 'the way things are' and show little inclination to detach themselves from these assumptions and look objectively and critically at the 'facts'. Even those of us adults who consider ourselves to be self-reflective, critical thinkers, fall back into our mythic mind a good deal of the time, because it is our mythical, narrative mind which provides our lives with meaning. We manage to stick to a particular narrative accepted in a group we support (associated with politics, religion, economics or football) and ignore or distort any alleged facts which contradict it. Myths are much more powerful than facts.

While I am busy telling you things that I think are important, you are busy sorting and selecting what I tell you. Some of it you may accept as being obviously true; you know it already. Some of it you may immediately reject as rubbish. Some of it you may filter or distort, so that what you hear and accept is different from what I think I am saying. Some of it you may put on hold; you need to reflect on it a bit more and check my references before you decide whether to accept it. You are automatically, and perhaps even unconsciously, checking this new information against a story you have spent years absorbing. Any tendency you may have to accept my ideas is impeded, or at least strongly influenced, by your tendency to hang on to your story.

When our students are refusing to learn what we want to teach them, it may be frustrating for us. From their point of view, however, it is entirely reasonable. What we are teaching them may threaten their present understandings, their value system, perhaps their notion of who they are, all of which flow into them from the past in their tribal narrative. Under this sort of threat they naturally choose to survive as they are, by sticking to their story and rejecting or ignoring the new story we want them to hear. Generally speaking, the story they are sticking to will be the one they have picked up from their family. Many children, adolescents and adults hang on grimly to the story that they are stupid, or bad, or incapable of success, in spite of teachers' attempts to persuade them to the contrary.

Whitehead distinguished between two kinds of perception. On the one hand, we perceive whatever appears to us in this instant. He called this kind of perception 'presentational immediacy'. At the same time, our experience at this instant is shaped by all our previous experiences. He calls this 'causal efficacy' because our present experience is caused by all past experiences (including experiences which occured only a micro-second ago). Our moment of aliveness is influenced by all the dead moments of the past. Our connection with all these dead moments is experienced physically rather than intellectually – in physical sensations and emotions rather than in thoughts. The past also shapes our experiences imaginally, in the stories we inherit from our family and culture. There is a constant tension between the past, which gives us continuity, identity and meaning, and the present, which provides an opportunity for novelty. Mimesis and myth make for a very stable culture and a stable personality, but they do not make much room for change. Where everyone is unconsciously copying themselves and those around them, and people keep repeating the stories that illustrate the way things are supposed to be, nothing changes very much. Fortunately, however, we have a capacity for more complex thinking than this.

Some of our students have basically the same stories about life as we have. They share our values and assumptions. Teaching them presents no problem as it poses no threat to them. The knowledge and skills we teach them can affirm them in who they are and enrich their understanding and behaviour. They do not have to reorganize their whole view of themselves and their world in order to take in this new knowledge. They just add it on. However, one thing that teachers get used to is the way some students resist learning. They have seen themselves for so long as people who can't or won't do certain things that, even when they declare that they want to learn, they still keep resisting the teaching. They may have identified with their inability to read, and don't yet know any other way to be. Their present experience is dominated by their past. We regularly come across children or adolescents whose public identity is bound up in being the one who gives teachers a hard time, or the one who does not join in games, or the one who hates poetry, or the one who can't read or do algebra. Giving up our identity and our story about ourselves, even an uncomfortable identity and an unpleasant story, can be scary.

We hang on very tightly to our values and assumptions, especially to our assumptions about ourselves. We can even argue that when people change, it is usually in order to remain the same. If we are forced to change the things we do and say, we look for ways of changing which leave our values, our assumptions and our sense of who we are unaffected. We generally stick to our story. So do our students.

However, as teachers we are often faced with the task of challenging students' stories. We are trying to teach them things which conflict with what they already 'know' about themselves. We may be trying to shift them from a sense of themselves as illiterate, ignorant or bored to a sense of themselves as literate, knowing or engaged. We may likewise be engaged in shifting them from living their lives within a racist, sexist or violent narrative and trying to persuade them to embrace a more morally and socially acceptable one. Not surprisingly, we sometimes find this difficult. And it is difficult because we are not just 'adding on' something to what is already known. When we are trying to teach someone something significant, as we often are, we must often deal with the fact that what we teach must connect with, and often conflict with, what is deeply 'known' already. Moreover, much of what is known already has become an aspect of their identity. In process terms, they have 'known' it again and again and again. Constant reiteration has established a field in which they are increasingly likely to know it again with each new experience.[298]

Mythic mind reinforces magic mind's tendency to conform to the ideas and assumptions of those around us. Attacking people's deeply held assumptions and taken-for-granted narratives is generally a good way to strengthen them. Disturbing their sense of who they are arouses a great deal of anxiety, and they often deal with this anxiety by defending themselves against this knowledge. When our sense of who we are is under threat we are inclined to opt for survival rather than risk it all for growth. And to survive we use whatever primitive, magical, ritualistic strategies seem to work.

Fortunately, magic mind and mythic mind can also support our attempts to change our students' views on life and give them skills they don't believe they are capable of. If students have self-destructive or anti-social ways of relating to the world we can change these by giving them experiences that contrast with the ones that shaped their assumptions, we can model attitudes, values, skills and ways of relating that they may tune into without being terribly aware that they are doing so. We can tell stories that engage them, so that they 'pick up' attitudes and values by identifying with characters in a story, without the need for us to tease out lessons or morals. The classroom is an environment where children's stories are transformed, for better or for worse, through hearing other stories in interaction with their teachers and friends.

Magic and myth enable us to live in a world which does not have to be constructed again at every moment. Together they give us a culture, a system of assumptions, behaviours and attitudes which we share with our tribe and rarely question. On the other hand a rational, individualistic consciousness enables us to detach ourselves from our physical experience, our culture and our environment, and have ideas about them. We need mentality, as well as magic and myth, for a full and rich life.

BEING A PERSON: MENTAL MIND

Mythical consciousness allows the emergence of what Damasio calls the *autobiographical self*. However, as long as we are in our mythical consciousness we are not truly individuals but members of a tribe whose understandings of the world we accept without question. However, the autobiographical self can do more than this. It can think critically about ourselves and the world, an exercise by which we really become individuals.[299]

Gebser associated the emergence of *mental* consciousness in European history with the discovery of perspective. Our archaic minds don't have much awareness of what they are looking at; our magic minds are aware of being entangled in the world; our mythical minds exist in a 'flat', two-dimensional world. They don't distinguish between true and false, right and wrong, significant and trivial. Our mental minds can make these distinctions by observing things one at a time and calculating their relationship with each other. Mental consciousness enables us to sort out reality, detaching ourselves from our experience, standing in a specific spot and looking in a specific direction. Science depends on this ability.

Robert Kegan suggests that a useful way of looking at cognitive development is to see it as a series of shifts in the ways we distinguish between our subjective and objective selves. In the beginning we simply experience the world and identify with this experience. Then our experience becomes an object and we identify with our awareness of that experience. Later we are able to identify with the person who is aware of the experience. By later childhood we are identifying with the contents of our minds which include our knowledge of who we are. The contents of our minds are all borrowed from other people, past and present, so the next development is to identify with our abilty to look critically at what we know and check it against the evidence from the outside, objective world. Kegan argues that this development of 'fourth order consciousness' is a central task of adolescence.[300] In Freud's language, it is the development of the ego.

Developmental psychologists are inclined to set out the phases of cognitive development in a neat sequence, but we know that it is more complex and messy than that. There are times when adults gladly let go of their sense of separateness and immerse themselves in the flow of collective emotion.

And we find children showing a capacity to distinguish between what is actual and what is possible and thinking rationally about it. However, we do have different expectations of children, adolescents and adults. When teaching children we may be disposed to focus on the *confluent* mode of physical experience. We expect our adolescent students to operate much of the time in the *discernment* mode of objective and detailed perception. We expect them to be able to think about their thoughts, to judge whether they match up to the evidence of the world as they experience it. We expect them to be able to sort out their experiences and make choices about their behaviour. We expect them to become individuals. We expect them to be able to handle abstract ideas. We expect them to be able to distinguish between true and false, right and wrong, better and worse.

It is our mental mind which makes these dualistic distinctions, and likewise the distinctions between subject and object, mind and body, me and you. It is our mental mind which quantifies time and space. It is our mental mind which focuses on assessing the evidence and drawing conclusions. We like to imagine ourselves as thinking, choosing individuals, even though neuroscientists are currently more likely to argue that we are emotion-driven individuals whose experience of making conscious decisions is somewhat delusional. The science suggests that our awareness of making a decision arrives *after* our brain has initiated the action that we are deciding to perform. It seems that our exercise of choice is limited to deciding not to do something that our organism has started to do.[301] Nevertheless, choice is at the centre of our subjective experience. Unfortunately when we conventionally think of choice we are inclined to think of it as something initiated by our mind, as distinct from our body. In the light of what we now know about our brains it makes more sense to think of choice as something which involves our whole organism, not just the part of our brain (the prefrontal cerebral cortex) which provides us with awareness of the choice we are making. We may not have much control over the thoughts and feelings which 'bubble up' in us, either stimulated by our senses or emerging from our ongoing unconscious processes, but we do have a choice in what we do about them. There is a passive side to our experience, which is dominated by the parts of our brain which provide archaic/physical, magic/emotional and mythic/imaginative experience. And there is an active, subjective side, which we associate with mental/critical mind. Schwartz puts it slightly differently:

> The brain may determine the content of our experience, but mind chooses which aspect of that experience receives attention.[302]

We acknowledge that growth comes from within, but not only from within. While the acorn cannot grow into a peach tree, it does have a lot of possibilities about the size, shape and vigour of the oak tree it will eventually become. Some of these possibilities are determined by the past, which has given the acorn a specific set of genes. Some of them are provided by the environment in which it is planted. However, the acorn does not do much choosing. The infant does rather more. At first her experience is essentially physical, dominated by the past through the confluent mode of being. As she grows and becomes more capable of discernment, choice becomes a more and more significant element in her experience. At the beginning, choices seem to be determined by her genes, her past experience and her immediate physical environment; later they are increasingly influenced by her social environment. As she grows, her choices become more and more conscious and deliberate and we encourage her to be aware of what she is choosing and why. We expect adults to be able to choose how they want to be, even if they only want to be the same as everybody else. However, when they feel trapped by their past and totally unable to choose for themselves, we suspect some kind of pathology.

We expect adolescents to develop what Jean Knox calls 'reflective function'. She argues that 'reflective function' is the root of our sense of meaning and capacity to symbolize.

> It begins to become clear that the concept of reflective function has enormous implications for our understanding of human psychological development and functioning and in particular for the development of a sense of meaning, a word that we all intuitively understand but which a moment's reflection shows to be rather vague and imprecise. What are the contributing factors to a sense of meaning, which is rooted in the capacity to find symbolic significance in our experience? I would suggest

there are four key and interrelated elements, all of which contribute to the development of reflective function.[303]

The four key elements she lists are *narrative competence* (the recognition of psychological cause and effect), *intentionality* (the capacity to pursue goals and desires), *appraisal* (the capacity to evaluate the significance of experiences) and *individuation* (the awareness of one's own and other people's independent subjectivity).

Knox bases her argument on current understandings of developmental psychology and the related field of attachment theory. On the one hand she proposes that the reflective function begins to emerge in early childhood. On the other she argues that not everybody manages to develop an adequate reflective function, and hence they 'lack the capacity to empathize with other people or place their own emotions in a meaningful context'.[304] She makes the case that this is a consequence of their failure to develop secure attachment as infants. In normal development children establish the capacity for empathy in infancy, in their connection with their carers through archaic and magic consciousness. If they do not spend their infancy in an environment which provides a satisfactory experience of attachment, it is possible to develop satisfactory relationships – and reflective function – later on, but they start with a considerable disadvantage.

The pull of magic and mythic consciousness is a pull towards conformity and continuity. Mental consciousness, which is able to look at 'the facts' objectively, brings with it the possibility of novelty. The tension between continuity and novelty may be thought of as a tension between the need to survive and the urge to grow. In educational terms, there is a competition between education as imitation (largely a function of magic mind) and education as individuation (a function of mental mind).

One of the things teachers try to do is to teach their students to observe the world critically and objectively and reach rational conclusions about it. We expect our students in late adolescence to be capable of standing outside their thoughts and reflecting on them critically. We encourage them to think abstractly about the world, to look at the evidence and decide what is most likely to be 'true'. We want them to realize that their current thoughts and 'the truth' are not identical and that other people have thoughts different from their own. We find that not all of them can manage it, at least not in areas where their image of themselves and their place in the world needs defending. We find that many adolescents, in their eagerness to discover 'the truth' become dogmatic about some absolute truth that does not really stand up to much critical scrutiny. They need a story to hang on to, and myths tend to be more powerful than facts. We have enough trouble in consistently avoiding this tendency ourselves. Our past experiences flow into the present moment and affect our ability to see what is actually there. Feelings and images flowing into our psyche from the past get projected on to our experience of the present moment. We find our students treating us as their indulgent father or controlling mother, their controlling father or indulgent mother, because when they look at us their experience of mother or father flows into their experience of us. Any new information we give our students is affected, and sometimes distorted, by what they 'know' already.

Gebser pointed out with some force that mental consciousness has both 'efficient' and 'deficient' expressions. He argued that, while mental consciousness gained some dominance in the classical period and the renaissance, the past three centuries have seen it take a wrong turn. During the era of scientific materialism mind has become largely identified with a crudely 'rational' ego-driven consciousness, which ignores intuition and emotion and sees the world only in terms of quantifiable material reality. This kind of consciousness, which is egocentric and detached from Nature, and which only accepts what is measurable and countable, has enabled the extraordinary development of Western science. However it has also got us into the position where we are destroying the planet. The rational thinking which ego-centred mental consciousness supports is often shaped by the myth of Herakles, and we know that Herakles, for all his good will, had a tendency to make a mess of things.

BECOMING WHOLE: INTEGRAL MIND

Magic and myth enable us to live in a world where we can make assumptions about life, a set of taken for granted behaviours and attitudes that we share with our tribe. On the other hand, a rational, individualistic, mental consciousness enables us to detach ourselves from our culture and have our own ideas about it. Gebser goes further and suggests that we have latent in us another kind of consciousness in which mental consciousness is integrated with the older and simpler kinds of consciousness into something new — an *integral* or *spiritual* consciousness.

In the mid-twentieth century he wrote with a sense of urgency of the need for new ways of thinking if we were to avoid what appeared to be an inevitable global catastrophe.[305] More optimistically, he went on to provide evidence from the arts and sciences that these new ways of thinking were emerging. A few decades later, similar observations were being made by Jacques Lyotard and other commentators on 'the postmodern condition'.[306] Gebser observed that not only were the magic and mythical modes of perceiving the world being once again widely accepted as legitimate, but that the magical and mythical structures of consciousness were being integrated with rational consciousness to produce a totally new way of perceiving and thinking.[307] It is central to Gebser's understanding that all the structures are co-present in us. However, the integral structure of consciousness is not merely the four previous structures 'jostling together' (to use Egan's phrase). It is an entirely new structure which enables us to apprehend not just the parts but the whole. He argues that 'it cannot dispense with the foundation of the mental structure any more than the mental structure can dispense with the mythical, and the mythical with the magic.'[308] The teacher's success in facilitating the emergence of integral consciousness in children depends on assuring that the child does not lose her archaic, magical and mythical identification with planet, species and community.

One of the key features of integral consciousness as Gebser imagines it is that it is free from the dualism which is at the core of rational thinking. Twentieth century science led inexorably to the unexpected conclusion that the rules of rational, dualistic thinking which have been so useful for us in the past may not be universally applicable.[309] Our mental minds are perspectival; they see the world from a particular position. Our integral minds enable us to see the world from every position at once. It is a notion that Picasso (an acquaintance of Gebser) incorporates in his paintings.

Egan argues, like Whitehead and Gebser, that there is more to human experience than the evidence of our senses and the rational conclusions we draw from it. A mature 'ironic' consciousness enables us to integrate our somatic experience with our capacity to think, and deal with the ambiguities which arise when there is a contradiction or tension between our thoughts and our senses. Our ironic consciousness enables us to cope with the conflict without disowning one kind of knowledge or another. Kegan argues that just as a modern society demands of its members that they be capable of fourth order (rational/critical) thinking, and expects teachers to develop it in adolescents, a postmodern society demands fifth order thinking. Unfortunately, we may not be capable of the complex subject-object differentiation involved.[310] We are comfortable enough with the fourth order notion that we should stop taking things for granted, look with fresh eyes at the objective facts and decide for ourselves what is true. However, Kegan suggests that in the world as it now presents itself we have to go further, and stop identifying with our way of thinking. We have to stop making the assumption that our way of observing and thinking is the only, or even the best, way of arriving at the truth. The truth does not reside in your perspective or in mine. It resides in both, and in the tension between them.

Whitehead was making a similar reflection when he suggested in *Modes of Thought* (1938) that science deals only with half the evidence available to human experience. By restricting themselves to the 'objective facts' scientists cannot find enjoyment, intention or creativity in nature. Yet we keep finding these in our experience. He also argued that truth is partial and plural and observed that both scientists and sceptics were falling for what he called 'the fallacy of dogmatic finality'. He urged us to avoid one-sided seeing, reminding us that here are no whole truths, only half truths.

Theories of the self used to focus on the importance of having a clear identity. Nowadays it has become conventional to talk about our many selves. Where once we were expected to develop a 'strong ego', we now find that we have many selves through which to express the fullness of our being, and that rigid identification with a single self, a single narrative, is an obstacle to our becoming what we can be. This way of thinking is consistent with the emergence of the integral structure of consciousness in our culture. (We might suggest that Buddhist psychology abandoned the egoic delusion some time ago!) The unfolding of integral consciousness in children demands a classroom which encourages and honors plurality in children's expressions of their 'personality' and talents, in contrast to the increasingly narrow and instrumental vision of mainstream education. However, integrality in education is not just a matter of facilitating the child's becoming all that she is capable of becoming as an individual. She is not only an individual. Indeed her individuality is not the most important thing about her. In Gebser's understanding the elicitation of integral consciousness inducts the child/adolescent/adult into awareness of a transparent whole of which he/she is an integral part.

Understanding who we are means getting past our egocentric and even anthropocentric assumptions about what sort of universe we are part of. Archaic mind give us experience with no awareness of being separate from what surrounds us. Magic mind gives us a sense of vegetative entanglement in a world in which everything is connected. Mythical mind separates us from Nature and gives us a sense of identification with a cultural group and the narratives which give meaning to its activities. Mental mind separates us from both the planet and the tribe and enables us to become individuals who have choices about who they are and what they do. Integral mind incorporates all the older, less complex minds and enables us to apply our whole attention (and our whole brain) to the transparent reality that we are both separate, thinking individuals and cells of a greater organism.

AND FINALLY

When we share a moment of consciousness and purpose with our students we need to remember that they are five-minded animals. In their archaic, somatic mind, they are one with their physical experience, united in experience with the species, creatures of instinct and habit. In their tribal, magic-mimetic mind, they share the collective emotion of the tribe and try to keep it safe through magic and ritual. In their mythical mind, they live embedded in the stories that carry their culture's values and attitudes. In their mental-rational mind they know themselves as individuals and seek to know the truth about the world. In their integral-ironic-spiritual mind they are capable of transcending the subject-object, self-other, truth-fiction, material-spiritual dualisms that shape rational consciousness.

There are clear parallels between the emergence of consciousness in our species as Gebser documents it, our individual cognitive development from infancy to maturity and the rhythm of learning. Cycles within cycles within cycles. The creative advance of our species manifests the rhythm of life.

In our individual advance from past to future all of our five minds are involved. To use Gebser's language once again, our archaic mind experiences the past through its identification with the physical world, our magic mind is emotionally engaged with the past and carries this emotion into our present experience, our mythical mind shapes its perceptions of the present experience according to the tribal narratives in which it is embedded and our mental mind has the capacity to escape from instinct, ritual, tribal narrative to see the past and present world objectively. The integral mind incorporates all of the older and simpler minds in a time-free, aperspectival, arational, pluralistic, ecocentric (not egocentric), constructive and creative experience of the world. For our integral mind, not only are 'my truth and 'your truth' incomplete without each other, but 'I' and 'you', person and planet, self and society, are likewise parts of each other, jewels in Indra's net.

NOTES Chapter 11. Being in Five Minds

[265] K. Egan, *The Educated Mind*, p. 80.
[266] See J. Gebser, *The Ever-Present Origin*.
[267] ibid, p. 42.
[268] M. Donald, *Origins of the Modern Mind*.
[269] M. Donald, *A Mind So Rare*, p. 262.
[270] See J. Hall, *Neuroscience and Education*.
[271] See P. MacLean, *The Triune Brain in Evolution*.
[272] See A. Damasio, *Self Comes to Mind*.
[273] Other contributors to the model of 'multiple minds' include Marshall McLuhan, who proposed that the evolution of consciousness should be viewed in terms of five successive quantum leaps in our capacity to communicate, and numerous writers who have focused on the shift from magical/mythical consciousness to mental/theoretic consciousness. See M. McLuhan, *Understanding Media*; J. Jaynes, *The Origin of Consciousness in the Breakdown of the Bicameral Mind*; M. Eliade, *The Myth of the Eternal Return*; K. Jaspers, *The Origin and Goal of History*.

274 It should be noted that Gebser's model is not based on an assumption of progress from a deficient to a more adequate experience of the universe. On the one hand the earlier, simpler structures provide just as valid a way of experiencing 'the ever-present origin' as the later, more complex structures. Second, the experience of time as linear and sequential (and consequently the very notion of evolution) belongs to a specific structure of consciousness – the mental/rational structure – and is in no way an essential attribute of time.

275 See R. Kegan, *In Over Our Heads*.

276 A. Damasio, *Self Comes to Mind*, pp. 143f.

277 ibid., p. 185.

278 Jung, CW 10, para. 105.

279 Jung, CW 8, para. 218

280 Jung, *Man and His Symbols*, p. 52.

281 See Meares, *Relief Without Drugs* (see chapter 8, above).

282 *A Way of Being*, p.134. It should be noted that Rogers understood this tendency to be a manifestation of a 'formative directional tendency in the universe ... This is an evolutionary tendency towards greater order, greater complexity, greater interrelatedness' (ibid., p. 133). Such statements naturally drew the accusation that he had ceased to be a serious scientist and had slipped into 'nature mysticism'.

283 R. Carson, *The Sense of Wonder*, p. 45.

284 See R. Louv, *Last Child in the Woods*.

285 See Sheldrake, *The Rebirth of Nature*, pp. 182f.

286 Gebser, *The Ever-Present Origin*, p. 49.

287 Current neuroscience suggests that mid-brain can function independently of the cerebral cortex, supporting Egan's assertion that our minds 'jostle together' and are 'somewhat distinct'. Kathryn Patten argues that

> there is overwhelming support that the systems that comprise affect function primarily in but not limited to the limbic region, and are distinct and capable of operating without cognitive regions of the brain, especially for primal levels of affect, such as fear. In other words, early appraisal of incoming stimuli need not involve higher order cortical processing or conscious appraisal in order to evoke basic emotions and produce bodily responses such as changes in heart rate, sweating, muscular tension, eye blinking, chemical responses and neuronal activation of other brain regions. The ability of the amygdalae to assess incoming stimuli for affective content and then activate other regions of the brain more rapidly and dramatically than the thinking part of the brain, the neocortex, lends credence to evidence that the amygdalae is capable of overriding the cognitive brain (*Educational Philosophy and Theory: Special Issue: Educational Neuroscience*, vol. 43, 1, p. 88).

Being in Five Minds

[288] Tuning in does not seem to be dependent on being in the same location. It is a common experience of twins or people in love to experience the emotional state of one another at a distance, and it is a common experience of mothers to sense the distress of an infant though out of sight and hearing. It appears to be a capacity common in pre-modern, collectivist cultures which people in modern individualistic cultures have largely lost. In Gebser's model it is a capacity belonging to the magic structure of consciousness which has been neglected, repressed and disowned in deficient rational cultures.

[289] These findings are largely based on the micro-analysis of films. Hall suggests that bodily rhythms are largely culture specific and that racism and intercultural misunderstanding is frequently a consequence of the inability to sync the bodily and vocal rhythms of a person from another culture. We sense our own rhythms as normal and are often confused by the rhythms of people from other cultures. See E. T. Hall, *Culture's Consequences*.

[290] Donald's understanding of the evolution of consciousness is similar in many respects to Gebser's, though his data comes from different sources – in neuroscience and cognitive science as well as anthropology and linguistics. He distinguishes three major cognitive transitions in human history and prehistory, producing three stages of cultural development which he calls mimetic, mythic and theoretic. Like Gebser, he argues that the older ways of representing reality still persist in us. There is still 'a vestigial mimetic culture embedded within our modern culture, and a mimetic mind embedded within the architectural structure of the modern human mind' (*Origins of the Modern Mind*, p. 163. See also *A Mind So Rare*).

[291] See V. S. Ramachandran, *The Tell-Tale Brain*, pp. 117ff. See also C. Hannaford, *Playing in the Unified Field*.

[292] Ramachandran notes that when the frontal inhibitory circuits have been damaged, the patient sometimes mimics gestures uncontrollably, a symptom call echopraxia. ibid., p. 125.

[293] This is obviously the case in team sports. When team members are in sync they can communicate intuitively and perform as a single organism. However, it can sometimes be an indication that things are going very badly – in mob behaviour, for instance. The difference is in the nature of the collective emotions which are being acted out.

[294] Patten, op. cit., pp. 87-97.

[295] Feelings are 'mental recognitions of the pattern of physiological, chemical, and neural responses evoked by certain brain systems when a person perceives or recalls objects or situations. Feelings involve cortical appraisal systems and therefore have a cognitive component' (ibid., p. 88).

[296] Damasio, op. cit,, pp. 167-8.

[297] Archetypal psychologists like James Hillman would argue that all of these stories are versions of the 'old stories' which carry the core ways of giving our lives value and meaning. The significant thing about them is that they

are essentially collective stories. We all have our personal versions of them, based on our own experience, but the essential shape of these stories (whether it is the victim story, the hero story, the ugly duckling story, the god's special people story, the inevitability of progress story or any of the others) belongs to our culture and we just take its truth for granted. See Hillman, *Revisioning Psychology*.

[298] Sheldrake's theory of 'morphic fields' suggests that not only does our past experience of 'knowing' pre-dispose us to know again in the same way, but we exist in fields created by others of our species:

> If behaviour is indeed governed by morphic fields then, when some members of a species acquire a new pattern of behaviour ... then others should tend to learn the same thing more quickly, even in the absence of any known means of connection or communication. The more members of the species that learn it, the greater should this effect become all over the world' (*The Rebirth of Nature*, p. 91).

[299] While the brainstem is coordinating our protoself and the thalamus is coordinating our core self, the cerebral cortex is coordinating our autobiographical self. Damasio suggests that

> In interplay with the thalamus and brain stem, the cortex keeps us awake and helps select what we attend to. In interplay with the brain stem and thalamus, the cortex constructs the maps that become mind. In interplay with the brain stem and thalamus, the cortex helps generate the core self. Last, using the records of past activity stored in its vast memory banks, the cerebral cortex constructs our biography, replete with the experience of the physical and social environments we have inhabited. The cortex provides us with an identity and places us at the center of the wondrous, forward-moving spectacle that is our conscious mind (*Self Comes to Mind*, p. 248).

[300] See Kegan, *In Over Our Heads*.

[301] Schwartz and Begley weigh up the neuroscientific evidence relating to the existence (or not) of free will. They conclude that, while it appears that our sense of choice is essentially limited to vetoing actions that our organism is about to perform, we can do more than this. While on the one hand our subjective experience (our mind) follows our brain's tendency to react automatically to the stimuli from our environment and our unconscious, on the other hand our mind is able to change the way our brain functions.

> It seems safe to conclude that the pre-frontal cortex plays a central role in the seemingly free selection of behaviours, choosing from a number of possible actions by inhibiting all but one and focusing attention on the chosen one (*The Mind and the Brain*, p. 368).

[302] Schwartz, op. cit., p. 370.

[303] Jean Knox, *Archetype, Attachment, Analysis*, p. 42.
[304] ibid., p. 139.
[305] In his preface to *The Ever-Present Origin* (1949), Gebser argues:
> The crisis of our times and of our world is in a process – at the moment autonomously – of complete transformation, and appears headed towards an event which, in our view, can only be described as 'global catastrophe'… We must certainly face the fact that only a few decades separate us from that event. This span of time is determined by an increase in technological feasibility inversely proportional to man's sense of responsibility – that is, unless a new factor were to emerge which would effectively overcome this menacing correlation (p. xxvii).

[306] See J. F. Lyotard, *The Postmodern Condition*.
There is a sense in much contemporary writing that rationality, like Christianity and Marxism, has been tried and has failed. We can detect a trajectory of thought, which runs through Kant, Schopenhauer and Nietzsche and diverges into a thousand parallel paths in this century which challenges the supremacy of reason and the logic of materialism, and points to the paradoxes and ambiguities that are characteristic of post-rationalist thought in every field. Lyotard and other commentators on the 'postmodern condition' point to the unrelenting exchange of information, leading to the deregulation of ideas, the dominance of the marketplace, the collapse of the 'grand narratives' and the heroic fantasy of controlling and possessing nature, and a postmodern science characterized by incomplete information, catastrophe and chaos, indeterminacy, paradox, discontinuity, and a tendency to uncover new questions rather than new answers. The postmodern mind's mode of dealing with reality is inclined to be aesthetic rather than rational, more comfortable dealing with images than with ideas, inclined also to give to direct, subjective (even mystical) experience a validity it seemed to have lost some time ago.

[307] When Gebser was writing in the 1940s, it was in the context of an apparent breakdown of the mental structure and a regression to magical and mythical consciousness – manifested in Nazism, fascism and tribalism. He argued then, as he would no doubt argue today, that the breakdown of one dominant structure (the mental) signals the possibility of a mutation to a more complex structure (the integral).

[308] Gebser, op. cit., p. 299.

[309] Gebser warns us against assuming that the only alternative to rational thinking is irrationality. He distinguishes the irrational thinking of mythic mind and the rational thinking of mental mind from the arational thinking of integral mind
> However we may wish to define it, arationality is never identifiable with irrationality or pre-rationality. There is a fundamental difference

between the attempt to go beyond the merely measurable, knowing and respecting it while striving to be free from it, and rejecting and disregarding the measurable by regressing to the immoderate and unfathomable chaos of the ambivalent and even fragmented polyvalence of psychic and natural interrelations (ibid., p. 147).

[310] Only fifth order thinking can meet the requirement of a postmodern culture that 'the epistemological construction of system, form or theory be relativized, moved from subject in one's knowing to object in one's knowing'. Kegan, *In Over Our Heads*, p. 321.

12

THE GODS IN THE CLASSROOM

The glorious gifts of the gods are not to be cast aside.

Homer

THE STORIES ABOUT THE GODS are not just stories we *tell*; they are stories we *live*. Our ancestors once lived in a world in which everything had already happened, in the time of the gods. It was a world in which mere mortals understood that they were simply re-enacting the stories of the gods. We are not far removed from our ancestors in evolutionary terms. Though our newly developed rational minds may be inclined to think of the great myths as stories which we have learned and may choose to tell to our children, our mythical minds experience them as stories which contain us, stories in which our lives are embedded.

The gods and myths of the classical Greeks are not the stories of a stone age tribe, though they may have begun as such. They are the gods and myths of an urban, sophisticated, self-reflective people, with a complex social and political system, and a highly developed cultural life. Yet the Greeks understood that there are forces in the cosmos that are bigger that any individual human – not just mechanical forces, but forces like power, love, fear and rage. They wove a web of myths from many sources to represent the complexity of life, a web of overlapping and interpenetrating stories which provided a rich source of meaning for the philosophers and poets of the European Renaissance and which now serves the same function for contemporary archetypal psychologists. The patterns we find in our lives in the twenty-first century are not new patterns. The stories through which we construct and express the meaning of our lives are not new stories. The conflicts between competing meanings and competing values are not new conflicts. The same squabbling gods whom Homer described are still present in our personalities, our technologies and our institutions. They are most definitely present in our classrooms.

Jung understood the gods and the myths surrounding them to be manifestations of archetypal patterns. He had several ways of explaining what he meant by archetype, and his different explanations seem sometimes contradictory. If we follow Jung, archetypes sometimes appear to be metaphysical entities, independent of human experience. Sometimes they appear to be biological structures, hard-wired in our genes and in our brains and manifested in instinctual behaviour. Sometimes they appear to be abstract mental structures which shape our experience, without being experienced themselves. Jung does not seem to have cared much about being logically consistent, and was content that philosophy, biology, psychology, anthropology and religious studies all pointed in the same direction – towards the notion that our behaviour is shaped by innate mental structures.

Since Jung's time, the word archetype has been used in so many different and inconsistent ways that we could argue that it is useless as a scientific term. Nevertheless, we do recognize patterns in individual and group behaviour, patterns which appear to be universal across cultures. We recognize that many of the patterns that we observe today are the same as those are recorded in ancient mythologies and associated with the personalities of the gods. And we now find that the sciences of brain and behaviour seem to point to something which, for want of a better word, we can continue to call archetype.

Cognitive scientists and evolutionary psychologists are not inclined to use that word, however, even when they are arguing that we are born with innate instinctual knowledge, inherited from our ancestors (for example, the instinctual tendency to use language, avoid danger and protect our children).[311] Others argue that our genes do not carry any sort of blueprint for our behaviour. They argue that, rather than carrying information, our genes carry a tendency to focus on particular patterns in our environment (for example, the human face) and interact with them. They suggest that we gradually construct a meaningful world through interacting with particular aspects of our environment. Our earliest experience is especially important. One of our first experiences – even before birth – is *containment*, from which we develop a sense of *inside* and *outside*. Other early experiences that we seem to be predisposed to notice are *path* (the sense of movement in a particular direction), *up-down*, *force*, *part-whole* and *link*. These *image schemas* can be thought of as our first step towards the appreciation of a meaningful universe.[312]

For anyone who is comfortable with the Jungian language of archetype this simply demonstrates what Jung intuited a long time ago. It made little difference to him whether we think there is a metaphysical entity which has a transcendent existence and manifests itself in our human experience of *containment* – a mother's womb, a mother's arms, a cave, a home, a family, a club, a gang, a profession, a classroom – or whether we believe that we are born with a cluster of molecules in our brains which have evolved through natural selection over thousands of years to enable us to have this experience and deal with it. If we find the theories contradict each other, this has more to do with our limited ways of thinking than with the nature of archetype. If we insist on imaging archetypes as 'things', it's easy enough to argue that there is no evidence that such 'things' exist. On the other hand, if we give up thinking of the universe as comprised of 'things' and imagine it rather as an emerging process, we will have no trouble seeing archetypal patterning as an aspect of this process.[313]

Giving these patterns the names of Greek gods (as people in the European classical world and the European renaissance did) brings our capacity for poetry into the service of our understanding. We can, if we like, believe in the gods as transcendent persons, but this is theology, not psychology. The question whether divinity is best imagined as singular or plural is certainly worth asking, but it is not the question asked by archetypal psychologists. They are more interested in exploring the narratives of the gods for insights into human behaviour and culture. They look for the gods in our personalities and in the way we live our lives. It leads them to a pluralistic understanding of values.

In the twenty-first century educators seem to have more capacity for thinking pluralistically about teaching than they did a few decades ago. It is now commonplace to talk about multiple intelligences, a variety of teaching and learning styles, different acceptable outcomes of education. If we take the lead from archetypal psychology, the Greek pantheon can provide us with a language for talking about a wide range of distinct philosophies, value systems, energies, feeling states, habits of behaviour and teaching styles as they can be observed in the classroom. The gods are many, and if we follow the advice of the ancient Greeks we will be careful not to neglect any of them – and not get too carried away in worshipping any single one of them.

GREAT ZEUS

I shall sing of Zeus, the best and greatest of gods,
far-seeing, mighty, fulfiller of designs who confides
his tight-knit schemes to Themis as she sits leaning on him.
Have mercy, far-seeing Kronides, most glorious and great.[314]

The Gods in the Classroom

Every god has his or her stories. We mere mortals are caught up in them. The way our culture has evolved we find that we are most powerfully caught up in the story of Zeus.

Zeus is the original Indo-European sky-god. His worship came to Greece with the waves of horse-riding cattle-herders who entered the Balkan Peninsula after 2000 BC. As the Greek invaders established their political domination, he became the personification of patriarchal power in the family, in the clan and in the emerging city-states. We find him first depicted as a punitive and unpredictable weather-god, the Cloud-gatherer who sends hail, thunder and lightening. Later he came to be seen as to an all-powerful creator and a benevolent and wise father of humanity 'in whom we live, and move, and have our being'.[315] Later still, we find him representing (for the philosophers at least) the notion of pure, eternal, all-embracing divinity. He is the same sky-father as is worshipped in the Judaic-Christian-Islamic tradition.

The stories of Zeus as told by the classical Greeks come from a number of different sources. There are stories of the origin of the Olympian gods, how Zeus was saved by his mother (Rhea) from being swallowed by his father (Kronos) and how he rescued his brother and sister gods who had already suffered this fate. There are stories of how Zeus led the Olympian gods in battle against the Titans and Giants for control of the world. There are stories of Zeus' marriages to numerous local goddesses, who were thus incorporated into the state cult. There are stories of his seduction of the various human princesses by whom he became the father of the heroes. There are stories of Zeus' exercise of power as ruler of the universe, and his punishment of those who defy his laws or think too much of themselves. There are stories of him, also, as the even-handed dispenser of justice, impartially resolving disputes between gods and men.

The archetypal pattern personified in Zeus and manifested in human history and individual psychology is the pattern of power, the power which brings order to chaos, the power which maintains itself either brutally or benevolently, the power which can both protect and punish, which provides security as well as fear. If we follow the cognitive scientists in looking for innate structures in our brain, we may see in the Zeus pattern a link between the *up-down* schema and the *force* schema. For Zeus, and for teachers who are infatuated with him, life is about the hierarchical exercise of force. They are still stuck in their infantile experience of finding that they can move things (the image schema *force*) and finding also that 'up' is a better place to be than 'down'.

Zeus, as patriarch, is the last of the line of 'old gods', who ruled by the brutal exercise of power. His grandfather, Uranus, and his father, Kronos, ruled before him but, being unwilling to relax their absolute control in any way, each found his power usurped by one of his sons. Zeus, however, having been advised by the cunning Titan, Prometheus, that he would preserve his power only by sharing some of it, was freed from this threat.

The narrative of Zeus remains powerful in European culture – in education no less than in politics. An education which places great value on authority, which believes in an absolute morality, which lives in a fantasy of 'the good old days' when 'kids had a bit of respect', which thinks about curriculum in terms of the transmission of established knowledge and values, is clearly dominated by the Senex gods – Zeus the benevolent despot, Kronos, who devours his own children, Uranus, who on the one hand represents the ancient golden age when the earth yielded its bounty without labour and on the other hand represents the brutal exercise of absolute power. Autocratic administrators or teachers may embody the positive qualities of Zeus, in providing staff or students with the security of clear expectations and unambiguous rules of conduct. They may also embody his negative qualities in their violent suppression of dissent. The Zeus-dominated curriculum ensures that what is taught is what is already known and already judged to be important for the preservation of the culture. The Zeus-dominated bureaucracy protects teachers and students from chaos. It also swallows up creative people and creative ideas the way Kronos swallows his children. The Zeus-dominated teacher wants to maintain strict control over his or her students, and allows no nonsense. Human beings generally prefer order, even autocratic order, to chaos. In times of crisis or confusion, Zeus' ability to take command and give clear directions is often essential to our safety. Even in classrooms.

The Gods in the Classroom

Zeus (and the Zeus-inflated teacher or principal) believes that he (usually he) does not have to answer to anyone. He makes all the decisions, sometimes after a show of consultation. He punishes those who offend him but rewards with great generosity those who please him. But his rewards are as unpredictable as his punishments. He acts according to whim rather than according to reason.

The Zeus-inflated teacher or principal may be benevolent and generous. Yet he is outraged when people block his schemes. And he may have some difficulty relating to women, unless they accept the daughter role and do not try to assert their independence. Yet there are lots of benefits in being part of a Zeus-dominated school or classroom, as long as you know how to carry out instructions and show adequate respect. Generally speaking, you know what is what. You know what counts for right and wrong. If you like having a strong leader, if you like to be respected for the power you share in, you may relate very well to Zeus. Zeus can be very efficient in producing results.

Nevertheless, the Zeus-inflated teacher is experiencing increasing difficulty in democratic societies where children's rights are taken seriously. Teachers used to have power over their students through their assumed right to punish or reward. Now, corporal punishment is outlawed in many places and many of the alternative punishments and rewards available have very little meaning for their students. In the past teachers could even control without punishment on the principle that their position in society gave them the right to demand obedience from children. They can't take that for granted any longer. They may keep insisting, 'Do that because I say so!', but increasingly they hear, 'You can't make me.' If they report misbehaviour to a child's parents they may find that the parents take the child's side. Their power is being usurped by their students.

Prometheus's advice to Zeus is still worth taking: 'Share your power or you will lose it.'

William Glasser describes the 'quality school' as one where children's basic needs are satisfied.[316] His list of basic needs has no surprises: power, belonging, freedom and fun. Children and adolescents no longer simply need power; they are aware when they haven't got enough, and inclined to demand it. If the teacher does not offer them any power, they manufacture it through defiance, resistance or apathy. However, if Zeus can let go of his sole right to power in the classroom, things can turn out differently. In the quality classroom students are involved in decision-making, take leadership roles, initiate action and experience responsibility. They don't need to attempt to satisfy their need for power in ways that damage themselves and others. They even learn to enjoy the power that comes from literacy, numeracy and understanding how things work.

Zeus did not abandon his authority when he learned to consult with the other gods. He remained very much in charge. The teacher's Zeus energy will keep the teacher in charge, also, even when she conducts her classes in radically democratic fashion. There are times when Zeus has to use his authority to deal with crisis or confusion, or to keep the classroom safe. We all, male and female, need his gifts. However, to keep ourselves nice we need something from the other gods as well.

GLORIOUS HERA

Of golden-throned Hera I will sing, born of Rhea,
queen of the gods, unexcelled in beauty,
sister and glorious wife of the loud-thundering Zeus.
All the gods on lofty Olympus reverence her
and honour her together with Zeus who delights in thunder.[317]

Hera, for the classical Greeks, was the goddess of marriage and the family, the Queen who shared in the power of King Zeus, the Wife who remained loyally in the background while the divine Husband attended to the affairs of the universe, and who jealously guarded her special status in the face of Zeus' inclination to pursue other goddesses and mortals. There are indications in the myths that she was a mighty goddess in the Balkan peninsula long before Zeus was thought of, and that the sacred marriage of Zeus and Hera represents the need of the Indo-European invaders to domesticate her.

The Gods in the Classroom

She is goddess of family, of social obligations, of the bonds of blood and the bonds of commitment, loyalty and fidelity which unite people. 'Lady' is a fitting title for her. On the one hand it denotes her dignity and the honour due to her as queen of the gods. On the other, it has an old-fashioned feel to it, with connotations of old-fashioned values and 'proper' behaviour and keeping up appearances. She is a great and glorious goddess who is capable of extraordinary pettiness and spite. She sometimes appears as an old woman, for she represents the wisdom of the old ways. She is more often represented as a mature and fulfilled woman, who can occasionally bend even Zeus to her will.

In the Greek imagination, Hera represents social stability. Homer and the other poets depict her as the god of marriage and the family, the god of all those familial and social bonds and shared expectations which keep a society from exploding into fragments. To use the language of *image schemas*, her behaviour is shaped to the patterns of *containment* and *force*. The container of the school or classroom, the container of shared values, the container of loyalty and commitment to the class or school family, are a means of control – on behalf of Zeus. The easy exercise of authority depends on having a stable society. To use the language of the *quality school*, Hera puts a high value on *belonging* and *power*, but has no interest in *freedom* or *fun*.

We might see her at work in a curriculum which takes note of such things as social education. We find her in the notion that the point of schooling is a social one, that the task of teachers is to educate their students in the appropriate ways of behaving in our society, that children should learn their responsibilities to society, should learn their proper roles and how to carry them out. She abhors change. She attaches no value to creativity or personal growth. Her priorities are responsibility, loyalty, respect, commitment, honour, stability, dignity. We often see Hera in the personality of the teacher who is queen of the classroom, or the female vice-principal (or principal's secretary) who plays Hera to the (male) principal's Zeus. She has her own religious language and her own religious rituals. She is jealous of her relationship with Zeus, and always does her work with his interests in mind. Contemporary educators think her somewhat old-fashioned.

For the teacher whose personality is dominated by the Hera image, the school and profession are 'family' and command complete loyalty. She will happily work long hours for little or no remuneration rather than let the school down. Students and colleagues are expected to give the school the same loyalty. There is no place in Hera's world for individuals who give priority to their own satisfaction and personal fulfilment. Every member of the school family must put commitment and loyalty to the school ahead of personal whims and satisfactions. It is important to the stability of the family that all its members know their roles and responsibilities and carry them out. Hera loves pointing this out to people.

The child who knows how to 'fit in' may flourish in the Hera style of classroom, because 'fitting in' is what it is about. The teacher who knows how to 'fit in' will flourish in the school where Hera is inordinately worshipped. He will be expected to act in the best interests of the school rather than out of personal ambition. She will treat senior members of the 'family' with great respect. He will not criticize the school to outsiders. She will appreciate that there is an established and 'proper' way of doing things. He may be made to feel that he is disloyal if he insists on his right to leave work at the official closing time. If she has any ideas that challenge the established way of doing things she will be wise to keep quiet about it.

In one way or another Hera is involved in many of the stories of the heroes. Sometimes as patron, sometimes as persecutor, she sends them off on their journeys, just as our families send us off still to fight or lose our battles and find or lose our kingdoms. There is always a tension between family and individual, between the values of Hera and the values of the hero. This tension is manifest in particular in Hera's persecution of two humans who eventually attained divinity – Herakles and Dionysos. These two represent two very different versions of what it means to be an individual, but both are in conflict with Hera values. For Hera, the notion of individual growth (Dionysos) is as meaningless as the notion of the individual struggle (Herakles). In a collectivist, Hera-worshipping culture the individual has identity, rights and status only as a member of the family. By contrast, in an individualistic, hero-worshipping culture the individual's right-to-be-me-and-to-do-my-own-thing is everything, and we need ultimately feel responsibility to no one.

The Gods in the Classroom

In a multicultural society there will always be a clash between Hera and the hero-gods. A mainstream culture which worships individual potential and initiative will produce teachers who want to see their students making their own choices and constructing their own lives. Many of their students will come from minority cultures where the child's responsibility is simply to do what the family demands. The polytheistic teacher may have no solution to the dilemma, but her awareness that her truth is not the only truth may at least help the child to find a way through the impasse.

POSEIDON THE EARTHSHAKER

I begin to sing of Poseidon, the great god,
mover of the earth and of the barren sea,
the sea-god who is lord of Helikon and the broad Aigai.
O Earth-shaker, two-fold is your god-given prerogative,
to be a tamer of horses and a saviour of ships.
Hail, Poseidon, black-maned holder of the earth!
Have a kindly heart, O blessed one, and come to the aid of sailors.[318]

According to myth, Poseidon is the elder brother of Zeus, who fought at his side in the war against the Titans and who, in the settlement which followed, took the sea as his domain while Zeus took the sky. According to history, he appears to have been originally the same Indo-European weather-god as Zeus, whose worship entered the Balkan peninsula with the Indo-European invaders. The earliest invaders, the Minyans, worshipped him as the Horse-god, the huge, divine Stallion who thunders over the northern plains and makes the earth shake under his galloping feet. Later, when they became a seafaring people, he was identified with the sea, and his earth-shaking activities made him responsible for earthquakes.

So Poseidon, like Zeus, is the personification of power, but he is a rather rougher character than his younger brother. He is distinguished from Zeus the way the sea and the sky are distinguished as metaphors for power. Poseidon-power is deep, unknowable, sometimes calm and friendly but often unpredictably violent. Mere mortals cannot resist it; their only hope is to ride out its turbulence. It is power expressed through emotional outburst rather than power manifested in order. It demands public sacrifice and private respect. There is no point in either denying its power or looking for a rational explanation for its behaviour.

We see Poseidon's power in the classroom where the students experience the storm of the teacher's emotional outbursts, expressed in verbal and sometimes physical violence. Teachers who shout at children are usually stressed themselves, and not inclined to identify with the storm which erupts without warning. If violence is in our shadow we tend to avoid owning it by means of the *I-wasn't-really-myself/something-came-over-me* strategy. Their students in the meantime learn to survive in a world where violent storms and earthquakes alternate with periods of deep calm. Even if the calm is only on the surface and powerful currents are circulating in the depths.

The absolute rule of the patriarchal gods has been under challenge for some time, and it may be that these gods will eventually be domesticated in their turn, the way the patriarchy domesticated Hera. For the time being, however, power is very much alive in education as elsewhere. Human beings in our society show an enduring tendency both to seek power for themselves and to respect it in others. Children are as likely to feel lost and resentful as to feel free and creative when their teachers refuse (or fail) to acknowledge and exercise their own power. Unfortunately, many teachers are unwilling to acknowledge either their own tendency to find satisfaction in power or the reality of the power which their role gives them to make an impact, for better or worse, on children's lives. Jungian theory supports the Greeks' conviction that unacknowledged gods are dangerous. If we do not give a particular aspect of our personality a place in our awareness, it will make itself felt in our unconscious behaviour, often destructively. Teachers who disown their power may find themselves unable to control its excesses. Poseidon brings not only the gift of power but the ability to use it gently.

When people see a decline of behaviour, morality, and academic standards from what they believe they experienced in 'the good old days' they are inclined to think that the remedy can only be found in a return to the patriarchal strategies of punishment and control. Punishment and control are certainly traditional ways of dealing with chaos and of satisfying our need for order and security. However, they do not have a very good record of success in changing people's attitudes and behaviour, or in helping people learn what they need to learn. Zeus and Poseidon represent only one aspect of our understanding and our needs. There are other gods to be worshipped, who represent other ways of dealing with chaos.

MOTHER DEMETER

> *Of Demeter, the lovely-haired and august goddess,*
> *and of her daughter, the fair Persephone, I begin to sing.*
> *Hail, O goddess! Keep this city safe, and guide my song.*[319]

Jung found that the image of *mother* as *container* is universal in human experience, and that it is psychologically significant. When he looked to mythology and religious belief he could find stories of the Mother Goddess which matched the observations that he and Freud had made about our infantile attachment to mother and our conflicting needs to escape from mother's embrace and remain in it.

The Great Mother of Greek mythology has many names – Ge (Gaia), Rhea, Themis, Maia, Cybele. She is the primeval womb from which we all come, the primeval breast which continues to nourish us. Primal humans had no sense of themselves as distinct from the earth, just as infants have no sense of themselves as being distinct from their mother. Rational consciousness broke our union with the earth, and we have been suffering the loss ever since.

The indigenous inhabitants of the Balkan Peninsula worshipped this Great Mother under her many names. The Greek invaders readily identified her with the consort of their Sky-god. The myths of Demeter, and the rituals associated with her worship, carry traces of the ancient cult of fertility. The central myth of Demeter's loss and recovery of her daughter Persephone is a narrative which resonates powerfully for people today, just as it did for the ancient Greeks.

Educating Psyche

There is clearly a pattern in human affairs which we call mothering, and Demeter personifies it. She gives birth, she suckles, she provides, she is anxious for her child, she grieves, she gives her child the love and support necessary for growth. This is a psychological pattern as well as a biological one, and men as well as women share in it. Teaching is a profession where mothering skills are often needed. For some children, the school and classroom provide the only container where they feel safe.

Teachers with strong Demeter values take mothering seriously. Central to their image of themselves is their task of providing a safe and supportive environment for their students. They take responsibility for the care of their students, exercising the power of the carer and nourisher. Rather than, 'Do what I say because I say so' which is the message of Father Zeus, Mother Demeter says, 'Trust me. I know what is best for you.' For their part their students may be content to be looked after.

It has been argued very plausibly that for a century or more we have been experiencing a gradual shift from a patristic to a matristic society. The grounds for this argument have been drawn from many fields and the argument has by no means been confined to feminist writing. There is a sense that the growth of feminism and the growth of the ecological movement are aspects of the same phenomenon. Many people at the beginning of the twenty-first century are energized by the conviction that the future, if there is to be a future at all, must belong to Gaia/Demeter.

The image of Gaia/Demeter points to a strong connection between earthcare and mothering. This connection may not be easily established through rational argument, but it is deeply felt in our magical consciousness, and is clearly marked in Demeter's myth. When we give our students information about environmental threats, when we try to give them a clear understanding of what is at stake, we are acting out of the perspective of Apollo, the clear-sighted god. When we suggest that science must find ways to combat pollution or global warming, we talk the talk of Prometheus. This is not enough. Apollo and Prometheus will never tell us that we must feel for the earth. It is the Demeter and Gaia myths which tell us that Earth is Mother to be loved and reverenced, not Territory to be defended or Resource to be exploited.

The Gods in the Classroom

There may be some shift towards Demeter values in schooling, but it is still hard to discern. Our society maintains a sentimental attitude towards motherhood, but remains essentially matriphobic. Freud must take some of the blame for the fact that it is socially approved to blame our mothers for everything we don't like about ourselves. Even many feminists have colluded with the patriarchy in ridiculing motherhood. When we find schools seriously devoted to mothering their students, protecting and nourishing them in a cycle of mutual affection and dependence, we may be concerned that children will not grow up 'tough' enough for the 'real' world. When we find teachers (women or men) engaged in 'mothering behaviour' with their students we may find it slightly ridiculous, or even unhealthy. We can see readily enough the negative aspects of the goddess in Demeter-inflated teachers. We see dependence, possessiveness, vicarious living, neediness, the manipulation of affection. It is reasonable to criticize teachers who are so inflated by Demeter energy, and so attached to 'their' students, that they cannot bear to let them grow up. However, awareness of Demeter's pathology leaves some educators unable to acknowledge the positive Demeter aspects – nurturance, protection, sacrifice, love. Demeter's right to be reverenced may be acknowledged in the infant class, where mothering needs little excuse, but it tends to be resisted elsewhere in the schooling system. Mothering is certainly resisted in men. Male infant teachers get used to seeing people raise their eyebrows when they say what they do for a living.

The patriarchal society is ambiguous about motherhood, yet the myth of Demeter suggests that if mothering is not honoured, Earth is not honoured, and if Earth is not honoured we all die. It is an education which is committed to nurturing the growing child (of whatever age) which is most likely to be committed to honouring the earth.

BRIGHT-EYED ATHENA

I sing of Pallas Athena, the glorious goddess,
gray-eyed, resourceful, of implacable heart.
This bashful maiden is a mighty defender of cities,

Educating Psyche

> *the Tritogeneia, whom Zeus the counsellor himself*
> *bore from his august head, clad with golden and resplendent*
> *warlike armour, as awe lay hold of all the immortal onlookers.*[320]

When the Sky-god arrived in Greece, he brought with him his consort and his warrior-daughter, whom people variously called Kore, Parthenos or Pallas, all of which simply mean the Girl. There was already a Girl-goddess worshipped in Greece, who was in some places called Athena. She was a sort of 'palace goddess', of Cretan origin,[321] responsible for protecting the peace and good order of the royal household, a goddess of practical wisdom and practical crafts. Since the Greek invaders happily adopted the gods of the conquered peoples rather than suppress their worship, these two goddesses were readily identified as one. As Pallas Athena she became the protector-goddess of the city-states, especially of the city-state of Athens, where her worship was most enthusiastic. With the development of both democracy and imperialism in the fifth century Athens she became, for the Athenians at least, the symbol of both. In late classical times she became the personification of wisdom, and stayed on in Christian times as Sophia, the Wisdom of God.

There is plenty of evidence in art and poetry that the ancient Greeks were deeply devoted to Athena. They told of her birth from the brow of Zeus, of her competing with Hera and Aphrodite in the divine beauty contest judged by the Trojan prince Paris, of her patronage of heroes like Odysseus, Jason, Herakles and Perseus, whom she assisted in their various adventures. They told of her help to those engaged in crafts, and her vindictive punishment of human women like Medusa and Arachne, who claimed to rival her beauty or skill.

Since Athena is the assimilation of the patriarchal daughter with one of the manifestations of the Great Goddess she represents a point where sky-worship meets earth-worship, where masculine meets feminine, where abstract culture meets concrete culture, where vertical power structures meet horizontal ones. She is, then, the goddess of balance, of normality, of common sense. Unlike the numerous gods of the bizarre, who manage to make our lives exciting, Athene represents our instinct for the normal, our tendency to avoid extremes. She is a goddess with attributes which we are now inclined to stereotype as masculine. She is, for instance, a god of war. Not vehement, sword-wielding, blood-lusting warfare, waged for the violence and the glory of it (like Ares, the other Olympian war god), but cool, intelligent, calculating, strategic warfare, waged to defend one's city and citizens. She is also a god of peace, and of the civilized living that comes with peace. She teaches us the arts and sciences which form the basis of this civilization. She also teaches us that we must fight to defend them. She is the goddess of common sense. She is the goddess of the democratic process. Yet she has little interest in relationships, except in so far as they have strategic value.

Athena still has many disciples in the education system. They believe in doing things well. They believe in participative decision-making. They use cooperative teaching methods. They see schooling as an apprenticeship in democracy. They are delighted when they find themselves teaching a group of children or adolescents who are really prepared to take responsibility for their behaviour, and are happy to negotiate curriculum and rules of classroom conduct with them. They favour a problem-solving approach to curriculum. In their teaching, they like to use a lot of group work, not because relationships are all-important, but because group work is a very functional and efficient method of teaching.

As administrators they believe in listening to every side of every argument, and have a great deal of faith in consensus. In the Athena style of administration decisions are made coolly and sensibly, after full debate, with full attention to practical implications. The preferred way of developing strategies or dealing with problems is a collaborative approach that recognizes and utilizes people's different kinds of expertise. Too much emotionality is frowned on. Principals who are committed to the values of Athena put great store by the professional expertise of their staff. However, for all their interest in the sharing of power they are certainly not revolutionaries. They accept the realities of a patriarchal society, and manage to work within it. Female teachers who wish to challenge the (male) principal's paternalistic assumptions may not be welcome. Athena may represent the independent, resourceful, clear-sighted feminine, but she accepts the ground-rules laid down by Zeus. She is content to work in a men's world.

Yet, while we find some Athena values honoured in contemporary education, we will have to look very hard to find some others. Many educators believe firmly enough that it is their task to champion civilization, to keep at bay the barbarians (inside and outside the education system) who would destroy it, but they do not find in themselves the will to fight fiercely in its defence. Many teachers encourage a problem-solving approach to their subjects, for instance, but neither teachers nor curriculum designers are inclined to list the development of wisdom as a primary objective of education. Educational policy-makers encourage teachers to give great emphasis to the learning of technical skills, but in order to produce wealth, rather than in order to produce civilization. The pathology of Athena can be found where students sit in classrooms, paralysed by boredom, having learned Athena's lesson of non-engagement and having applied it to everything they experience, but not having learned the point of that non-engagement, which is to enable a clear-sighted and focused attack on a critical problem. It is apparent also in schools where democratic processes are seen to be so central that no decision can ever be made until everyone's opinion has been taken into account – with the result that often decisions are not made at all, or Zeus decides to ignore everyone's opinion and just do it his way.

SHINING APOLLO

I shall remember not to neglect Apollon who shoots afar.
The gods of the house of Zeus tremble at his coming,
and indeed all spring up from their seats
as he approaches, stringing his splendid bow.[322]

Like Athena, Apollo seems to be an assimilation of two similar deities. There is one line of evidence which points to an origin in Asia, and another which suggests that he was an Indo-European god who entered Greece with the invading Dorians.[323] There were actually two distinct cults of Apollo, one centred in the Aegean island of Delos, and the other in the mountain shrine of Delphi on the mainland, where Apollo spoke through his oracle.

The Gods in the Classroom

In addition, there was a tendency to identify him with Helios, the sun, and by Roman times this identification was complete.

Whatever his origins, he became a thoroughly Greek god, the eldest son of Zeus, the symbol of what it meant to be Greek and civilized: art, music, poetry, physical and moral beauty, respect for law, athletic prowess, a sense of moderation. He was, besides, the god of prophecy and healing. However, the myth of Apollo shows him to be very inept when it comes to relationships.

Since Freud and his friends started telling us what is wrong with us, we have tended to assume that solitary thinkers must be miserable. We have been told that we need to have lots of friends and be in an intimate relationship to be happy. Indeed, some still argue that humans can neither be happy nor healthy unless they are in a satisfying sexual relationship. History appears to say otherwise.

Many of the great achievements in European arts, philosophy and science have been the work of men who were single, celibate and solitary. Some of them even appear to have led satisfying lives.[324] The hermit in the silence of the mountain or desert, the philosopher in his library, the sculptor in his studio and the scientist in his laboratory, have all been driven by Apollo energy in their quest for understanding. This has usually been perceived to be a peculiarly masculine obsession. Regardless of any evidence to the contrary, women were generally assumed to have little capacity for thought.

If we look specifically at the basic assumptions behind traditional notions of education, we will find Apollo, the god of clarity, understanding, civilization, enlightenment and order claiming our attention and demanding our worship. However, Apollo's claim to this domain has been under challenge for some time. It used to be assumed without question that, while there were certain skills which everyone ought to learn, and certain habits that everyone ought to acquire, the real purpose of education was knowledge, understanding, even wisdom. This Apollonine fantasy may have persisted in universities longer than it has at other levels of education, but at present it seems to be hanging on grimly even in that sanctuary, in the face of a challenge from other more fashionable gods.

Educating Psyche

In the classroom Apollo establishes order and the rule of law. Not autocratic do-it-because-I-say-so law (which is the law of Zeus), but rational law, based on a reasoned estimation of what constitutes good and bad behaviour. He is the god who gives children and adults the capacity to think clearly, to understand how the world works, to find meaning and beauty, to organize their lives in an ordered way. He demands that we seek moderation in all things and look at the world in a detached and reasonable way, without being carried away by emotion.

Teachers or principals who are sensitive to Apollo values will place a high value on a rational approach to their work. Individual whims and impulsive decision-making are strongly discouraged and emotional outbursts are looked on with distaste. It is assumed that all problems can be solved and all crises dealt with through the application of cool intelligence. Considerable emphasis is placed on developing and maintaining structures which are truly rational – not based on mere tradition, superstition or personal taste. People, including children, are expected to behave rationally and there is some surprise when they do not. There is an assumption that if matters are clearly explained to people, they will understand and act on that understanding. Above all. they take it for granted that a key function of schools is to teach children to think.

Where reason is not honoured, Apollo appears in the form of rationalizations and rationalisms of various kinds. When we cease to respect our sense that reason can guide us towards truth, we find ourselves in a groundlessness which some people escape by embracing dogma. The pathology of Apollo emerges in a tendency to dogmatism and rigidity. Once the Apollonine principal or teacher sees the way things are, he or she has little tolerance for those who cannot. He (usually he) wants things to be obvious, and has little patience with ambiguity and illusion. He is inclined to insist that the people accept his assessment of a situation because its reasonableness is perfectly clear to him and those who can't see this must be stupid or bloody-minded. He is blind to the critical influence of emotions, relationships and unconscious drives on people's behaviour, and sometimes makes bad decisions because his perspective prevents him from taking in certain kinds of information.

Apollo's pathology also emerges in his hostility to women, whom he marginalizes as trivial, intuitive, emotional, sensual and irrational. In mythology, Apollo appears to be unable to have any sort of satisfactory relationship with a female – goddess, nymph or mortal – except with his mother and sister.

The polytheistic classroom is not a place where anything goes, where nothing is true. Each of the gods gives us a different meaning for our being, a different truth, and all these meanings and truths must be held in balance. It is Apollo, the clear-sighted one, to whom we turn to make the discriminations and judgments we must constantly make to act humanly in a human classroom.

ARTEMIS THE HUNTRESS

I sing of Artemis of the golden shafts, the modest maiden
who loves the din of the hunt and shoots volleys of arrows at stags.
She is the twin sister of Apollon of the golden sword,
and through shady mountains and windy peaks
she delights in the chase as she stretches her golden bow
to shoot the bitter arrows.[325]

Artemis was originally an Asian goddess of wild animals, who was worshipped on mountain tops. When the Greeks made her part of their Olympian family she became the virgin daughter of Zeus and twin sister of Apollo. As a young girl she begged Zeus to let her remain a virgin, avoiding the male-dominated world and going off to live in the wilderness with her girlfriends. Zeus assented, and Artemis tries to protect the virgin forest and her virgin followers from male exploitation and oppression.

Artemis, or Diana as the Romans called her, is the goddess of sisterhood. She is the virgin goddess of the woods and mountains, the goddess of the moon, a goddess who is both a hunter and a protector of animals. Having assisted her mother, Leto, with the birth of her twin brother Apollo, she is the goddess of childbirth. She is surrounded always by a band of nymphs with whom she enjoys her freedom from any relationship or obligation to men. She has neither the need nor the desire to make herself pleasing to men or to give them power. As goddess of wild animals she shares their natural grace, their ability to live in harmony with nature and their fierceness. As goddess of childbirth she has a special role in the protection of children. As a nature-goddess she is clearly distinguished from Demeter, as the virgin forest is distinguished from the nurturing earth.

The picture of Artemis and her girlfriends living in the forest tells us something about the particular sensibility of Artemis-dominated education, which is much more likely to be found in a girls' school than a boys' school – though this need not be the case, for boys also are not complete without a connection with Artemis. An Artemis education is based on an ideal of companionship rather than hierarchy, natural rhythms rather than abstract order. It values its difference, sees itself not only as special, but as constantly under threat from an outside world which would destroy it. The bonds between people, which are very important in such an arrangement, are based as much on the sharing of an ideology as on intimacy. Teachers in such an environment are expected to be passionate about their mission, which is generally concerned with the assertion of the feminine and the protection of the fragile, the natural and the oppressed. Where this sensibility is strong there is often an attempt to do away with formal management structures in order to engage in more 'organic' decision-making. Intuition is highly valued, and there is considerable distrust of bureaucracies.

Artemis is paranoid as well as powerful. She ruthlessly exacts absolute loyalty from her followers. Artemis offers to satisfy their need for belonging, but on her own terms. Her myth includes the story of Callisto, a companion of Artemis who was raped by Zeus (who had disguised himself as Artemis for the purpose). When her pregnant condition became apparent Artemis turned her into a bear and drove her away. Companion-nymphs who cast their eyes curiously or affectionately or lustfully towards a man were punished severely. When the young hunter Actaeon chanced upon the goddess as she was bathing, he was so enraptured by her beauty that he was, for the moment, unable to move. She assumed without evidence that he had come to mock her nakedness. Accordingly, she turned him into a deer, so that he was torn to pieces by his own hounds. Nature is not always gentle, and the goddess whose task it is to preserve and protect the natural and feminine from the managed and masculine is inclined to adopt ruthless and violent means of doing so. Her ruthlessness, like her single-mindedness, she shares with her brother Apollo. Like him, also, she is not particularly successful in her relationships.

However, it must be observed that the values of Artemis, the heroic feminine, provide an essential counterbalance to the images of the masculine hero which have played a dominant part in our culture. Modern European images of the hero continue to follow the Greek classical masculine model. Heroes are fighters. (Artemis herself carries some of this meaning: she is closely associated with the Amazons.) Heroes overcome obstacles, escape from captivity, kill monsters, conquer evil, are pathologically competitive, tame the wilderness, often leaving a trail of wreckage behind them. It is a perspective which has been the source of a great deal of the achievement of Western society; it is also the source of much of the damage that we continue to do to our planet and to our relationships. It can be argued that our culture and our educational institutions have been suffering from a hero-pathology for some time. When we talk of education in terms of 'mastery', 'comprehension' and 'achievement', we are caught in this hero fantasy. Artemis brings us a very different vision of educational priorities: to develop in children a sense of community, a love of wilderness, ecological sensitivity and a respect for non-human creatures.

This is not to suggest that education must give up the hero-image completely. Heroism belongs to adolescence – at whatever age it occurs. Popular culture provides the archetypal image of Herakles (Rambo, Superman), which feeds the developing male ego. The archetype of the feminine hero, of which Artemis is one personification, demands expression also. Both girls and boys, both women and men, have suffered from the devaluation of the qualities peculiar to Artemis: the ability to live within the rhythms of nature, to move lightly over the earth, to deal with crises precisely and gracefully, to build community, to be self-contained, to protect the weak. Next to Artemis, the masculine hero Herakles appears as a good-hearted and enthusiastic buffoon, who is as likely to wreck the world as save it. The truth of Artemis, that we must live in harmony with nature, not in opposition to it, is one which must be fought for, ruthlessly if need be.

Artemis, like the other Nature-god, Dionysos, exercises her influence over her disciples through personal power. She is not dependent on roles and structures, but on a sort of animal bonding which is sometimes called charisma. Teachers who have this power should recognize it as a gift, but a dangerous one. It can help them immeasurably in the work if they can acknowledge it without embarrassment. It can enable them to do great harm if they refuse to own it or if they identify with it too completely. Artemis and Dionysos must be worshipped, but so must their brother, Apollo, who understands such things and knows how to discriminate.

GOLDEN-HAIRED APHRODITE

Sing to me, O Muse, of the works of golden Aphrodite,
the Cyprian, who stirs sweet longing in gods
and subdues the races of mortal men as well as
the birds that swoop from the sky and all the beasts
that are nurtured in their multitudes on both land and sea.[326]

Aphrodite, for the Greeks of classical times, and for European culture ever since, is the goddess of beauty and sensuality. She is overtly and unself-consciously sexual, the only goddess who appears naked to mortals. She believes in fun, in immediate gratification, in the ultimate power of beauty. She has none of Hera's concern for respectability and social obligations. She is irresponsible and self-indulgent, careless of the consequences of her actions.

When we consider that, in classical Greece, Aphrodite was perhaps the most popular of all the gods, it is interesting to note that she was a foreigner. She is a Greek version of the Great Goddess of Western Asia. It was probably through Cyprus that the worship of this Semitic mother-goddess made its way to Greece, for the most popular story of her origin has her emerging from the sea near that island, having sprung from the foam around the genitals of the old god Uranus when his son Kronos sliced them off and cast them over the sea. The Greek-Phoenician culture of Cyprus began Aphrodite's transformation from a fertility goddess to a goddess of beauty and pleasure. In classical Greece and in European culture since then she is Beauty personified, whose particular domain is sexual attraction. She gets plenty of attention in popular culture, but she does not get much acknowledgment in an education system dominated by other gods.

People living in an environment dominated by Aphrodite may pay a lot of attention to personal appearance; they may be obsessed with the need to be attractive; they may be more interested in the elegance of what they do than with its usefulness or efficiency; they may not have much interest in doing anything at all if it is not fun. However, there are not many classrooms where educational activity is driven by the pursuit of beauty, where poems are read, stories are told, photographs are looked at, mathematical formulations are admired, scientific experiments are performed, systems of government are examined, objects are crafted, languages are practised, simply because they are beautiful. The teachers who see their teaching of mathematics, language, drama or chemistry in terms of the pursuit of beauty tend to be considered a little odd, if indeed they are rash enough to confess to their obsession. Yet it can be argued that our constant physical and conceptual exploration of our universe is driven as much by a need for beauty as by a need for power or understanding. In the myth of Psyche, it is Aphrodite, Beauty, who drives the human soul to the depths of the Underworld in her reluctant quest for the meaning of it all, and it is Beauty which she finds there. There are many writers for whom the right phrase is the most beautiful one rather that the most accurate one. There are many mathematicians who will seek the most elegant solution to a problem rather than the most useful one. Yet the school forces the worship of Aphrodite to be carried on in secret, if at all. The 'appreciation' of art, or music, or literature, or nature no longer has a proud place in the curriculum, and we are all a little sicker for it. Furthermore, many of us, teachers and students are starved of beauty in the places where we work.

Teachers who are under the influence of Aphrodite see themselves as engaged in an art rather than a job, and will not stay in the profession unless they can find beauty and pleasure in their work. They want teaching to be fun for them and fun for their students. Colleagues whose interest in the profession is based on different expectations may find them difficult to understand. Unfortunately, teachers who are inspired by Aphrodite to think that they and their pupils should be having fun are sometimes looked on askance, as though taking education seriously is incompatible with enjoying it. Yet, as Glasser argues, the world which children and adolescents take seriously is the world in which they can have fun. If they find all their fun outside the classroom, they'll do their learning outside the classroom. Classrooms without fun are classrooms without engagement. What children learn through fear, anxiety or boredom is not worth learning, and they are probably better off without it.

One way in which Aphrodite makes herself present in the classroom is through seduction. This may be an expression of either the positive or negative polarity of the archetype. Good teachers are all involved in seduction. They want to seduce their students into learning. They want to seduce them into loving history or physics or yoga. They attempt to present their subject as attractively as possible so their students will share their own love for it. They are also involved, consciously or unconsciously, in presenting their own personalities attractively, for it important to them to be liked by their students. It requires no great effort to imagine the ways this can tip over into the negative in the teacher who has no other gods to worship, or whose need for beauty gets no satisfaction elsewhere. Exploitative sexual seduction in 'helping' professions such as teaching, counselling and medicine is too common to be ignored.

John Keats proclaimed the fantasy that

> Beauty is truth, truth beauty, that is all
> We know and all we need to know.[327]

While there may indeed be other perspectives on truth, and there may be other things we need to know, we ought to recognize that Beauty is a powerful and demanding goddess in her own right, who needs no other god's approval to legitimize her. It may not be conventional any more to think of beauty as a goddess, or even as an instinct or drive or need, but she/it has had a powerful part in shaping our culture and our sensibility. Her presence is to be found in the delight people find in their work and the elegance with which they do it. The Greek myths warn that she ruthlessly punishes those who ignore her. She certainly has her pathology – sexual seduction, bitchiness, vindictiveness, superficiality, self-obsession and self-indulgence, inability to tolerate the grittiness of reality – and her influence must be balanced by the presence of other, more responsible gods. Nevertheless, without her education has no charm and provides no delight.

WINGED EROS

Eros, the fairest of the deathless gods
... unstrings the limbs and subdues both mind
and sensible thought in the breasts of all gods and all men.[328]

The power of Eros is felt by humans and gods alike, in their propensity to fall obsessively in love. It is felt in both the delight and the anguish of intimacy. Eros is singularly the god of relationship, and of the creativity that is generated by relationship.

According to one tradition, Eros was the most ancient of the gods. It was Eros who brought Sky (Uranus) and Earth (Gaia) together to generate the gods, who presided over the unions of gods and mortals, who is ultimately the source of life. This personification of cosmic harmony was present at the birth of the gods and mortals and present also in their lovemaking, for love and the generation of life are obviously manifestations of the same god, the god of union, harmony and creativity.

When the Greeks of later times imagined this god it was as an adolescent boy, for their experience of love included more than the simple drive to union. Eros, as they imagined him, was unpredictable and irresponsible and destructive as well as delightful and creative. In imagining him in this way, they did not diminish his power, for Eros, when he chooses to, can control even Zeus. In the Olympic pantheon, he is pictured as the son of Aphrodite.

We find Eros in the classroom where the teacher is convinced of the critical importance of relationships. We find him in the teacher who is able to say that she loves mathematics, loves Shakespeare, loves teaching, loves her pupils. Much has been written about the place of Eros in education. He is easily recognized in the work of the sane and healthy teacher who goes to great pains to establish a climate of non-dependent trust in his classes, who genuinely loves his students and has their good always in mind. He can be recognized just as easily in the insane and unhealthy teacher whose life is bound up entirely in his relationships with his students, so that they seem to exist principally to satisfy his emotional needs.

In the classroom dominated by Eros, the highest value is intimacy. The ideal emotional climate is positive, supportive, free of risk. Notions of hierarchy, or even of authority, have no place in Eros' value system. What makes the classroom a great place to grow and learn is the quality (and intensity) of the relationship between teacher and students. They may have a sense of common purpose, they may be productive in many ways, they may have established ways of going about their work, but these are secondary to the satisfactions of relationship, the satisfaction of belonging. It is love which makes teaching creative and productive.

Eros pathology readily appears when Eros is the only god being honoured. If intimacy and openness are good, we might suppose that more intimacy and openness are better, and that still more openness and intimacy are better still. However, experience of closeness is not always as unambiguously positive as this. Sometimes, relationship maintains its intensity while reversing its meaning. Teachers and students can get so caught up in with relating to each other that they forget that their purpose in being together is to learn something. Unless Eros is accompanied by more responsible gods like Hera and Apollo, he may become destructive.

MIGHTY ARES

Mighty Ares, golden-helmeted rider of chariots,
stout-hearted, shield-carrying and bronze-geared saviour of cities,
strong-handed and unwearying lord of the spear, bulwark of Olympos
father of fair Victory, and succorer of Themis,
... from above shine a gentle light on my life
and my martial prowess, that I may be able
to ward off bitter cowardice from my head.[329]

The Gods in the Classroom

In the Greek pantheon, Ares would seem to have assured status as the only son of the marriage of Zeus and Hera. However, his parents don't seem to be particularly fond of him and the Greek people were suspicious of him. Homer makes him look somewhat ridiculous in his stories of how Ares was trapped in a net by Hephaistos while making love to Aphrodite, and of how he was beaten in battle by Athena (who detests him) and by the human hero Diomedes. His worship seems to have originated with the Thracians of Northern Greece, who were much fonder of war than the urbanized people of the South. As a war-god, Ares represents battle-fury, blood-lust, the exhilaration of conflict and conquest. This may have suited the Thracians, but most Greeks preferred to give their devotion to Athena, who personified intelligent, strategic warfare.

Ares is recognized easily enough in his negative aspect. The centuries are strewn with the consequences of Ares-pathology, both personal and tribal, and we have good reason to be suspicious of him. However, Ares has a significant place in our lives, and even in our classrooms. He is the god of energy, of vehemence, of conflict, of challenge, of activism, of fire in the belly and fire in the eyes. If as teachers we are devotees of Athena, Eros or Hermes we are not likely to have much time for Ares. If we are religiously committed to the values of cooperation, relationship and dialogue, we are likely to see conflict and competition in an entirely negative light, and give them no place in our classrooms. Because we believe cooperation is good we may be inclined to believe that competition is bad. Yet some of the worst teaching comes from Athena, Eros and Hermes, and some of the best teaching comes from Ares.

It is certainly not a good idea to hand over the classroom entirely to Ares; he is emotionally immature and not very smart. Classrooms where children and adolescents are taught that life is about competition, where they learn to see success solely in terms of beating the opposition, are destructive both for those who always win and those who always lose. Nevertheless, the classroom where Ares is properly worshipped is full of challenge and excitement; conflict is not avoided but welcomed and enjoyed; the satisfactions of competition are acknowledged; children are encouraged to be passionate about the things that matter to them, teacher and students revel in each other's energy. The need of many adolescents to resist authority is acknowledged, and they get the fight they want. Intellectual subtleties may be neglected, but there is real engagement in what is happening. Ares is often mistaken, but never boring. Ares does not care much what is taught, as long as it is taught energetically.

It is particularly important that Ares be given some attention in the education of girls. When Pandora, the first woman, was crafted by Hephaistos, the gods each gave her a gift. Ares' gift was the fire which flickers within her. It is a fire which the Senex culture prefers to keep under strict control. Our society generally makes sure that most boys pick up more than enough of Ares values. Girls, on the other hand, are not encouraged to engage in the friendly physical rough and tumble that boys grow up with; they are taught not to assert themselves, or fight for their rights; they do not get a chance to learn the rituals of 'fighting fair'. Vehemently activist women are perceived as 'unfeminine'. Many women feel great resistance to the notion of learning to defend themselves against physical assault. Yet both men and women are incomplete without Ares, just as both women and men are incomplete without Artemis.

To allow Ares to be undeveloped and unacknowledged in us is to risk having him run out of control. To deny him proper worship in the classroom is to invite the emotional and physical violence which characterize his pathology.

HERAKLES THE ADVENTURER

> *I have a splendid theme: Herakles*
> *Is the son of Zeus;*
> *And has surpassed the glory of his birth*
> *With the labours of his noble life;*
> *By destroying beasts by which men lived in terror*
> *He won for us the tranquillity we enjoy.*[330]

The Greek myths are full of heroes, men who lived a long time ago and dealt with the gods directly – often, it appears, on equal terms. The most popular of the hero stories were the stories of Herakles, the hero who was not only a man but a god.

King Amphitryon married his niece, Alcmene, the wisest and most beautiful of women. She refused to sleep with him until he had gone to war and avenged the murder of her brothers. One evening Zeus disguised himself as the battle-weary Amphitryon. He arrived at the palace and announced that vengeance had been exacted. Then he spent the night with Alcmene. She was somewhat surprised when the real Amphitryon arrived home next morning. The outcome of these events was the birth of Herakles, the greatest of the heroes.

There are many tales of Herakles. The picture we get is of a man of great energy and drive, plenty of good will towards people and a tendency to take the most direct path to any goal. He is good-humoured, generous and courageous. On the other hand, compared to other heroes like Odysseus, Perseus and Jason, he is not very clever, and not particularly charming. His lack of subtlety is symbolized in his choice of the club as his preferred weapon. He has a violent temper and an enormous appetite. He is macho man, the superhero.

We all seem to be hardwired to follow the path of the hero, the adventurer. (This may be more evident in a boy than a girl, if her parents' contribution to her development is to constantly praise her for being pretty and obedient rather than for being brave or independent.) We can see the Herakles energy emerging in children early in life. When they are born, infants do not have any sense of separation from their mother, but they gradually become independent beings. Four-year-olds are notorious for developing a need to show their independence and make their own decisions. As they grow older they become aware of the tension between the need to be close to their parents and the need to break away from them. When they reach adolescence the desire to be 'their own person' can become very strong, and may lead them to resist the authority of their parents and anyone else who tries to tell them what to do. Like the other gods, Herakles has his positive side and his negative side. We will find Herakles behind both courage and recklessness, behind both spirited independence and blind resistance to authority.

Educating Psyche

We can find Herakles in every classroom. There are children and adolescents in whom this drive to independence is underdeveloped or frustrated, who will automatically do what they are told, but seek ways to sabotage it. There are those in whom Herakles is balanced with the other gods, who weigh up the appropriateness of doing exactly what they are told and make their own decisions with a view to who they want to be and where they want to go. There are children and adolescents who automatically resist directions, even when it is to their advantage to follow them.

Parents and teachers would find life much easier if their children or pupils simply did what they were told, or at least only did things they approved of. However, this is not the way that children become adults. They develop their identity as independent adults by resisting authority. It may only be in small ways (like playing the kind of music their parents hate), but they have to do it nevertheless. To grow up, they need something to resist. Parents and teachers who let adolescents do whatever they like are not doing them any favours. Adolescents, in particular, occasionally need something to push against – family, school. society, adult culture. This sometimes involves risky behaviour. Parents and teachers who find their authority resisted should appreciate that they are dealing with growing people who both need to be directed and need to resist it. They certainly do not want their children or pupils to grow up automatically doing anything a person who is bigger or more powerful tells them to do.

Herakles, like Dionysos and Hermes, was originally the child of the Great Mother. (Alcmene was almost certainly a goddess whom the patriarchal culture re-visioned as a human lover so that Herakles would become the son of Zeus.) The archetypal struggle between Mother and Child, Society (which wants everyone to be the same) and Individual (who wants to be different) is represented in the conflict between Hera and Herakles. Herakles is a favorite of Zeus, but Hera hates him.

Hera does not have much time for the notion that life is an adventure. People should just do what society expects of them. Our students need the courage of Herakles to go through life with a sense of purpose and commitment and handle the various pressures to conform to others expectations.

The Gods in the Classroom

Unfortunately, courage does not often figure prominently in the school curriculum, and young people have to find adventure elsewhere.

It does not have to be like this. There is plenty of room for adventure in the classroom. The philosopher Alfred North Whitehead insisted that learning should always be an adventure. It should begin with a new experience, engage the student emotionally, and lead to new ideas. This is not the usual sequence. Many teachers find it easier to start with old ideas and ignore emotion and experience altogether – except the experience of rehearsing the old ideas and committing them to memory.

Most of the stories about Herakles are concerned with the tasks he had to perform to expiate his crime of killing his own wife and children. (It was Hera who was actually responsible for this. In her unrelenting persecution of Zeus' illegitimate children she had driven Herakles mad, so that he believed he was hunting wild animals.) In expiation of his blood-guilt he had to serve as a slave, clear the sea of pirates. capture or kill various monsters, steal the girdle of Hippolyta, queen of the Amazons. He had to find the garden of the Hesperides, at the very edge of the world, and bring back the golden apples that grew there. In the course of these journeys he had many adventures. For instance it was Herakles who shot the eagle that was devouring the liver of Prometheus, and set the Titan free. He also had many sexual adventures. He made love to the fifty daughters of King Thespius in a single night. Wanting to make the most of the presence of so great a hero in his house, the king got Herakles drunk so that he thought he was with the same girl all night. Of course, each of the daughters bore him a son.

Adolescents and young adults may be driven by Herakles energy, engaging in risky or dangerous behavior for the adrenaline rush it gives them or for the status they seek in their peer group. For most of them it is not a permanent way to be, and they eventually get reconciled to Hera (goddess of the family) and find a way of life that acknowledges other gods besides Herakles. For some of them, however, being a hero comes to define their personality. The Herakles personality has a quest to fulfill, a mission to perform. There are giants to wrestle, dragons to slay, maidens to rescue, tyrants to overthrow, rivers to divert, mountains to flatten, forests to clear. There is a sense of having to do all this single-handedly. If they are teachers they may bring this energy into the classroom, and invite their students to an adventure.

Such teachers may not have the loyalty to the school that Hera demands. They do what they do because they choose to, not because of the directives or expectations of others. They may even lead their class in resisting school rules. They are not satisfied with conventional ways of doing things (which is Hera's preference). They want to test themselves by doing something new, and they want the same for their students. Some of their colleagues will appreciate their energy and activism. Others will be annoyed or embarrassed by it.

Sometimes a whole school staff is inflated with Herakles energy, especially in times of crisis. The principal in the Herakles-inflated school is an individual whose authority is respected and unquestioned and who leads by example. However, outside the school, authorities are likely to be regarded with contempt. Short-sighted and narrow-minded authorities and bureaucracies are constantly getting in the way of the school's right to do whatever it likes. Worse, they may even be trying to shut the school down. Perhaps the school is determined to go where no school has gone before and finds that the system insists that they conform. The school resists being pushed around, and is ready for a fight.

Unfortunately, Herakles has little capacity for reflecting on the consequences of his actions, and has little sense of social obligation or responsibility. For all his good intentions he can be randomly and unintentionally destructive.

It can be argued that Western culture has suffered from a hero-pathology for some time. In collective as well as personal life we have been too much inclined to think of the goals of life in terms of 'mastery' and 'achievement' and to ignore the random destruction that goes with this perspective. We can see this happening in a classroom where all the energy is put into achieving 'outcomes' and other important gods like Eros and Athena are ignored. This is not to suggest that we should abandon the hero-image. We should, however, avoid being stuck, personally or collectively, in what is essentially an adolescent way of being. It is always dangerous to give too much worship to a single god.

The Gods in the Classroom

SKILLED HEPHAISTOS

Sing, O clear-voiced Muse, of Hephaistos, renowned for skill,
who along with grey-eyed Athena taught fine crafts
to men of this earth; indeed before that time
they used to live in mountain caves like wild beasts.
But now, thanks to Hephaistos, the famous craftsman,
they have learned crafts and easily for the full year
they lead a carefree existence in their own homes.
But have mercy on me, Hephaistos, and grant me virtue and happiness.[331]

Hephaistos is the only god who works. He is the divine blacksmith, the god of craftwork. His status as a god rose and fell with political and economic conditions in ancient times, as in our own. Originally an Asian god of fire,[332] he moved from Asia to Greece, where he is represented in the *Iliad* and *Odyssey* as a crippled and comical god of metal-working, who is definitely numbered among the Olympians. His status and responsibilities rose enormously during the golden age of Athens, along with the status of his worshippers, and fell again as the metal-workers, potters, sculptors, wood-workers and jewellers fell in the social hierarchy. His role as husband to Aphrodite shows how deeply he is obsessed with beauty, and the myths reveal how little reward he gets for his devotion. Hephaistos is the ugly god, who creates beauty through pain and tedium. He is the god who drives the dancer or gymnast or musician or sculptor to craft something beautiful through the aches and pains of practice and performance, and to bear the calluses and other physical deformities that are the price of this obsession.

Hephaistos is honoured in the arts, but gets little worship in the normal classroom. There is too little value put on beauty to expect children or adolescents to endure pain to create it. There is too little value put on teaching as craft to properly reward teachers who make each of their lessons a work of art. It is no longer fashionable to see work as a good in itself, and many teachers are reluctant to demand hard work from their students. In a commodity-driven society such as our own there is too little value put on any sort of crafting to give it a respected place in the classroom. Teachers who are committed to teaching the crafts of living and who regard their own profession as a craft are really a bit old-fashioned, like Hephaistos and his mother, Hera.

The gods will be worshipped, however. The Hephaistos stories are told and retold in teachers' staff-rooms. There is the story about teaching being a greatly undervalued profession, whose practitioners slave day and night down at the forge while fancier, more fashionable gods enjoy themselves upstairs in the palace. There is the story about how all problems can be solved by working harder. There are stories about trapping Hera or Ares or Aphrodite in compromising or embarrassing situations and having a good laugh at their expense. Hephaistos complains a lot about the way he is treated but he stays where he is, for he has no doubt that he is superior to those who lord it over him.

AUNTY HESTIA

Hestia, you who tend the sacred dwelling
of the far-shooting lord, Apollon, at holy Pytho,
from your tresses flowing oil ever drips down.
Come to this house! Come in gentle spirit
with resourceful Zeus and grant grace to my song.[333]

Hestia is another fire-god, but the fire which she personifies is the domestic fire, the hearth. For the Indo-European nomads, keeping the fire alight from day to day was a crucial responsibility which was given to a woman, generally an unmarried sister or daughter who was given the status fitted to such an important function. Naturally, the Sky-father and his family had someone to perform this task for them, so we find that Zeus has an elder sister, a maiden aunt among the gods, who looks after the divine fire. Hestia is hardly personified at all in Greek mythology. She was felt as a place rather than as a person or an energy; she dwelt in the heap of glowing coals which was the clan's source of warmth. She dwelt in the hearth which was the focus of each home, and in the communal fire which was the focus of each village or city.

Hestia is the centre of things. She is the centre of the individual, the centre of the family, the centre of the city, the centre of the world. She represents the place of stillness from which we come and to which we go, the focus towards which everyone faces, the point around which everything revolves. She does not enter into the squabbles of the gods, but sits quietly and works at her weaving. She is quiet and self-effacing, but demands considerable honour from humans. It was to Hestia that the Greeks said 'grace' before and after their meals.

There are societies whose notions of education give Hestia a central place, where 'just sitting' is regarded as a legitimate activity. Obviously, our mainstream society is not one of them. There in not much value placed on introversion, on stopping to rest in what is essential. Things have been falling apart for so long that there is little sense of a focal point around which everyone is happy to gather from time to time. Yet Hestia, like the other gods, represents both an individual and a collective need. Where she is present in the classroom she gives children the sense of containment they yearn for.

Some people learn to satisfy this need through meditation. Indeed, meditation is gaining more and more legitimacy as the pace of life increases. People can identify themselves as meditators without arousing more than the mildest curiosity. 'Just sitting' is a permissible activity in the most unlikely places. However, schools generally manage to keep themselves remote from such activities. When teachers want to argue for the value of meditation in the classroom, they are forced to fall back on utilitarian arguments, and evidence of the way meditation will increase their students' attention and productivity. Fortunately, there are plenty of such arguments and plenty of such evidence available, so we are able find a handful of teachers and their students practising centring or meditation with their students. They may not be able to argue persuasively that there is a Hestia perspective on education which must be taken seriously in the development of curriculum, but they are able to manifest the presence of Hestia in the serenity of their classrooms, in their students' balance and focus and in the ease with which they learn.

If Hestia is honoured she sometimes gives us an extraordinary experience of focus. Our students are totally focused on what they are doing. The outside world disappears. Past and future disappear. Time appears to stop. We are with them in this moment, in the safe container of the classroom, and nothing else matters much. The experience may be rare, but even in its rarity it makes our work deeply rewarding.

DIONYSOS THE ENLIVENER

Hail, child of Semele with the fair face! There is no way one can forget you and still compose sweet songs.[334]

When Semele,[335] Zeus' human lover, persuaded the god to swear to grant her a request, and then demanded that he show her his face, Zeus had no choice but to keep his word. He showed himself as he is and she was scorched to death by his glory. He snatched the child from her womb as she died, and sewed it into his thigh. The child, when he was born for a second time, was called Dionysos.

Like other children of Zeus' lovers, Dionysos was persecuted and pursued by Hera, as were all those who assisted and protected him. To fool Hera, Zeus arranged for him to be raised as a girl, and at one stage turned him into a goat. He spent many years in Asia, followed by crowds of female worshippers, punishing with madness all those who would not acknowledge him, and rewarding those who acknowledged him by granting them fertility, ecstasy and his gift of the grape. Eventually he returned to Greece and was welcomed as a god by the other Olympians.[336]

The authorities found his worship somewhat unsettling and did not at first approve of it. Here was a god to be worshipped through mystical rites, whose followers sought ecstatic communion with him, who ran enthusiastically into the mountains to give themselves over to madness and orgiastic celebrations. Eventually, however, the worship of Dionysos was incorporated into the state cults; the god of licence and chaos was worshipped side by side with Apollo, god of order and moderation. In particular, the development of the theatre came under his sponsorship, so that the exploration of the most intense human experience was pursued through a sophisticated and highly structured art form.

The Gods in the Classroom

The authorities are still suspicious of Dionysos, and acknowledge him very reluctantly. He gets very little honour in schooling, and that only on the fringes of the curriculum. For one thing, Dionysos has no respect for authority and no regard for social expectations, and schools are supposed to turn children into good citizens. He is the god of go-with-the-flow and do-my-own-thing. He brings both joy and grief. He is the god of the adrenaline charge, the god of tragedy, of feeling, of play, of suffering, of exhilaration, of charisma, of performance, of ecstasy, of newness, of freedom. Certainly, like the other gods, he has his nasty manifestations as well as his nice ones. However, he demands acknowledgment and it is dangerous to deny him.

It is hardly necessary to point out that there is not much ecstasy apparent in schools. Feeling of any kind does not have much of a place in a schooling entirely given over to turning both children and knowledge into commodities. Dionysos would have our students dance, sing, perform, be creative and spontaneous, experience the animal flow of life, be utterly engaged in what they are learning, experience both fun and freedom – but there is little time for such things in most schools now. One fruit of this neglect is apathy, the absence of feeling. Another is the uncontrollable explosion of feeling whose expression has been frustrated. If policy makers in education persist in their primitive, narrow, simple-minded worship of the marketplace, and if civilized teachers stop resisting the pressure join in this worship, we will find that we are performing education not as farce but as tragedy.

We can think of the gods as representing instinctual needs or drives. We may not often think of ecstasy and intoxication in terms of needs or drives, unless we are focusing on addiction. Yet there seems to be plenty of evidence that we have a psychological need for at least an occasional experience of ecstasy or intoxication, a need to escape from the ordinariness of existence. Historically people have sought and found such experience in religious ritual, in sexual orgasm, in the exhilaration of battle or in hallucinogenic drugs (which were often closely associated with religious experience). We are familiar enough with the consequences when students seek ecstasy in dangerous ways – through train-surfing, risky sex, alcohol or other drugs, yet we are not generally inclined to see this as a substitute for the ecstatic religious experiences which have ceased to be accessible. Fortunately we can still seek ecstasy and intoxication in lots of less problematic ways as we let ourselves be caught up in the joy of play, or in the tribal enthusiasm of a football match, a concert, a religious celebration or a dance party. Or we can try mountain-climbing or jumping out of planes. One of the most useful things a teacher can do for adolescents is to teach them ways to have fun without getting drunk or stoned.

The Greeks recognized intoxication as Dionysos' gift to humanity. Schools should appreciate it more.

CLEVER PROMETHEUS

But Zeus was angered in his heart and hid the means to life
because Prometheus with his crooked schemes had cheated him.
This is why Zeus devised sorrows and troubles for men.
He hid fire. But Prometheus, noble son of Iapetos,
stole it back for man from Zeus, whose counsels are many.[337]

In the Academy in Athens, there was a shrine dedicated to Prometheus, the divine patron of the arts and sciences. Prometheus was not one of the Olympians, but he was greatly honoured, revered as the saviour of humanity, the god who took the side of humanity against the will and wrath of Zeus.

Prometheus actually fashioned men[338] out of clay in the first place. Zeus did not like them much and wanted them to perish in the cold and dark. To live like men, and not in caves like animals, they must have fire. Prometheus had to save them. He stole fire from the gods – the fire of Hephaistos, the blacksmith-god – and brought it down to earth in a fennel stalk. With this gift of light and heat he brought men technology, freeing them from the pain and frustration of groping around in the cold and dark, teaching them the crafts that would enable them to gain control over their world instead of being always at the whim of the gods. For this men have been grateful ever since.

The Gods in the Classroom

The image of Prometheus has been enormously significant in European consciousness. He is the creative mind. He is the god who took humanity's side. He is the hero who defied the patriarchy in the name of individual freedom, who brought light into our darkness. He is the saviour who sacrificed himself for the sake of humankind,[339] the benefactor who brought the gift of technology down from heaven, the teacher who showed us that we are not at the whim of the gods any more, who showed us how to use our intelligence to take control of the world. He is the individual who proclaims his and our right to be an individual.

In the nineteenth century, the capitalist version of the Promethean myth expressed the fantasy of achieving freedom from poverty through the development and management of technology. This has proved remarkably resilient, in spite of the fact that anyone who wants to look can see how our obsession with technology has brought us to a point where we may have damaged the planet irreversibly and put the future of the species at considerable risk. Anyone who wants to look can see that technology has proved at least as effective an instrument of enslavement as it has been an instrument of emancipation. It has become increasingly clear that belief in the inevitability of progress has little evidence to support it. Yet the fantasy survives. Now, in the middle of what may be the last dying spasm of the industrial age, we are still being exhorted to focus on the technology which will save us. Education is constantly re-shaped and re-aligned so that its entire justification is that it will make students more technically skilful and thus potentially more productive. The primary purpose of education, we are told, is the skilling of our society. There has been a reorientation from low tech to high, but it is still technology which will make us free and rich and happy, and take us into the golden age. The Greeks of the classical age may have seen in Prometheus the patron of the artist and scientist.[340] In the past two hundred years he has undoubtedly become patron of the engineer.

When the Promethean fantasy takes over education we hear a great deal of talk about technology, as we might expect. We also hear talk about education as an instrument of social change, of emancipation. (The very notion of social engineering belongs to a Promethean fantasy.) But most of all we find ourselves immersed in a rhetoric of skilling and training. The Prometheus' view of education is a very simple one: skilling brings empowerment for the individual and productivity for the society, and the simplest and most efficient and most technically sound way of teaching skills is through training. It is also the way most congenial for those who perceive human beings as machines. Training as a mode of education can be satisfying and useful. Or it can be boring and irrelevant. There is a dimension to our humanity which is machine-like, which responds to having our buttons pushed, learns through repetition and rehearsal and exalts in the power that we find in new skills. Yet there is more to education than teaching skills. Nevertheless, those who oppose this focus on skilling and training, who suggest that there might be more to education than this, are likely to be branded as fuddy-duddies who collude with the establishment to keep the people in chains.

It can readily be argued that the modern, Promethean era has ended, that we have entered a post-industrial, post-modern era with a different dynamic and a different sensibility, that the myth of progress has been abandoned in the face of the realities of recent history and present crisis. Yet educational policy in many industrialized and industrializing countries is still in the grip of the Promethean fantasy. Modern mythical thinking connects the images of liberation, technology, control, and masculine heroism in a narrative in which our dedication to gaining control of our destiny through an ever-improving technology, and the devotion of all our resources to this great project, takes us inevitably to a glorious future.

Aischylos, in *Prometheus Bound*,[341] had to remind the fifth century Athenians — who had a strong tendency to be infatuated with their own cleverness — that the image of Prometheus represents the limits, as well as the promise, of being human. Prometheus' gifts of science and technology are precious, but they can only do so much for us. When Prometheus fashioned the first man he had no way of bringing him to life, and had to ask Athena to breathe a soul into him.

Those who are stuck in Prometheus myth think that we can solve the social and ecological problems of the planet by being clever and developing our skills, and they fail to see that in a world of accelerating change the skills we teach our students today may prove inadequate or irrelevant by tomorrow. There are other gods to be acknowledged.

The Gods in the Classroom

HERMES THE COWBOY

Of Hermes sing, O Muse, the son of Zeus and Maia,
lord of Kyllene and Arcadia abounding with sheep,
helpful messenger of the immortals, whom Maia bore,
the fair-tressed and well-loved nymph, when she mingled
in love with Zeus.[342]

If there was any god more popular in classical times than Aphrodite, it was Hermes, the god of travellers, shepherds, thieves, merchants and scholars. It appears that the god known to the classical Greeks as Hermes was an amalgamation of several more ancient deities. There was a god who protected the flocks of the native peoples, and who lived in the stone-heaps they set up as boundary-markers. When the Greek invaders took their lands the natives saw this god as their protector in whatever guerrilla activities they undertook to make life unpleasant for their oppressors. He became the god of thieving and trickery. The Cretans also, during their cultural domination of southern Greece, had introduced their own god of the stone-heap, the master of wild animals (and therefore protector of shepherds and travellers), who seems to have been a version of the earth-mother's son and consequently a god of fertility. The Greeks saw, naturally enough, that they were dealing with one god rather than two, and associated him also with trade, good luck, protection of the house, the bearing of messages from the gods and the conduct of the souls of the dead to the Underworld. Like other Indo-European peoples, they already worshipped a god of trickery and magic,[343] and readily identified him with this god of the conquered natives, making Hermes a very complex character.

The myth of Hermes, as recounted in the Homeric hymn in his honour, makes Hermes a very slippery character indeed, an opportunist without any respect for conventional morality, a trickster, a liar and a thief. He is elusive, unpredictable and mischievous. He is also very charming. We may distinguish between the infantile Hermes who steals the cattle of the gods, subverts Apollo's attempts to get to the truth of things in a rational way, and cannot resist a chance to make a profit on a deal, and the mature Hermes who is the healer and guide of souls; yet we would do well to watch him carefully. The Greeks believed him to be friendly to mortals, but they were careful not to trust him too much.

In recent years the myth of progress has been replaced by the myth of the marketplace, and Hermes, god of the marketplace, has taken a strong hold on our consciousness. This is manifested in the way we now look at education. The marketplace is becoming the dominant metaphor. Teachers in times past have been seen as custodians of the culture (Zeus), developers of social responsibility (Hera), givers of parental care (Demeter), providers of understanding (Apollo), protectors of the fragile and vulnerable (Artemis), guides to the appreciation of beauty (Aphrodite), defenders of civilization (Athena) or facilitators of personal growth (Dionysos); now they are asked to be retailers of marketable skills. Many educational institutions are now happy to take their offerings into the market and to hawk them to whoever will buy. They happily base curriculum decisions not on what best serves the culture, or what most intelligently examines it, but on what sells best.

In the Hermes-driven classroom, there is plenty of interest in communication, but not so much concern about what is worth communicating. There is plenty of interest in the process of learning, but not so much concern about what is worth teaching. Hermes is the messenger, but has no messages of his own. He does not believe that some things are intrinsically more worthy of study than other things. Image is all-important. He is more interested in seeming than in being. In such a classroom the learning of dry facts is not regarded very highly. Students don't have to accumulate knowledge. What matters is being able to access the information you need and getting it to serve you. Teachers and students get their buzz out of being clever rather than being learned, finding ways to 'beat the boredom', constantly moving on, being entrepreneurs rather than workers or artists.

The contemporary classroom strongly reflects the Hermes energy which drives the broader culture. Once upon a time we lived in a society. Now we live in a marketplace. Once upon a time our students were in our care. Then they became our customers, or at least their parents did – purchasing skills and information which they could later trade in for a prosperous life. Now we are encouraged to see our students as commodities. Our customers are their future employers.

While there is much to appal us in a tendency to worship Hermes uncritically, whether in politics, economics or education, it is well to remember that Hermes is the god of magic, of transformation. He subverts the conventionally accepted order of things, disrupts all our certainties, unties all our knots, and makes change possible. Schools, and education systems generally, get stuck in repeating themselves, doing things the way they have always done them simply because this is the way they have always done them. We need Hermes' gifts of flexibility, adaptability and imagination, even his opportunism and persuasiveness, to initiate change. In a world where we are told 'change is the only constant' a Hermes consciousness is essential. But in education, as in business, it must be balanced by the other gods or it will quickly bankrupt us.

Hermes does not hold to values of his own. Zeus tells us to respect rightful authority; Apollo tells us to act rationally; Hera tells us to fulfil our social obligations; Aphrodite tell us to pursue beauty; Artemis demands that we live in harmony with Nature; Hephaistos tells us that work is honourable; Eros insists that we love one another; Poseidon tells us to be connect with our power; Dionysos challenges us to become fully ourselves; Athena tells us to keep things in balance; Prometheus requires us to use our intelligence to make a better world; Ares wants us approach our tasks with passion; Hestia gently suggests that we stay centred, not get fussed, and focus on what is essential.

Hermes insists that we worship all the gods.

DREAD HADES

How did you dare to come below to Hades' realm,
where the dead live on without their wits as disembodied ghosts?[344]

When the gods had won their battle with the Giants and Titans for control of the universe, Zeus and his two older brothers divided up the world between them by casting lots. Zeus won and got the sky for his kingdom, Poseidon got the sea and Hades won the Underworld. They decided that the earth could be shared between the three of them. So Hades ruled in the realm of the dead, and stayed there except for a brief excursion to the living world.

The occasion was the abduction of his niece, Persephone, daughter of his sister, Demeter. Eros, eager to demonstrate his power even over the Lord of the Underworld, wounded Hades with an arrow, causing him to fall in love with the young goddess. Hades made the necessary enquiries and learned her identity. With Zeus her father's permission he drove up from the darkness in his chariot and carried her off to be his queen. When the enraged Demeter brought famine on the earth, Zeus sent Hermes to negotiate with his brother for the release of Persephone. Before she returned to earth, Hades tricked her into eating some pomegranate seeds so that, having eaten the food of Hades, she was obliged to return to the kingdom of the dead for four months each year.

Hades has no interest in the upper world, and humans do not waste time building temples to worship him. He can do nothing for them now, and he will get them in the end no matter what they do.

Hades, which is the name of the place as well as the name of the god, is a fit image for certain classrooms. The classroom dominated by Hades is not much interested in what is going on in the outer world but focuses on its own processes. It is inhabited by lost souls, who lead a flavourless existence in a place without life or light. They make no attempt to escape for they do not have the energy, and escape is impossible in any case. They have no power over their situation, nor is there any point in seeking it. They go through the motions, but without hope, purpose or feeling. Life in a Hades classroom is dreary and mechanical, without the prick of ambition or the joy of social intercourse. Power is held by someone remote, cold and detached. It makes no connection with the outer world. Nothing changes. It seems to go on forever.

Talk about school engagement focuses on many different things. Students are disengaged because the curriculum is irrelevant. They are disengaged because traditional ways of teaching don't work for an iPad-savvy

The Gods in the Classroom

generation. They are disengaged because their parents don't value education and don't encourage their children to take it seriously. They are disengaged because there are too many interesting things competing for their attention. They are disengaged because their peers are disengaged. They are disengaged because they can't see how taking school seriously is going to help them get a satisfactory job and a prosperous life. They are disengaged because classes are too large. They are disengaged because their teachers can't even be bothered learning their names. They are disengaged because they have too short an attention span to concentrate on anything. (Video games are apparently responsible for this.) And so on. What doesn't get mentioned often enough is that they are disengaged because they are BORED!

Sometimes Hades takes over a whole school. Toxic management leads to the collapse of morale. People stop caring. They stop believing in what the school is doing or even clinging to any idea of what the school ought to be doing. Staff even lose the energy to attempt to change things. Since there is no spark of life within the school they find their interests elsewhere.

Hades is the image of death. Hades rules his kingdom with absolute power. He is grim and inexorable, but not malicious. He is certainly not a manifestation of pure evil, like the Devil. He has no favorites; he applies the rules without discrimination. He keeps his kingdom locked, and has a three-headed watch dog, Cerberus, to prevent anyone from leaving. A handful of the inhabitants, mostly defeated Giants and Titans, are subject to eternal torture for crimes against the gods, but most wander as phantoms, mere shadows of their former selves, without their bodies and forgetful of their former lives. They exist without passion. Their forgetfulness is a result of drinking from the river Lethe, a merciful requirement, for memories of the pleasures of life up in the light would cause them intolerable pain. On rare occasions, a hero manages to enter the kingdom of Hades on special terms and leave again[345] but most of the shades must wander forever, without joy or pain or sensation of any kind, over plains of asphodel.

Hades may not be evil, but it is difficult to say anything nice about him other than that he is simply doing his job! Apparently, the Greeks did not bother worshipping Hades. They understood that, because he was responsible for ruling the dead, he would have no interest in the living.

A school that is dead or dying is likely to be dominated by a Hades culture. There may be a few Giants and Titans who rage against the dying of the light, but most of the inhabitants accept their fate without much protest. The loss of morale, the loss of the will to fight, is one of the first symptoms of the condition. Occasionally a hero may arrive, create a stir and leave, without changing the condition of the shadowy beings who continue to go about their mechanical tasks without hope of change.

Sometimes a political decision is made to close a school down and Hades is called on to facilitate the task. This involves taking away light and power and hope. Decisions are best made by people who are remote and, most desirably, invisible. Those who wish to challenge them will find no one to whom they can put their case. Compassion is not only unnecessary but impossible. Hades' key maxim is, 'This is the way it is, and there's nothing to be done about it.'

Hades is apparently the assimilation of two quite different gods. In his Indo-European origins he is probably the same god as Zeus. In his Mediterranean origins, he is an earth-god, a god of fertility and plenty. In the old fertility cult the same divine earth-force devoured life and created it. In a mythical consciousness, life and death are not mutually exclusive; they are opposing aspects of a single reality; there is no new life without death. Hades is death, but in the Orphic rituals he was identified with Dionysos, the god of new life. Persephone is new life, but she is also Queen of the Underworld. The personality of Hades carries two contradictory images; the image of the permanence of death, and the image of the rhythmical cycle of birth, death and rebirth. Hades was also called Plouton (Pluto), which makes him the god of wealth. On the one hand, this was a euphemism, for the Greeks preferred not to use his real name. But it also represents a relic of Hades' origin as a fertility god, child of the Great Mother. Wealth, both vegetable and mineral, comes from under the ground. When we die we return to earth and even, in some societies, are planted in it. The domination of Hades culture in an organization such as a school may signal the total cessation of life. Paradoxically, acceptance of this situation may be the only way to a new birth.

Sometimes an organization such as a school has to go through a period of doubt, to experience Hades. In the organizational decay the seeds may sprout if the environmental conditions are right, and we can see a transition to a new life. It may be useful here to make a distinction between change and transition. Change can be forced on an organization but, unless the members of the organization undergo a psychological process of transition, the attempted change is likely to be destructive. For a change to be effective, people must own it. They have to stop denying that the school is dead or dying. Sometimes there has to be a death to allow new life to emerge, but the death has to be acknowledged if this sort of energy is to be generated from it. Change can be implemented very quickly, but transition can take a long time. Nevertheless, leaders with an understanding of the process and appropriate strategies can accelerate it significantly. Unfortunately, the usual story of the Hades culture is not one that involves either change or transition. In Greek mythology, only a handful of heroes ever come back from Hades.

SUMMONED OR NOT

Zeus and his family, who dwelled on Mount Olympus, were not the only gods demanding worship.

Pan and Persephone and Priapus, Hades and Hecate and Herakles, the Graces, the Muses, the Fates and the Furies, were all alive in the Greek awareness of the world, and they are still competing for our attention when we turn our minds to wondering about the point of education.

Each of the gods has his or her special gifts to give. Each represents a different notion of the aims of education, a different perspective on curriculum. Each appears differently in the personalities of teachers and in their ways of teaching and learning. Each is present in her or his distinctive form in the truths we adhere to, in the instincts which drive us and the visions which draw us, in teaching as in the rest of our lives. In our current arguments about the purposes of education and the best ways of providing it, the ancient and immortal gods are still involved in their old arguments.

While we must honour them all, we are unlikely to honour them all equally. We each have particular gods which shape our personality, our values and our perceptions. And while there is no single god who can claim the classroom as his or her personal sphere of influence, some of them may have a greater claim on it than others. Each god has her or his sacred time or place, and the gods which rule our childhood and adolescence may not be the gods which govern us as adults.

We may like to see the eternally squabbling gods simply as colourful images, and their worship simply a useful metaphor to help us explore a multi-dimensional approach to education. On the other hand we may wish to take them more seriously, to acknowledge that the Greeks, like other polytheistic cultures, knew something about cosmology and psychology which we have forgotten. We may as readily approach ultimate reality through a fantasy of the Many as through a fantasy of the One. Whatever our religious beliefs, it can be argued that psychologically we are polytheistic. Whether we summon them or not, the gods are present.[346]

NOTES Chapter 12. The Gods in the Classroom

[311] See S. Pinker, *How the Mind Works*. Pinker suggests that our genes carry even such abstract notions as a sense of justice and a sense of self.

[312] For discussion of image schemas see M. Johnson, *The Body in the Mind*; G. Lakoff, *Women, Fire and Dangerous Things*.

[313] Alfred North Whitehead speaks of the universe as being composed of 'drops of experience', an expression he borrowed from William James. See chapter 10.

[314] Apostolos Athanassakis, *The Homeric Hymn*, 1976, p. 64. The Homeric hymns are a collection of devotional songs once ascribed to Homer but apparently the work of various poets between the eighth and fifth century BC.

Themis is an early earth-goddess. In Olympian myth she is a Titaness, the second wife of Zeus. She was honoured in classical Greece as a goddess of order, responsible specifically for public assemblies. Zeus is called Kronides as the son of Kronos, who was probably originally a harvest-god (the Roman Saturn).

[315] Epimenides (c. 500 BC), quoted by St Paul in Acts 17:28. The idea the Greek philosophers developed of Zeus as a supreme and benevolent deity owed a great deal to the increasing influence of Judaism.

[316] See *The Quality School*.

[317] Athanassakis, ibid., p. 59. Rhea is an ancient earth-goddess. In the Olympian myth she is wife to Kronos and mother of Hestia, Demeter, Hera, Poseidon, Hades and Zeus.

[318] ibid., p. 64.

[319] ibid., p. 60. Persephone, daughter of Demeter and Zeus (or Poseidon) was abducted by Hades, god of death, to be his bride. After Demeter brought famine on the earth by withholding her bounty, the gods negotiated to allow Persephone to return for part of each year to live with her mother and make the earth fertile again.

[320] ibid., p. 66. The name Tritogeneia is of pre-Greek origin. Its meaning is uncertain.

[321] The Cretans (Minoans) had cultural (and occasionally political) dominance of southern Greece between 2000 and 1400 B.C. The bronze-age Mycenean culture which is described by Homer in the *Iliad* and *Odyssey*, was the product of an enthusiastic acceptance of the Cretan civilization by the invading Minyans.

[322] ibid., p. 15.

[323] The Dorians were a Indo-European people who seem to have entered the peninsula c. 1200 BC and settled in central and southern Greece.

[324] In *Solitude*, Anthony Storr argues that our capacity for being alone is just as important an aspect of psychological health as our capacity for relationship.

[325] ibid., p. 65.

[326] ibid., p. 47.

[327] John Keats, 'Ode on a Grecian Urn'.

[328] Hesiod, *Theogony* (trans. A. Athanassakis), p. 16.

[329] Athanassakis, ibid., p. 58.

[330] Euripides, *Herakles*, lines 691-696.

[331] ibid., p. 63.

[332] Hephaistos, whose (non-Greek) name probably means fire, seems to have originally been worshipped as such, specifically as a jet of flaming gas near the summit of Mt Olympos in Lycia, the south-western region of Asia Minor. The myth of Hephaistos' conception and birth from Hera, without any involvement by Zeus, would seem to refer to this emergence as fire from the belly of the Great Mother.

[333] ibid., p. 64.

[334] ibid., p. 58

[335] Semele may have been the Phrygian earth-goddess Zemelo. The Greeks were inclined to identify her with the mother of the Egyptian god Osiris, whose myth shares common elements with that of Dionysos.

[336] While the myth carries the Greek understanding that Dionysos was an Asian import, there is evidence that Dionysos was worshipped in Greece before the Indo-Europeans arrived, and that the conquered peoples continued to worship him under Greek domination. He was the personification of new life, the child-lover of the fertility goddess. The official acceptance of the cult of Dionysos in public worship in the sixth century BC was an acknowledgment that this god of the common people could not be ignored any longer.

[337] Hesiod, *Works and Days*, lines.47-51, in A. Athanassakis (ed.).
[338] Men, not women. Women were created later, by the gods, to prevent men from doing too much damage.
[339] Zeus eventually lost patience with Prometheus and nailed him to a rock at the farther reaches of the universe. Eventually Hermes negotiated a deal in which Prometheus was accepted among the gods and Zeus learned the secret to maintaining his power.
[340] It is interesting to note that, unlike ourselves, the classical Greeks made no distinction between art and skill. The word 'techne' served for both.
[341] Aischylos wrote at least four plays about Prometheus, of which *Prometheus Bound* is the only one to have survived in full.
[342] ibid., p. 31. Maia (mother) is another personification of goddess-earth.
[343] Compare the Nordic Loki, the Irish Lugh and the Roman Mercury.
[344] Homer, *The Odyssey*, 11: 444.
[345] Herakles descended to the Underworld to capture the watch dog, Cerberus. Orpheus came to rescue his wife, Euridice. Aeneas came to speak to the shade of his father, Anchises. Theseus and Pirithous came to carry off Persephone, but were imprisoned by Hades in the chains of forgetfulness.
[346] Above the door of his home Jung carved the words: *Vocatus aut non vocatus deus aderit.*

Bibliography and Further Reading

Abell, A. *Talks with Great Composers*, Schroeder-Vertog, Garnisch-Pastenbuchen, 1964.
Adler, A. *Understanding Human Nature*, Fawcett Premier, New York, 1957.
Adler, G. (ed.). *The Letters of C. G. Jung*, Princeton University Press, 1973.
Apuleius, *Metamorphoses*, Cambridge University Press, Cambridge, 1963.
Arieti, S. *Creativity: The Magic Synthesis*, Basic Books, New York, 1976.
Aspy, D. & Roebuck, F. *Kids Don't Learn from Teachers They Don't Like*, Human Resources Development Press, Amherst, 1977.
Assagioli R. *Psychosynthesis*, Penguin, UK, 1970.
—— *The Act of Will*, Penguin, 1974.
Athanassakis, A. (trans. and ed.). *The Homeric Hymns*, Johns Hopkins University Press, 1976.
—— (ed.). *Hesiod: Theogony, Works and Days*, Shield, Johns Hopkins University Press, 1983,
Avens, R. *Imagination is Reality*, Spring, Dallas, 1980.
Bandler, R. *Using Your Brain for a Change*, Real People Press, 1985.
Bandura, A. *Social Foundations of Thought and Action: A Social Cognitive Theory*, Prentice Hall Englewood Cliffs, 1986.
Bateson, G. *Mind and Nature*, Bantam, New York, 1980.
Benfey, O. 'August Kekule and the Birth of the Structural Theory of Organic Chemistry in 1858', *Journal of Chemical Education*, 1958, 1, pp. 21-23.
Benson, H. *Beyond the Relaxation Response*, Avon, New York, 1975.
Benson, H. 'Looking Beyond the Relaxation Response', *Revision*, 7, 1, 1984.
Bharati, A. *The Light at the Centre: Context and the Pretext of Modern Mysticism*, Ross-Erikson, Santa Barbara, 1976.
Birch, C. *Science and Soul*, Templeton, West Conshohocke, 2008.
Blatner, A. *Acting In*, Springer, New York, 1973.
Bohm, D. *Wholeness and the Implicate Order*, Routledge, London, 1980.
Brown, M. Y. *The Unfolding Self*. Psychosynthesis Press, Los Angeles, 1983.
Brown, F. & Graeber, R. *Rhythmic Aspects of Behaviour*, Erlbaum Associates, Hillsdale, 1892.
Bry, A. *Visualisations*, Harper, New York, 1986.

Buber, M. *Between Man and Man*, Fontana, 1961.

—— *The Knowledge of Man*, Harper and Row, New York, 1966.

Burke, A. *Self-Hypnosis: New Tools for Deep and Lasting Transformation*, Crossing Press, 2004.

Burnet, J. *Early Greek Philosophers*. A & C Black, London, 1930.

Buzan, T. *Using Both Sides of Your Brain*, Dutton, New York, 1976.

Bynne, W. *The Way of Life According to Lao-Tse*, Capricorn, New York, 1962,

Carrington, P. *Freedom in Meditation*, Anchor, New York, 1978.

Carson, R. *The Sense of Wonder*, Harper and Row, New York, 1984.

Cleveland, B. F. *Master Teaching Techniques*, Connecting Link Press, Muskego, 1986.

Corell, C. (ed.). *Multiple Intelligences: Howard Gardner and New Methods in College Teaching*. New Jersey City University, 2003.

Cornelius-White, J. 'Learner-Centred Teacher-Student Relationships Are Effective: A Meta-Analysis', *Review of Educational Research*, 77 (1), 2007, pp. 1123-43.

Corsini, R. (ed.). *Current Psychotherapies*, Peacock, Itasca, 1979.

Coué, E. *How to Practice Suggestion and Auto-Suggestion*, American Library Service, New York, 1923.

Czikszentmihalyi, M. *Beyond Boredom and Anxiety*, Jossey-Bass, New York, 1975.

Damasio, A. *The Feeling of What Happens: Body and Emotion in the Making of Consciousnes*, Mariner Books, New York, 2000.

—— *Self Comes to Mind: Constructing the Conscious Brain*, Pantheon Books, New York, 2010.

Davies, M., McKay, M. & Eshelman, E. R. *The Relaxation and Stress Reduction Workbook*, New Harbinger, Oakland, 1982.

Davies, P. *The Mind of God*, Penguin, UK, 1992.

De Bono, E. *New Think*, Basic Books, New York, 1967.

—— *The Mechanism of Mind*, Jonathan Cape, London, 1969.

—— *Lateral Thinking*, Harper and Row, New York, 1970.

De Quincey, C. *Radical Nature: Recovering the Soul of Matter*, Invisible Cities Press, Montpelier, 2002.

—— *Radical Knowing: Understanding Consciousness through Relationship*. Park Street Press, Rochester, 2005.

Delaney, G. *Living Your Dreams*, Harper and Row, San Francisco, 1975.

Dell, W. *Notes for a New Mind: Brain Lateralization, Deconstruction and the New Myth*. Universal Publishers, 2005.

Dement, W. *Some Must Watch While Some Must Sleep*, San Francisco Books, 1976.

Désoillé, R. *Le Rêve Eveillé en Psychotherapie*, Presses Universitaires, Paris, 1945.

Bibliography and Further Reading

Dickens, C. *Hard Times*, Penguin Classics, UK. 1985.
Dixon N. F. *Subliminal Perception: The Nature of a Controversy*, McGraw-Hill, New York.
—— *Preconscious Processing*, Wiley, New York, 1981.
Donald, M. *Origins of the Modern Mind*, Harvard University Press, 1991.
—— *A Mind So Rare*, Norton, New York.
Duhen, P. *The Aim and Structure of Physical Theory*, Princeton University Press, 1954.
Durand, G. 'Psyche's View', *Spring Journal*, 1981, pp.1-13.
Eason, A. *The Secrets of Self-Hypnosis: Harnessing the Power of Your Unconscious Mind*. Network 3000 Publishing, 2005.
Egan, K. *The Educated Mind*, University of Chicago Press, 1997.
Eliade, M. *The Myth of the Eternal Return*, Princeton University Press, 1954/1991.
Eliot, T. S. *Complete Poems and Plays*, Harcourt Brace, New York, 1971.
Erickson, M., Rossi, E. & Rossi, S. *Hypnotic Realities*, Irvington, New York, 1976.
Ferrucci, P. *What We May Be*, Tarcher, Los Angeles, 1982.
Freeman, L. *Light Within: The Inner Path of Meditation*, Darton Longman & Todd, London, 1987.
Freire, P. *Pedagogy of the Oppressed*, Penguin, UK, 1972.
Freud, S. *The Problem of Lay-Analysis*, Brentano, New York, 1927.
Galin, G. 'Implications for Psychiatry of Left and Right Cerebral Specialisations', *Archives of General Psychiatry*, 1974, 31, pp. 572-593.
Gallwey, W. T. *The Inner Game of Tennis*, Pan, UK, 1974.
—— *Inner Skiing*, Pan, UK, 1977.
Gardner, H. *Frames of Mind: The Theory of Multiple Intelligences*, Basic Books, New York, 1985.
Gawain, S. *Creative Visualization*, Berkley Books, New York, 1978.
Gebser, J. *The Ever-Present Origin*. Trans. A. Mickunas. Ohio University Press. 1949/1990.
Gendlin, E. *Focusing*, Bantam, New York, 1980.
Ghiselin, B. (ed.). *The Creative Process*, UCP, Berkeley, 1952.
Gibb, J. R. *Trust: A New View of Personal and Organizational Development*, Guild of Tutors, Los Angeles, 1978.
Glasser, W. *The Quality School*, HarperCollins, New York, 1990.
Globus G., Maxwell, G. & Savodnik, I. (eds). *Consciousness and the Brain*, Plenum Press, New York, 1976.
Graves, D. *Children Writing*, Collins Dove, Melbourne, 1986.

Green, E. E. & Green, A .M. *Beyond Biofeedback*, Delta, New York, 1978.
Greenberg, I. *Psychodrama: Theory and Technique*, Souvenir, London, 1974.
Grinder, J. & Bandler, R. *The Structure of Magic, Science and Behaviour*, Palo Alto, 1976.
Grof, S. *Ancient Wisdom and Modern Science*, SUNY Press, Albany, 1984.
Gurdjieff, G.I. *Meetings with Remarkable Men*, Dutton, New York, 1969.
—— *Beelzebub's Tales to His Grandson*, Dutton, New York, 1975.
—— *Views from the Real World*, Dutton, New York, 1975.
Hadamard, J. *An Essay on the Psychology of Invention in the Mathematical Field*, Princeton University Press, 1954.
Haisch, B. *The God Theory: Universes, Zero-Point Fields and What's Behind It All*, Weiser Books, San Francisco, 2006.
Haley, J. *Uncommon Therapy*, Norton, New York, 1971.
Hall, E . T. *Culture's Consequences*, Random House, New York, 1976.
Hall, J. 'Neuroscience and Education: A Review of the Contribution of Brain Science to Teaching and Learning', Occasional Paper No. 12, University of Glasgow, 2005.
Hampden-Turner, C. *Maps of the Mind*, Collier, New York, 1981.
Hannaford, C. *Playing in the Unified Field*, Great River Books, Salt Lake City, 2010.
Harman, W. & Rheingold, H. *Higher Creativity*, Tarcher, Los Angeles, 1984.
Harper, L. *Classroom Magic*, Twiggs Communications, Troy, 1982.
Hendricks, G. & Wills, R. *The Centering Book*, Prentice-Hall, New York, 1975.
Heracleitus, *Cosmic Fragments*, Cambridge University Press,1937.
Hillman, J. *The Myth of Analysis*, Northwestern Universities Press. 1972.
—— *Revisioning Psychology*, Harper and Row, New York, 1976.
—— *Archetypal Psychology*, Spring, Dallas, 1983.
—— *Inter Views*, Harper Colophon, New York 1983.
—— *Kinds of Power: A Guide to its Intelligent Uses*, Doubleday, New York , 1995.
Houston, J. *The Possible Human*, Tarcher, Los Angeles, 1982.
Jaynes, J. *The Origin of Consciousness in the Breakdown of the Bicameral Mind*, Houghton Mifflin, New York, 1976.
Jantsch, E. *The Self-Organising Universe*, Pergamon, Oxford, 1980.
Jaspers, K. *The Origin and Goal of History*, Yale University Press, 1953.
Johnson, M. *The Body in the Mind: The Bodily Basis of Meaning, Imagination and Reason*, University of Chicago Press, 1987
Johnson, R. *She*, Harper & Row, New York, 1976.
—— *Inner Work*, Harper & Row, New York, 1986.
Johnson, Willard, *Riding the Ox Home*, Rider, London, 1982.

Bibliography and Further Reading

Johnson, William, *Silent Music*, Harper & Row, New York, 1986.

Johnstone, K. *Impro*, Methuen, London, 1981.

Jung, C. G. *Collected Works*, Princeton University Press, 1953-1963.

―――― *Modern Man in Search of a Soul*, Harcourt Harvest, 1955.

―――― *Man and His Symbols*. Doubleday, New York, 1964.

―――― *Psychology and Religion*, Princeton University Press, 1969.

―――― 'Psychological Commentary on Kundalini Yoga', *Spring Journal*, 1975.

Jungerman, J. A. *World in Process: Creativity and Interconnection in the New Physics*, SUNY Press, Albany, 2000.

Keats, J. *The Complete Poems of John Keats*, Modern Library, 1994.

Kegan, R. *In Over Our Heads: The Mental Demands of Modern Life*, Harvard University Press, 1994.

Kelly, G. *The Psychology of Personal Constructs*, Norton, New York, 1955.

Kiersey, D. & Bates, M. *Please Understand Me*, Prometheus Nemesis, Del Mar, 1984.

Kipling, R. *Something of Myself*, Doubleday, New York, 1937.

Knowles, M. *Self-Directed Learning*, Association Press, New York, 1975.

Knox, J. Archetype, *Attachment, Analysis: Jungian Psychology and the Emergent Mind*, Brunner-Routledge, New York, 2003.

Koestler A. & Smythies J. *Beyond Reductionism: New Perspectives in the Life Sciences*, Hutchinson, London, 1968

Krippner, S. *Human Possibilities*, Doubleday, New York, 1980.

Kuhn, T. *The Structure of Scientific Revolutions*, University of Chicago Press, 1962.

LaBerge, S. *Lucid Dreaming: A Concise Guide to Awakening in Your Dreams and in Your Life*, Sounds True, Incorporated, 2009; Tarcher, Los Angeles, 1985.

Lakoff, G. *Women, Fire and Dangerous Things: What Categories Reveal about the Mind*, University of Chicago Press, 1987.

Lanza, R. & Berman, B. *Biocentrism: How Life and Consciousness are the Keys to Understanding the True Nature of the Universe*, Benbella Books, Dallas, 2009.

Laszlo, E. *The Connectivity Hypothesis*, SUNY Press, Albany, 2003.

Laszlo, E. *Science and the Akashic Field: An Integral Theory of Everything*, Inner Traditions, Rochester, 2004.

Le Shan, L. *How to Meditate*, Bantam, New York, 1974.

Louv, R. *Last Child in the Woods: Saving Our Children from Nature Deficit Disorder*, Alonquin Paperback, Chapel Hill, 2008.

Lovelock, J. *Gaia: A New Look at Life on Earth*, Oxford University Press, 1979.

―――― *The Vanishing Face of Gaia*, Penguin, UK, 2010.

Lozanov, G. *Suggestology and Outlines of Suggestopedy*, Gordon and Breach, New York, 1978.

Lyotard, J. F. *The Postmodern Condition*, Manchester University Press, 1984

McKinnon, P. *Living Calm in a Busy World: Stillness Meditation in the Meares Tradition*, David Lovell Publishing, Melbourne, 2011.

MacLean, P. *The Triune Brain in Evolution*, Plenum Press, New York, 1990.

McLuhan, M. *Understanding Media: the Extensions of Man*, McGraw Hill, New York, 1965.

Mahareshi Maresh Yogi. *The Science of Being and the Act of Living*, SRM Publications, Los Angeles, 1966.

Maltz, A. *Psychocybernetics: A New Way to Get More Living Out of Life*, Pocket Books, New York, 1969.

—— *Psychocybernetic Principles for Creative Living*, Pocket Books, New York, 1974.

Maslow, A. *The Further Reaches of Human Nature*, Harper & Row, New York, 1973.

Masters, R. & Houston, J. *Listening to the Body*, Delta, New York, 1978.

Maturana, H. & Varela, F. *Autopoeisis and Cognition: The Realization of the Living*, Reidl, London, 1980.

Meares, A. *Strange Places, Simple Truths*, Fontana, London, 1973.

—— *Relief Without Drugs*, Hill of Content, Melbourne, 1985.

—— *The World Within*, Hill of Content, Melbourne, 1987.

Mesle, C. R. *Process-Relational Philosophy*, Templeton Press, West Conshohocke, 2008.

Miller, D. *The New Polytheism*, Spring Publications, Dallas, 1981.

Moreno, J. L. *Who Shall Survive?*, Nervous and Mental Diseases Publishing Co., Washington, 1934.

—— *Psychodrama*, Beacon, New York, 1946.

—— 'The Magic Charter of Psychodrama', *Group Psychotherapy and Psychodrama*, 25, 4, 1972.

Murphy, M. *Golf in the Kingdom*, Delta, New York, 1972.

Myers, I. B. *Gifts Differing*, Consulting Psychologists Press, Palo Alto, 1980.

Needleman, J. & Lewis, D. *On the Way to Self-Knowledge*, Knopf, New York, 1976.

Neumann, E. *Amor and Psyche*, Bollingen, New York, 1956.

Ornstein, R. *The Psychology of Consciousness*, Penguin, UK, 1986.

Osborn, A. F. *Applied Imagination: Principles and Practice of Creative Problem-Solving*, Scribner, New York, 1953.

Ouspensky, P. D. *In Search of the Miraculous*, Harcourt Brace, New York, 1949.

Bibliography and Further Reading

Panksepp, J. *Affective Neuroscience: The Foundations of Human and Animal Emotions*, Oxford University Press, New York, 1998.

Papadopoulos, R. & Saayman, G. *Jung in Modern Perspective*, Wildwood, Houston, 1984.

Patten, K. 'The somatic appraisal model of affect: Paradigm for educational neuroscience and neuropedagogy', *Educational Philosophy and Theory* 43, 1, 2011.

Pauli, W. *The Interpretation of Nature and Psyche*, Bollingen, New York, 1955.

Payne, P. *Martial Arts: The Spiritual Dimension*, Thames and Hudson, London, 1982.

Peale, N. V. *The Power of Positive Thinking*, Gibson, Norwalk, 1959, 1970.

Pelletier, K. *Mind as Healer, Mind as Slayer*, Delta, New York, 1977.

Perkins, D. N. *The Mind's Best Work*, Harvard University Press, 1981.

Pinker, S. *How the Mind Works*, Penguin, UK, 1997

Price, L. (ed.). *Dialogues of Alfred North Whitehead*, Nonpareil Books, Boston, 2001.

Progoff, I. *Depth Psychology and Modern Man*, McGraw-Hill, New York,1959.

Ramachandran, V. S. *The Tell-Tale Brain: A Neuroscientist's Quest for What Makes Us Human*, Norton, New York, 2011.

Restak, R. M. *The Brain*, Doubleday, New York, 1979.

Rico, G. *Writing in the Natural Way*, Tarcher, Los Angeles, 1983.

Riffert, F. (ed.). *Alfred North Whitehead on Learning and Education*, Cambridge University Press, 2005.

Roczak, T., Gomes, M.E. & Kanner, A.D. (eds). *Ecopsychology*, Sierra Club Books.

Rogers, C.R. *On Becoming a Person*, Constable, London, 1971.

——— *Freedom to Learn for the Eighties*, Chas Merrill, New York, 1983.

——— *On Personal Power*, Delacorte, New York, 1977.

——— *A Way of Being*, Houghton Mifflin, Boston ,1980.

Romen, A. S. *Self-Suggestion and Its Influence on the Human Organism*, M. E. Sharpe, Amonk, 1981.

Rosenblum, B. & Kuttner, F. *Quantum Enigma: Physics Encounters Consciousness*, Oxford University Press, 2006.

Rossi, E. 'Hypnosis and Ultradian Cycles, a New State(s) Theory of Hypnosis', *The American Journal of Clinical Hypnosis*, 1982, 1, p. 26.

Scarfe, A. C. (ed.). *The Adventure of Learning: Process Philosophers on Learning, Teaching and Research*, Rodopi, New York.

Schultz, J. H. & Luthe, W. *Autogenic Training*. Greene and Stratton, New York, 1959.

Schwartz, J. & Begley, S. *The Mind and the Brain: Neuroplasticity and the Power of Mental Force*, Harper Perennial, New York, 2002.

Schwarz, J. *Voluntary Controls*, Dutton, New York, 1978.

Shaker, P. 'The Application of Jung's Analytical Psychology to Education', *Journal of Curriculum Studies*, 1982, 14, 3.

Sheikh, A. A. *Imagery: Current Theory, Research and Application*, Wiley, New York, 1983.

Sheldrake, R. *The Rebirth of Nature: New Science and the Revival of Animism*, Rider, London, 1990.

Shorr, A. *Psychotherapy Through Imagery*, Thieme-Stratton, New York, 1983.

Silva, J. *The Silva Mind Control Method*, Grafton, London, 1977.

Silver, H. F., Strong, R. W., & Perini, M. J. *So Each May Learn: Integrating Learning Styles and Multiple Intelligence*, Association for Supervision and Curriculum Development, 2000.

Simonton, O., Matthews-Simonton, S. & Creighton, J. *Becoming Well Again*, Tarcher, Los Angeles, 1977.

Singer, J. & Pope, K. *The Power of Human Imagination*, Plenum, New York, 1978.

Stone, R. *Autohypnosis*, 1987.

Storr, A. *Solitude*, Fontana, 1988.

Suzuki, D., Femin, E. et al. *Zen Buddhism and Psychoanalysis*, Allen & Unwin, London, 1960.

Tart, C. *Waking Up: Overcoming the Obstacles to Human Potential*, Shambhala, Boston, 1986.

—— *Altered States of Consciousness*, Doubleday, New York, 1972.

Trungpal, C. *Meditation in Action*, Shambhala, Berkeley, 1970.

Vernon, P. *Creativity: Selected Readings*, Penguin, UK, 1970.

Waddington, C. H. *The Nature of Life*, Unwin, London, 1961.

Wallas, G. *The Art of Thought*, Harcourt Brace, New York, 1976.

Watkins, M. *Waking Dreams*, Spring Publications, Dallas, 1988.

White, J. *Frontiers of Consciousness*, Julian Press, New York, 1985.

Whitehead, A. N. *An Introduction to Mathematics*, Oxford University Press, 1911.

—— *Science and the Modern World*, Cambridge University Press, 1927.

—— *Process and Reality: An Essay in Cosmology* (corrected edition). D. R. Griffin & D. W. Sherburne. (eds.). Free Press, New York, 1929/1978.

—— *The Aims of Education and Other Essays*, The Macmillan Company, New York, 1929.

Whitmont, E. *The Symbolic Quest*, Princeton University Press, 1978.

Whitmore, D. *Psychosynthesis in Education*, Destiny Books, Vermont, 1986.

Bibliography and Further Reading

Wilber, K. *Eye to Eye*, Shambhala, Los Angeles, 1985.
—— 'Of Shadows and Symbols: Physics and Mysticism', *Revision*, 7, 1, 1984, p.4.
Williams, A. *The Passionate Technique*, Routledge, London, 1989.
—— *Forbidden Agendas*, Routledge, London, 1990.
Winson J, Brain and Psyche, Random House, New York, 1986.
Wolman, B. & Ullman, M. Handbook of States of Consciousness, Van Nostrand, New York, 1986.
Young, P. *Personal Change through Self-hypnosis*, Angus & Robinson, 1986.

Index of Names

Abell, A., 209
Actaeon, 402
Adler, A. 24, 54-55, 64, 140
Adler, G. 132
Aeneas, 432
Aischylos, 422, 432
Alcmene, 411, 412
Alexander, 64
Allan, G., 334, 344
Amazons, 26, 403, 413
Amphytryon, 411
Anchises, 432
Antoinette, Marie., 230
Aphrodite, vii, 1-3, 6, 27, 144, 147, 212, 269, 284, 321, 341, 396, 404-7, 409, 415, 416, 424, 425
Apollo, 3-23, 27, 123, 131, 144, 146, 147, 208, 218, 268, 269, 279, 285, 290, 321, 394, 498-401, 403, 404, 408, 423, 424, 425
Apollon (Apollo), 398, 401, 416
Apuleius, 1, 4, 28
Arachne, 396
Archimedes, 178, 231
Ares, 25, 144, 147, 397, 408-10, 416, 425
Ariadne, 321, 322
Arieti, S., 185, 199, 202, 204, 209
Aristotle, 328
Artemis, 15-18, 26, 29, 147, 289, 321, 401-4, 410, 424, 425
Aspy, D., 323

Assagioli, R., vii, 24, 29, 103, 110, 113, 116-7, 120, 133, 134, 140, 144, 168, 201, 212, 233, 235, 237-9, 248, 250, 256-60, 280, 319
Athanassakis, A., 430, 431, 432
Athena, 26, 147, 395-8, 409, 424, 425
Augustine, St, 143
Aurora, 321
Avens, R., 171
Bach 44
Bandler, R, 66, 77, 95, 135
Bandura, A., 334, 335, 344
Bates, M., 167, 172, 173
Bateson, G., 30
Baudouin, 139
Beethoven, 44, 179, 189, 204, 239-40
Bell, E. T., ix
Begley, S., 378
Benfey, O., 209
Benson, H., 61, 254, 262-3, 273, 280
Bergson, 25
Berman, B., 437
Berne, 238, 239
Bharati, A., 281
Birch, C
Blake, W., 11, 189
Blatner, A., 248
Bohm, D., 343
Bohr, N., 326
Bonaventure, St, 274
Brahms, 44, 179
Brown, M., 133, 134

Brown, F., 135
Bry, A., 133
Buber, M., 287, 303, 317, 322
Buddha, 31, 272, 331
Budzinski, T., 63
Burke, A., 63
Burnet, J., 395
Burney, C., 132-3
Butler, S., 65
Buzan, T., 193, 209
Bynne, W., 323
Callisto, 402
Cameron, 77
Carrington, P., 279
Carson, R., 354, 376
Cerberus, 427, 432
Chaos, 321
Charcot, 238
Chase, S., ix
Christ, Jesus, 10, 27, 154, 229
Cicero, 122
Cleveland, B. F., 95, 129, 135, 136
Coleridge, S. T., 197
Combs, A., 293
Corbin, H., 171
Corell, C., 136
Corelli, 44
Cornelius-White, J., 323
Corsini, R., 248
Coué, E., vii, x, xiii, 33-36, 39, 41, 47-55, 58, 61-62, 64, 139, 221, 272, 273
Creighton, J., 440
Cybele, 393
Czikszentmihaly, M., 227, 248, 280

Index of Names

Dahl, N., x, 35
Damasio, A., 170, 348, 350, 351, 354, 360, 361, 367, 375, 376, 377, 378
Danton, 230
Darwin, C., 25, 110, 144, 178
Darth Vader, 161
Davies, M., 63
Davies, P., 434
De Bono, E., 194, 209
De Chardin, Teilhard, 25
De Quincey, C., 342
Deikman, A., 276-7, 281
Delaney, G., 134
Dell, W., 30
Dement, W., 134
Demeter, 110, 144, 147, 289, 297, 321, 393-5, 402, 424, 426, 430, 431
Désoillé, R., 101-2, 117, 133
Descartes, 328
Desdemona, 110
Devil, the, 427
Diana, 147, 401 (see Artemis)
Dickens, C., 164-5, 172
Diomedes, 409
Dionysos, 4, 15-18, 23, 26-29, 144, 148, 167, 218-221, 228-9, 232, 234, 237, 248, 268, 269, 278, 279, 286, 289, 312, 316, 322, 363, 390, 404, 412, 418-20, 424, 425, 428, 431
Dixon, N. F., 63
Donald, M. D., 64, 347, 357, 362, 375, 377-8
Dostoevsky, 110-1
Duhen, P., 209
Durand, G., 3-4, 28
Eason, A., 63
Eccles, J., 170
Eddington, 253, 280

Egan, K., vii, 58-60, 64, 202, 345, 346, 348, 349, 350, 357, 372-3, 375
Einstein, A., 108, 178, 186, 189, 190, 197, 204, 209, 231, 249, 326
Eliade, M., 375
Eliot, G., 189
Eliot, T. S., 3, 28
Epicharmos, 343
Epimenedes, 430
Erickson, M., vii, xi-xii, 37, 51, 54, 66-96, 272, 319
Eros, 3-6, 10, 12, 15-20, 23, 26-28, 55, 96, 123, 131, 144, 146, 147, 205, 279, 284-5, 286, 287, 288, 289, 290, 291, 292-3, 296, 297, 307, 309, 310, 312, 314-7, 319, 320-1, 322, 341, 407-8, 409, 425, 426
Eshelman, E. R., 63
Euridice, 432
Euripides, 234, 431
Fates, the, 429
Federer, R., 115
Federn, 238
Feldenkrais, 64
Femin, E., 440
Ferrucci, P., 106, 133, 134
Fine, L., 248
Fox, J., 248
Frankl, V., x, 3, 7-9
Freeman, L., 280
Freire, P., 287, 304, 320, 322, 323
Freud, S., x, 3, 7-9, 32-33, 55-58, 98, 113, 138-143, 151-5, 170, 197, 212, 238, 247-8, 250, 285, 286, 290, 319, 367, 393, 395, 399
Friedman, 134-5

Furies, the, 429
Gaia, 321, 362, 393, 394, 407
Galileo, 178
Galin, G., 170
Gallwey, W. T., 280
Gardner, H., 135-6
Gauss, 200, 231
Gawain, S., 133
Ge, see Gaia
Gebser, J., vii, 59-61, 64, 280-1, 346-7, 349, 354, 357, 360, 361, 362, 371, 372, 374, 375, 376, 377, 379
Gendlin, E., 117, 134, 202
Ghiselin, B., 208, 209
Giants, 385, 425, 427, 428
Gibb, J. R., 293-8, 299, 300, 302, 303, 304, 305, 306, 307, 312, 314-7, 320, 322, 323
Given, 360
Glasser, W., 387, 406
Globus, G., 170
Godzilla, 27
Goethe, 11, 25, 179
Gomes, M. E., 439
Graces, the, 429
Gradgrind, T., 164-5
Graeber, R., 135
Graves, D., 300, 322
Green, A .M., 61-63, 134, 209
Green, E. E., 61-63, 133, 134
Greenberg, I., 248
Grinder, J., 66, 77, 95
Griffith, F., 281
Grof, S., 133, 209
Gurdjieff, G. I., 56-58, 64, 264
Hadamard, J., 209
Hades, 425-9, 430, 431, 432
Haisch, B., 436
Haley, J., 66, 95

443

Hall, E. T., 356, 377
Hall, J., 375
Hampden-Turner, C., 248
Handel, 44
Hannaford, C., 377
Harman, W., 52, 63, 136, 208, 209
Harper, L., 95
Hecate, 321, 429
Heilbroner, R. L., ix
Hekate, 373
Helios, 399
Hendricks, G., 281
Hephaistos, 26, 147, 268, 409, 410, 415-6, 420, 425, 431
Hera, 27, 55, 147, 218, 234, 341, 388-91, 396, 404, 408, 409, 412, 413, 416, 418, 424, 425, 430, 431
Herakles, 25, 212, 371, 390, 396, 403, 410-4, 429, 431, 432
Heraclitus, 21, 29, 331-2, 335, 343
Hermes, 4, 12, 15-18, 29, 96, 286, 287, 321, 341, 363, 409, 412, 423-5, 426, 432
Hesiod, 431, 432
Hestia, vii, 268-9, 277, 278, 279, 416-8, 425, 430
Hillman, J. T., 10, 21, 28-9, 145, 168, 171, 318-9, 321, 323, 362, 377
Hippolyta, 413
Hitler, A., xii, 54-55
Holy Ghost, the, 190, 270
Homer, 17, 325, 381, 409, 430, 431, 432
Horney, K., 140, 201
Hotstadter, D., ix
Houston, J., 64, 133
Huxley, A., 184, 273, 275
Iapetos, 420

Icarus, 286
Inana, 4
Indra, 331, 332, 384, 427
Isis 4
Izanami, 4
James, W., 41, 430
Jantsch, E., 436
Jason, 396, 411
Jaynes, J. T., 170, 375
Jaspers, K., 375
Jeans, J., 252-3, 280
Jesus, see Christ
Johnson, M., 430
Johnson, R., 29, 132
Johnson, Willard, 270-1
Johnson, William, 278, 280, 281
Johnstone, K., 219-20, 243
Jones, J., 54-55
Jourard, S., 293
Judson, H. F., ix
Jung, C. G., vii, xi, 8-10, 14, 20, 24-25, 28, 97, 98-103, 113, 117, 131, 132, 136, 137, 140-170, 171-2, 188, 190, 191, 198, 201, 204, 212, 238, 239, 250, 289, 292, 318-9, 323, 351-2, 362, 376, 382-4, 392, 393, 432
Jungerman, J. A., 395
Kanner, A.D.
Kant, I., 10, 143, 431
Karenina, A., 230
Keats, J., xi, 283, 404, 431
Kegan, R., 61, 64, 346, 349, 363, 367, 373, 376, 378, 380
Kekule, A., 178, 187, 209
Kelly, G., 205-6, 210
Kiersey, D., 167, 172, 173
Kipling, R., 179, 189, 208
Knowles, M., 300, 322
Knox, J., 369-70, 379

Koestler, A., 64
Kore, 396
Krippner, S., 62, 248
Kronides (Zeus), 384, 430
Kronos, 144, 268, 286, 298, 385, 386, 404, 430
Kuhn, T., 206, 210
Kuttner, F., 439
LaBerge, S., 134
Lakoff, G., 430
Lamarck, 25
Lanza, R., 437
Lao Tse, 287, 323
Laszlo, E., 437
Le Shan, L., 263, 280
Leibniz, 328
Leto, 401
Leuner, 117, 121, 134
Lewis, D., 29
Loewi, O., 183
Loki, 432
Louv, R., 376
Lovelock, J., 327
Lozanov, G., vii, x, 41-52, 62, 184, 195, 221, 222
Lugh, 432
Luthe, W. 61
Lyotard, J. F., 372, 379
MacLean, P., 59, 64, 348, 349, 354, 360, 375
McKay, M., 63
McKinnon, P., 280
McLuhan, M., 375
Magna Mater, 321
Mahareshi Maresh Yogi, 262, 280
Maia, 393, 423, 432
Maltz, A., 61, 63
Maslow, A., 24, 29, 201, 293
Masters, R., 64, 133
Matthews-Simonton, S., 440
Maturana, H., 438
Maxwell, G., 435
May, R., 293
Medea, 212

Index of Names

Meares, A., 37, 61, 254, 264-6, 272, 273, 278, 280, 353, 376
Mercury, 432
Medusa, 396
Menander, 175
Mendeleev, 178, 179
Menuhin, Y., 254
Mesle, C. R., 330, 343
Mesmer, 32
Metis, 321
Mickunas, A.
Miller, D., 171
Milton, 179
Moreno, J. L., vii, 140, 168, 212-4, 217-24, 228-30, 232-243, 245-48, 250, 312, 319
Moriarty, Dr, 161
Mozart, 44, 109, 178, 179, 190
Murphy, M., 280
Muses, the, 373
Myers, I. B., 172
Namagiri, 189, 190
Narcissus, 286-7
Needleman, J. 29
Neumann, E., 29
Newton, I., 178, 209, 328, 343
Nietzsche, 379
Odysseus, 396, 411
Oedipus, 212
Ogden, 350
Ornstein, R., 30
Orpheus, 432
Osiris, 431
Osborn, A. F., 193, 197, 209
Ouspensky, P. D., 64
Paganini, 239-40
Pallas, 395, 396
Pan, 429
Pandora, 410
Panksepp, 348
Papadopoulos, R., 132, 209

Paris, 396
Parthenos, 396
Patanjali, 274
Patten, K., 360, 376, 377
Paul, St, 430
Pauli, W., 23-24, 29, 190
Pavlov, 12, 30, 38, 42
Payne, P., 280
Peale, N. V., 61
Pelletier, K., 133
Penia, 321
Perini, M. J.
Perkins, D. N., 196, 209
Perls, F., 80
Persephone, 4, 15, 20-22, 27, 29, 321, 393, 426, 428, 429, 431, 432
Perseus, 396, 411
Philemon, 98
Picasso, P., 234, 424
Piaget, 59, 346
Pinker, S., 430
Pirithous, 432
Plato, 25, 143, 252, 279
Plouton (Pluto), 428
Poincaré, H., 176-8, 185, 204, 205, 208, 209
Polanyi, 202
Pope, K., 134
Poseidon, 391-3, 425, 426, 430, 431
Priapus, 429
Price, L., 29, 344
Progoff, I., 24, 29, 144
Prometheus, 4, 12, 16-18, 29, 96, 126, 130-1, 146, 147, 208, 268, 279, 285, 291, 362-3, 386, 387, 394, 413, 420-2, 425, 432
Psyche, 1-29, 39, 46, 123, 131, 205, 208, 218, 268, 284, 342, 405
Puer, 144, 286, 287, 290, 294, 316, 317, 318-9, 322
Pythagoras, 10

Rachmaninoff, 35
Raikov, 239
Ramachandran, V. S., 377
Ramaniyan, 189, 190
Rambo, 204, 403
Rank, O., 24, 140
Reich W., 2, 27, 140
Reingold, H., 63, 136, 208
Restak, R. M., 170
Reynolds, A., xii-xiii
Rico, G., 193, 209
Riffert, F., 334, 344
Rhea, 385, 388, 393, 430
Robespierre, 230
Roczak, T., 343
Roebuck, F., 323
Rogers, C. R., 24-26, 29, 80, 96, 201, 228, 287, 290-293, 300, 305, 309, 312, 314-7, 319, 320, 322, 323, 339-40, 353, 376
Romen, A. S., x, 38-42, 48-51, 58, 61, 273
Rosenblum, B., 439
Rossi, E., 63, 66, 96, 134, 135
Rossi, S., 96
Rousseau, J. J., 223
Saaynam, G., 132, 210
Saint-Saens, 179
Santa Claus, 363
Satan, 10
Satir, V., 80
Saturn, 27, 286, 297, 298, 316, 319, 322, 430
Savodnik, I.
Scarfe, A. C., 396
Schopenhauer, 143, 431
Schultz, J. H., x, 36-38, 41, 47, 58, 61-62, 101-2, 121, 133, 257
Schuman, 179
Schwarz, J., 281, 367, 378
Semele, 321, 418, 431

445

Senex, 55, 144, 146, 147, 286, 287, 290, 291, 293, 297, 305, 307, 309, 312, 314-7, 318-9, 320-1, 322, 407
Shaker, P., 173
Shakespeare, W., 2, 11, 317, 319, 351
Sheikh, A. A., 133
Sheldrake, R., 327, 342, 353, 376, 378
Shorr, A., 134
Silva, J., x, 44, 47-51, 58, 61-62, 121-3, 273
Silver, H. F., 136, 172
Simonides, 122
Simonton, O., 133
Singer, J., 134
Smythies J. 64
Socrates, xiii, 20, 287
Sophia, 396
Spinoza, 328
Stanislavsky, 38
Steiner, R., ix
Stevenson, R. L., 179
Stone, R., 63
Storr, A., 431
Strauss, 189
Strong, R. W.
Suinn, P., 133
Superman, 403
Suzuki, D., 29
Sysiphus, 144
Tart, C., 56, 64, 281
Tartini, 179
Tesla, N., 131-2
Thanatos, 286, 317
Themis, 389, 393, 408, 430
Theseus, 432
Thespius, 413
Titan, 386, 413
Titans, the, 232, 248, 385, 391, 425, 427, 428
Tolaas, J., 210
Tolstoy, 2
Tooth Fairy, the, 363

Trungpa, C., 264, 280
Ullman, M., 63, 134, 210
Uranus, 286, 321, 386, 404, 407
Urvasi, 4
Uznadze, 39-40
Van Gogh, V., 197, 209
Van Rapport, R., 209
Varela, F.
Vergil, 11
Vernon, P., 208
Vesta, 268, see Hestia
Vogt, x, 36
Voluptas 28
Waddington, C. H., 343
Wagner, R., 178, 197
Wallas, G., vii, 177, 204, 207, 208
Watkins, M., 132
Watt, J., 179
White, J., 281
Whitehead, A. N., vii, 25, 28-29, 62, 325, 326, 344, 346, 361, 364, 372, 373, 412, 430
Whitmont, E., 134, 171, 172
Whitmore, D., 108, 133
Wilber, K., 172, 253, 280
Williams, A., 248
Wills, R., 281
Winson, J., 170
Wolman, B., 63, 134, 210
Woods, Tiger, 115
Wordsworth, 25
Yeats, W. B., 211
Young, P., 441
Zemelo (Semele), 431
Zeus, 14-15, 17, 131, 144, 232, 284, 286, 289, 298, 321, 341, 363, 384-8, 389, 391, 394, 396, 397, 398, 400, 401, 402, 407, 409, 410, 411, 412, 413, 416, 418, 420, 423, 424, 425-6, 428, 429, 430, 431, 432

Also by Bernie Neville

OLYMPUS INC.
Intervening for Cultural Change in Organizations
Bernie Neville & Tim Dalmau
452 pp 235 x 170 mm pb Bibliography & index
ISBN 978 192114 296 3

Bernie Neville and Tim Dalmau use the ancient Greek gods to explore the values, practices and beliefs that underpin businesses, schools, corporations and the like, and through this they illuminate the complex forces and currents that are at work in modern organizations.

By combining ancient myths with archetypal psychology, they deliver an approach to the complex issues of organizational change. Their approach is creative and engaging, but also down to earth and practical.

The authors' approach to organizational change is shaped by five guiding ideas which they elucidate in the first chapter: contemporary organizations exist in the postmodern world; organizational behavior has unconscious components; patterns of behavior in organizations are archetypal; the whole organization is more than the sum of its parts; and intentional cultural change is unpredictable.

This stance takes them to a discussion of culture and cultural change in organizations, the Jungian understanding of archetype and myth, and then to an exploration of the gods of the Greek pantheon as representing the specific energies, perspectives, ways of understanding and patterns of behavior which characterize contemporary organizations, whether they be corporations, institutions or social clubs.

Olympus Inc. includes a discussion of the DNAI – the Dalmau-Neville Archetypology Indicator – a powerful and easily applicable tool that distills the theory of archetypal psychology in ways that enable organizations to see themselves not only as they are but as they want to be. A further bonus is the appendix: A Toolbox for Change Agents. Here the authors outline a number of change intervention strategies based on the principle that sustainable cultural change involves dealing with the unconscious dynamics of an organization, and cannot be limited to manipulating the organization's rhetoric, structures and procedures.

Also by Bernie Neville

THE LIFE OF THINGS
Therapy and the Soul of the World
228 x 152 mm 240 pp pb   ISBN 978 186355 144 1

This book is alive, as a wonderfully rich, well-informed and searching conversational journey of inquiry and wisdom. It pulsates with ideas joined in a continually extending landscape of meaning.
Godfrey Barrett-Lennard, from the Foreword

What would psychology look like if we took the planet seriously?

This is the question addressed by ecopsychologists, who reject the notion that the earth is a huge machine clunking along within the larger machine which is the clockwork universe. They argue that we should trust our experience and understand that the earth is not composed of dead matter but is a living system of which we are a part. Ecopsychologists are more interested in our relations with the earth than our relations with each other. They do not find much inspiration in conventional psychology, and generally have little to say about counselling and psychotherapy.

Meanwhile, counsellors continue to work as though counselling is essentially an exercise carried out in private between two individuals, one of whom is undertaking to help the other deal with a personal problem. Surely, as Bernie Neville puts it in *The Life of Things*, 'Our efforts should be spent on saving the planet. After that we can worry about whether we are happy or not.'

In discussions of the human predicament these two points of view rarely meet, but here they are brought together lucidly and coherently. Bernie Neville takes both personal counselling and the planet seriously. He gets his inspiration from philosophers and psychologists who have puzzled over our relationship to the planet and each other. Arne Naess, Alfred North Whitehead, Jean Gebser, Carl Rogers and Carl Jung have had a significant influence on his ideas. These five thinkers all have enthusiastic followers, but they don't talk to each other very much. *The Life of Things* may be unique in fitting all five between the same covers. It is unique also in its achievement of dealing with these rich, diverse and complex ideas with eloquence and clarity.

Dr Bernie Neville originally trained as a primary teacher, though most of his school teaching career was spent in secondary schools in Adelaide, Sydney and Melbourne as a teacher of English, LOTE and Drama. He holds an MA in Classics from Adelaide University and a PhD in Education from La Trobe University. He is currently Honorary Professor of Education at Swinburne University of Technology and Professor of Holistic Counselling at the Phoenix Institute of Australia.

Dr Neville has been involved in the pre-service and inservice education of teachers since 1972. He has researched and written extensively on the interpersonal aspects of teaching and learning and the application of counselling theory to the teaching-learning process. As a university teacher in both of education and counselling, he has had a keen interest in applying the thought of Carl Rogers and Carl Jung to the practicalities of teaching and counselling.

He is also the author of *Olympus Inc: Intervening for Cultural Change in Organizations* (2004, 2011) and *The Life of Things: Therapy and the Soul of the World* (2013).

www.ingramcontent.com/pod-product-compliance
Lightning Source LLC
Chambersburg PA
CBHW052041220426
43663CB00012B/2394